T0326341

PEOPLE, MARKETS, GOODS:
ECONOMIES AND SOCIETIES IN HISTORY
Volume 9

People, Places and Business Cultures

PEOPLE, MARKETS, GOODS:
ECONOMIES AND SOCIETIES IN HISTORY

ISSN: 2051-7467

Series editors
Barry Doyle – University of Huddersfield
Nigel Goose – University of Hertfordshire
Steve Hindle – The Huntington Library
Jane Humphries – University of Oxford
Willem M. Jongman – University of Groningen

The interactions of economy and society, people and goods, transactions and actions are at the root of most human behaviours. Economic and social historians are participants in the same conversation about how markets have developed historically and how they have been constituted by economic actors and agencies in various social, institutional and geographical contexts. New debates now underpin much research in economic and social, cultural, demographic, urban and political history. Their themes have enduring resonance – financial stability and instability, the costs of health and welfare, the implications of poverty and riches, flows of trade and the centrality of communications. This paperback series aims to attract historians interested in economics and economists with an interest in history by publishing high quality, cutting edge academic research in the broad field of economic and social history from the late medieval/ early modern period to the present day. It encourages the interaction of qualitative and quantitative methods through both excellent monographs and collections offering path-breaking overviews of key research concerns. Taking as its benchmark international relevance and excellence it is open to scholars and subjects of any geographical areas from the case study to the multi-nation comparison.

PREVIOUSLY PUBLISHED TITLES IN THE SERIES ARE
LISTED AT THE END OF THE VOLUME

People, Places and Business Cultures

Essays in Honour
of Francesca Carnevali

Edited by

Paolo Di Martino, Andrew Popp and Peter Scott

THE BOYDELL PRESS

First published 2017
The Boydell Press, Woodbridge

ISBN 978-1-78327-212-9

The Boydell Press is an imprint of Boydell & Brewer Ltd
PO Box 9, Woodbridge, Suffolk IP12 3DF, UK
and of Boydell & Brewer Inc.
668 Mt Hope Avenue, Rochester, NY 14620–2731, USA
website: www.boydellandbrewer.com

A catalogue record for this book is available
from the British Library

The publisher has no responsibility for the continued existence or accuracy of URLs for
external or third-party internet websites referred to in this book, and does not guarantee
that any content on such websites is, or will remain, accurate or appropriate.

This publication is printed on acid-free paper

Typeset by BBR, Sheffield

To the memory of Francesca Carnevali, 1964–2013

Contents

PART I
INTRODUCTION

PART II
BETWEEN ECONOMICS AND CULTURE: EXPLAINING
BUSINESS PRACTICES IN THEIR HISTORICAL CONTEXT

PART III

MAKING PEOPLE MATTER: EMERGING
APPROACHES IN ECONOMIC HISTORY

PART IV

CONCLUSIONS

Illustrations

Tables

Contributors

Andrea Colli has a Ph.D. in Economic and Social History (Bocconi University, Milan) and is Professor of Economic History at the Department of Policy Analysis and Public Management, Bocconi University, Milan. His research interests range from the history of family firms, to small and medium-sized enterprises, to the role played by international entrepreneurs and firms in the global economy, and to corporate governance in historical perspective. He has also devoted research activity to the study of the history of entrepreneurship in different contexts.

Paolo Di Martino is Senior Lecturer in International Business and Economic History at Birmingham Business School, University of Birmingham (UK). His research interests are financial history, business history and the history of legal institutions. He has published extensively in edited books and journals, including *Business History*, *Economic History Review* and *Enterprise and Society*. He is an active member of the Economic History Society.

Leslie Hannah lives in Japan and is a visiting professor at the London School of Economics. He previously held posts at various American, Asian and European universities and was pro-director of LSE and dean of two business schools. He was Francesca Carnevali's Ph.D. supervisor and co-authored an article with her, and also published a history of Barclays Bank, jointly with Margaret Ackrill. His writings are now focused on the comparative business history of twentieth-century Europe, America and Japan.

Matthew Hilton is Professor of Social History at Queen Mary University of London. He has published widely on the history of charities, social activism, consumption and NGOs. His most recent books are *Prosperity for All: Consumer Activism in an Era of Globalisation* (Ithaca, NY, 2009) and, with James McKay, Nicholas Crowson and Jean-François Mouhot, *The Politics of Expertise: How NGOs Shaped Modern Britain* (Oxford, 2013). He has co-edited several collections of essays, including *The Ages of Voluntarism* (Oxford, 2011) and *Transnationalism and Contemporary Global History* (Oxford, 2013). He is co-editor of *Past & Present* and is currently engaged on a history of British approaches to humanitarianism. The article presented in this volume is the product of ongoing conversations between members of the Centre for Modern British Studies at the University of Birmingham.

Kenneth J. Lipartito is Professor of History in the Department of History at Florida International University. He has been a Newcomen Fellow (1991) and a Thomas McCraw Fellow (2009) at Harvard Business School. He is the author or editor of six books, most recently, *Corporate Responsibility: The American Experience*, published in 2012 by Cambridge University Press. His articles have appeared in the *American Historical Review*, *Journal of Economic History*, *Technology and Culture*, *Industrial and Corporate Change* and the *Business History Review*. He was editor of *Enterprise and Society: The International Journal of Business History* (2003–07) and President of the Business History Conference.

Lucy Newton is Associate Professor in Business History in the School of International Business and Strategy, Henley Business School, University of Reading. She has published her work on financial history and nineteenth-century consumer durables in a variety of business history journals. She has been an active member and Trustee of the Business History Conference (USA) and twice elected as Council member of the Association of Business Historians (UK).

Andrew Popp is Professor of Business History at the University of Liverpool Management School. He has published on a wide range of topics in British business and industrial history, principally of the nineteenth century. His most recent book is *Entrepreneurial Families: Business, Marriage and Life in the Early Nineteenth Century*, published by Pickering & Chatto in 2012. He is Editor-in-Chief of *Enterprise and Society: The International Journal of Business History*.

Alberto Rinaldi is Associate Professor of Economic History at the University of Modena and Reggio Emilia. He has published extensively on contemporary Italian economic history, focusing in particular on industrial districts, trade, economic growth and the structure of the corporate system. His works are published in leading international journals, such as *Explorations in Economic History*, *Cliometrica*, *Business History* and *Enterprise and Society*.

Peter Scott is Professor of International Business History at Henley Business School, University of Reading. He has written extensively on the history of British and American mass retailing; consumer durables sectors; household consumption; housing; and related topics – mainly for the early twentieth century. His most recent book, *The Making of the Modern British Home: The Suburban Semi and Family Life Between the Wars*, was published by Oxford University Press in 2013.

Anna Spadavecchia is Associate Professor at Henley Business School, University of Reading, and gained her Ph.D. in the Department of Economic History at the London School of Economics. Her field of expertise includes the growth of small and medium-sized enterprises and clusters; regional and national policies for SMEs; innovation in British regions; innovation and Italian economic performance in the long run. Her publications include book chapters and articles in *Business History*, *Enterprise and Society*, the *Economic History Review* and *Oxford Economic Papers*.

James Walker is Professor at Henley Business School, University of Reading, and Head of International Business and Strategy. His overall research agenda is characterised by the application of empirical methods to solve real world problems and issues past and present. He has published in journals as diverse as *Journal of Applied Economics* and the *Journal of Economic History*, examining the spatial competition in product markets and between firms, varieties of capitalism, academic performance and pay, and attitudes to multi-national enterprises.

Chris Wickham is Chichele Professor of Medieval History (Emeritus) at the University of Oxford. Among his recent books are *Framing the Early Middle Ages* (Oxford, 2005), *Medieval Rome* (Oxford, 2014) and *Medieval Europe* (New Haven, CT, 2016). He is currently working on the economic history of the eleventh century.

Acknowledgements

Preliminary versions of the chapters appearing in this volume were presented at a workshop held at the University of Birmingham in March 2014. The editors and contributors wish to thank the University of Birmingham for its generous hospitality and the Economic History Society for the funding that made the workshop possible. We, the editors, are also indebted to the participants in the workshop (in particular Julie-Marie Strange, Corey Ross and Adam Tooze), as well as two anonymous readers of this volume, for the comments received.

PART I

INTRODUCTION

Francesca Carnevali (Boston, 2008)

Editors' Introduction

Economic History 'As If People Mattered'

PAOLO DI MARTINO, PETER SCOTT AND ANDREW POPP

This book seeks to celebrate and to continue the career, work and legacy of Francesca Carnevali (1964–2013) by presenting new perspectives on debates in economic, social and business history and, indeed, history more generally. Driven by curiosity and a refusal to settle for easy answers, Francesca produced work that was multifarious in its themes, methods and styles; but all of it was underpinned by a desire to reveal the complex historical interactions between economy and society, always placing people at the centre of that nexus. Whether individually or collectively, we cannot hope to emulate Francesca's unique elan but we do hope that we can pick up and carry forward what mattered most to her in her work as an historian. That hope is what has motivated this project. Thus we have identified the debates and questions with which Francesca was most preoccupied, as well as the various methodological avenues she used to explore them, and have asked a distinguished groups of scholars to consider where they might be taken next. This is very apt as Francesca was most prescient – or agenda setting – in her work: this introduction outlines that agenda and the various chapters through which we attempt to extend it.

In the early 1990s, when Francesca and several of the contributors to this volume were working on their doctoral theses, economic history was undergoing a period of contraction as an academic discipline, both in the UK and internationally. Simultaneously, it was experiencing a narrowing focus towards the 'new economic history', an approach that reduced complex historical phenomena to ones explicable by simple neoclassical economic models and studied via quantitative, *cliometric* methods. Francesca's legacy has been to help recast economic history as a discipline where people *matter* – that is: they make a *difference*. If everything – economy, society – is connected then it was people who built those connections and rendered complex the historical interactions between economy and society. This role for people as agents who really matter was revealed in Francesca's work in many different ways: thus, she consistently showed people as being at the heart of the processes shaping political economies, institutions and the creation and meaning of 'value'. This theme – that people are at the very centre of the dense web of interconnections between economy, society and culture – represents the *fil rouge* of this book, around which our various authors develop their own argument, each starting from Francesca's own contribution either to a specific topic or from particular methodologies and perspectives. In the remainder of this introduction we will set out the structure of the book and outline the contributions made by each chapter.

Structure and contributions

This volume is composed of four elements. The first, introductory, section comprises both this editors' introduction and a more in-depth and personal review of Francesca's life and academic legacy, written by Paolo Di Martino. Inspired by Francesca's work, he revisits a number of key debates in British and American economic and business history. These debates include: Britain's alleged relative economic decline since the late nineteenth century; the importance of national systems of political economy in modifying the predictions of market-based models of bank–industry relations; industrial districts and their systems for co-ordinating business activity and tempering opportunism; the development of a mass 'luxury' market in jewellery and the segmentation strategies used to simultaneously demarcate and underpin the mass and elite sections of the trade; the importance of sociological factors in both the functionality and promotion of industrial districts; and the central roles of segmentation, branding, marketing and distribution strategies for household goods' manufacturers and retailers. As we can readily see, Francesca's work was very far-reaching in its interests.

This chapter further explores Francesca's contributions to each of these debates, focusing on her rejection of simplistic neoclassical economic arguments in favour of richer approaches that also incorporate political economy; interest groups and lobbying; opportunism; socialisation; and the ways in which marketing can create that particularly intangible and subjective quality – 'value' – in the eyes of the consumer. These all emerge as important correctives to what had become, in the eyes of many of its younger practitioners, a rather sterile dominant paradigm in economic history, one that too often reduced the world to narrowly defined economic motivations, which were tested using only statistical data (sometimes employing models that would validate the author's hypothesis given any plausible data). In many ways, and as already suggested, reactions to that once dominant paradigm permeate this whole project.

In the second section, five chapters provide up-to-date analysis of thematic areas of economic and business history to which Francesca directly contributed: industrial districts and networks as forms of organisation of production; the political economy of finance; Britain's post-1870s 'decline'; marketing and consumption in interwar Britain; and the production, distribution and consumption of household goods in Victorian and Edwardian Britain.

The section opens with Andrew Popp's chapter on 'Custom and Spectacle: The Public Staging of Business Life'. Focused on the mercantile industrial district of Liverpool, this chapter takes its inspiration from Francesca Carnevali's pioneering study of social action in the Providence jewellery district, particularly the way her study is framed by an introduction that dwells on the spectacle of a parade staged by the New England Manufacturing Jewelers and Silversmiths Association.[1] Empirically, the chapter starts from an anomaly: why did Liverpool's cotton brokers continue to insist on public, open-air trading for many years after they had access to a purpose-built cotton trading room? This idiosyncratic behaviour is hard to rationalise.

Popp's chapter draws on several strands of literature – new and old – to explore how business historians can fruitfully consider what could be called the public staging of business life; a rich array of events and occasions that might stretch from the annual Lord Mayor's procession in the City of London to City workers crowding into pubs at the end of the day. In particular, it examines the persistence of such performances and their relationships to the spaces in which they take place and the communities that perform them. This requires a shift from viewing these occasions and behaviours as merely expressive, to considering them as forms of 'symbolic action' with constitutive power. In so doing, Popp, drawing on older traditions in social history, asserts that we should see the way Liverpool's cotton brokers persisted with open-air trading as a 'custom in common'. Enactment of customs was part of the process through which the brokers claimed rights and legitimacy and made themselves as good market subjects.

The next chapter, 'The Political Economy of Financing Italian Small Businesses, 1950–1990s' by Alberto Rinaldi and Anna Spadavecchia, looks at small and medium-sized enterprises (SMEs) and industrial districts (IDs) in Italy, where they are widely regarded as the backbone of the regional economy. Received wisdom claims that SMEs within IDs finance themselves by reinvesting their profits. Rinaldi and Spadavecchia argue that in fact a complex financial structure was created in Italy to finance SMEs. The 1936 Banking

---

1 Francesca Carnevali, 'Social Capital and Trade Associations in America, c.1860–1914: A Microhistory Approach', *Economic History Review* 64 (2011), 905–28.

Law empowered the Bank of Italy (BoI) to shape the banking sector in terms
of market specialisation (i.e. medium- versus short-term credit) and territorial competence. After 1945 the BoI favoured the opening of new branches
by regional banks, as these would provide finance to SMEs. Moreover, from
the early 1950s regional institutions specialising in the provision of medium-
term credit to SMEs were established: the Mediocrediti Regionali – together
with their refinancing institution, the Mediocredito Centrale.

Yet another institution, the Artigiancassa (Artisan Bank) was established
in 1947 to provide loans to artisan firms. In the first five years of activity the
Artigiancassa funded only 1% of Italian artisan concerns, prompting a 1952
reform that abandoned the idea of a specialised national institution for such
lending. The Artigiancassa was transformed into a rediscount institute for
the banks, which were henceforth authorised to grant medium-term loans to
artisan firms – the banking network, as a system of ordering, was in flux.
Drawing on work highlighting the Italian state's political and economic
interest in SMEs and how this contributed to a banking structure tuned
towards the SMEs' financial requirements (a major theme in Francesca's
work on Italian banking), their chapter further develops these approaches,
providing a comprehensive analysis of the Italian financial system for SMEs.

Leslie Hannah's chapter, 'Banks and Business Finance in Britain Before
1914: A Comparative Evaluation', starts with a discussion of the pivotal role
of the City pre-1914 in the international financial system. London had both
the largest stock exchange in the world and the largest number of overseas
bank head offices and branches, as well as a substantial and (still) competitive domestic commercial and investment banking industry. The impact on
the UK's structure of both large and small companies, and on multinationals
and firms with a domestic focus, was palpable. As Francesca's own work
on European banking demonstrated, these kinds of effects can often best
be appreciated in comparative context and the contrasting cases of France,
Germany and the USA are examined. The UK had a stock of giant firms
fully comparable with those of the USA, despite the latter already being an
economy with twice the UK's real GDP, largely because of the more global
reach of UK manufacturing and service firms, and the (politically determined)
unusually small-scale and inward focus of American banking.

If there was a mild UK 'climacteric' before 1914 it was primarily the result
of factors which would later equally afflict European followers, such as an
unusually rapidly ageing population (in the UK, the combined early result of
precocious birth control and high propensity of its young men to emigrate)
and catch-up growth by followers, as much as from inherent weaknesses in
its competitive domestic economy with its strong financial, commercial and
new technology sectors, but some emerging weaknesses in human capital
formation. The structure of the UK's economy was, however, much less appropriate for meeting the problems of de-globalisation, financial crowding out by

government securities and crony capitalist banks, and structural adjustments that were to afflict the world from 1914 onwards. The political response – providing a system of ordering and legitimation – reinforced elements of sclerosis. While the growth of limited liability enterprises continued to outstrip such firms in France and Germany, the economy had lost much of the flexibility which characterised it before 1914 and which increasingly drove American growth.

Next, Peter Scott and James Walker examine 'Large-Scale Retailing, Mass-Market Strategies and the Blurring of Class Demarcations in Interwar Britain'. As Paul Johnson has noted, before 1914 working-class people were commonly regarded as a class apart, separated from the rest of society not only by their income, but their entire way of life. Social segregation was strongly evident in access to shops, with working-class, lower-middle-class and higher-income groups patronising different retailers. Moreover the 'independent' retailers who mainly served the working-class market had an often problematic relationship with their customer base – tying their patronage via credit provision, treating their own staff in ways that shocked even contemporaries, using their collective political power to lobby for the restriction of competition from other retail formats and advocating 'economy' in government – seeking to block or limit measures to improve conditions for the working classes, such as state education, council housing, or social welfare provision.

Conversely, while some retail class segmentation remained in 1939, there had been a real transformation, with the development of 'popular' retailers accessible to (and, in some cases, patronised by) all classes. Variety store chains – Woolworths, Marks & Spencer and British Home Stores – represented the fullest development of this trend, though it was evident among a much broader range of retailers, from 'popular' department stores, to multi-product and line-specialised multiples such as Boots, Montague Burton and Drage's.

Lower-income families benefited substantially from a number of inter-related innovations by the new popular retailers. Clearly marked prices increased the confidence with which consumers could make purchases, without fear of finding that the price was more than they could afford. Moves to semi-self-service retailing methods reinforced this trend, by removing the sales assistant as the arbiter of what goods were offered following a customer's request. Moreover, by cutting out the wholesaler and pressing manufacturers to introduce greater standardisation and mass production techniques, stores such as Woolworths and Marks & Spencer succeeded in achieving substantial price reductions over a wide range of goods. Their stores also served as 'social centres' where people of all classes could meet and browse at their leisure, without pressure to purchase. Finally, as key pioneers of 'industrial welfare' they instituted new employment practices that not only improved the work conditions of their own employees but had a powerful demonstration effect on other sectors. Together these innovations reordered the UK retailing system and helped to legitimate working-class consumption.

Finally, Lucy Newton's chapter on '"Made in England": Making and Selling the Piano, 1851–1914', assesses the range of household goods made in England before the First World War. This chapter emerges directly from a project that was very close to Francesca's heart and one on which she and Lucy had embarked but were unable to complete. While the literature on the development of the staple goods industries (e.g. tobacco, clothing) and of capital goods (e.g. iron and steel, coal, shipbuilding) is extensive, we know less about the manufacturing of the goods with which the Victorians and Edwardians filled their homes, such as furniture, carpets, glass, pottery, cutlery, papier mâché goods and so much more. Although studies on some individual industries exist, there is no overview of the role played by consumer goods 'Made in England' in the Second Industrial Revolution. One of the reasons for this gap in the literature is that no data exists at a macro level to isolate the impact of these industries, as output, employment and export data are available only in aggregate form (e.g. glass with bricks; furniture together with timber).

Newton's chapter approaches the issue via a case study of the piano industry and from a microhistorical perspective: by assessing first the location of these industries (expanding Alfred Marshall's list of industrial districts), then whether they were represented by trade associations and described in trade journals and 'lifestyle' magazines, such as *Hearth and Home* and *The Furnisher and Decorator*. More qualitative information on the marketing on these goods is obtained from exhibition catalogues and the archives of department stores.

The third section comprises four chapters discussing methodological issues and the interaction between different branches of history, including: emerging trends in modern British economic, cultural and social history; trust and social capital in historical perspective; the methodologies of microhistory and, finally, comparative history. Matthew Hilton's 'Twentieth-Century British History: Perspectives, Trajectories and Some Thoughts on a Revised Textbook' surveys the field and points to new directions and narratives that might guide future research, taking as its starting point the last edition of *20th Century Britain: Economic, Cultural and Social Change*, edited by Francesca Carnevali and Julie-Marie Strange, and published in 2007. It asks what a revised edition might look like today. What are the most important topics and themes that ought to be included? What have been the latest innovations in research? And what new lines of historical exploration have begun to emerge which might warrant separate treatment?

Hilton pays particular attention to the narrative framing devices we might use to provide an intellectual coherence to any such volume and, drawing upon the recent intervention by the Centre for Modern British Studies at the University of Birmingham, considers the extent to which an emphasis on 'cultures of democracy' might be used to make sense of twentieth-century Britain, again urging us to think about processes of ordering and legitimation. It argues that the transition to mass affluence and mass democracy ought to be regarded as a phenomenon which can only be understood with reference to the economic, the social, the cultural and the political. In this way, it seeks to reintegrate economic and cultural history in a manner towards which Francesca Carnevali's final research and publications were striving.

Kenneth Lipartito's chapter, 'From Social Capital to Social Assemblage', takes a critical look at how economists and historians have applied concepts such as trust, social capital and embeddedness to understand how economic actors sometimes operate in co-operative or non-self-interested ways. Their reliance on such concepts speaks to their recognition that models built purely on reductive, rational self-interest cannot explain how firms, networks, or other collective forms of enterprise operate in the real world. They thereby attempt to bring the social and the cultural back in to economic theory and history.

Utilising the concept of 'assemblages', Lipartito argues that the landscape of social capital must map a genuinely separate realm of human interaction, with its own rules and meaning. If it is reduced to a market or economic interaction by another name, then it loses this characteristic. At the same time, it must be treated as a form of capital, and thus connected in a fundamental way to the economy. To put it succinctly, the economic is inherently social, and vice versa. Following Francesca's breakthrough study of the Providence and Birmingham jewellery industries, his chapter makes the case for thinking of social capital not as an overarching structure, but a process – a contentious process that can be changed and inflected by human agency; one with winners and losers.

Likewise, trust should be seen not in utopian terms – as a way to happily unite people – but as a precarious relationship that puts actors at risk when they interact, with trust a potential tool of guile and deception. By emphasising process, time, risk and the full range of human emotions, we shift the story from the ways economic action relies on or is embedded in prior existing social institutions (trust, social capital) to the way that the economic and social are mutually constituted, and inevitably contested. In his conclusion Lipartito observes that we 'began with trust and we end with the conclusion that trust does not offer much help in understanding how agents undertake collective economic action'. Reflecting on Francesca's recognition of the importance of time and process – that time is the lever that moves all things – Lipartito argues against reductive, teleological and determinist models of the social, the economic and the relationship between them. Relationships are never organic or fundamental, nor are they stable and enduring. The notion of assemblages forces us to confront the constant work of time and process.

At the very outset of his chapter on 'Economic History and Microhistory',

Chris Wickham notes that microhistory was 'perhaps the most significant original contribution by Italian historians to historiography since the Second World War'.[2] It was a methodology in which Francesca became increasingly interested and she remains one of the pioneering scholars to have applied it to modern economic history. It is an approach to historical scholarship that could hardly be more different from the 'new economic history'. In fact, Wickham's analysis focuses specifically on the potential for a stronger relationship between microhistory and economic history – indeed he notes that, while microhistory's glamour is now somewhat faded, the one area in which it retains the potential to play a 'subversive role' is precisely economic history, not least because of that subdiscipline's predilection for grand overarching theories. For Wickham, Francesca's work on the jewellers of Providence exemplifies what an economic microhistory might look like. Looking to the future, microhistory is positioned as a way of questioning the indivisibility of all economic systems, one of the central assumptions of economic history.

The point of departure for Andrea Colli's chapter on 'Europe's Difference and Comparative History: Searching for European Capitalism' is the recent renewal of interest in the study of the 'European Corporation', both by scholars and practitioners. Part of this interest derives from the perpetually vibrant debate on the 'varieties of capitalism', which vigorously stresses the presence of different 'regional' models of capitalism and capitalist enterprise. The differences in organisational, financial and ownership structures between (very broadly speaking) North American, Continental European and Asian corporations are analysed and investigated in several research domains: as for instance in strategy and management, organisation studies, finance and corporate governance, but also economic sociology and, of course, business and economic history. Colli explores not only the differences and similarities among capitalist archetypes, but – more importantly – the impact that each model of capitalism has on the 'performance' of the corporate sector and, in consequence, the 'wealth of the nation'.

Colli's chapter also explores whether we can really talk about a 'European Corporation' model, or do we have to admit that regional variations prevail over homogeneities? Is it possible to identify similarities which, taken together, allow us to identify a sort of genetic code shared by European enterprises? Moreover, which kind of 'European Corporation' are we talking about, given that each country has a 'corporate demography', with different mixes of large, medium, small and microenterprises, while it is unclear to what extent the 'European Corporation' model covers all these variants? To answer these questions, Colli takes a comparative, longitudinal approach – an approach adopted by Francesca in her own study of European banking

2   Chris Wickham, 'Economic History and Microhistory', this volume, p. 193.

– reflecting the fact that the roots of present similarities across Europe date back to the origins of industrialisation and its progressive diffusion over the Continent. The chapter thus focuses on a number of elements common to the European corporations in the long run, while also recognising exogenous influences, common to all European countries.

The fourth and final section of the book will offer conclusions and includes both a general editors' conclusion and a bibliography of Francesca's published work.

Conclusion

By building on the work of Francesca Carnevali as an exemplar of a critical and multidisciplinary approach to historical research, we have sought, collectively, to re-establish the need for deeper and wider dialogue between different types of historical approaches (economic, social, cultural) and between history and other social sciences (economics, sociology, politics, marketing and management) in the search for innovative and original views on the worlds of production, distribution and consumption, and in the analysis of economic performance, economic change and social life. This research agenda is not only conceptually richer than that adopted in most studies with a narrow disciplinary focus, but reflects the approach of such classic thinkers as Adam Smith, Alfred Marshall, Thorstein Veblen, Joseph Schumpeter and Pierre Bourdieu, who made their great leaps in understanding precisely by being prepared to challenge existing paradigms and boundaries. If this volume can encourage new scholars to cast their theoretical and methodological nets more widely, it will indeed have succeeded in its aim of honouring Francesca's work and legacy.

In light of this, we should aim at extracting specific concepts and themes that permeate all, or most, of the chapters of the book, explicitly or implicitly. As Hilton notes in his chapter, even a relatively cohesive field such as British modern history is characterised by what 'an optimist might describe as pluralism and a pessimist as fragmentation'.[3] Such fragmentation exponentially increases as soon as fields start to be divided and then subdivided between economic, business, social, political history and so on. By identifying some concepts that (maybe unconsciously) cross chapters and themes, the hope is that their exploration might become a thematic challenge that would unify rather than divide.

The first of these concepts or themes is that of the *market* – or to be more

---

3   Matthew Hilton, 'Twentieth-Century British History: Perspectives, Trajectories and Some Thoughts on a Revised Textbook', this volume, p. 157.

precise it is an acknowledgement that we need to complicate and problematise the notion of 'the market'. In the light of the chapters presented in this volume, it is evident that behind what is often seen as a mechanical structure accommodating – more or less efficiently – demand and supply, there lies a number of dimensions and perspectives. First, as Scott and Walker and then Newton show, demand and supply are, at the very least, both managed and shaped (if not created), challenging the idea of *automatism*, and the 'market' as the physical, physiological and cultural space in which this happens. The very existence of such space, however, is in itself a creation; as Popp and Lipartito show, cultural elements are not just (or only) able to interfere in the relation between *individuals* and *markets* but, to a large extent, they themselves *make* the market. A market is as much its rituals and customs as it is the commodities traded, the money exchanged, or the services provided. If this is true, then a further question naturally emerges: who sets the rituals, the norms, the rules? From the analysis of Rinaldi and Spadavecchia, Hannah and Colli, a continuous conflict seems to emerge in a struggle for power between different components and actors in markets, and what surprises the reader is the kaleidoscopic and diverse nature of the players across time and space: small versus big, finance versus production, firms versus political forces, and technocrats versus democratic powers.

The complex and diverse *natures* of the market and of market exchange over time and space call for an attempt at providing an explanation of the *meta rules* of behaviour that allowed such complexity to survive. This leads to a second theme of the book, that of *trust*, which can be analysed in terms of that which drives economic agents to operate together. In a way, the forces that shape trust can be seen as a mirror image of those that make the market: trust creation through socialisation (Lipartito), via rituals and customs (Popp), through effective formal rules (Hannah), repeated transactions (Newton), or a mix of social norms and rules (Rinaldi and Spadavecchia). Thus, just as we complicate the market we also seek to complicate trust as something richer – and stranger – than mere bargaining between actors. The concept of trust, however, can be seen as an epiphenomenon of a deeper issue running through the functioning of economies and society – that of legitimacy. How are the boundaries of legitimacy drawn? Who are the key 'gatekeepers'? What are the critical traditions, precedents and values that are drawn on? These issues emerge repeatedly in the chapters that follow. These struggles for legitimacy reflect the fact that the economy is as much a system of ordering – of order creation – as it is one of production, exchange or consumption. But it is also vital, we believe, to stress that these systems are cultures as much as they are structures. This is perhaps especially true of markets in fact. And so, finally, if markets are cultures then people are not simply actors; they are, first and foremost, humans. That is the overriding message of both this introduction and of the volume as a whole.

Politics, Society and Culture in the World of Production: Some Reflections on Francesca Carnevali's Legacy

PAOLO DI MARTINO

Introduction

There are historians who spend their entire academic careers inquiring into all possible details, perspectives and angles of pretty much the same topic. Some leave the scholarly community a complete reassessment of a key aspect of history, others seem to repeatedly publish the same article. Either way, summarising the intellectual achievements of their careers is relatively straightforward, although not necessarily easy.

There are some historians, on the other hand, who seem to get intellectual satisfaction only by moving from topic to topic, by radically changing perspective and methodology, by mixing quantitative with qualitative analysis, the national with the international dimension, the domestic with the comparative view. Francesca Carnevali (1964–2013) certainly belonged to this latter category. She was primarily interested in the economy and the business environment – 'how things are made', she would say – but this naturally led her to engage with the impact that society, culture, politics and gender had on the world of production she wanted to understand and study. This sensitivity towards the bigger picture made her an all-round historian, whose contribution is so fascinating to read and so hard to reduce to a few consistent lines of enquiry. Nonetheless this is a challenge which is worthwhile to take on, with the hope that in this exercise in rationalisation we do justice to Francesca's creativity and originality.

This chapter is a reflection on Francesca Carnevali's academic legacy, aimed at analysing – via perspectives from her work – some key debates in economic and business history, as well as some possible further lines of inquiry. It is based on published work, reviews of her books, presentations to conferences, grant applications, and notes for future research projects, as well as some personal memories. It takes a chronological approach, starting from the beginning of Francesca's career in the UK in the mid-1990s, to her last completed paper, published in 2013.[1]

The chapter is organised as follows. In the first section the background to Francesca's research is set out. The following two sections analyse her contribution during the early years of her career, notably the study of comparative banking and financial history, and how industrial districts function. The next three sections focus on the period that followed Francesca's rethinking of the nature and scope of economic history which took place around the mid-2000s: these analyse Francesca's interest in the idea of luxury, the renewed attention for social and cultural elements in explaining economic agents' behaviour, and her late project on 'small things'. Finally, some concluding remarks on Francesca's legacy follow.

The decline that never was?

In the first half of the 1990s, when Francesca was working on her Ph.D. at the London School of Economics, one of the most discussed topics in economic history was the alleged (and relative) decline of the British economy, in particular over the decades from the 1870s to the First World War. The case for that decline was based on the argument that the new capital-intensive technologies of the Second Industrial Revolution were fully developed in the USA and Germany, but not so much in the UK, which started to fall behind these nations and, eventually, lost its prime position.[2] The explanations for such 'failure' varied, but three main non-conflicting views emerged. The first, often referred to as the 'cultural critique', pointed the finger at the upper-class attitude that regarded engagement in manufacturing as some kind of inferior activity. In an attempt to pander to such social norms, the second generation of the productive middle class emerging from the industrial boom of the 1820s to 1850s moved away from manufacturing to embrace other more aristocratic activities (or so they were perceived). This led to a progressive decline in the nature and scope of British entrepreneurship, with the consequent progressive inability to adopt

---

1 Before embarking on her Ph.D. and then an academic career in the UK, Francesca had already carried out research on Italian economic and business history as a result of her undergraduate degree and MA dissertations. Some of the results of that research were subsequently published in international journals. See, for example, Francesca Carnevali, 'A Review of Italian Business History from 1991 to 1997', *Business History* 40 (1998), 80–94 and Francesca Carnevali, 'State Enterprise and Italy's "Economic Miracle": The Ente Nazionale Idrocarburi, 1945–1962', *Enterprise and Society* 1 (2000), 249–78.

2 Bernard Elbaum and William Lazonick, eds., *The Decline of the British Economy* (Oxford, 1986).

more advanced technologies, explore new markets, and so on.[3] Independently from this approach, but with a view fully compatible with it, other scholars started arguing that the marriage between the landed aristocracy, part of the previously productive middle class, and the pre-existing lobby of finance and commerce, produced in Britain a unique type of 'gentlemanly capitalism', where the interests of industry (and of workers) became ancillary to that of services.[4] In this interpretation the decline of British industry (and its economy) was seen as the result of an adverse institutional and political setting whose decisions, from imperial policy to tariffs, never supported manufacturing. The third interpretation of this malaise was again compatible in many ways with the cultural critique/gentlemanly capitalism view and looked at the deficiencies of the British financial and banking sector. While American businesses could rely on the support of the stock market and German firms on the commercial banks, British industrial concerns collided with the reluctance of credit institutions to fund long-term capital-intensive projects and the orientation of the financial market towards imperial businesses.[5] Both phenomena, it was argued, find their origin (or were at least compatible) in a cultural divide between the middle-class productive sector in the north of the country, and the London-based upper-class (or aspiring to be upper-class) financial and service industries.

Although during the 1980s the idea of decline had become 'the orthodoxy of British history',[6] the following decade saw the emergence of different, often opposing views: the cultural critique was dismissed on the grounds of a lack of solid and incontrovertible evidence;[7] the gentlemanly capitalism hypothesis was accused of having overlooked the complexity of British social relations and the dynamic of social mobility;[8] and the failure of banks (and of the stock market) to support manufacturing was seriously reconsidered and/or explained in terms of market efficiency.[9]

By the mid-1990s the debate thus found itself in what looked like an

---

3 Martin Wiener, *English Culture and the Decline of the Industrial Spirit, 1850–1980* (Cambridge, 1981).

4 Peter Cain and Antony Hopkins, 'Gentlemanly Capitalism and the British Expansion Overseas II: New Imperialism, 1850–1945', *Economic History Review* 40 (1987), 1–26.

5 William Paul Kennedy, *Industrial Structure, Capital Markets and the Origins of British Economic Decline* (Cambridge, 1987).

6 Martin Daunton, '"Gentlemanly Capitalism" and British Industry 1820–1914', *Past & Present* 122 (1989), 119–58 (p. 126).

7 William Rubinstein, *Capitalism, Culture, and Decline in Britain, 1750–1990* (London and New York, 1994).

8 Daunton, 'Gentlemanly Capitalism'.

9 Forrest Capie and Michael Collins, *Have the Banks Failed British Industry? An Historical Survey of Bank/Industry Relations in Britain, 1870–1990* (London, 1992); Mark Edelstein, *Overseas Investment in the Age of High Imperialism: The United Kingdom, 1850–1914* (London, 1982); Sidney Pollard, 'Capital Export, 1870–1914: Harmful or Beneficial?', *Economic History Review* 38 (1985), 489–514.

intellectual cul-de-sac. Francesca, who was deeply interested in bank–industry relations, realised that the traditional approaches to the question of the possible financial origins of British decline were doomed to fail in the face of growing criticism. Convinced that an economic decline had taken place in Britain during the Victorian and Edwardian years and that the banking sector had played a part in it, Francesca had to find new approaches and perspectives to make her case.

This need for alternative views on this topic shaped Francesca's early career, and led to the emergence of two ideas. The first was to try to go beyond the mere perspective of market-based efficiency in the analysis of the banking and financial sector, and to embrace wider aspects, including political economy. The second was to abandon the domestic view (or at least the standard comparison of Britain versus Germany or the USA) to measure the performance and impact of the British financial sector in a truly comparative way.

Politics matters, does *the* market? (1996–2002, and 2005)

As we saw in the previous section on the debate about the alleged decline of the British economy, finance and banking played a central role. Francesca offered her contribution to the topic first in various articles and book chapters published between 1995 and 2002 and, eventually, with her monograph *Europe's Advantage*, which appeared in 2005.[10] Although she had already moved on to the study of other topics (for example, the functioning of industrial districts) by the time it appeared, this volume was conceived and developed mainly during the mid-to-late 1990s and it makes sense to analyse its content together with other works published during these years as an integral part of her early academic career.

The core of Francesca's argument, which somehow often escaped both enthusiastic and critical reviewers alike,[11] is that the historical evolution of

---

10   Francesca Carnevali and Leslie Hannah, 'The Effects of Banking Cartels and Credit Rationing on UK Industrial Structure and Economic Performance Since World War Two', *Anglo-American Financial Systems: Institutions and Markets in the Twentieth Century*, ed. Michael Bordo and Richard Sylla (Homewood, IL, 1995), pp. 65–88; Francesca Carnevali, 'Between Markets and Networks: Regional Banks in Italy', *Business History* 38 (1996), 83–100; Francesca Carnevali and Peter Scott, 'The Treasury as a Venture Capitalist: DATAC Industrial Finance and the Macmillan Gap, 1945–60', *Financial History Review* 6 (1999), 47–65; Francesca Carnevali, 'Did They Have it So Good? Small Firms and British Monetary Policy in the 1950s', *Journal of Industrial History* 5 (2002), 15–35; Francesca Carnevali, *Europe's Advantage: Banks and Small Firms in Britain, France, Germany, and Italy Since 1918* (Oxford, 2005).
11   For the former, see Duncan Ross, 'Review of: *Europe's Advantage: Banks and Small Firms in Britain, France, Germany, and Italy Since 1918*', *Economic History Review* 59 (2006), 862–3; Christophe Lastecoueres, 'Review of: *Europe's Advantage: Banks and Small Firms in Britain,*

banking in Europe cannot be understood by looking at market-based factors alone. A number of decisions were in fact directly (or indirectly via strong incentives) the result of a process of political economy which led to extreme levels of functional and structural bank diversity between the UK, France, Germany and Italy.

This argument was first developed by looking at specific aspects of the evolution of British and Italian banks, and their behaviour in specific circumstances, in particular regarding the financing of small businesses. In a book chapter published in 1995, written together with Leslie Hannah, Francesca started from the premise that, in theory, credit rationing might take place even in a competitive market, as the result of risk evaluation of various avenues for investment being affected by the different degrees of asymmetric distribution of information between borrowers and lenders. In practice, however, other factors can interact with the natural asymmetric state of information distribution in the credit market, making the risk of credit rationing more severe in some cases and less in others. In the British case, for example, cartelisation allowed relatively higher profits in return for the same or even lower risk. In such situations, the relative risk/return spectrum of some investments artificially worsened, with credit to small business in particular becoming progressively less appealing, leading to an artificial contraction of supply to those clients.[12] Cartelisation, in itself a response to economic policies (or lack thereof), was not the only case of incentives resulting from political decisions influencing bank behaviour. In an article co-written with Peter Scott in 1999, for instance, Francesca showed how criteria set up by the Treasury, in terms of the promotion of those industries dominated by big business, reinforced the aversion of British banks to lend to small firms.[13] This argument was further developed in a paper published in 2002, where it was argued that British monetary policies adopted as part of the stop-go approach of the 1950s, and in particular the sudden increases of central bank rates, had a negative impact on the growth of firms in general but much more so to small businesses, given their lack of alternative sources of financial support.[14] This picture stood at odds with case in Italy, which was considered to be the quintessential example of political promotion of small banks and small firms. In a paper published in 1996, Francesca showed how – thanks to their embeddedness in the local economy – small banks in Italy were able to produce and

France, Germany, and Italy Since 1918', Financial History Review 15 (2008), 98–100; and John Wilson, 'Review of: Europe's Advantage: Banks and Small Firms in Britain, France, Germany, and Italy Since 1918', Business History 48 (2006), 605–6. For the latter, see Forrest Capie, 'Review of: Europe's Advantage: Banks and Small Firms in Britain, France, Germany, and Italy Since 1918', Business History Review 80 (2006), 610–12.

12   Carnevali and Hannah, 'The Effects of Banking Cartels'.
13   Carnevali and Scott, 'The Treasury as a Venture Capitalist'.
14   Carnevali, 'Did They Have it So Good?'.

share key information. The consequences for banks' policies, however, were strongly reinforced by a legislative intervention that limited the customer base for many banks; in such situations credit institutions had to opt for fully exploiting their natural advantage of dealing with a local clientele, rather than expansion and diversification.[15]

These considerations were generalised and qualified in Francesca's book which analyses, in comparative perspective, Great Britain, France, Germany and Italy in both the interwar period and that of the 1950s and 1960s. Francesca began from the standpoint that no capitalist system emerges and develops by simply responding to market forces: the strength and impact of lobbying, as well as the way in which this is channelled through the political system, determines key aspects, including the features of the financial sector. To use her words: 'the differences between the economies of Britain, France, Italy, and Germany are the result of the interplay between social, economic, and political groups and of the victories and defeats of different groups at different times'.[16] The first implication is that focusing on the alleged superiority or inferiority of given economic models is futile, as none of them is actually fully tested on pure market logic, thus efficiency in a strict sense does not exist. In fact, different systems serve different interests and have different aims. However, insofar as the size segmentation of firms and the parallel existence of small, medium or big business can be seen as an advantage, then size segmentation of banks too is a positive attribute, as only a segmented credit market sector has the ability to reduce the information gap vis-à-vis different borrowers and serve all types of business. This is what happened, although to different degrees, in Continental Europe via the pressure of local business lobbies. Britain stands out as an exception, and not because a more concentrated banking sector was the only possible response to market challenges and opportunities, but mainly because of the political weakness of local interests. Although often confused for a book arguing for the existence of a specific British malaise, Francesca was indeed very careful to also stress the advantages of the British system, such as the greater stability of its financial and banking sector.

Small yet beautiful (2003–04)

Analysis of banking in comparative perspective thus unveiled to Francesca the complexity of the dual interaction between finance and political economy on the one hand, and finance and production on the other. The latter point dictated the direction of the next step in Francesca's research; if, as shown,

---

15   Carnevali, 'Between Markets and Networks'.
16   Carnevali, *Europe's Advantage*, p. 2.

the limited development of small local banks in Britain was engineered rather than market-produced, than it became worthwhile to analyse how British small firms had managed to swim against the tide of limited institutional financial support.

This line of inquiry led Francesca to analyse the functioning of a particular industrial district: the Birmingham jewellery quarter. At the beginning, it was a technical issue that mainly attracted Francesca's attention: the fact that this district was able to produce great quantities of relatively cheap items, despite most firms being of an extremely small size. Francesca then showed how this took place via complex networks of contracting and subcontracting, with firms sharing buildings and having the ability to 'rent' workers from each other in order to balance the needs of individual concerns and accommodate fluctuations in demand.[17] The picture that emerged was a fascinating and original mix of the various ideal types of industrial districts identified by Sabel and Zeitlin in their seminal work on the subject.[18] In Birmingham it was quite common, in cases where there was a rapid increase in demand, for integrated firms to subcontract the production of parts to local artisans with a logic that resembled that of the 'municipality' model. At the same time, the habit of local craftsmen in sharing the use of the same premises to save on the cost of machinery echoed the features of the 'paternalistic' type of industrial district, while the strategy of firms banding together to buy raw materials in bulk echoes that of the 'federated' system. Some of the features of the district, however, went beyond the ideal type identified in the literature: the establishment of the school of design to help training and retraining was co-financed by various firms, in an organisational model halfway between paternalistic and municipality.

The analysis of the virtuous interactions that characterised firms in the Birmingham jewellery sector opened the door to further questions and, in particular, to the study of the reasons why a number of firms concentrated in a small geographic area would compete fairly but also co-operate efficiently. At the time Francesca was inquiring into these aspects, the literature on districts was dominated by economic sociologists, mainly Italian, who provided an explanation that pointed towards a natural tendency to share cultural elements and social norms which was automatically provided by geographic proximity.[19] Being physically close to each other, so the argument runs, led to the rise of natural trust among economic agents, deriving from

17 Francesca Carnevali, 'Golden Opportunities: Jewellery Making in Birmingham Between Mass Production and Specialty', *Enterprise and Society* 4 (2003), 272–98.

18 Charles Sabel and Jonathan Zeitlin, 'Historical Alternatives to Mass Production: Politics, Markets and Technology in Nineteenth-Century Industrialization', *Past & Present* 108 (1985), 133–76.

19 For example, Giacomo Becattini, Marco Bellandi, Gabi Dei Ottati and Fabio Sforzi, eds., *From Industrial Districts to Local Development* (Cheltenham, 2003).

sharing the same cultural environment; to use the famous expression by Granovetter, economic actions were embedded in social relationships.[20] Trust shaped socially in this way was, in turn, the glue that held together industrial districts and allowed firms to co-operate without having to rely exclusively on expensive and often incomplete contracts, as would have happened in 'normal' market-based transactions. From the very beginning, such explanations left Francesca very cold for two reasons. The first concerned the nature of such social relationships, what exactly they were and meant, and their supposed 'natural' derivation from geographic proximity. In a book chapter published in 2003, Francesca thus demonstrated how, in the case of nineteenth-century Birmingham, social norms were in fact slowly and patiently constructed, and she also carefully analysed exactly how they operated in facilitating economic transactions among agents and firms.[21] Very little of the supposed natural and automatic trust creation was at work, nor did trust among economic agents, once established, function in a predictable and straightforward way.

The second line of criticism levelled at economic sociology runs even deeper. According to Francesca, most of the sociological literature risked falling into a tautological trap by arguing that firms co-operated because they trusted each other, but they also trusted each other through the repetition of co-operative games. In other words, even if social norms and cultural views played a part in Francesca's early analysis of the functioning of industrial districts, she found them progressively less and less convincing. Starting from this disaffection for culture-based explanations, Francesca turned her attention to the institutional analysis that had emerged in economics out of the classic works by Oliver Williamson.[22] The result of this approach appeared in a paper by Francesca published in the *Economic History Review* in 2004, again analysing the functioning of the Birmingham jewellery quarter.[23] From the very title, 'Crooks, Thieves, and Receivers', it seems to be clear just how little of this natural trust actually existed among the members of this industry, opening up the question of what other forces were actually at work in ensuring long-term co-operation. The answer was to be found in the analysis of formal institutions, such as the establishment of trade associations

20   Mark Granovetter, 'Economic Action and Social Structure: The Problem of Embeddedness', *American Journal of Sociology* 91 (1985), 481–510.

21   Francesca Carnevali, '"Malefactors and Honourable Men": The Making of Commercial Honesty in Nineteenth-Century Industrial Birmingham', *Industrial Clusters and Regional Business Networks in England, 1750–1970*, ed. John F. Wilson and Andrew Popp (Aldershot 2003), pp. 192–207.

22   Among many others, Oliver Williamson, 'The Modern Corporation: Origins, Evolutions, Attributes', *Journal of Economic Literature* 19 (1981), 1537–68, and Oliver Williamson, *The Economic Institutions of Capitalism* (New York, 1985).

23   Francesca Carnevali, '"Crooks, Thieves, and Receivers": Transaction Costs in Nineteenth-Century Industrial Birmingham', *Economic History Review* 57 (2004), 533–50.

and the rules that they promoted and enforced. Pushed by phases of declining demand, jewellers organised a series of institutional devices revolving around the trade association (quality control; a school of design; acquisition of stocks of failed firms) to avoid the collapse of prices and unfair cannibalisation among firms. It was the threat of being expelled from such an association, and the consequent loss of reputation and business connections, that created a credible enforcement. Proximity had nothing to do with the development of natural trust, as argued by the sociologists, rather it facilitated the circulation of information and reduced the cost of monitoring behaviour, as claimed by the new institutional economists. In other words, formal institutions reduced transaction costs in a credible way, and for economic agents it became more convenient to play by the rules and enjoy long-term business stability, than free-ride in the search for short-term solutions to demand contraction.

Luxury for the masses (2007–11)

Francesca's long (and successful) struggle with institutional analysis, culminating in the publication of her first paper in the *Economic History Review* in 2004, together with the delivery of her book in 2005, represented a watershed in her research. Between 2005 and 2006, her growing disaffection with what she perceived as the oversimplification of pure economics-based, and narrowly conceived, economic history, led to the emergence of three new perspectives.

The first saw her attempt to expand the borders of economic history by incorporating elements and methodologies from different disciplines and types of history. Francesca's knowledge of a wide spectrum of diverse literatures made her realise that while the study of *production* had become a monopoly of economic history, the other side of the coin, *consumption*, was mainly if not exclusively analysed by social and cultural historians. Bizarrely, the link between the two spheres, *distribution*, was again mainly confined to a third disciplinary field, business history, and in particular the history of marketing. In Francesca's view, however, this was little short of intellectual suicide, as no one aspect could be fully understood without looking at the other two. Very likely, the awareness of the research potential implicit in bridging these literatures was also the result of her editing, together with Julie-Marie Strange, the second edition of the textbook *20th Century Britain*. This was an ambitious and successful volume, providing a wide and diverse perspective – social, cultural and economic – on the main issues of twentieth-century British history.[24]

24 Francesca Carnevali and Julie-Marie Strange, eds, *20th Century Britain: Economic, Cultural and Social Change* (Harlow, 2007).

Starting from her profound knowledge of the jewellery industry, Francesca realised that she already had the concept and the topic to try to combine these three literatures: luxury. In a paper published in 2007,[25] Francesca analysed the dynamic between the jewellery industry in Birmingham and London in the late nineteenth century, and in an original way managed to link the issue of the identity of different types of consumers, and of the cities in which they lived, to the technological and distributional aspects of various categories of jewellery. Thanks to advances in high-volume machine-based technology, Birmingham managed to successfully imitate and adapt the expensive designs made in London, allowing for the democratisation of jewellery consumption during the Victorian period. The spread of such technology, combined with the possible mass distribution of cheap goods, however, could have resulted in dramatic consequences for the industry in general, given that London-made goods came with a perceived exclusiveness, in turn linked directly to status and class identity. What emerged, instead, was a high degree of planned market segmentation which led to a dynamic equilibrium between production and identity, whereby 'the existence of Birmingham, known as the place where cheap, imitation jewellery was made, allowed the consumer to "forget" or ignore the fact that cheaper, mechanised jewellery was also made in London'.[26] In a subsequent paper,[27] Francesca analysed similar issues occurring in a different market: Providence, Rhode Island, USA. Francesca's interest in the Providence industrial district – which also specialised in the production of cheap jewellery – could be seen in many ways to be the obvious next step as it represented a natural comparator to Birmingham. The paper starts with the analysis of the cultural issues that shaped customers' taste in jewellery in the USA, and explains the layers of entrepreneurship needed to turn such cultural constructs into the actual democratisation of jewellery consumption. Entrepreneurs faced two challenges: first, the complex struggle to understand (and to some extent influence) taste in a scattered market with a high degree of asymmetry of information between consumers and producers; and, secondly, the need to adapt and develop technologies able to deal successfully with such a volatile market.

What it is and why it sticks together (2007–11)

Parallel to the study of luxury, a second new line of inquiry, emerging during 2005–06, arose from the risk of under-socialisation often noted in the mainstream institutional economics of the time. The world described in

25 Francesca Carnevali, 'Luxury for the Masses', *Entreprises et Histoire* 46 (2007), 56–70.
26 Carnevali, 'Luxury for the Masses', p. 58.
27 Francesca Carnevali, 'Fashioning Luxury for Factory Girls: American Jewelry, 1860–1914', *Business History Review* 85 (2011), 295–317.

the classic works by Oliver Williamson left little, if any, actual role for social norms and beliefs. Although Williamson himself was aware of this gap (but saw it as little more than a necessary methodological device), the literature that followed his path-breaking approach ended up forgetting such caveats and analysed economic agents as totally non-social constructs, all identical in their bounded rationality and unmitigated opportunism. On the other hand, economic sociology was coming to terms with what was perceived by many, including Francesca, as the opposite problem: *over*-socialisation and the risk of mistaking basic economic incentives and efficacy-based mechanisms for the results of social interaction alone.[28]

In what remains a rather unusual and brave move, Francesca thus realised that it was possible to challenge her own previous institutional economics-based view, to reach a more complete and satisfying understanding of what shapes economic behaviour in local industrial networks. To achieve this aim, Francesca decided to focus on trade associations and social-capital formation in the USA, leading to the publication of a paper on the Providence industrial district.[29] Francesca starts her piece:

> On a sunny June morning in 1905, the twenty-sixth annual summer outing of the New England Manufacturing Jewelers and Silversmiths' Association took place in Providence, Rhode Island. The day started with a parade, headed by a twenty-piece band, followed by the Association's president, its officers, and members. According to their annual custom the men wore straw boater hats and carried opened Japanese paper sunshades.[30]

From the very beginning of the article, then, the reader understands the relevance that the author puts on cultural elements. Rather than just exploring them for their own sake, however, the paper pushes cultural history a step further, into investigating what the construction of symbols and performance of rituals can also reveal about economic behaviour. This brave methodological move is not the only one in the paper, as it is married with the rediscovery (at least in economic history) of the forgotten device of *microhistory*. This New England jewellery association, and the behaviour of its members, thus became the Trojan horse by which to investigate a wider and 'neglected topic in the history of American capitalism, that of trade associations'.[31] In this way, the paper shows how the construction of symbols and performance

28   The emergence of a new branch of economic sociology, known as 'new institutionalism in economic sociology', represented an important step in this direction. See Mary Brinton and Victor Nee, eds, *The New Institutionalism in Sociology* (New York, 1998).
29   Francesca Carnevali, 'Social Capital and Trade Associations in America, c.1860–1914: A Microhistory Approach', *Economic History Review* 64 (2011), 905–28.
30   Carnevali, 'Social Capital and Trade Associations', p. 905.
31   Carnevali, 'Social Capital and Trade Associations', p. 905.

of rituals was, to an extent, the public reaffirmation of cultural norms and beliefs about the 'rightness' of producing goods, while also fighting unionism, controlling competition and co-operating in key economic matters. But the re-establishment of such 'rightness' was not only an aim in itself; forging a strong identity was also functionally important in attracting further members, enforcing behaviour via peer pressure, and channelling individual voices into stronger and more cohesive political lobbying.

Small things and 'toys for boys' (2008–13)

Since 2007 Francesca had thus been exploring and elaborating in an original way the complex connections between the economic, the social and the cultural spheres, via a reassessment of the nature of the links between economic agents in industrial districts. On the other hand, her research on luxury was revealing the potential for a dialogue between history, economics and marketing. Together, these two directions were developing into a kind of double entry matrix that, implicitly, was setting up a further path for Francesca to follow and a new personal challenge: the idea of resurrecting the study of *production* using a totally novel approach.

Traditionally, the attention of economic historians has focused on the production of 'big' things, the sectors where scholars thought it would have been most likely to find the roots of comparative advantage, rapid productivity growth and technological revolutions. Thus, steel and cotton first, then shipbuilding, chemicals, cars and the like have been the main protagonists of economic history papers and books. Big, strong, heavy, hard; the adjectives alone that were used to describe these industries suggested to Francesca that the passion for these sectors by a traditionally male-dominated discipline could have concealed something more than, and different from, their mere economic or technological relevance. Possibly inspired by some of Deirdre McCloskey's essays,[32] Francesca started wondering whether other industries had been traditionally neglected not because of lack of relevance, but rather because they were not 'hard' enough to qualify as 'toys for boys'.[33] If so, what about looking instead at the production, consumption and distribution of household goods? Francesca realised that in Britain the impact on production and employment of industries related to the manufacture of household goods – from furniture to carpets to curtains to musical instruments – was far from negligible. In 1907, for example, they amounted to about 8–12% of

32 Francesca particularly appreciated some of the essays published in Deirdre McCloskey, *How to Be Human, Though an Economist* (Ann Arbor, MI, 2000).
33 So Francesca claimed in her presentation at the 2010 Annual Conference of the Economic History Society.

net output of total manufacturing.[34] Just as important, if not more so, the history of such objects could reveal an enormous amount of information about not only producers, but also consumers and distributors, bridging the gap between economic, social and business history. Together with her friend and colleague Lucy Newton, Francesca embarked on a new adventure entitled 'Made in Britain', which offered the potential for a complete rewriting of the history of production, consumption and marketing of household goods in Britain between 1850 and the First World War.

The pilot project of this ambitious agenda focused on pianos and resulted in the publication of a paper called 'Pianos for the People: From Producer to Consumer in Britain, 1851–1914'. This paper shows the challenges posed for both producers and distributors alike by an increasing demand for pianos following the steady increase in household income from the mid-nineteenth century onwards and on the dynamic that existed between them. Thus the production of cheaper pianos via a process of increasing mechanisation pushed towards the need for clever market segmentation. This took place through advertising, expositions and other marketing techniques, as well as opening up new distribution points, including department stores. Cheaper pianos were therefore marketed, distributed and advertised in ways that, de facto, insulated this product from comparisons with expensive pianos, which remained different objects in the eyes of consumers. As with jewellery, the democratisation of piano consumption took place via a complex interaction of producers and distributors, ensuring that increasing demand did not jeopardise the inherent status of the object, the extent of the market and the viability of the industry.

'Pianos for the People' is the last completed academic work to which Francesca contributed. Accepted for publication in late 2012, it appeared a year later, and in 2014 received an award for the best paper published in 2013 in the journal *Enterprise and Society*.[35]

Journey's end? Some conclusions

At the end of this fascinating journey, it seems clear that Francesca's route between different themes, perspectives and methodologies was indeed led by a *fil rouge*, her love of inquiry and refusal to settle for easy answers. With the

---

34 Source: Francesca Carnevali, notes for presentation at the 2010 Annual Conference of the Economic History Society.

35 Francesca Carnevali and Lucy Newton, 'Pianos for the People: From Producer to Consumer in Britain, 1851–1914', *Enterprise and Society* 14 (2013), 37–70. A book chapter, edited by Jennifer Aston, was published posthumously in 2015 as part of an edited collection: Francesca Carnevali and Jennifer Aston, 'Victorian Capitalists and Middle-Class Formation: Reflections on Asa Briggs' Birmingham', *The Age of Asa: Lord Briggs, Public Life and History in Britain Since 1945*, ed. Miles Taylor (Basingstoke, 2015), pp. 79–89.

benefit of hindsight we may now try to draw such a *fil rouge* clearly, establishing connections and links that look logical to us. Personally, however, I doubt that such logical connections were the compass that helped Francesca in her travels. Francesca, probably, just loved to reach her scheduled destination for the mere pleasure of being able to keep dreaming of new and wider horizons, and of being able to imagine, in the far distance, the borders of a new terra incognita for future exploration.[36]

Francesca had a fantastic feeling and sense for history; to use Steve Broadberry's words, she 'loved it and lived it'. In Francesca's view, history was a product of the lives of women and men and, like life, was complex and mysterious or, as Gerschenkron claimed, 'a messy housewife'. This appears even more true when we try to reconstruct these complex lives with the help of sources that, when they do exist, are incomplete, fragmented, biased in good and in bad faith, and often not conceived for the purpose of writing history.

However, in research (as well as in life) complexity might be unsettling, mystery scary and mess unpleasant, and over the centuries social scientists have given us devices to deal with all of this, promising us the holy grail of universal laws. But at what point does the search for universality across time and space just become an excuse to give in to the allure of simple and unsatisfying explanations, which might happen to coincide with our established view of the world, or allow us to publish a paper in time for the next REF evaluation or job application? At what point do expressions such as 'robustness of results' and 'rigour of analysis' stop being legitimate academic aims, and become a shortcut for narrowmindedness that shelters us from the vertigo we feel when we truly try to explore the unknown?

In her love and feel for history Francesca never feared its complexity and mystery, courted doubts rather than repudiated them and was always open to changing her mind. She left us a number of exquisitely crafted pieces of scholarship, but it is the courage to always try to look into the eyes of our intellectual fears that is, and will remain, her deepest and truest legacy.

---

36 In fact, in 2012 Francesca was exploring research on social mobility in late-nineteenth-century Britain. Some provisional results of this study were presented at the last Economic History Society Annual Conference she attended in Oxford in 2012, where the title of her presentation was 'Not Quite Gentlemen? Capitalism and Middle-Class Formation in Late Victorian England'.

PART II

BETWEEN ECONOMICS AND CULTURE: EXPLAINING BUSINESS PRACTICES IN THEIR HISTORICAL CONTEXT

I

Custom and Spectacle:
The Public Staging of Business Life

ANDREW POPP[1]

Introduction

On 6 January 1854, heavy snows fell on the great port city of Liverpool, enough to disrupt and eventually halt the open-air trading that was the preferred practice of the city's vibrant community of cotton brokers, who could, on any normal working day, be found flocked together on the 'Change Flags, the paved courtyard of the Exchange building in the heart of the business district (in Liverpool, the word Exchange was habitually shortened to 'Change). Left idle and frustrated with the unwonted interruption to trade, the cotton brokers were soon engaged in a pitched snowball fight with rival brokers from other commodity trades. Hundreds were involved. Windows were smashed and town council proceedings interrupted. When the town's police attempted to intervene they were met with volleys of both snowballs and insults; the contending brokers now had a common enemy. Perceived ringleaders, all of them prominent brokers, were taken into custody, but on their release battle simply recommenced. Now the police attempted to enter the Exchange newsroom but were roughly ejected. In the end it was only nightfall that brought an end to the three-sided hostilities.

Soon the day's events were being celebrated in rhyme, in a piece of doggerel written by local poet John Pedler and published in the *Liverpool Mercury*, and in image, local artist John R. Isaac producing a fine lithograph of the scene. The event is remembered to this day and receives extensive coverage on the website of the International Cotton Association (ICA), a trade association still based in Liverpool.[2] Pedler's pseudo-epic records how:

1   I gratefully acknowledge the generous support of the Visiting Professor Programme and Unit for Economic History of the University of Gothenburg. I also want to thank Ken Lipartito and Barbara Hahn for their insightful comments on drafts of this chapter.
2   http://www.ica-ltd.org/about-ica/our-history/1830-1913/.

> So without more ado, they the matter cut short
> And snowballs they threw, at each other for sport
> Thus forgetting awhile, both the cotton and grain
> To resume the arch smile, of their boyhood again.[3]

Pedler's verse seems to emphasise that this was a moment of play, a suspension of normal behaviour: a moment of *misrule*, significant, if at all, only in its exceptionality. Are not those moments in which we are confronted with a 'world turned upside down', in the end, only ever about a reinforcing of the status quo? In this light, the snowball fight appears a mere 'intrusion … compulsive, rather than self-conscious or self-activating'.[4] What I want to argue, instead, is that the great snowball fight, and its celebration, was an assertion, and a highly public one, of prerogatives the brokers saw as central to their identities and practices.

Exactly fifty years after the great snowball fight an anonymous postcard of the Liverpool Exchange was posted from the city. It was covered in a series of cryptic and mysterious annotations and drawings, but the picture printed on it is remarkably mundane: the 'Change Flags on what is very likely simply an ordinary working day (Figure 1.1).[5] However, this picture comes alive when viewed against almost any other similar postcard of the same view – and there are many, easily found in online searches. What had appeared to be a random distribution of figures is suddenly thrown into high relief and we begin to see the ways in which it is, in fact, strongly patterned. Specifically, in many images the majority of the figures are arranged in a series of tight knots of men clustered over towards the left margin of the scene, where the Cotton Rooms were to be found.[6] There they stand, in near-mirror images, appearing like characters on a stage, performing a role, the winged Exchange Building itself standing in as a magnificent proscenium arch, a framing fit for the dramas, variously tragic, comedic and mundane, taking place in the centre.

The men in these postcards are once more the city's vital cotton brokers and, in a much quieter but no less powerful way, they are asserting the same prerogatives that were at stake during the mêlée of 1854 – expressed as the

---

3   http://www.bbc.co.uk/news/uk-england-merseyside-16070003.
4   Edward Palmer Thompson, 'The Moral Economy of the English Crowd in the Eighteenth Century', *Past & Present* 50 (1971), 76–136 (p. 76).
5   For a study of this postcard see Andrew Popp, 'The Broken Cotton Speculator', *History Workshop Journal* 78 (2014), 133–56.
6   A cursory search reveals numerous, broadly contemporaneous postcards of the Exchange. Some do show the Exchange Flags either empty or sparsely populated, or very densely but evenly crowded, but the majority clearly show the same basic distribution of figures as seen in the image reproduced here.

Figure 1.1. Postcard of the Liverpool Exchange, 1904

right to trade in the open air.[7] It was a claim barely diminished by such innovations as the establishment of the Liverpool Cotton Clearing House (1874), the Liverpool Cotton Bank (1878), the Liverpool Cotton Association (1882) or, indeed, the construction of a new Exchange Building, complete with dedicated cotton trading room, in the mid-1860s. This chapter begins with a simple question: what did open-air trading mean to Liverpool's cotton brokers that they would persist with it for so long?

This public open-air trading is an example of what we might call the public staging of business life, which might include the performing of a rich array of events and occasions, spectacular and mundane, unique and repeated, ranging from galas, dinners and parades through riots, revelry and disputes, to patterns of behaviour during commutes, lunch hours and gatherings before and after work. Though everywhere, these elements to business life have been largely neglected in the historical literature. One striking aspect of such performances tends to be their persistence. A second is their relationship to the

7   Open-air trading nominally ended on 4 January 1896 when the Liverpool Cotton Association moved to new premises in Brown's Buildings, overlooking the Exchange Flags. The evidence from later pictorial representations suggests an at least vestigial survival after that date. In 1906 a purpose-built Cotton Exchange was opened on Old Hall Street, just two or three minutes walk from the main Exchange. This development probably did sound the death knell for open-air trading.

spaces in which they take place and the communities that perform them. We
might view these occasions and behaviours as 'communicative events' or 'forms
of symbolic action' with constitutive power, giving them an interest beyond
their surface display.[8] The brokers were making a market – especially that for
cotton futures – possessing material, cultural and expressive dimensions. They
were, in the end, making financial capitalism and themselves as capitalists
and market subjects. These processes of making were rooted as much in
the subjectivities of the brokers as in any presumed economic rationality. These
subjectivities expressed themselves through practices that I position as customs.
Though nominally capitalism's winners, Liverpool's cotton brokers still had to
stake their claim and they did so, in part, through enacting customs.

I will use a range of sources and literatures in making an argument
that is perhaps more provocative than definitive. Sources include, among
others, images, memoirs and novels. Thus I follow a method of clues.[9] This
microhistory-inspired method seems doubly appropriate; being apt not only
to the fragmentary and allusive sources from which I draw my hints but also
to Francesca Carnevali's questing methodological spirit. Indeed, the piece of
Francesca's work from which I take my starting point is explicitly subtitled 'A
Microhistory Approach'.[10] I cannot here begin to do justice to the complexity
and subtly of this methodological tradition, not least as this volume carries
an authoritative essay on the subject from Chris Wickham, but I apply it as
best I can.[11]

For interpretive lenses I draw not simply on business and economic history
but also economic sociology, anthropology, the history of capitalism and,
above all else, the work of social historian E. P. Thompson. In doing so I
hope to further the disciplinary and methodological dialogue that was so
important to Francesca and is central to this present volume.

The chapter is structured, somewhat unusually, thus. In the first section I
will begin by laying out how this chapter emerges in response to problems and
questions that were central to Francesca's own work. I will then examine the
Liverpool cotton market in the nineteenth century before turning to the role
of open-air trading within that market. Thereafter I will introduce the notion
of custom, first theoretically and then applied, as a lens through which to
understand the persistence of open-air trading in Liverpool's cotton markets.
A final section presents conclusions.[12]

---

8   Peter Burke, 'Performing History: The Importance of Occasions', *Rethinking History* 9
(2005), 35–52 (p. 38).
9   Carlo Ginzburg, *Clues, Myths and the Historical Method* (Baltimore, 1989).
10   Francesca Carnevali, 'Social Capital and Trade Associations in America, c.1860–1914: A
Microhistory Approach', *Economic History Review* 64 (2011), 905–28.
11   Chris Wickham, 'Economic History and Microhistory', this volume.
12   This structure emerges from a microhistorical desire to read outwards from the anomalous
phenomenon examined.

Performing the market?

Francesca, with her undeniable flair and style, understood the importance of spectacle and display. She opened her 2011 *Economic History Review* article on associationalism in Providence, Rhode Island, with a fine flourish of parades, bands and paper parasols.[13] It is, I think, my favourite passage in all her writing. Critically, the intent was not merely to add colour (though that effect is splendidly achieved) but to make a serious point, one I only began to grasp as I looked at images of the Liverpool Exchange, placed side by side. In so opening this late piece, Francesca presented us with an interpretative choice:

> We can interpret concerts, banquets, picnics and clambakes as just the leisurely pursuits of an aspiring middle class or as having a deeper meaning ... [we] can see these events, such as the annual parade, as deeply symbolic, meant to create a collective and public experience based on occupational identity that would forge ties between individuals.[14]

The interpretive choice that Francesca made was clear. She opened her article with the staging of the parade in Providence on that day in 1905 precisely in order to emphasise that this event was not mere froth or *mise en scène*, embroidery on the surface of the fabric of social and economic interaction. Rather, it is *itself* part of the very warp and weft of that fabric; an occasion through which vital social interactions were staged and performed and through which activities both markets and market subjects were actively made and remade.

Francesca's work on the jewellers of Providence emerged from a sustained concern to better understand regional economic development, particularly via the concept of the 'industrial district'. This was a literature in which she and I shared a strong interest and to which she made significant contributions from a business history perspective. A central problem of the industrial district literature is the distinctive balancing of competition and co-operation held to be a characteristic of these spatial concentrations of industries and firms. It is worth briefly considering how this problem is typically treated in the industrial district literature in order to highlight, by way of contrast, the argument I want to make here, an argument towards which I think Francesca was already moving.

Firms in industrial districts, inhabiting structures marked by high degrees of vertical and horizontal dis-integration, face considerable problems of market co-ordination. Following Ronald Coase's insights, in an industrial district,

---

13 Carnevali, 'Social Capital and Trade Associations'.
14 Carnevali, 'Social Capital and Trade Associations', p. 918.

many activities are carried out and co-ordinated via market mechanisms rather than by managerial authority within large, integrated organisations. Crucially, firms in districts use markets to both co-operate *and* to compete along the value chain (in both intermediate and final product markets). The market is both boon and bane. It is the source of stimulating competitive pressures but also poses a near constant danger that district firms will compete each other into the ground.[15] A mechanism is needed to co-ordinate (and mediate) competition, while simultaneously promoting co-operation. This is a problem of some difficulty, both for actors on the ground and for theorists. As Sabel and Zeitlin succinctly state, in industrial districts 'the central problem of industrial organization was ... the coordination of decentralization'.[16] Alfred Marshall's concept of external economies of scale and scope might explain *why* decentralisation can have powerful competitive effects, but it does not explain *how* it works and, in particular, how it can be productively channelled.

An economist, Alfred Marshall believed decentralisation could be 'thoroughly effected without conscious effort'.[17] More recent theorists have though taken inspiration from a relatively opaque line of Marshall's work – that industrial districts possess an 'industrial atmosphere' that is 'as it were ... in the air'. From this single under-examined observation, they have developed a central role for trust between economic actors in industrial districts, with trust being promoted by spatial, social and cultural proximity, and sustained through ongoing interactions within the marketplace (via a history of successful transacting).

Most of us probably experience trust as a largely psychological and emotional state. In the industrial district literature it is often treated as a matter of rationality; the product of game-theoretic processes that reward forbearance from opportunities to exploit asymmetries in economic relationships. Trust so conceived deracinates individuals, reducing their relations to the sum of the (economic, contractual) interactions in a reified marketplace. As Francesca argued, the 'danger with this functionalist approach ... is that cooperation is reduced to little more than a coordination game, in which economic self-interest is the only driving force and the institutions created to reduce transaction costs are always efficient'.[18] Though markets are seen as socially embedded their basic constitution is left unexamined because the existence of the market is assumed to be unproblematic, conforming to an almost platonic ideal.

---

15   Andrew Popp, *Business Structure, Business Culture and the Industrial District: The Potteries, c.1850–1914* (Aldershot, 2001).
16   Charles Sabel and Jonathan Zeitlin, *World of Possibilities: Flexibility and Mass Production in Western Industrialization* (Cambridge and New York, 1997), p. 21.
17   Alfred Marshall, *Industry and Trade* (London, 1919), p. 601.
18   Carnevali, 'Social Capital and Trade Associations', p. 908.

Similarly, from a perspective of social embeddedness, actors no longer appear as simple *Homo economicus*, instead they come imbued with identities and subjectivities formed by a range of social determinants – gender, kinship, religion, ethnicity, ideology – but they bring these identities and subjectivities to an encounter with a reified market that exists independently of them and their actions. The rationalities of the market are interpreted and navigated via these identities and subjectivities, but it is the market rationalities that are both prior and central in this encounter; market rationalities are filtered through the subjectivities of actors but remain at root unmodified. Moreover, as Francesca highlighted, over-socialised embeddedness arguments often risk sliding into the tautological, in which trust explains co-operation, which explains trust.

What, though, if we were to enquire into the constitution of markets and of market subjects? Though she was not able to proceed to a detailed consideration of this question it is, I believe, one towards which Francesca was moving. Across an increasing number of fields – including the new history of capitalism, economic sociology and ethnography – it is argued that markets and capitalism are made and remade. They have powerful performative dimensions, through which they are constituted. Market subjects – a Liverpool cotton broker, for example – are created through the same processes, at the core of which lie *subjectivities*, not *rationalities*.

Ethnographer Caitlin Zaloom, for example, in her study of contemporary futures exchanges, stresses that 'when thousands of [traders] gather every day, they help create something larger – the market'.[19] They do so using 'existing materials ... [and] existing habits', locating the processes through which the market is constituted in time and space.[20] Zaloom places considerable emphasis on the materiality of these processes, arguing that in the nineteenth century the Chicago Board of Trade (CBOT):

> began to construct a site of trade that reconciled an abstract notion of the market with the physical structure of the city and the architecture of the CBOT's marketplace ... the space of the city became the space of their trade.

This relationship to space was not one of merely containing or locating the marketplace but was also constitutive, such that 'each iteration of the market was an opportunity to renegotiate how to make markets in stone, wood, and steel'.[21] The Exchanges constructed by the CBOT were 'an experiment in the

---

19 Caitlin Zaloom, *Out of the Pits: Traders and Technology from Chicago to London* (Chicago, 2006), p. 2.
20 Zaloom, *Out of the Pits*, pp. 4–5.
21 Zaloom, *Out of the Pits*, p. 17.

social shape of the market'.[22] These Exchange buildings became arenas for a 'cultural infrastructure', spaces that 'define the actions that *can* happen there and the actions that *must* happen' and places in which brokers could 'congregate as men', that is as constituted market subjects.[23] In these spaces, drawing on a cultural infrastructure, attempting to conform to 'norms of economic action' (and what is a norm but a *subjectivity?*), traders were simultaneously 'being the market and acting in it'.[24] The market was not constituted and expressed only through the materiality of architecture and the city but also in and through the bodies of traders, their eye and hand movements, the sounds of their voices. Critically, even as the spaces, technologies and cultures of trading changed over the twentieth-century and into the twenty-first, the 'CBOT's historical attachment to open-outcry trading was not easily broken. The members' collective commitment to the cultural life and form of labor based in the trading pits was as fierce as the spirit of Chicago commerce.'[25]

A similar approach is evident in the work of sociologist Donald MacKenzie, who argues that practices are produced and reproduced in concrete, bodily contexts repeated over time. One telling example he gives is of how:

> The bodily aspects of arbitrage are most prominent when it is performed in open-outcry trading 'pits': stepped amphitheatres, traditionally octagonal. Dozens or hundreds of traders stand on the rungs of a pit, making deals by voice or by eye contact and an elaborate system of hand signals.[26]

We are immediately alerted to profound continuities of behaviour across gulfs of space and time – from nineteenth-century Chicago (or Liverpool) to twenty-first-century London. There is not space here to do justice to the sophisticated work done by MacKenzie and his collaborators. Nonetheless, one key idea is that of assemblages or *agencement*, a notion that 'helpfully directs us to the conditions of possibility of economic actors: the often-ignored infrastructure that enables them to be the actors they are'. Thus, Mackenzie, like Zaloom, sees the making of the market taking place through repeated embodied enactments located in specific *materialities*. Critically, MacKenzie also sees economic theory as itself performative, another source of subjectivities through which markets and actors are made.

The emergent history of capitalism also argues for a more contingent view of the market and its constitution. In *The Cotton Kings*, for example, Bruce Baker and Barbara Hahn paint a picture of global cotton markets – spot

22 Zaloom, *Out of the Pits*, p. 25.
23 Zaloom, *Out of the Pits*, pp. 11, 26 and 37.
24 Zaloom, *Out of the Pits*, pp. 5 and 6.
25 Zaloom, *Out of the Pits*, p. 49.
26 Daniel Beunza, Iain Hardie and Donald MacKenzie, 'A Price is a Social Thing: Towards a Material Sociology of Arbitrage', *Organization Studies* 27 (2006), 721–45 (p. 731).

and futures – at the turn of the twentieth-century that while at least partly independent of the actors populating it is also full of fallibility, malleability, irrationality and competing subjectivities. Supply, demand and their matching, in particular, emerge as notions and processes riddled with irrationalities and based in prices almost entirely detached from the commodities to which they are meant to relate. Market subjects' *beliefs*, whether those of bears or bulls, had far more bearing on the constitution of the market for cotton than either the crop growing in the fields or the demand pent up in Lancashire's mills.[27]

We might also draw on the performative turn in history. Burke, arguing for the 'importance of occasions', suggests that this performative turn 'reveals a reinterpretation of the old dramaturgical model. Instead of drawing analogies between society and the theatre, the new approach dissolves the boundaries between them', reinforcing the idea advanced here of the staging of business life.[28] Critically, aligning with the emphasis on the constitutive power of social action to be found in ethnography and sociology, Burke goes on to stress how 'studies of ritual emphasize that "performance is never mere enactment" or expression, but has an active role to play'.[29] Areas of life to which Burke believes a performative turn can help bring light include rituals and festivals, architectures, executions, processions and other performances and customs of the state, law and power, and all '"framed" events that are deliberately set apart from everyday life'.[30]

I next sketch the rise of cotton broking as a key element in Liverpool's growth and development during the nineteenth century before introducing the long-lasting attachment of the city's cotton brokers to the public spectacle of open-air trading.

Making a market for cotton in Liverpool

During the nineteenth century Liverpool became the dominant location in global cotton markets. Perhaps physical resource endowments (geographical location at the mouth of the River Mersey, facing the Atlantic) enabled this concentration but they did not guarantee its success. Instead, through a progressive and cumulative process of expansion, learning and innovation, the city increasingly specialised in and excelled at a range of activities associated with seaborne international trade: shipping and ship-ownership; merchanting; banking and finance; insurance; the construction and provision

---

27 Bruce E. Baker and Barbara Hahn, *The Cotton Kings: Capitalism and Corruption in Turn-of-the-Century New York and New Orleans* (Oxford, 2016).

28 Burke, 'Performing History', p. 41.

29 Burke, 'Performing History', p. 41.

30 Burke, 'Performing History', p. 43.

of port facilities; warehousing; and the leisure, hospitality and retailing services needed to cater for a growing bourgeoisie, both resident and visiting. There was some manufacturing but it was dwarfed in scale and importance by trade and its attendant services. And among the many commodities traded from and passing through the port cotton was by far the most important. Alongside the flourishing port and docks there emerged an increasingly sophisticated central business district that constantly physically remade itself without ever moving from a relatively compact site a few minutes walk from the waterfront.[31] Here new experiments were launched in, for example, how office space might be provided, designed, built and serviced. Alongside or within this evolving physical fabric, the 'soft' tissue of the mercantile industrial district was comprised of a wide range of formal and informal institutions, many of them of a highly innovative kind. Equally striking was the innovation of new business practices, for example the rapid 'invention' and diffusion of futures trading in the 1850s. As it grew in size and prosperity the city grew in civic and cultural confidence, fostering a local elite connected to but not dependent on the metropolis. During the nineteenth century Liverpool truly came into its own as the second great port of Empire. And the courtyard-like space of Exchange Flags, enclosed within the wings of the Exchange building, was at the physical, psychical and active heart of this city. And perhaps no other group claimed the Exchange as their own more than a growing cohort of cotton brokers.

Cotton broking emerged in Liverpool in an ad hoc fashion during the second half of the eighteenth century. This emergence was a response to the growing opportunities for intermediation presented by the increasingly rapid growth of the cotton textile industries of north-west England and took place as Liverpool began to supplant London as the principal port for the import of raw cotton, a shift that was itself primarily a response to shifting sources of supply, specifically the growth in importance of cotton-growing states in the southern USA. Given the vital role played by brokers and brokerage in the growth of both Liverpool and the cotton textile industry the brokerage function is remarkably little researched and in some ways Ellison's book of 1886 remains the definitive work, with subsequent additions to knowledge made by Dumbell, Hyde *et al.* and Hall, among others.[32] Nonetheless, despite

---

31 Joseph Sharples and John Stonard, *Built on Commerce: Liverpool's Central Business District* (Swindon, 2008).
32 Thomas Ellison, *The Cotton Trade of Great Britain, Including a History of the Liverpool Cotton Market and the Liverpool Cotton Brokers' Association* (London, 1886); Stanley Dumbell, 'Early Liverpool Cotton Imports and the Organisation of the Cotton Market in the Eighteenth Century', *The Economic Journal* 33 (1923), 362–73; Francis E. Hyde, Bradbury B. Parkinson and Sheila Marriner, 'The Cotton Broker and the Rise of the Liverpool Cotton Market', *Economic History Review* (new series) 8 (1955), 75–83; Nigel Hall, 'The Emergence of the Liverpool Raw Cotton Market, 1800–1850', *Northern History* 38 (2001), 65–81; Nigel

this relative neglect a broad outline of the development of the role of the cotton broker is possible.

Liverpool's first cotton brokers were not specialists, they were often initially brokers in other commodities or, indeed, also followed completely unrelated professions. For example, George Holt, one of the most important early cotton brokers, maintained the business of stay-maker for some time after his first entry into brokerage.[33] However, more or less specialist brokers were certainly in existence by the end of the eighteenth century, though their numbers remained small. Nonetheless, the Cotton Brokers' Association, founded in 1841, began with a membership of ninety firms and Mäenpää has identified almost seven hundred cotton brokers as active at some point during the second half of the nineteenth century.[34]

Ellison claims that most were either selling or buying brokers, that is either selling on behalf of Liverpool and overseas-based merchants, or buying on behalf of either cotton dealers, largely based in Manchester (and whom they gradually ousted from the trade), or spinners in the surrounding cotton textile districts. In all these scenarios brokers worked on commission. Both Ellison and Hyde *et al.* also claim that cotton brokers very rarely if ever traded on their own account; that is, as merchants or dealers. Hyde *et al.* claim that 'opinion was developing that a broker's business depended for its success on the avoidance of personal speculation' and that he 'did not buy and sell on his own account'.[35] Hall convincingly demonstrates that the reality was in fact much more clouded, with probably most brokers acting for both buyers and sellers at times and many, at least occasionally, acting as merchants, dealers and speculators, sometimes on a sustained basis.[36]

Hall, 'The Business Interests of Liverpool's Cotton Brokers, c.1800–1914', *Northern History* 41 (2004), 339–55.

33 Ellison, *The Cotton Trade*, p. 67.

34 Sari Mäenpää, 'Combining Business and Pleasure? Cotton Brokers in the Liverpool Business Community in the Late 19th Century', unpublished paper, p. 1.

35 Hyde, Parkinson and Marriner, 'The Cotton Broker', p. 78.

36 Hall, 'Business Interests'. Daniels provides an account of the possible consequences of speculation in this market as 'described in a pamphlet written in 1816 by a Liverpool broker who was actually in the midst of things. After referring to the arrival of the news regarding the defeat of the French at Leipzig he continues: "No sooner was this news known than an immediate speculation took place in buying goods not only in Manchester, but by numbers of houses in Liverpool in buying cotton, as there was nothing equal to cotton to speculate upon, not only regular merchants, but brokers, grocers, corn merchants, timber merchants, tobacconists, coopers, etc., etc. By this speculation cottons were run up beyond all bounds, which not only seriously injured the manufactures, but many of the speculators became themselves heavy sufferers, and almost every artifice was adopted to raise unfounded reports which got inserted in the London newspapers as news from Liverpool, but which had no other foundation than merely report without cause"': George W. Daniels, 'Cotton Trade with Liverpool Under the Embargo and Non-Intercourse Acts', *The American Historical Review* 21 (1916), 276–87 (p. 286).

Intermediators are always at risk of being excluded from markets by buyers and sellers making direct contracts, but this did not happen to Liverpool's cotton brokers. In part they were aided in this by the geographical separation of markets and, initially, poor lines of transport and communication (though Liverpool's brokers were later to make good use of the arrival, in turn, of the railway, the telegraph and eventually the telephone). What they offered clients, beyond very keen rates of commission (typically 1%, considerably less than the margins normally sought by Manchester's dealers), was highly specialist knowledge and superb access to information. Ellison captured their competitive advantages with precision. The commission they earned was:

> remuneration for the special technical knowledge and for the time which in those days had to be consumed by the broker, who had to attend the warehouse and examine and select such bales as in the matter of quality and staple met the requirements of his client.[37]

The brokers were able to consistently enhance these advantages throughout the nineteenth century. That they were able to do so speaks to some very important aspects of a strong, shared culture that began developing very early. Though their claim that brokers avoided all speculation is certainly exaggerated, Hyde, Parkinson and Marriner were very probably justified in quoting Baines to the effect that the brokers possessed a code of 'strict probity and honour'.[38] In his memoir Liverpool cotton broker and politician Samuel Smith averred that any broker, if he wished to be successful:

> must work for the future, not the present. He must realize that the slow upbuilding of character brings its reward in course of time. Of nothing am I more certain than that 'Honesty is the best policy,' if spread over a lifetime, and that there is no opposition between the 'Golden Rule' and sound commercial success ... I doubt whether I ever knew of permanent success where the fundamental laws of honesty were not observed.[39]

---

37 Ellison, *The Cotton Trade*, p. 166.
38 Hyde, Parkinson and Marriner, 'The Cotton Broker', p. 79. They continued: the 'integrity of the broker [was] as much an essential feature as his skill, experience and capital in establishing him as a successful central figure in a rapidly expanding market'.
39 Samuel Smith, *My Life-Work* (London, 1902), p. 35. However, it should be noted that Smith, who entered the trade in 1853 but wrote his memoir at the very close of the nineteenth century, also argued that 'All the old landmarks of those days [the 1850s] have been swept away ... Speculation has enormously increased ... At each stage strong opposition was offered to the speculative and "demoralizing changes" as they were then styled, but nothing could stop the "the Rake's Progress" downward.' Smith seemed to strongly associate this degradation with a move away from 'bona-fide transfers of cotton in warehouse' with the result that the 'great mass of business done has long been in contracts for future delivery' (p. 17).

Perhaps the strongest and most important mark of that culture was the brokers' early-established, deep and unwavering commitment to information sharing. Commercial intelligence on the state of markets (of both supply and demand) became and remained among them a public good; one they actively gathered, collated and shared, both among themselves and with others. In this informational effort they acted as a collectivity. Daniels called them 'the intelligence department of the economic system'.[40] As Dumbell notes, 'the eighteenth-century brokers established a custom which was later to become of considerable importance, namely the circulation of market information'.[41] But what was once merely customary became increasingly formalised and was enshrined, along with the arbitration of disputes, in the foundation of the Liverpool Cotton Brokers' Association in 1841. Baker and Hahn also emphasise the role of information in the functioning (and the manipulation) of cotton markets (futures and spot) in New York and New Orleans. Conventional economic theory too privileges information – it is perfect information that permits the frictionless market. But Baker and Hahn's study stresses the extent to which information is *not* perfect. Even when not subject to deliberate corruption, and even when rooted in statistics, information always remains a subjective representation of, not mirror to, the world. Further, the strenuous information gathering efforts of Liverpool's cotton brokers shows that information is very far from being a naturally occurring good. It too is deliberately constituted and in the process is infused with the subjectivities of its authors.

These institutional urges built on and strengthened rather than created the shared culture of the brokers.[42] They were further bound together by other, more informal institutions, such as the distinctive and rich modes of dress described by Ellison.[43] Occupational dress codes, creating a distinctive and recognisable visual image, can be a particularly powerful way of reinforcing a sense of collective identity, something still encoded in the colourful jackets worn by traders to this day.[44]

Moreover, many of the earliest generations of brokers not only worked but also lived in the warren of streets around the Exchange at the centre of the

---

40 Daniels, 'Cotton Trade with Liverpool', p. 277.
41 Dumbell, 'Early Liverpool Cotton Imports', p. 360.
42 Moreover, Ellison claims that 'For many years after the formation of the Association, the business of the market was conducted on the lines of an unwritten code, which clearly defined the functions, and plainly set forth the rights and duties, of both merchants and brokers, in their individual capacities and in their conduct towards each other': Ellison, *The Cotton Trade*, p. 272.
43 Ellison, *The Cotton Trade*, p. 169.
44 Andrew Popp and Michael French, '"Practically the Uniform of the Tribe": Dress Codes Among Commercial Travellers', *Enterprise and Society* 11 (2010), 437–67.

emerging central business district.[45] More than anything else though, the very strong, shared culture displayed by the brokers across the nineteenth century might be attributed to the remarkable shared business genealogy traced in great depth by Ellison. Liverpool's cotton-broking community engaged, over many decades, in an extremely productive process of fertilising new firm formation, as the industrial district literature predicts. By the mid nineteenth century the rapidly branching community of firms could be mapped as though drawing a family tree (in many cases, of course, these new shoots and outgrowths did have a basis in family and friendship), very many of them, normally organised as small partnerships, tracing a direct descent from the earliest generation of specialist cotton brokers. The ties created were strong and fraternal, but at the same time flexible – ability, as much as connections, were key to gaining a footing in the trade and, ideally, a partnership. Writing in the 1870s, Orchard observed how:

> On every side are brokers, merchants, agents, who from the clerk's stool have been raised to the private room of the firm, because they deserved the promotion. Half the partnership firms in Liverpool twenty years old contain a partner who was once a clerk.[46]

Partnerships frequently evolved in their composition to accommodate new talents, without ever losing identity, cohesion, or, in the case of spin-offs, traces of their lineage. The depth to which Ellison was able to reconstruct this history in the 1880s, looking back over more than one hundred years, is testament to a kind of 'folk' or living memory among the community of brokers. New entrants were inducted and integrated via marriage, leisure, 'clubbability' and service.[47] It is possible this culture began to break down, or at least started to become more exclusive and insular, towards the close of the nineteenth century. Social mobility from the outer office to the inner sanctum began to decline. At the same time, in 1888, *The Clerks' Journal* complained that:

> We have too many speculators, too many brokers ... too many opportunities for commercial pitch and toss . . . [brokers are] parasites of commerce – a class of men who foster and prolong financial anarchy and the ruin of businessmen.[48]

---

45   Graeme Milne, 'Business Districts, Office Culture and the First Generation of Telephone Use in Britain', *International Journal for the History of Engineering & Technology* 80 (2010), 199–213.
46   Benjamin Guinness Orchard, *The Clerks of Liverpool* (Liverpool, 1871), p. 41.
47   Mäenpää, 'Combining Business and Pleasure?'.
48   *The Clerks' Journal*, 1 June 1888, quoted in Gregory Anderson, *Victorian Clerks* (Manchester, 1976), p. 45.

Of course, there is an element of special pleading to this complaint, but that does not mean it should be entirely discounted. Socially, the elite were in headlong flight to the suburbs and, perhaps critically, early and enthusiastic adoption of the telephone was reducing the need to leave the office.[49] Nonetheless, the Liverpool cotton-broking community and culture had remained remarkably robust over a period of more than one hundred years, one that had witnessed dramatic growth and innovation.

Open-air trading in Liverpool

One of the more notable features of the culture of cotton broking in Liverpool, examined above, was a strong predilection for open-air trading. The Liverpool cotton broker lived his life at large in the heart of the city, whether heaving snowballs or doing deals. Samuel Smith described how in 1857 he 'obtained the management of the cotton saleroom [in the firm he worked for] ... and so had to go "on 'change"; and much of my time was spent "on the flags," as the open area was styled where the cotton-brokers assembled "sub Jove frigido" to transact their business'.[50] Note how Smith said that he 'had' to go on the Exchange flags. Ellison gave some space to describing (if not analysing) open-air trading, but subsequent authors have paid it little attention. Perhaps it was not the most important aspect of the brokers' work and practice; nonetheless, its persistence appears both puzzling and, potentially, revealing.

The habit of meeting to trade in public, in the 'open air', was well established among Liverpool cotton brokers before the end of the eighteenth century, early in their emergence as a distinct group.[51] Initially, their 'commercial rendezvous ... was at the top of Castle Street', close to the original Exchange building. However, re-designation of the Exchange as the Town Hall:

> had no influence upon the merchants and brokers of the day, who still insisted upon congregating on the spot which had been the meeting-place of their mercantile forefathers; and this notwithstanding the complaints constantly made that they were more or less obstructing the thoroughfare,

---

49 Graeme Milne, 'British Business and the Telephone, 1878–1911', *Business History* 49 (2007), 163–85.
50 Smith, *My Life-Work*, p. 16.
51 Of course, outdoor 'kerb' trading had taken place around Exchanges for a long time and in many locations. See, for example, Natasha Glaisyer, *The Culture of Commerce in England, 1660–1720* (Martlesham, 2006).

to say nothing of their inconveniencing the neighbouring tradesmen by sheltering in the shop door-ways on wet days.[52]

In 1808 a new, purpose-built Exchange was opened. Billinge's *Advertiser* was to describe Monday, 7 March 1808, as:

> a day of much importance in the commercial annals of Liverpool, as on that day the merchants abandoned their usual place of meeting, at the upper end of Castle St, and assembled for the first time in the grand area of the New Exchange. No place in the world affords so elegant and commodious a situation as this for the purposes of a public exchange, and we have often been surprised to hear it observed that it would be difficult to bring the merchants to abandon their old situation to which they were so much attached by the strong ties of habit and early prepossession. In opposition to this common opinion, we are happy to observe that the transference was absolutely perfect the first day, not a single person being found loitering about his old haunts during the whole 'Change hours.[53]

But although they moved location, they did not move indoors, for Ellison describes how:

> The upper portion of the Exchange [e.g. the 1808 Exchange] was used for municipal business; the lower portion, with the open area which at that time existed in the centre of the building, was intended for the use of the merchants and brokers of the day. But they preferred assembling outside, *a custom kept up to the present day by the cotton trade.*[54]

Thus, open-air trading was still strongly in evidence in the 1880s, when Ellison was writing. It is not clear at what point it began to break down, but perhaps in the final quarter of the nineteenth century. John Owen's novel *The Cotton Broker*, published in 1921 but set a little earlier, locates almost all of its most important scenes indoors: in offices, in sample rooms, restaurants and private homes, and in the premises of the Cotton Association, where 'the mere presence of a Belstock in the Cotton Associations' "Room" had got to have its meaning'.[55] In particular, trading activities also take place indoors, among 'the well-dressed men in their morning coats or dressy sporting tweeds, ... [pushing] their way down the steps towards the "Ring"'.[56] Moreover, Owen, who had been a Liverpool cotton broker, portrays the world of the broker as

---

52   Ellison, *The Cotton Trade*, p. 171.
53   http://www.ica-ltd.org/about-ica/our-history/.
54   Ellison, *The Cotton Trade*, p. 169, emphasis added.
55   John Owen, *The Cotton Broker* (London, 1921), pp. 20–1. In the novel, the Belstocks are an old and elite cotton-broking family firm.
56   Owen, *The Cotton Broker*, p. 49.

one set apart, physically, socially and psychologically, from its context in the city; to enter it was to move 'not merely from one room to another. It was rather a passage from one country – a half civilized country – to another where society was infinitely more complex and where not even the language was the greatest difficulty.'[57] Nonetheless, he also shows the traders 'Mixing daily and trading together, instead of keeping each one to his own office ... the cotton brokers kept their sense of adventure.'[58] Even the flagstones of the 'Change still had their place, albeit now largely as the haunt of those 'grey, shabby fellows, those ghosts of their own prime ... who still encumber the outer places of "the Flags"'.[59] Perhaps the figures in the postcard with which this paper began are little more than the vestigial remnants of the practice of open-air trading.

However, regardless of the precise timing of when, and of the extent to which, the practices involved may have evolved and mutated, it is clear that this pattern of behaviour was prolonged and valued. Critically, the pattern was one that had its co-ordinates in communities, spaces and practices. Moreover, it also survived and adapted to very significant innovations; the coming of futures trading in the 1850s, the foundation, in turn, of Liverpool Cotton Clearing House (1874), the Liverpool Cotton Bank (1878) and the Liverpool Cotton Association (1882), and the construction of no less than two new Exchange buildings. Was open-air trading part of the process through which the Liverpool cotton market was made and through which Liverpool's cotton brokers were constituted as market subjects?

Open-air trading as a custom in common?

Two conjoined features of open-air trading seem most salient; its public nature and its persistence. Of course, if reputations for 'strict probity and honour' were as critical as Hyde *et al.*, claim (and there is no reason to think they were not) then a degree of visibility and transparency for trades

---

57 Owen, *The Cotton Broker*, p. 79. Zaloom describes how the walls of a new trading floor built in Chicago in the 1990s 'create a boundary for the market, severing it from the city streets beyond and ensuring that no information can be exchanged between inside and outside. There is no public entry to the building': *Out of the Pits*, p. 47. Thus, Chicago underwent a transformation Liverpool had experienced almost a century earlier.

58 Owen, *The Cotton Broker*, p. 152.

59 Owen, *The Cotton Broker*, pp. 47–8. Half a century earlier, during the cotton famine of the 1860s, Samuel Smith had observed vast fortunes made – and lost. The losers appeared to him pathetic: 'They had last their legitimate business and their habit of patient industry, and many of them sank into chronic poverty. It was pitiable to see men who had bought fine mansions and costly picture galleries, hanging about "the flags," watching the chance of borrowing a guinea from an old friend': *My Life-Work*, p. 35.

was important.[60] But visibility *to other brokers*, which is what mattered, could have been achieved within the much more private spaces of the rooms provided inside the Exchange. But we should note Billinge's remarks on the opening of the new Exchange in 1808, namely that: 'No place in the world affords so elegant and commodious a situation as this for the purposes of a *public* exchange.' In other words, open-air trading made market participation and market activity visible and transparent not only to other brokers but to the wider public as well. It was an arena that anyone might enter, or at least observe, if they chose to. So, if not actually spectacular then open-air trading was certainly *spectacle* and over time it even became a notable sight of Liverpool, one that visitors and sightseers would make a point of seeing. It was well known that 'There at 'high Change might be seen' all of Liverpool's most prominent and important brokers.[61] If performance is a 'cultural behaviour for which a person assumes responsibility to an audience', then the brokers were performing their custom; they cannot have been unaware of the attention it attracted, that they had an audience.[62] Perhaps it was this reputation as a tourist attraction that led publishers to produce postcards of the Exchange flags on a working day. Over time the Exchange flags became a kind of theatre and, eventually, one of the key points in a wider 'site of memory' comprising the entire Liverpool waterfront and central business district.[63] The notion of open-air trading was thus very firmly tied in people's minds to a highly specific space, to its 'proper material abode'. Open-air trading was remarkably immobile. This identification of open-air trading with a specific space was reinforced by its highly visual (and no doubt aural) nature. As Ellison noted of the early days, 'The scene at high 'Change a hundred years ago was, therefore, a much more picturesque sight than at the present day, as it was also, no doubt, much less bustling' – a vast increase in the scale of activity on the flags clearly went some way to compensating for the replacement of more flamboyant modes of dress with the drab black that became universal among businessmen during the second half of the nineteenth century.[64] As well as public and site-specific, open-air trading was also extremely persistent and long-lasting, for at least a century, as has been emphasised several times. As well as being unnecessary, dedicated provision for indoor trading being made from 1808 onwards, this persistence was also

60   Hyde, Parkinson and Marriner, 'The Cotton Broker', p. 79.
61   Ellison, *The Cotton Trade*, p. 169. 'High 'Change' refers to the hours of peak trading, all accounts having to be settled and resolved by mid-afternoon.
62   Dell Hymes, 'Breakthrough Into Performance', *Folklore: Performance and Communication*, ed. Dan Ben-Amos and Kenneth Goldstein (The Hague, 1975), pp. 11–74, quoted in Burke, 'Performing History', p. 38.
63   Laura Balderstone, Graeme J. Milne and Rachel Mulhearn, 'Memory and Place on the Liverpool Waterfront in the Mid-Twentieth Century', *Urban History* 41 (2014), 478–96.
64   Ellison, *The Cotton Trade*, p. 170.

irrational in many ways. I will consider advantages it may have conferred later (though it is not clear any of these would have been completely unavailable in an appropriate indoor setting) but it also undoubtedly imposed definite disadvantages and inconveniences, many of them highly practical. As the great snowball fight demonstrated, the weather was not the least of these. As Samuel Smith remembered, in 'all weathers, cold and wet, winter and summer, we stood outside, sometimes sheltering under the arches when the rain and cold were unendurable. It was a discipline which killed off weakly men and made the healthy still hardier.'[65] In any case, it is difficult to appeal to economic rationality as explanation for either of these key characteristics of open-air trading. Zaloom's judgement on late-twentieth-century Chicago is strikingly similar: 'commitment to the pit, a specific place ... contradicted the logic of ubiquitous circulation'. Nonetheless, the pit remained the CBOT's 'emblem and key tool for making markets'.[66]

In looking elsewhere for an explanation of what I believe is as largely neglected phenomenon in the history of business life I want to appeal to the notion of customs, as conceived of by social historians, and I want to distinguish that notion of customs and the customary from ideas of 'culture' as commonly applied by business historians (with the notion of customs positioned as complementary to that of culture). I draw in particular on the work of E. P. Thompson in his book *Customs in Common*. Business historians rarely turn to Thompson, who was an historian first and foremost of the working or labouring classes.[67] We need to be very careful in seeking to transfer his concept of custom to the entrepreneurial or capitalist classes; nonetheless, there are insights to be won. Moreover, older generations of business historians grasped the idea and importance of custom; for example, both Ellison and Dumbell several times use either 'custom' or 'customary' in referring to the practices of Liverpool cotton brokers.[68]

One of the best definitions of culture in business history writing remains that given by Lipartito in 1995; namely that:

> Culture ... [is] a system of values, ideas, and beliefs which constitute a mental apparatus for grasping reality. Business culture is that set of delimiting and organizing concepts that determine what is real or rational for [actors], principles that are often tacit or unconscious.[69]

65   Smith, *My Life-Work*, p. 16.
66   Zaloom, *Out of the Pits*, p. 49.
67   Though he is a source in the emerging history of capitalism.
68   Dumbell claims, for example, that 'it was customary for brokers to report informally what transactions' each had made: 'Early Liverpool Cotton Imports', p. 371.
69   Kenneth Lipartito, 'Culture and Practice of Business History', *Business and Economic History* 24 (1995), 1–41 (p. 2).

In contrast, a custom can be defined as a practice, but one that is underpinned by a claim to a right or prerogative. Thompson notes that, while a
custom may reflect or embody an 'ambience, *mentalité*', placing it close to
culture, it is also a 'whole vocabulary of discourse, of legitimation and of
expectation'.[70] The attempt to legitimate a practice or identity is made by
drawing on precedent – thus, customs necessarily are also located in time.
Actively engaging in a custom, repeatedly over time, is an attempt to assert,
maintain and, sometimes, to defend a legitimating claim. Customs *do* things
and it is their repeated performance that gives them constitutive power.
Customs are always collective (and typically conceived as operating at the
level of class). As an assertion to a claim they perform a different, perhaps
less flexible, role from the interpretive function assigned to culture. And as
both collective and public they are different in important ways from habits
and routines, which tend to be more specific to either the individual or the
organisation and to be more intimate or even private.

As noted, we must be careful not to do too much violence to a concept
that Thompson developed in the very specific context of the English working
classes in the eighteenth century. Given this context, his framing inevitably
stresses customs with extremely deep historical roots, often of many centuries
(such as, for example, public access to common lands). They emerge out of
both folklore and a kind of natural law. Such roots cannot be claimed for the
customs of Liverpool's cotton brokers.[71] Nonetheless, Thompson does allow
that other classes, such as patricians, might also display customs, so it is not
an exclusively working-class concept. Further, we might see the nineteenth
century as a period when customs and the customary began to be co-opted
or captured by elites, a process culminating in the civic passion for historical
pageants that emerged towards the close of the nineteenth century.[72] In a
sense, the emergence of new capitalist customs might have been a necessary
corollary to the diminishment or subjugation of the older 'true' customs of
the labouring classes. Moreover, Thompson himself says that some of the

---

70   Edward Palmer Thompson, *Customs in Common: Studies in Traditional Popular Culture*
(London, 1991), p. 2.

71   Eric Hobsbawm and Terence Ranger, eds, *The Invention of Tradition* (Cambridge, 1983).

72   Mark Freeman, '"Splendid Display; Pompous Spectacle": Historical Pageants in Twentieth-
Century Britain', *Social History* 38 (2013), 423–55. As Thompson explores, there was a
dynamic shift in the meaning and practice of custom in the nineteenth century, probably driven
equally by politics and economics: 'The ceremonies and processionals of the trades, which had
once been built into the calendar of the corporate year … might still be celebrated on special
occasions in the eighteenth century. But in the nineteenth century such processionals lost their
consensual "trade" endorsement, they were feared by employers and corporations as occasions
for high spirits and disorder (as indeed they sometimes were), and St Clement was honoured
not in the streets, but in the trades club or friendly society meeting in the tavern': *Customs in
Common*, p. 5.

plebeian customs of the eighteenth century were 'of recent invention ... and were in truth claims to new "rights"'.[73] Thus new rights, and new customs through which to assert claims to those rights, might be possible. Indeed, Thompson says that 'custom was a field of change and of contest, an arena in which opposing interests made conflicting claims'.[74]

Nonetheless, even in asserting new rights, brokers had to draw on practices that would be recognisable and comprehensible to observers. And so, in their persistence in and insistence on publicly staged, open-air trading, the brokers might be seen as trying to draw on pre-industrial, or even pre-capitalist, understandings of the market, one that inhabited a very real space – the public marketplace.[75] At the very moment when the market was being sundered from its material bases, rendered abstract and immaterial, for example through futures trading, the brokers were, whether consciously or not, evoking a much older custom of exchange, one recognisable to all, even if the details of what they did remained obscure. Futures trading can be considered a disruptive technology. Zaloom argues that the market was once 'a *place* to buy and sell' but the telegraph 'helped create *the* market, a new entity that existed all the time and everywhere'.[76] In Liverpool, open-air trading rematerialised trade, regrounded it in an age of increasing abstraction.

Thompson argues that we need to 'examine the components [of customs] with ... care: rites, symbolic modes, the cultural attributes of hegemony, the inter-generational transmission of custom and custom's evolution within historically specific forms of working and social relations'.[77] Customs generate 'ritualized or stylized performances', exemplified in open-air trading by the drama and tension of 'high 'Change', accompanied by the visual spectacle of costume, the aural effect of hue and cry as trades are made, the ringing of signal bells, all followed by the dramatic rush to settle accounts at an arbitrary hour.[78] Moreover, every custom has its 'proper material abode', just as it is always located in time through precedent. For open-air trading, this 'proper material abode' was the literal marketplace of the Exchange flags.[79] Unmoored from place and time it is no longer custom.

We note how Ellison says brokers 'insisted' on their continued use of public thoroughfares for trading and that their refusal to desist was 'spite of several attempts made to remove them'.[80] Thus open-air trading contained

73 Thompson, *Customs in Common*, p. 1.
74 Thompson, *Customs in Common*, p. 6.
75 The literal and metaphoric marketplace was, of course, central to Thompson's work on customs and the moral economy.
76 Zaloom, *Out of the Pits*, p. 22.
77 Thompson, *Customs in Common*, p. 13.
78 Thompson, *Customs in Common*, p. 8.
79 Thompson, *Customs in Common*, p. 7.
80 Ellison, *The Cotton Trade*, pp. 171 and 169.

the requisite assertion of a claim, one made through its repeated enactment; a claim to the right to continue their practice in this place and through the assertion of that right the brokers also made a claim to their centrality to the commercial life of the city.

In turn, the great snowball fight of 1854 can be read as another, if exceptional, example of the assertion or enactment of the claims inherent in customs. In another seminal essay, this time on the moral economy of the English crowd, Thompson argues that it is 'possible to detect in almost every eighteenth-century crowd action some legitimating notion. By the notion of legitimation I mean that the men … in the crowd were informed by the belief that they were defending … rights or customs.'[81] Again, we must very careful to push our claim too far; nonetheless it is revealing to posit the 'riotousness' of the snowball fight as both active resistance to the disruption or dislocation of a custom, and to see in its exceptionalness an indication of the strength of attachment on which the custom of open-air trading was founded. Alternatively, adopting a subtly different position, we can see the 'misrule' of the snowball fight as only possible because there were norms to be suspended; it was in fact only possible because of the custom, not despite it.[82]

What was custom for?

Thompson noted that past generations of folklorists had 'lost sight of the rational functions of many customs within the routines of daily and weekly labour'. In other words, customs *do* things, or enable those who practise them to do things, linking Thompson's perspective to more recent emphases on the performative in ethnography, sociology and history. What did open-air trading *do* for cotton brokers? First, its mere existence as a custom helped them to span and reconcile discontinuities in other aspects of their working lives, from the considerable growth in their numbers to such radical innovations as futures trading or the founding of institutions such as the Cotton Clearing House. Open-air trading as custom enabled an oral transmission of brokers' lore. Samuel Smith, for example, reflected that 'On the whole [open-air trading] was a good commercial training, and much better than sitting in a counting house.'[83] In this the custom of open-air trading might also act as a bulwark against some of the unwanted effects that came with relative openness to newcomers. With its obvious emphasis on precedent, custom asserts the importance of continuity. In this sense and context,

81   Thompson, 'Moral Economy', p. 78.
82   Natalie Zemon Davis, 'The Reasons of Misrule: Youth Groups and Charivaris in Sixteenth-Century France', *Past & Present* 50 (1971), 41–75.
83   Smith, *My Life-Work*, pp. 16–17.

custom achieved something within brokers as a group. Perhaps this public yet, in some way, impenetrable display of community also helped brokers preserve the air of mystery that gave them power over the work.[84]

Custom, counter-intuitively, could also be a source of innovations in practice. As we have already seen, Thompson saw custom as a field of change as well as contest and continuity. Custom was not only enactment of a claim but could also be the ground from which sprang new modes of being and new practices. In a changed context custom can generate novelty. Thus we can see the trading pit or ring, still so central to modern exchanges (and themselves now saturated in custom) as emerging from the natural way in which brokers might group themselves to trade in a large and open space such as a market-place like Liverpool's Exchange flags.

But if customs are fields of 'change and contest, an arena in which opposing interests made conflicting claims', the other wider context in which this custom operated was that of the broad mercantile, financial and industrial revolutions unfolding with such force in Britain at that time.[85] If we can 'read much eighteenth-century social history as a succession of confrontations between an innovative market economy and the customary moral economy of the plebs', then perhaps the nineteenth century can be read as a succession of attempts to assert the customs of the market economy – an as yet incomplete financial revolution – over those of a plebeian culture that was not yet completely defeated.[86] Cotton brokers aggressively claimed the public spaces of the city as theirs; the proper space for the performance of the market and its relationships at the very moment they were being remade by the brokers themselves. And more than that, though referencing the past via the spectacle of the marketplace, they staked their claim on the future, a claim to *be* the future. The message was complex though; in so boldly, publicly, stating this claim they also excluded: the very fact of visibility emphasised, rather than cloaked, the almost hermetically sealed world of the broker. Non-brokers could watch, but not enter this world: the right to constitute and represent the market was the property, the right of the brokers. These were perhaps custom's most important function. It helped in publicly legitimating the moral standing and claims of an increasingly marketised economy and of the role of the brokers within it.[87]

84 I am grateful to Barbara Hahn for this insight.
85 Thompson, *Customs in Common*, p. 6.
86 Thompson, *Customs in Common*, p. 12. Thompson describes plebeian culture as 'rebellious in defence of custom' and against 'the innovation of capitalist process' (p. 9).
87 For similar but later claims for the moral basis of Exchanges and markets, see Julia C. Ott, '"The Free and Open People's Market": Political Ideology and Retail Brokerage at the New York Stock Exchange, 1913–1933', *The Journal of American History* (2009), 44–71.

Conclusion

This chapter's deep origins lay in the challenges of understanding co-ordination and embeddedness in industrial districts but, spurred by the inspired éclat with which Francesca opened her article on the jewellers of Rhode Island, it has strayed far from that point of departure. Nonetheless, I think it still has something to say on that original topic. Embeddedness explanations, such as essentially private networks of transacting, reciprocity, affiliation, affinity and actual kinship, focus on attempts to build cohesion, trust and co-operation within groups. Thus, the jewellers' parade in Rhode Island, or the brokers' snowball fight in Liverpool, can be seen as part of this effort to build group solidarity among members. Francesca knew this, emphasising how, like many other trade associations, 'the NEMJSA did not neglect to promote the social life of its members, through banquets, picnics, baseball games, and ... quarterly dinners and dances ... including a "Ladies" Day'.[88] As she said, it 'was through the annual dinners and the summer outings that the jewellers found the space and opportunity to "become better acquainted"'. This sociability mattered because it could 'help reduce conflict'.[89] The jewellers recognised this too, arguing that:

> There is a disposition among many to regard this organization as purely a social one. This is undoubtedly the general purpose of the association, but intercurrent with an informal program comes the opportunity of making and strengthening friendships and the informal interchange of business opinions which mutually benefit the members and in a measure, lessen antipathies and petty rivalries.[90]

We can plainly see that, to an extent, this rationale is framed in a language of benefits, interests and competition. This fits the ways in which the problem of co-ordinating co-operation and competition in districts has been framed within a highly rational, economistic model.

However, important though these effects were, I do not think they tell the whole story. Francesca herself observed how occasions like parades, dinners and galas were 'meant to create a collective and public *experience*'.[91] The emphasis on 'experience' bespeaks a very different set of effects; more embodied, more emotional, less rational. Indeed, it forces us to confront the possibility of *irrationalities* and, ultimately, *subjectivities*. These possibilities are a challenge to over economistic readings of business life.

---

88 Carnevali, 'Social Capital and Trade Associations', p. 916.
89 Carnevali, 'Social Capital and Trade Associations', p. 917.
90 Carnevali, 'Social Capital and Trade Associations', pp. 917–18.
91 Carnevali, 'Social Capital and Trade Associations', p. 918, emphasis added.

Moreover, that challenge is reinforced when we remember how Francesca stressed that these were *public* experiences. The notion that they were public is as hard to reconcile with conventional explanations as the idea that they were experiential. Searching for a way to recast these phenomena I have argued that they represented a form of custom, whether they be routine and quotidian, such as open-air trading, or more spectacular, such as the parades and galas studied by Francesca. Custom and the customary, publicly performed, is a hitherto neglected thread in the social fabric into – or from – which business is woven. It would be interesting to search out and explore other examples. In the City of London, for example, the annual Lord Mayor's Show draws on ancient guild (and thus artisanal) customs to project and re-legitimate the continuing economic and political power and influence of finance capital.

Thus, business groups sought through custom not only to build their own internal cohesion but also to actively assert a claim, one demanding legitimation for their position in society, markets and the economy. Just as CBOT members did, cotton brokers 'committed themselves to carving out a place in the city that would match their growing stature'.[92] Through customs they communicated those claims to their rights to others. We can see Liverpool's cotton brokers, through the public enactment of open-air trading, in which they themselves embodied exchange within the 'proper material abode' of the 'change flags, as both drawing on pre-industrial visions and memories of the physical and moral arena of the marketplace and, simultaneously, using this evocation to project forward to the abstracted, *despatialised* world of financial capitalism in the early twenty-first century. Remarkably, our contemporary world is one in which traces of the customs the brokers inherited, remade and passed down persist, testament to both the durability and malleability of customs. The notion of customs allows us to see over the very long run, helping us to notice how customary notions of the market are mobilised time and again to re-legitimate a radically evolving understanding of trade and exchange. Emptied of the content ascribed to it by the plebeian communities studied by Thompson, the 'market' was recruited to support the rights of financial capitalism. In the open-air trading of Liverpool we see that process in a microcosm. Open-air trading was a part of the process through which Liverpool's cotton brokers made the market and made themselves. Thus, attention to the notion of customs, which are always the property of collectives, also directs business history back towards an interest in class in a sense wider and deeper than the mere recognition of shared economic interests. Capitalists, as much as workers, faced the necessity of staking their claim and engaging in cultural struggles for their identity and position.

92 Zaloom, *Out of the Pits*, p. 25.

2

The Political Economy of Financing Italian Small Businesses, 1950–1990s

ALBERTO RINALDI AND ANNA SPADAVECCHIA

The political economy of the banking sector

Banking history has traditionally represented the evolution of the banking sector in various nations as essentially a market-driven path: financial systems worked quite efficiently and capital markets were perfectly rational in supplying firms with funds. If there were credit restrictions, criticism should be levelled at *macro policy* and not at banks.[1] Francesca Carnevali challenged this view by arguing that in the four largest European economies the structure of the banking sector is shaped by the interaction of social, economic and political groups, rather than by invisible market forces.[2]

In the twentieth century, Britain became the economy with the most concentrated banking sector and industrial base in Western Europe. Conversely, the French, German and Italian banking systems remained segmented, with Italy showing the highest degree of segmentation. The interplay that took place between the state and social and economic groups representing small firms in France, Germany and Italy did not happen in Britain. In the three Continental nations small firms occupied an important place in the cultural identity, where they were seen as preservers of social stability and as valuable sources of votes. Small firms in Britain had little lobbying power or political

---

1   See, for the UK, Michael Collins, *Money and Banking in the UK: A History* (London and New York 1988); Forrest Capie, 'Commercial Banking in Britain', *Banking, Currency and Finance in Europe between the Wars*, ed. Charles H. Feinstein (Oxford, 1995), 395–413; David Chambers, 'The City and the Corporate Economy Since 1870', *The Cambridge Economic History of Modern Britain*, vol. 2: *1870 to the Present*, ed. Roderick Floud, Jane Humphries and Paul Johnson (Cambridge, 2014), pp. 255–78.
2   Francesca Carnevali, *Europe's Advantage: Banks and Small Firms in Britain, France, Germany, and Italy Since 1918* (Oxford, 2005).

representation, and neither the Conservative nor the Labour party developed policies in their favour.

As local banks disappeared in Britain, nothing replaced them to make use of the information possessed by local networks, in order to fund viable investment projects of small and medium-sized enterprises (SMEs) clustered in regional economies. In France, Germany and Italy, however, local and regional banks retained the larger share of commercial lending, and the state intervened with the promotion of additional public and semi-public lending institutions. Here, a segmented banking system allowed different types of banks to specialise in different types of customers in different geographical areas, ensuring the fulfilment of the credit needs of SMEs.

Studies on the financing of SMEs in the USA, an economy closer to the 'Anglo-Saxon' model than the Continental European one, strengthen Carnevali's argument, with analysis of SMEs in the late nineteenth and early twentieth centuries, and also in the late twentieth century, showing the importance of local commercial banks.[3] Research on the later period also highlights the importance of 'relationship' lending, where the connection between banks, firms and their business environment occurs over a prolonged period of time, which in turn reduces the problem of asymmetric information associated with lending to SMEs. Like the Italian banking system, American banking was specialised geographically and in terms of market segment. In 1933 the Glass–Steagall Act restricted ordinary banks to their traditional activity of accepting deposits and lending, prohibiting them from buying shares in corporations or undertaking investment banking activities. Moreover, commercial banks – both national (federal) and state banks – were restricted to opening branches within the boundaries of their home state.[4] Although banks did try to overcome this by forming associations with banks in other states, it was not until the early 1990s that the wave of cross-state consolidations took place, with the repeal of the interstate banking restrictions.[5]

By taking Carnevali's view as its point of departure, this paper explores how political action in Italy gave rise to the most intense case of banking regulation and provision of medium-term subsidised finance, with the explicit aim of promoting the expansion of the small firm sector. This was one of the factors, after the Second World War, which led to the development

---

3   Robert Cull, Lance E. Davis, Naomi R. Lamoreaux and Jean-Laurent Rosenthal, 'Historical Financing of Small- and Medium-Size Enterprises', *Journal of Banking and Finance* 30 (2006), 3017–42; Allen N. Berger and Gregory F. Udell, 'Relationship Lending and Lines of Credit in Small Firm Finance', *The Journal of Business* 68 (1995), 351–81.

4   Richard S. Sayers, *American Banking System* (Oxford, 1948), pp. 19–20.

5   Allen N. Berger and Gregory F. Udell, 'Small Business Credit Availability and Relationship Lending: The Importance of Bank Organisational Structure', *The Economic Journal* 112 (2002), 32–53.

of industrial districts (IDs) – geographic clusters of small firms, each special-ising in one or several phases of the same production process – some of which are internationally competitive.

This paper is structured as follows. First, there is a review of the role of politics and institutions in fostering the expansion of the small firm sector in Italy. Secondly, there is an analysis of the role of the Bank of Italy in strength-ening local banks as these were crucial to the funding of SMEs. Thirdly, there is a focus on the establishment of those institutions charged with the provision of medium-term finance for SMEs, followed by a discussion of the financial infrastructure created to support micro-firms, i.e. artisan firms.

Politics, institutions and small firms in Italy

Italy's industrial structure is in many respects unique among the most advanced economies, as it is characterised by a dominance of SMEs, often clustered in IDs, and with a marginal role for large firms.[6] In the last thirty years, a widely held rhetoric has seen SMEs as a sort of natural path of Italian industrialisation which is essentially market-driven. This view emphasises the dynamic role of SMEs in traditional sectors, and their ability to exploit the comparative advantage of a country with very easy access to labour without any relevant government or public policy support.[7] From this perspective, some long-term coincident factors are seen to be crucial to the success of Italian small firms: the Italian extended family; the preservation of aspects of late-medieval communal civilisation in central and northern Italy and, in particular, of traditional craft skills; the existence of merchant traditions connecting the Italian provinces to the world markets; the sophisticated and fragmented distribution channels that represent a demanding intermediate buyer which generates enormous variety in 'Made in Italy' products; and the willingness of local governments to create the infrastructure and services to support the development of small firms.[8] Moreover, since the 1970s Italian SMEs have benefited from a number of important trends in the world economy. One is the shift from standardised, mass-produced products towards more customised, sophisticated and higher-quality goods. Another is the movement of production technology away from rigid, scale-intensive processes towards

---

6 Fabrizio Onida, *Se il piccolo non cresce. Piccole e medie imprese italiane in affanno* (Bologna, 2004).

7 Luciano Cafagna, *Dualismo e sviluppo nella storia d'Italia* (Venice, 1989); Giovanni Federico, ed., *The Economic Development of Italy Since 1870* (Aldershot, 1994); Giacomo Becattini, *Distretti industriali e made in Italy. Le basi socioculturali del nostro sviluppo economico* (Turin, 1998).

8 Michael J. Piore and Charles F. Sabel, *The Second Industrial Divide: Possibilities for Prosperity* (New York, 1984), pp. 227–9.

those with more flexibility that are suitable for, and adaptable to, small production runs.[9] This perspective acknowledges the contribution of institutions to the development of SMEs. However, these institutions were mainly local, such as local governments, associations of artisans and industrialists and chambers of commerce, which provided valuable services.[10]

At the same time, this rhetoric holds that large companies in capital-intensive oligopolistic sectors are somewhat unnatural for Italy and were established thanks only to government support. As a result, only a few big companies could thrive; these were often protected by the state and enjoyed considerable market power in the industries in which they operated.[11] State interventionism brought about a kind of 'political capitalism' inside which entrepreneurs pursued growth not for economic reasons (i.e. to exploit economies of scale and have the scope to cut unit costs and increase market share) but to strengthen their bargaining power with political authorities.[12]

A recent work by Colli and Rinaldi[13] has challenged this view by holding that Italy's peculiar industrial structure is to a minor extent the result of the spontaneous action of market forces, i.e. the entrepreneurial failures of big business and the dynamism of small entrepreneurs. Colli and Rinaldi stress the role that politics and institutions played in determining the relative performances of both big business and small firms. Institutional failures took place across all the areas in which big business could be supported: internationalisation, human capital formation, technological leadership and corporate finance. As a result, large firms in Italy grew, protected as they were in the domestic market; they were strong and in a monopolistic position at home, but relatively small and weak by international comparison. Conversely, other work has stressed that after the Second World War institutions fostered the expansion of the small firm sector through a variety of measures: artisanship policy, subsidised credit to SMEs, banking and labour market regulation, and insolvency legislation.[14]

---

9 Michael E. Porter, *The Competitive Advantage of Nations* (London and New York, 1990), pp. 421–53.
10 Michael H. Best, *The New Competition: Institutions of Industrial Restructuring* (Cambridge, 1990), p. 208.
11 Cafagna, *Dualismo e sviluppo*; Federico, *The Economic Development*; Giorgio Mori, *Il capitalismo industriale in Italia. processo d'industrializzazione e storia d'Italia* (Rome, 1977); Franco Bonelli, 'Il capitalismo italiano: linee generali di interpretazione', *Storia d'Italia*, vol. 1: *Dal feudalesimo al capitalismo*, ed. Ruggero Romano and Corrado Vivanti (Turin, 1978), pp. 1195–255.
12 Franco Amatori, 'Entrepreneurial Typologies in the History of Industrial Italy: Reconsiderations', *Business History Review* 85 (2011), 151–80.
13 Andrea Colli and Alberto Rinaldi, 'Institutions, Politics and the Corporate Economy', *Enterprise and Society* 16 (2015), 249–69.
14 Linda Weiss, *Creating Capitalism: The State and Small Business since 1945* (Oxford, 1988); Anna Spadavecchia, 'Financing Industrial Districts in Italy, 1971–91: A Private Venture?',

Such institutional action was consequent on a favourable view towards SMEs which was expressed by all the Italian political parties and by the Bank of Italy (BoI) in the post-war years. The major governing party, the Christian Democratic Party (DC, to use its Italian acronym), had a social project that assigned a positive value to the *petite bourgeoisie*, seeking to swell their ranks and thereby extend the ideals of economic independence – small firms, skilled craftsmen – throughout society.[15] In emphasising the role of small-scale ownership, the DC was heir to the very problem that had urged Catholics into the political arena: the struggle to deflect the proletariat from the attractions of socialism. This 'great labour question', as Pope Leo XIII defined it in the *Rerum novarum* of 1891, 'cannot be solved save by assuming, as a principle, that private ownership must be held sacred and inviolable. The law should, therefore, promote ownership, and its policy should be to induce as many people as possible to become owners.'[16] In effect, the proletariat could be redeemed not as workers, but by conversion to something else, by restoring all the means of production that are indispensable for sustaining one's own livelihood.

Thus, in the DC's analysis, the solutions to the labour problem centred on the diffusion of property. In the view of the DC, the small producer was the very symbol of integral society: he was both employer and labourer; he worked alongside his or her assistants and related to them in a highly personal way. Consequently, in the small firm, the organisation of work was 'more human', the worker's dignity 'better protected, the sense of responsibility and collaboration more keenly developed'. If large firms engendered the class struggle, small firms fostered solidarity, thus transcending the capital–labour divide.[17]

Moreover, this analysis was influenced by the views of the Catholic economists of the early twentieth century, who had stressed the economic rationality of small firms.[18] The DC never regarded technological progress as a prerogative of large factories, but maintained that its benefits could also be exploited by small firms. Thus, small enterprises were not considered as

Business History 47 (2005), 569–93; Giuseppe M. Longoni and Alberto Rinaldi, 'Industrial Policy and Artisan Firms (1930s–1970s)', *Forms of Enterprise in 20th Century Italy: Boundaries, Structures and Strategies*, ed. Andrea Colli and Michelangelo Vasta (Cheltenham and Northampton, MA, 2010), pp. 204–24; Paolo Di Martino and Michelangelo Vasta, 'Companies Insolvency and "the Nature of the Firm" in Italy, 1920s–1970s', *Economic History Review* 63 (2010), 137–64.

15   Weiss, *Creating Capitalism*.

16   Cited in Richard L. Camp, *The Papal Ideology of Social Reform* (Leiden, 1969), p. 84.

17   Democrazia Cristiana (DC), *Atti e documenti (1943–67)*, 2 vols (Rome, 1968), vol. 1, p. 246.

18   Gianni Toniolo, *Osservazioni e discussioni durante le giornate sociali di Milano. Resoconto delle giornate sociali di Milano (7–9 febbraio 1907)* (Vatican City, 1951).

backward or inefficient, but as an essential element for economic development that was to play a central role in the reconstruction of Italy's economy.[19]

As a party that defined itself as 'of the centre moving towards the left', the aspiration of the DC was to forge a broad alliance of workers, peasants and the middle classes. A policy that fostered small firms made good political sense for two reasons. First, the diffusion of small business would reinforce the class structure of the solidaristic state and at the same time expand what the party saw as its social base of consensus. Secondly, by dispersing labour among a myriad of small firms, the potential for collective action from left-wing trade unionism would be minimised and conflict defused. The fundamental concern for the DC was the preservation of a particular class structure whose disappearance would have polarised Italian society between the industrial proletariat and a very small class of large business owners. An expanding middle class of small entrepreneurs would allow the DC to occupy a large 'middle ground' and tackle the rise of the Communist Party.[20]

When the DC won Italy's first post-war general election in 1948, it was heavily dependent on sources of support that were outside the party's direct control. Its outstanding electoral victory[21] had been obtained with the massive backing of the Church, the financial assistance of big business and the clientelistic support of the southern notables (landowners and the professional classes): in short, groups expecting a thoroughly conservative policy from the DC. However, after a lacklustre result at the next general election in 1953,[22] the balance of power within the DC shifted to the left. Under the new leadership of Amintore Fanfani, the party decided to strengthen its penetration in civil society, breaking away from dependence on its traditional backers which had restricted the level of support available from other social strata. The DC had to stand on its own two feet from an organisational perspective, seeking less binding sources of finance and reducing the level of influence wielded by traditional power structures. In this scenario, the party became more predisposed towards a policy in favour of small firms.[23] This involved the granting of special fiscal regimes and subsidised credit to small and artisan firms, on condition that such firms joined business associations independent from the Confindustria (General Confederation of Italian Industry) and other regulatory bodies, such as chambers of commerce. In

19   Weiss, *Creating Capitalism*.
20   Weiss, *Creating Capitalism*.
21   The DC got 48.5% of the vote and secured an absolute majority of seats in the Chamber of Deputies, the lower house of Parliament.
22   Support for the DC dropped to 40.1% of the vote in the election for the Chamber of Deputies. Nonetheless it was still far ahead of the second-largest party (the Communist Party) that got 22.6% of the vote.
23   Liborio Mattina, *Gli industriali e la democrazia. La Confindustria nella formazione dell'Italia repubblicana* (Bologna, 1991).

turn, small firm and artisan associations became not only weighty pressure groups, but also the conduit of the state's industrial policy.[24]

Also the major opposition party, the Italian Communist Party (PCI, to use its Italian acronym) recognised the importance of attracting the middle classes and small entrepreneurs. According to its leader, Palmiro Togliatti, large enterprises were the most efficient way of organising production, but, in some circumstances – and the Italian case was one of them – they may lead to monopoly or oligopoly, both of which tend to limit production in order to maximise profits. Small firms are not – contrary to the DC's thinking – a form of enterprise, by its very nature different from large concerns. Moreover, small firms are not economically efficient. They are, instead, the first stage in the life cycle of capitalist firms, which must either grow or eventually fail. In either case, the presence of small firms opposes the tendency to economic stagnation which stems from the predominance of monopolies. Thus, the expansion of the small firm sector must be encouraged because it facilitates an increase in production, employment and wages, and therefore provides an improvement in the living standards of the working class.[25] This reasoning was intertwined with other considerations regarding the need for the PCI to distract the middle classes from the influence of right-wing forces in order to strengthen Italian democracy and avoid a return to an authoritarian regime. On this basis, small entrepreneurs should become 'strategic allies' of the working class.[26] Thus, these considerations eventually led the PCI to pursue policies in favour of SMEs and artisan firms that were very similar to those of the DC.[27]

Local banks and the small firm sector

The political and economic rationales highlighted in the previous section shaped a banking system geared towards meeting the financial requirements of SMEs. The reorganisation of the Italian banking system had its origin in the Banking Law of 1936.[28] This conferred upon the BoI the power of

24 Marco Maraffi, 'L'organizzazione degli interessi in Italia, 1870–1980', *L'azione collettiva degli imprenditori italiani. Le organizzazioni di rappresentanza degli interessi industriali in prospettiva comparata*, ed. Alberto Martinelli (Milan, 1994), pp. 137–96.
25 Palmiro Togliatti, 'Ceto medio e Emilia rossa', *Critica Marxista* 2 (1964), 130–58; Partito Comunista Italiano (PCI), *La dichiarazione programmatica e le tesi dell'VIII Congresso del PCI* (Rome, 1957).
26 Sebastiano Brusco and Mario Pezzini, 'Small-Scale Enterprise in the Ideology of the Italian Left', *Industrial Districts and Inter-Firm Cooperation in Italy*, ed. Frank Pyke and Werner Sengenberger (Geneva, 1990), pp. 142–59.
27 Longoni and Rinaldi, 'Industrial Policy'.
28 The Italian banking system has undergone three major transitions: in 1893–95, from commercial credit to 'universal' banking; in 1931–36 with the end of universal banks and the

shaping the banking sector in terms of market specialisation and territorial competence, which were in turn related to the legal status of the banks, and from 1975 to the size of their deposits.[29] The BoI divided the credit system into two branches, one comprising institutions entitled to take short-term savings and provide short-term finance for working capital (hereafter ordinary banks), and the other consisting of institutions permitted to take medium- and long-term savings, and extend medium- and long-term finance and industrial credit (hereafter medium-term credit institutions, MCIs).

The separation between the short- and medium-term credit markets[30] should have ensured stability in the banking system, as it implied harmony between bank assets and liabilities. It also avoided the excessive freezing of capital that had characterised the universal banks and their collapse,[31] leading to huge losses for the depositors and political repercussions.[32] However, if this had been the only aim, it would have sufficed to impose a clear equilibrium between medium-term assets and liabilities on the banks, and restricting the banks to the short-term credit market would have not been necessary. The decision, supported in particular by Donato Menichella (general manager of the Institute for Industrial Reconstruction (IRI, to use its Italian acronym)[33] 1933–44; deputy governor of the BoI 1946–48; governor of the BoI 1948–60) and Alberto Beneduce (president of the IRI 1933–39; senator of the Kingdom of Italy 1939–44) was more about reducing the role of banks in the Italian

establishment of a clear distinction between short- and medium-term credit; and in the early 1990s when banks were again authorised to operate on the medium-term market (in accordance with the second EU Banking Directive). See Alfredo Gigliobianco, Giandomenico Piluso and Gianni Toniolo, 'Il rapporto banca–impresa in Italia negli anni Cinquanta', *Stabilità e sviluppo negli anni cinquanta*, vol. 3: *Politica bancaria e struttura del sistema finanziario*, ed. Franco Cotula (Rome-Bari, 1999) 225–302 (p. 229); Giovanni Federico and Gianni Toniolo, 'Italy', *Patterns of European Industrialization: The Nineteenth Century*, ed. Richard Sylla and Gianni Toniolo (London and New York, 1992), pp. 197–217 (p. 204); Elisabetta Gualandri, 'The Restructuring of Banking Groups in Italy: Major Issues', *The Recent Evolution of Financial Systems*, ed. Jack R. S. Revell (Basingstoke, 1997), pp. 157–80 (p. 157); Giandomenico Piluso, 'From the Universal Bank to the Universal Bank: A Reappraisal', *Journal of Modern Italian Studies* 15 (2010), 84–103.

29   Sabino Cassese, *È ancora attuale la Legge Bancaria del 1936? Stato, banche e imprese pubbliche dagli anni '30 agli anni '80* (Rome, 1987).

30   The definition of the short- and medium-term market changed over time. From 1952 onwards it was defined as short-term credit up to one year and medium-term credit from one to ten years, with the exception of southern Italy where it was up to fifteen years: Vincenzo Pontolillo, 'Aspetti del sistema di credito speciale con particolare riferimento all'intervento dello Stato', Banca d'Italia *Bollettino*, 1971/1 (1971), 105–22 (p. 109 and n. 3).

31   Rodolfo Banfi, 'Gli Istituti di Credito Speciale e il sistema del credito agevolato', *Rivista Bancaria – Minerva Bancaria* 1981/1–2 (1981), 30–67 (pp. 30–1).

32   Gigliobianco, Piluso and Toniolo, 'Il rapporto banca–impresa', p. 229.

33   The Institute for Industrial Reconstruction (Istituto per la Ricostruzione Industriale) was a state-owned holding company established in 1933 to take over the three largest universal banks (Banca Commerciale Italiana, Credito Italiano and Banco di Roma) and their industrial securities.

economy, for in the 1920s banks had become the leaders of industrial and financial groups, were the central actors in a tightly connected corporate network, and were ultimately determining the direction of the country's industrial development.[34] Therefore, the ultimate aim of the distinction was to bring the banking system within the realm of state economic planning.

The financial structure of the country that emerged after the Second World War was to a large extent the result of the intense debate that took place in 1946 in the Ministerial Committee of Inquiry on Finance and Insurance. One of the most important recommendations of the committee was that the separation between banks and the provision of medium- and long-term finance to firms should persist. However, the committee did not see the stock market as an important alternative source of capital for industry. Instead, it recommended that the funds held by investors should be passed on to firms through the MCIs, as these would lend to firms and finance their activity by the sale of industrial bonds to the public. In particular, Luigi Einaudi (governor of the BoI 1945–47; Italy's Finance Minister 1947–48; President of the Italian Republic 1948–55) and Menichella saw a system in which funds were channelled through institutions, such as the banks and the MCIs, which were largely state-controlled, as more easily manoeuvrable than a market-based system. Most importantly, the government and the BoI also believed that SMEs and artisan concerns would be left out of the transfer of money, if the supply of credit was solely left to the market.[35]

Thus, in the post-1945 years Italy's banking system was restructured to strengthen the position of local banks that were embedded in IDs, with the growth of the former strongly associated to that of the latter. In fact, throughout the years after the Second World War, the national banks within IDs had a much lower share of the local credit market than elsewhere. Lower assessment, monitoring and enforcement costs, and social connections between local banks' managers and local entrepreneurs, gave local banks a competitive edge within IDs. As a result, credit to small firms within IDs was abundant.[36]

---

34   Gigliobianco, Piluso and Toniolo, 'Il rapporto banca–impresa', pp. 229–30; Gianni Toniolo, 'Il profilo economico', *La Banca d'Italia e il sistema bancario, 1919–1936*, ed. Giuseppe Guarino and Gianni Toniolo (Rome-Bari, 1993), pp. 5–101 (p. 72). On the structure of corporate interlocks in Italy in the interwar years, see Michelangelo Vasta and Alberto Baccini, 'Banks and Industry in Italy, 1911–36: New Evidence Using the Interlocking Directorates Technique', *Financial History Review* 4 (1997), 139–59.

35   Carnevali, *Europe's Advantage*, pp. 184–5. As part of this policy, savings banks were transformed from institutional investors that mainly subscribed to state securities and extended loans to local governments into banks that became increasingly involved in financing the manufacturing sector: Giuseppe Conti, 'Le banche e il finanziamento industriale', *Storia d'Italia*, vol. 15: *L'industria*, ed. Franco Amatori, Duccio Bigazzi, Renato Giannetti and Luciano Segreto (Turin, 1999), pp. 441–504.

36   Giuseppe Conti and Giovanni Ferri, 'Banche locali e sviluppo economico decentrato', *Storia del capitalismo italiano dal dopoguerra a oggi*, ed. Fabrizio Barca (Rome, 1997), pp. 429–65.

The BoI played a decisive role in strengthening local banks. Thus, regulations were put in place to restrain bank competition and thereby protect small banks from large national banks. The main instruments the BoI used to achieve this goal were a limit on permits for new bank branches and a restriction on mergers of existing banks: when granting authorisation to open new branches, the BoI favoured the banks of a local character, while at the same time limiting the expansion of the bigger banks to a few large or medium-sized cities.

Competition was also stifled through the limitation of the territorial area in which the banks could operate, which varied according to the size of the bank and where it had its head office. Only those three financial institutions (Banca Commerciale Italiana, Credito Italiano and Banco di Roma) defined as being 'banks of national interest' in the 1936 Banking Law, and directly controlled by the IRI, had branch networks throughout the country. The other large banks (defined as such by the extent of their deposits) could operate in a whole region only if their head office was located in the regional capital, otherwise they could operate only in the province in which their branches were concentrated. The other banks could collect deposits and make loans in the whole province only if their head office was based in the provincial capital, otherwise their territory was limited to the municipality in which their branches were located.

Another important area of bank regulation was the imposition of a limit on the size of advances. The banks required authorisation from the BoI before they could grant a loan to a single customer which would raise that customer's total liability to the bank to over one-fifth of the bank's paid-up capital and reserves. This regulation linked the size of the advances to the size of the banks, which segmented the market as small banks could only cater for small loans. As a further measure to control bank competition, the Banking Law made the creation of a banking cartel compulsory to avoid price wars that would have eliminated the smaller banks, thus protecting them from competition regarding deposit rates.[37] Nonetheless, competition among local banks inside local economies was often ferocious and this ensured that small firms were not deprived of necessary credit.[38]

Alongside the genuine belief in the importance of small firms and small banks for the nation's economic development, support for small banks was also a tool used to strengthen the grip of political parties on the banking

---

37 Carnevali, *Europe's Advantage*, pp. 179–81. The banking cartel expired in 1952, but it was reconstituted in 1954 as a banking agreement on a voluntary basis recognised by the BoI. Nonetheless, breaches of the cartel were not infrequent, especially as regards deposit rates and the amount of advances that banks offered to their clients: Giorgio Albareto, 'Concorrenza e politica bancaria', *Stabilità e sviluppo negli anni cinquanta*, vol. 3: *Politica bancaria e struttura del sistema finanziario*, ed. Franco Cotula (Rome-Bari, 1999), pp. 198–206.

38 Gigliobianco, Piluso and Toniolo, 'Il rapporto banca–impresa', pp. 238–9.

sector. In fact, the only banks that could be controlled by private or financial groups were the ordinary commercial banks, which accounted for little more than 10% of the total banks operating in Italy. The other banks were public bodies (savings banks), foundations (the public law banks), co-operative banks (popular banks and also rural and artisan banks), or joint-stock companies controlled by public bodies (the three 'banks of national interest' that were controlled by the IRI). Thus, boards of local banks mostly comprised bankers from other banks and directors appointed by municipal and provincial governments on the recommendation of local political parties.[39]

The establishment of medium-term credit institutions

The establishment of MCIs was a major novelty that stemmed from the 1936 Banking Law. The rigid separation between medium-term savings and credit meant that ordinary banks could not access the medium-term market, and thus could not transfer surplus funds from short-term operations to the medium-term credit market.[40] In order to get round this barrier, ordinary banks established departments of industrial credit (DICs) and MCIs, so that they could transfer short-term deposits to the medium-term market and provide firms with medium-term credit. The transfer took place by acquiring DIC and MCI bonds, which was a profitable investment in itself, considering that these bonds paid higher yields than state securities and were risk-free. A further source of profit for the banks was the sale of such bonds to the public. Moreover, by establishing DICs and MCIs, ordinary banks created an intermediary, providing firms with assistance in placing their shares on the market.[41]

The main public law banks were the first to establish DICs, the proliferation of which took place in connection with the economic growth of the post-war period and the capital availability that it required.[42] The DICs exploited the existing banking networks, and their operations could thus be diffused throughout the country. The DICs at the southern banks (Banco di Sicilia and

---

39 Conti and Ferri, 'Banche locali', pp. 435–40. As an example of the connection between political power and banks, in 1975 seventy of the eighty-nine savings banks had presidents belonging to the DC while another twelve had presidents affiliated to the DC's junior government coalition parties: Luciano Barca and Gianni Manghetti, *L'Italia della banche* (Rome, 1976), p. 169.

40 Banfi, 'Gli Istituti', p. 33.

41 Francesca Carnevali, 'British and Italian Banks and Small Firms: A Study of the Midlands and Piedmont, 1945–1973' (Ph.D. thesis, London School of Economics, 1997), pp. 201 and 205.

42 Pier Francesco Asso and Gabriella Raitano, 'Trasformazione e sviluppo del credito mobiliare negli anni del governatorato Menichella', *Stabilità e sviluppo negli anni cinquanta*, vol. 3: *Politica bancaria e struttura del sistema finanziario*, ed. Franco Cotula, pp. 309–589 (p. 331); Pontolillo, 'Aspetti', p. 108.

Banco di Sardegna in 1944 and Banco di Napoli in 1946) and the ISVEIMER[43] were designated by the BoI to be the institutions in charge of financing the industrialisation of southern Italy with a particular focus on southern SMEs from 1947.[44] Between 1946 and 1949 other medium-term credit institutions were established by ordinary banks breaking into the medium-term market. The popular banks established Centrobanca (1946); the three banks of national interest, the Banca d'America e d'Italia and various insurance companies established Mediobanca (1946). Finally, Efibanca was established in 1949 by public law banks and other financial institutions by transforming an existing institution.[45]

This first stage in the creation of institutions dedicated to medium-term finance marks a decentralisation of the provision of that type of credit and the progressive blurring of the distinction between short- and medium-term finance, particularly when considering that few of the DICs were distinct from the establishing banks from a legal point of view.[46] In the second stage, which was marked by the establishment of regional medium-term credit institutions (RMCIs), the Mediocrediti Regionali, the issue of decentralisation is combined with the provision of medium-term credit to SMEs. With the establishment of the RMCIs the banking sector assumed the structure that it would retain until the reforms of the early 1990s.

Research into the establishment of RMCIs and their rediscount institute, the Mediocredito Centrale (MCC), claims that the decision to provide medium-term finance to SMEs in the early 1950s was based on political rather than economic considerations. When the bill establishing the first RMCI (Law 445/50) was discussed in Parliament, the dominant view was that SMEs were economically inefficient and relics from the past, although in the speeches of some MPs such small firms were defined as the backbone of the

---

43   The Istituto per lo Sviluppo Economico dell'Italia Meridionale (ISVEIMER), or Institute for the Economic Development of Southern Italy, was established in 1938 as an MCI and as a development bank. Its aim was to promote and increase industrial production in southern Italy.

44   From 1947 those institutions were endowed by the state, with the latter agreeing to guarantee up to 70% of possible losses: Banca d'Italia, *Relazione Annuale* (Rome, 1948), p. 151.

45   These MCIs were authorised to issue medium-term loans throughout the country and were supposed to finance themselves by placing bonds and securities on the market, which were also bought up by the deposit banks. Only Mediobanca financed itself with time deposits (1–5 years) placed by the public at the three banks of national interest and could not issue bonds and securities: Simona Pergolesi, *Il credito agevolato alle imprese industriali. Le incentivazioni gestite dal Ministero dell'Industria, 1962–1984* (Milan, 1988), p. 25; Vera Zamagni, *The Economic History of Italy, 1860–1990* (Oxford, 1993), p. 359; Stefano Battilossi, 'L'eredità della banca Mista. Sistema creditizio, finanziamento industriale e ruolo strategico di Mediobanca 1946–1956', *L'Italia Contemporanea* 185 (1991), 625–54.

46   The distinction between short- and medium-term credits has also been partly overcome by authorising banks to increase their share of medium- and long-term operations: Vincenzo Pontolillo, *Il sistema di credito speciale in Italia* (Bologna, 1980), pp. 14–15.

economy and important for the reconstruction of the country. Italian international competitiveness was seen as resting on large corporations introducing American mass production systems. Nevertheless, preserving SMEs was seen as important in order to avoid a society polarised between the proletariat and capitalists, and an economy dominated by monopolies and state bureaucracy, which the ruling Christian Democratic Party considered akin to communism. An important push in favour of RMCIs came from Piedmont, where various banks were willing to establish a regional financial institution specialising in providing credit to SMEs and able to rediscount their bills at a favourable rate at the BoI. This should have been financed through a fund made available by the government. Small business associations in the Lombardy and Marche regions also expressed interest in this project.[47]

The discussion was particularly concerned with the organisation of medium-term credit for SMEs. One solution, envisaged in Parliament and supported by several MPs, was to authorise some of the existing banks to provide medium-term credit for SMEs, rather than creating addition regional institutions. Donato Menichella and Giuseppe Pella (Italy's Treasury Minister 1948–53 and Prime Minister 1953–54) were not prepared to compromise on the division of the credit system into short- and medium-term credit. Therefore, ordinary banks would not be authorised to provide medium-term credit directly to SMEs; Menichella and Pella preferred to create a dedicated circuit. Moreover, some MPs pointed out that not all Italian regions were endowed with a banking system attentive to the needs of SMEs and sufficiently well developed to satisfy such needs. MPs to the left of the political spectrum advocated direct government intervention. This would make funds available for medium-term credit to SMEs which could be managed by some of the existing banks. In 1950 all parties in Parliament took the view that the state must organise the credit system. Credit was seen as a tool to achieve the common good, and could not be conceived as independent of collective aims. Menichella and Pella, however, were not in favour of letting the government act as a banker and wanted to defend the autonomy of the banking system from the control by the government.[48]

Ultimately, authorising regional banks to establish RMCIs, which would rediscount the new institutions' bills at very favourable rates, was a compromise solution to make medium-term credit available to SMEs while avoiding various undesirable scenarios such as: ordinary banks entering the medium-term credit market; the BoI losing control of the savings banks; the state acting as a banker and financing industry directly; or the BoI printing money to finance credit to industry. This was a compromise solution also

47 Paolo Peluffo and Vladimiro Giacché, *Storia del Mediocredito Centrale* (Rome-Bari, 1997), pp. 6–18.
48 Peluffo and Giacché, *Mediocredito Centrale*, pp. 17 and 28.

in the sense that credit was not directly controlled by the government, but it was being directed towards specific sectors of the economy. The determination with which this project was pursued rested on the belief that credit had a 'socio-economic purpose', as the Minister of Industry, Giuseppe Togni, expressed it in his speech to Parliament.[49]

Two years after the establishment of the first RMCI in Piedmont the refinancing institution MCC was established. This was deemed necessary to promote the creation of RMCIs in those regions where local banks did not have the capacity to establish them, and to co-ordinate RMCIs and the banking system. Menichella wanted the MCC as his strategy was to create filters between the BoI and the banking system on the one side, and credit aimed at supporting specific sectors of the economy and regulated by law on the other. These considerations led to the establishment of the MCC in 1952, working at the interface between RMCIs and the central bank, and providing an initial rediscounting of the RMCIs bills.[50] Moreover, the MCC was deemed necessary by the BoI because the funds available to other RMCIs were insufficient to allow them to function adequately and their ability to finance themselves by issuing bonds was questioned. The MCC would have also enabled RMCIs not to depend excessively on the banks that had set them up.[51]

The MCC refinanced the RMCIs by discounting their bills; buying their medium- and long-term bonds; by extending loans using returns from the issuing of its own bonds; and by grants to cover part of the financing for SMEs.[52] The MCC was regulated by the Interministerial Committee for Credit and Savings (ICCS), which fixed its rediscounting rate, the lending limit and the size of firms eligible for loans.[53] These were defined as firms with fewer than five hundred workers and fixed assets below 1.5 billion lire. The fact that the MCC was not placed under the control of the BoI, but under the ICCS, also indicates that the MCC was conceived as an instrument of government intervention, which was placing SMEs at the centre of its intervention in favour of industry.[54]

Following the establishment of the MCC there was a proliferation of RMCIs in northern and central Italy. Only at a much later stage – the

---

49   Peluffo and Giacché, *Mediocredito Centrale*, p. 27; (Law 445/50) did not specify a definition of an SME but did fix the maximum loan at 15 million lire. This ceiling was increased to 50 million lire in 1954, and in 1960 it was further enhanced to 20% of the paid-up capital of the borrowing firm: Associazione Bancaria Italiana (ABI), *La legislazione italiana sul credito speciale all'industria e al commercio* (Rome, 1963), pp. 179–80.

50   ABI, *Legislazione italiana*, pp. 31–6.

51   Banca d'Italia, *Relazione Annuale* (Rome, 1952), p. 289; Guido Carli, 'Le origini del Mediocredito Centrale', *Credito Popolare* 1984/6 (1984), 261–7 (p. 261).

52   Banfi, 'Gli Istituti', p. 54.

53   Giuliano Amato, ed., *Il governo dell'industria in Italia* (Bologna, 1972), p. 23.

54   Asso and Raitano, 'Trasformazione', pp. 427–32.

beginning of the 1980s – did the ICCS authorise the establishment of four RMCIs in southern Italy (in the regions of Puglia, Calabria, Basilicata and Sicily) to assist the existing institutions – the ISVEIMER and the Istituto Regionale per il Finanziamento alle Industrie in Sicilia (IRFIS) – in their lending to SMEs.[55]

Additional finance was available to SMEs located in southern Italy through the regional policy, managed by the Cassa per le Opere Straordinarie per il Mezzogiorno, established in 1950. Its establishment was the result of action by internal economic and political forces but also by international institutions such as the International Bank for Reconstruction and Development (IBRD), which was willing to finance a long-term plan of investment in southern Italy, with the request that this should be managed by one institution rather than several ministries.[56]

The provision of financial subsidies, including subsidised credit and grants, to southern SMEs was part of the wider Cassa intervention in industry, which began in 1957. The definition of SMEs, and therefore eligible firms, as applied in the south was broader than in other regions of the country, i.e. fewer than five hundred employees and fixed assets below 3 billion lire. The focus on SMEs has been interpreted as reflecting the intention of developing an organic network of SMEs in the south. However, the eligibility criteria were soon abandoned such that, by 1962, limits on employees and fixed assets were lifted and grants could be awarded on the first 6 billion lire of investment for firms of any size.[57] This diversion from the original intention was due to the need to attract modern industries to the south and investment from large northern companies. Moreover, it also enabled state-owned enterprises to gain access to subsidies.[58]

The Artigiancassa

The policy in favour of artisan firms is a further instance of the interplay between government and economic forces leading to a financial structure geared towards the requirements of SMEs. This policy was based on the provision, on the one hand, of lower tax, as well as employers' contribution and welfare

55 Pietro D'Onofrio and Roberto Pepe, 'Le strutture creditizie nel Mezzogiorno', Banca d'Italia, *Il sistema finanziario nel Mezzogiorno*, special issue of *Contributi all'analisi economica* (Rome, 1990), pp. 207–50 (p. 235).
56 Salvatore Cafiero, *Storia dell'intervento straordinario nel Mezzogiorno (1950–1993)* (Manduria-Bari-Rome, 2000), pp. 25–6.
57 Pergolesi, *Il credito agevolato*, pp. 39–40.
58 Sergio Conti, 'Industrialization in a Backward Region: The Italian Mezzogiorno' (Ph.D. thesis, University of London, 1979), p. 126; Giovanni Federico and Renato Giannetti, 'Italy: Stalling and Surpassing', *European Industrial Policy The Twentieth-Century Experience*, ed. James Foreman-Peck and Giovanni Federico (Oxford, 1999), pp. 124–51.

benefits at reduced premiums, and on the other, of 'substitution factors': subsidised credit, services and promotional initiatives by state agencies.[59]

In 1947 the Artigiancassa (Artisan Bank) was established, charged with the task of providing subsidised loans for artisan firms, either directly or through the banks participating in its capital. The State provided half of its endowment fund, which amounted to 500 million lire, with the remaining half provided by the following five banks: the Istituto di Credito delle Casse di Risparmio Italiane, Istituto Centrale delle Banche Popolari Italiane, Monte dei Paschi di Siena, Banco di Napoli and Banco di Sicilia, which each provided 50 million lire.

In addition to resorting to its endowment fund, the Artigiancassa could fund its operations by rediscounting bills and issuing bonds and securities, but was not authorised to collect deposits. Actually, until its transformation into a joint-stock company in 1993 – apart from a short time and for a limited amount of money in the 1970s – the endowment fund was the only source used.[60]

The problems that emerged in the first five years of activity led to reform of the Artigiancassa in 1952. It was transformed into a rediscount institute for the banks participating in the endowment fund and all the credit societies, savings banks and rural and artisan banks, which were henceforth authorised to grant medium-term capital equipment loans to artisan firms. By contrast, short-term loans were excluded from the facilities. In the application of the law, firms eligible for funding by the Artigiancassa at this time were those defined as 'artisan' by the 1948 decree on family allowances.[61]

In 1956 the Italian Parliament, after overcoming the resistance of the MPs linked to the Confindustria and of those linked to the two largest trade unions (the left-wing CGIL and the Catholic CISL), approved the Artisan Act (Law 860/56) that defined the boundaries of artisanship. Unlike the German and French systems, where the artisan qualification was defined on the basis

59 Although most frequently employers of labour, Italian artisans are taxed at the same rate as their workers and receive equivalent family allowances; they pay less onerous social security contributions than other employers and are exempted from those same taxes for their apprentices; they benefit from a generous health and pension scheme, subsidised by the state; they receive technical and marketing assistance from various government agencies and have access to low-cost investment and running capital, publicly subsidised and guaranteed: Weiss, *Creating Capitalism*, pp. 55–60.

60 Alberto Baccini, *Artigiancassa. Artigiancassa. Da Istituto di Credito Speciale a banca per le imprese artigiane* (Florence, 2002), p. 13.

61 According to this decree, a firm was considered to be artisan if the proprietor participated in the manual work carried out by the firm; the firm carried out one of the activities included in a specific list prepared by the Ministry of Labour; and the firm employed no more than five workers, or no more than three workers – depending on the type of activity carried out – excluding apprentices and members of the proprietor's family: Piero Gualtierotti, *L'impresa artigiana* (Milan, 1977).

of professional lists of activities, the Italian artisan firm was defined on the basis of the number of employees.[62] The 1956 Act established an extension of the legal definition of an artisan firm that was unequalled in Europe. Artisanship was therefore defined not as a professional category, but as a legal regime, membership of which entitled the owner to a wide variety of benefits, including access to subsidised credit.[63] This legal arrangement opened the doors of artisanship to a variety of newcomers having little to do with activities of a strictly artisanal nature, resulting in a dramatic increase in the number of artisan firms, i.e. of the pool of potential beneficiaries of the subsidised credit provided by the Artigiancassa.[64]

A subsequent law of 1958 increased the Artigiancassa endowment fund from 5,500 to 10,500 million lire. Moreover, this law established that the net profits resulting from the Artigiancassa's financial statements, after deducting a rate of 20% to be allocated to the reserve fund, were to be disbursed to the banks participating in the endowment fund, up to an amount equivalent to 4% of the stake held by each of them. In this manner, from 1958 onwards, the state was awarded a dividend on its stake in the endowment fund, which was intended to supplement the interest relief grant fund. This measure was extremely important because it established the interest relief grant fund on a permanent basis, while the 1952 law had financed it for only five years.[65]

From 1964 to 1986 there were fifteen further allocations to the endowment fund, which at the end of that year stood at 1,788.5 billion lire. No further allocations took place in the following ten years until the privatisation of the Artigiancassa and its acquisition by the Banca Nazionale del Lavoro in 1996. Allocations took place in a sporadic way until the mid-1970s. They became more frequent and substantial between 1975 and 1986, which saw a concentration of eleven out of the eighteen allocations, accounting in real terms for 77.7% of the total funds allocated to the endowment fund.[66] Over time the interest relief fund provided by the government became the most important intervention by the Artigiancassa. From 1958 to 1996 it benefited from forty-one allocations, amounting to 9,157 billion lire overall. These took place on a more regular basis than those to the endowment fund. Nonetheless, most of them also occurred in the years 1976 to 1986, which accounted for 69%

---

62   The Artisan Act established a maximum of ten persons employed (or twenty including apprentices), with exceptions for co-operatives, artistic trades (e.g. ceramics, fashion, etc.), limited companies and partnerships, 'as long as members are personally involved in the work, and as long as such work has a pre-eminent role on capital'.
63   Corrado Barberis, 'L'Artigianato in Italia', *L'artigianato in Italia e nella Comunità Economica Europea*, ed. Corrado Barberis, Gabriella Harvey and Olga Tavone (Milan, 1980), pp. 7–82.
64   Weiss, *Creating Capitalism*.
65   Baccini, *Artigiancassa*, pp. 32–7.
66   Baccini, *Artigiancassa*, pp. 32–7.

of the total money allocated to the fund in real terms. In this case, and by contrast with the endowment fund, allocations also continued in the decade from 1987 to 1996, even if it was to a lesser extent.

The more plentiful resources that had been made available to the Artigian-cassa were used to increase the total amount of subsidised loans, but not their average value, which decreased from 72.7 million lire during 1967–76 to 64.0 million during 1977–88 (at 1998 prices). Thus the impression is that until the mid-1970s, when funding was relatively scarce, available resources were channelled to a relatively small number of artisan firms, selected from those that presented the best prospects for development, which were boosted by granting them loans of an increasing average amount. Conversely, the increased funding of the Artigiancassa from the mid-1970s to the late 1980s seems to have responded to a different logic, that is to make subsidised credit available to everybody (or at least to as many artisans as possible) by distributing a large number of loans of a smaller average size. This seems a strategy more coherent with the DC's original social project that was to foster the proliferation of micro-firms and not to boost the growth of individual companies. However, such a change in the Artigiancassa's policy is also compatible with a consensus-building strategy aimed at appeasing a vast stratum of the middle-class whose support was perceived as very important to the electoral fortunes of both the DC and the PCI at a time when lobbying by artisan associations had become more pressing than in the previous decades.[67]

The distribution of loans to the largest number of applicants possible seems even more impressive (or puzzling) if we observe that it occurred at a time when the expansion of the artisan sector had come virtually to a halt. In fact, the number of artisan firms registered with provincial chambers of commerce rose by 68% in the period from 1958 to 1966 and by another 17% from 1967 to 1976. Numbers grew more slowly after 1977, reaching a peak of 1,455,547 in 1984 before dropping to 1,421,762 in 1988, despite the new 1985 Artisan Act (Law 448/85) that had further increased the size limit of artisan firms.[68] Thus, the overall increase in the number of artisan firms in the period 1977–88 amounted to just 9%, which – from an economic perspective – would probably justify an opposing strategy to that pursued by the Artigiancassa, that is, to concentrate the provision of subsidised credit in a smaller number of loans of a higher amount to stimulate the growth of more promising concerns.

---

67   Dino Pesole, *L'artigianato nell'economia italiana. Dal dopoguerra a oggi* (Milan, 1997).
68   The new size limits were as follows: a) if no mechanised production was undertaken: up to 18 employees (including up to 9 apprentices) or a maximum of 22 if the additional employees were apprentices; b) if mechanised production was undertaken: up to 9 employees (including up to 5 apprentices) or a maximum of 12 if the additional employees were apprentices; c) transport firms: up to 8 employees; d) construction firms: up to 10 employees (including up to 5 apprentices) or a maximum of 14 if the additional employees were apprentices.

Conclusion

Italian SMEs and IDs came to the forefront of scholarly research in the late 1970s when their resilience to the oil-shock crises became evident. This pattern of business organisation gained international attention with seminal work by Brusco, Piore and Sabel, Best, and Sabel and Zeitlin.[69] While stressing their importance, this literature also interpreted SMEs and IDs as a spontaneous industrial pattern and a revival of modes of production pre-existent to the emergence of mass production systems. Researchers did acknowledge the contribution of institutions to the development of SMEs and IDs. However, those institutions were mainly local, such as local government, associations of artisans and industrialists, and chambers of commerce.

The path-breaking work by Francesca Carnevali brought to our attention the nexus between a suitable banking structure and the development of SMEs in Italy, as well as Germany and France. Conversely, this nexus helps explain the decline of SMEs in Britain. The fragmented Italian banking system – both geographically and in terms of market segment – enabled local banks, mainly co-operative and savings banks, to flourish together with the local business community. As banks and firms belonged to the same regional economic fabric it was much less costly for the former to acquire non-formalised information on the latter, thus reducing asymmetric information.[70] Studies on the financing of SMEs in the USA, an economy closer to the 'Anglo-Saxon' model than to the Continental European one, strengthen Carnevali's argument.

The central tenet of Carnevali's thesis is that the banking structure was not the result of market forces, but rather was shaped by political and economic institutions on the basis of political, social and economic considerations. Linda Weiss had already pointed out the non-neutrality of the Italian state towards the nation's industrial structure. However, rather than focusing on the banking system, Weiss explained the introduction of policy tools and financial subsidies for SMEs and artisan firms as the Christian Democratic Party's attempt to promote a diffused ownership, so to avoid a polarisation of society between large firms and the proletariat. The ruling party saw in the middle classes a strong component of its constituency.[71]

This chapter has discussed the political and economic rationales behind

69 Sebastiano Brusco, 'The Emilian Model: Productive Decentralization and Social Integration', *Cambridge Journal of Economics* 6 (1982), 167–84; Piore and Sabel, *The Second Industrial Divide*; Best, *The New Competition*; Charles F. Sabel and Jonathan Zeitlin, 'Historical Alternatives to Mass Production: Politics, Markets and Technology in Nineteenth-Century Industrialization', *Past & Present* 108 (1985), 133–76.
70 Francesca Carnevali, 'Between Markets and Networks: Regional Banks in Italy', *Business History* 38 (1996), 83–100; Conti and Ferri, 'Banche locali'.
71 Weiss, *Creating Capitalism*, pp. 55–80 and 104–26.

the structure of Italy's banking system and explored the system of medium-term credit and financial subsidies established in the country to promote the development of SMEs, which were viewed as an important component of the Italian economy by the end of the Second World War. It has also explained how major political parties, as well as economic institutions such as the Bank of Italy, agreed to foster SMEs. This led to the establishment of a fragmented banking system, in which local banks were preserved to serve the needs of SMEs clustered in local production systems, and to the establishment of the medium-term credit institutions (the Mediocrediti and the Artigiancassa) which provided additional financial support to SMEs and to artisan firms.

Finally, this chapter and Carnevali's comparative work on banking systems can be placed within the context of Rondo Cameron's nexus between a country's financial institutions and its industrialisation. Most importantly the basis of their arguments is fully consistent, i.e. financial systems are shaped by legal, social and political traditions as well as the country's economic conditions.[72]

---

72 Rondo Cameron, Olga Crisp, Hugh T. Patrick and Richard Tilly, *Banking in the Early Stages of Industrialization: A Study in Comparative Economic History* (New York, 1967), p. 290.

3

Banks and Business Finance in Britain Before 1914: A Comparative Evaluation

LESLIE HANNAH[1]

Introduction

The work which I co-authored with Francesca Carnevali at the London School of Economics (where I was her Ph.D. supervisor) in 1995 suggested that British economic sclerosis relative to continental Europe after the Second World War was partly caused by the banking sector.[2] We came to this conclusion independently from complementary directions. Francesca in her Ph.D. thesis compared finance in the British Midlands unfavourably with Piedmont's *local* banks[3] and my history of Barclays Bank highlighted its successful strategy for gaining UK market share by giving more discretion to *local* directors.[4] Francesca developed these ideas on banking – and international comparisons supporting them – in her book *Europe's Advantage*, published in 2005.[5] Most British banks, she argued, were too big, centralised and uncompetitive, while elsewhere in Europe smaller, local and regional banks provided stronger support for SMEs, shaping a different political economy of flexibility and

---

1   I am grateful to Adam Tooze, Peter Scott, Richard Grossman, Mark Billings and participants in the workshop held at the University of Birmingham in March 2014 for comments on an earlier version. The usual dispensation applies.
2   Francesca Carnevali and Leslie Hannah, 'The Effects of Banking Cartels and Credit Rationing on UK Industrial Structure and Economic Performance Since World War Two', *Anglo-American Financial Systems: Institutions and Markets in the Twentieth Century*, ed. Michael Bordo and Richard Sylla (Homewood, IL, 1995), pp. 65–88.
3   Francesca Carnevali, 'British and Italian Banks and Small Firms: A Study of the Midlands and Piedmont, 1945–1973' (Ph.D. thesis, London School of Economics, 1997).
4   Margaret Ackrill and Leslie Hannah, *Barclays: The Business of Banking 1690–1996* (Cambridge, 2001).
5   Francesca Carnevali, *Europe's Advantage: Banks and Small Firms in Britain, France, Germany, and Italy Since 1918* (Oxford, 2005).

innovation in continental post-war economies. Her approach meshed with the new growth theory's emphasis on banks' role in the screening and monitoring of projects rather than the traditional functions of money transmission to facilitate trade, pooling of savings and maturity transformation (in which scale might be more of an advantage). British problems derived from a toxic mix of government complaisance in the banking cartel (for misguided macro-economic policy reasons), from oligopolistic concentration (dominance by the 'Big Five' banks) and from bankers' weak local roots and motivation (as Sir John Hicks said, the best of all monopoly profits is a quiet life). These issues were only partly resolved at the time we were writing with greater competition, modified regulation and hyperactive bankers; the unresolved problems of excessive concentration and flawed centralised lending models arguably contributed to the 2008 global financial crisis and its aftermath. Before and during that crisis bankers had very good lines of communication with (generally supportive) UK politicians. Conservative ministers did refer bank mergers to the Monopolies Commission and were concerned about the quality of services to small business constituents, but critical views such as ours resonated more with the pragmatic left before recently becoming more widely shared.[6]

The present paper focuses on the financial sector in the UK in a very different period: before the First World War. It is hard to see lack of compe-tition as a problem in business finance then, though this has not discouraged many attempts to find it. There were several dozen UK stock markets and even more commercial banks, so finance was smaller in scale and still had strong roots in vigorous regional economies. The view that British banks performed well in the pre-1914 period – in some respects usefully and creatively providing loan accommodation beyond the conservative limits that bankers publicly purported to follow – has been vigorously argued by leading financial historians,[7] though Francesca was never entirely convinced by their more optimistic interpretations, especially when applied to later periods.[8]

6 Such as the views of Patricia Hewitt, privately expressed to HSBC's chairman: see Richard Roberts and David Kynaston, *The Lion Wakes: A Modern History of HSBC* (London, 2015), pp. 428–9.
7 Forrest Capie and Michael Collins, *Have the Banks Failed British Industry? An Historical Survey of Bank/Industry Relations in Britain, 1870–1990* (London, 1992); Forrest Capie and Michael Collins, 'Industrial Lending by English Commercial Banks, 1860s–1914: Why Did Banks Refuse Loans?', *Business History* 38 (1996), 26–44; Forrest Capie and Michael Collins, 'Banks, Industry and Finance, 1880–1914', *Business History* 41 (1999), 37–62; Michael Collins, *Money and Banking in the UK: A History* (London and New York, 1988).
8 Francesca duly acknowledged Forrest Capie's help in the preface to her Ph.D., but the scepticism was deep and mutual: see his hostile review of *Europe's Advantage* in *Business History Review* 80 (2006), 610–12. Anna Schwartz also expressed habitual free-market scepticism (about UK lending discrimination against small firms), blithely ignoring clear evidence on the competitive and political economy forces that led to *contrasting* lending differentials in the USA,

Banks

A key – but historically neglected – indicator of whether banks were taking reasonable risks in their lending portfolios is their bad debt ratio, which is plausibly related to the performance of their critical screening role by an inverted U-shaped function.[9] A high ratio – loans written off of well over 1% of the loan portfolio annually – is undesirable, because, as much of the world discovered in 1932 and 2008, it can wipe out the capital of banks. On the other hand, low ratios below 0.1% – as averaged by Barclays in the period 1940–69 – indicate that lending was too timid. The intermediate (0.5%) loss ratio that Barclays registered in the interwar period reflects the severe challenges of those troubled years and was arguably the maximum tolerable at then typical lending rates of 3–5%. Only in the dire years of 1922, 1932 and 1939 did Barclays' bad debt write-offs rise above 1%: still comfortably below the loss ratios which then bankrupted thousands of overseas banks. There is only sparse archival data on bad debts prior to this, but Barclays' earliest consistently recorded write-offs (for 1914–19) averaged 0.2% and for other banks before 1914 varied between 0.05% and 0.5% annually.[10] It is arguable, then, that at least some banks were less conservative than became the later norm and were taking the lending risks necessary to back enterprise and maximise bank profits.

Germany, Italy and Japan (Anna Schwartz, 'Stability, Efficiency and Credit Controls', *Anglo-American Financial Systems*, ed. Bordo and Sylla, pp. 94–100 (pp. 98–9)); and 1960s evidence of the unusually low British ratio of private bank credits to GDP (see the World Bank summaries in Charles Calomiris and Stephen Haber, *Fragile by Design* (Princeton, NJ, 2014), p. 139). On the other hand, Billings and Capie offer a careful, nuanced and measuredly critical analysis of initially only modestly anticompetitive bank behaviour, intensifying after 1945: Mark Billings and Forrest Capie, 'Evidence on Competition in English Commercial Banking, 1920–1970', *Financial History Review* 11 (2004), 69–103.

9 Bruce Greenwald and Joseph Stiglitz, 'Information, Finance and Markets: The Architecture of Allocative Mechanisms', *Finance and the Enterprise*, ed. Vera Zamagni (San Diego, CA, 1993), pp. 1–36.

10 The best measure of bad debt experience – actual write-offs, rather than advance provisions – is available only for Barclays over a long period: see Mark Billings and Forrest Capie, 'Profitability in English Banking in the Twentieth Century', *European Review of Economic History* 5 (2001), 367–401, n. 37, and Mark Billings and Forrest Capie, 'Financial Crisis, Contagion, and the British Banking System Between the World Wars', *Business History* 53 (2011), 193–215 (pp. 205–8). See also Ackrill and Hannah, *Barclays*, pp. 448–55; Charles Goodhart, *The Business of Banking, 1891–1914* (London, 1972), pp. 161–4; Ranald Michie, 'Banks and Securities Markets, 1870–1914', *The Origins of National Financial Systems: Alexander Gerschenkron Reconsidered*, ed. Douglas J. Forsyth and Daniel Verdier (London and New York, 2003), pp. 43–63 (p. 55). Baker and Collins show the banks sensibly supported financially distressed industrial clients and estimate a 0.19% loss ratio (but over various periods not the annual standard in bank accounts): Mae Baker and Michael Collins, 'English Industrial Distress Before 1914 and the Response of the Banks', *European Review of Economic History* 3 (1999), 1–24.

Banks might take *too many* risks (as they have recently), but Grossman and Imai argue that distinctive (partially unlimited) liability rules for British banks before 1914 removed some of the moral hazard to which their modern counterparts have succumbed.[11] However, earlier Grossman had worried that – even before the 1914–20 UK merger boom doubled the national level of concentration – numerous bank amalgamations inflated bank profits, suggesting this 'may have rendered English banks less efficient as allocators of capital and may have contributed to Britain's industrial decline'.[12] At the peak of private banking in 1810, there were around 1,100 British retail banks, but over the following century the spread of joint-stock banks dramatically reduced their numbers, both by competitive attrition and by mergers and acquisitions.[13] Of the UK's 381 domestic commercial banks remaining in 1875 fewer than a quarter survived to 1913, while the mean number of offices per bank increased tenfold to ninety-eight.[14] Grossman acknowledged not distinguishing efficiency gains (deriving from this larger scale and risk-sharing) from monopoly profits in measuring post-merger returns. Most of the world's bankers were nearer the British than the American model, not seeing banking as exempt from the contemporary trend of managerial efficiency gains from increasing scale, diversification, co-ordination and integration (memorably championed by Alfred Chandler outside banking) or the need for their resources and resilience to shocks to keep pace with the rising scale of non-bank enterprises that were a major part of their customer base.[15] Moreover, Grossman's calculation allowed for other factors that – as contemporaries recognised – were actually *reducing* shareholder returns on bank stocks, including increased competition from non-bank lenders, notably insurance companies and securities issues on stock exchanges. Grossman's econometrics suggest that price leadership was accentuated by mergers, but not that there was a *net* reduction in competition.[16]

---

11   Richard Grossman and Masami Imai, 'Contingent Capital and Bank Risk-Taking Among British Banks Before the First World War', *Economic History Review* 66 (2013), 132–55. The effect is surprising since insurance against contingent liabilities was available at only 0.125% pa premiums (*Economist*, 23 May 1914, p. 1203). Many US banks at the time had double liability, though Continental European banks veered more and earlier to the modern norm of full shareholder liability limitation.

12   Richard Grossman, 'Rearranging Deck Chairs on the Titanic: English Banking Concentration and Efficiency, 1870–1914', *European Review of Economic History* 3 (1999), 325–49 (p. 325).

13   Philip Garnett, Simon Mollan and Alexander Bentley, 'Complexity in History: Modelling the Organisational Demography of the British Banking Sector', *Business History* 57 (2015), 182–202.

14   Collins, *Money*, pp. 52–3.

15   For a deterministic population ecology interpretation, see Garnett, Mollan and Bentley, 'Complexity'.

16   Grossman, 'Rearranging'. Contemporaries did believe banking profits were higher than necessary, as suggested by the market-par ratios of bank shares being above the norm, but

American banking was different.[17] The USA had hundreds of times more *banks* than the UK and even 50% more commercial bank *offices* per capita in 1913,[18] but (since businesses in both countries mainly banked locally) such national data are inappropriate indicators of market concentration or competition. The USA had a less integrated national market, with more people living in small towns (some with only a single one-unit bank) than more highly urbanised Britain (with multiple national and regional chains). London was clearly a more competitive banking market than New York[19] and in mid-sized city markets the two countries looked much the same and increasingly competitive. For example, in Oxford (a city of about 65,000 by 1913), there had been only two private banks (the oldest dating from 1771) and one branch of a national joint-stock bank chain in 1875;[20] the Oxford Savings Bank, unable to compete with them, had closed down in 1865. In 1900 and 1909 both private banks were acquired by Barclays (an expanding federation of formerly private bankers that had incorporated in 1896),[21] but this was after six additional national chains had opened new branches with full current account and lending services. Also a new private bank, Gilletts (founded in 1877), had expanded to three Oxford offices, investing surplus funds with the London discount house owned by relatives.[22] This brought Oxford's commercial bank total in 1913 to nine (with fifteen offices): three times the 1875 level for banks and four times for offices. Thus the Oxford

---

put this down to customers' desire to foster good relationships and unwillingness to bargain on deposit or loans rates with their bankers (though this was clearly possible: see Ferdinand Lavington, 'The Social Importance of Banking', *Economic Journal* 21 (1911), 53–60). Companies then usually had only one banker and rarely changed banks: see Fabio Braggion and Steven Ongena, 'A Century of Firm–Bank Relationship', unpublished paper (2014).

17   In 1912, there were four French, four British, three German, one Spanish and no American banks with an equity market capitalisation above £14 million ($68 million).

18   Comptroller of the Currency, *Annual Report of the Comptroller of the Currency 1913* (Washington, DC, 1914), and David Sheppard, *The Growth and Role of UK Financial Institutions* (London, 1971), p. 114.

19   To the extent that one US historian, abandoning free-market priors, was reduced to implausibly claiming that lower competition in New York promoted superior quality: Bradford De Long, 'Did J. P. Morgan's Men Add Value: An Economist's Perspective on Financial Capitalism', *Inside the Business Enterprise*, ed. Peter Temin (New York, 1990), pp. 205–49, and compare to Leslie Hannah, 'J. P. Morgan in London and New York Before 1914', *Business History Review* 85 (2011), 113–50.

20   *Banking Almanac 1876*, p. 413.

21   Wootten & Co. (joining Barclays in 1909) had declined to trivial size, but Parsons, Thomson & Co. (which joined in 1900) had three prosperous branches and the former partners maintained considerable decision-making independence in their local head office.

22   A national chain provided it with London clearing services, so Gilletts was not seriously hobbled by the clearing house cartel. On Oxford banks see *Bankers' Almanac 1913* (London, 1913), p. 669 and *Kelly's Directory of Oxford, Abingdon and Neighbourhood 1913–14* (London, 22nd annual).

market had become more competitive *despite* local mergers and *because of*
the expansion of national chains. Not all cities were as lucky but larger cities
had even more competitors and it is difficult to identify counties which had
become *excessively* concentrated by 1913.[23]

There were also many quasi-banks, though their ability to compete effectively in money transmission was limited by the London clearing house cartel
until the 1980s. Savings bank[24] and money order facilities were available at
Oxford's twenty-three post offices (accepting deposits up to the government
cap of £200). Deposits were also taken by building societies,[25] friendly
societies and branches of the national Lipton grocery chain and local retail
co-operatives (though they provided little or no business lending).[26] Other
providers of financial/business services included forty-eight solicitors (some
arranging private mortgages), eight accountants, one business transfer
agent (who, with more specialist expertise than solicitors and accountants,
organised the sale of private businesses or partnerships)[27] and one stockbroker
(southern cities were not as well served by local exchanges as their northern
counterparts, but there were four stock markets with thousands of brokers
within a 100 kilometre radius of this broker's central Oxford office, accessible
by telephone or same-day post: he was a convenience not a monopolist). There
were also twenty-three insurance offices, offering both savings products and
business loans (usually secured by mortgage, life policies or private debenture)

---

23   Manchester had more than a dozen regional and national chains (the largest with twenty-
three branches) and several unit-banks and foreign banks. For a county-level analysis see
Fabio Braggion, Narly Dwarkasing and Lyndon Moore, *The Economic Impact of a Banking
Oligopoly: Britain at the Turn of the 20th Century*, University of Melbourne Working Paper
(Melbourne, 2015).

24   The Trustee Savings Bank did not open an Oxford office until 1933.

25   By 1914 there were 1,506 UK building societies with £66 million in assets. Although only
one building society is shown with an Oxford office in the 1913 city directory, the Church of
England Society in London also advertised its services in the directory (paying 3.5–4.5% on
various accounts) and others also took deposits by post.

26   Sir Thomas Lipton offered a banking service at his retail grocery stores, attracting £150,000
of savings deposits earning 3.5% (less than he had to pay on debentures but better than
depositors could get elsewhere: *Economist*, 14 June 1913, p. 1448); Oxford had two branches of
Lipton's. It had once been common for businesses such as cotton mills and breweries to accept
deposits but this had become rarer. Co-operatives mainly paid dividends related to purchases
not ownership, but the CWS bank in Manchester (which mainly served retail societies and trade
unions) also offered individual accounts (though not to rival tradesmen) from 1910, encouraging
co-operators who had invested the maximum £200 in their local society to deposit any surplus
with them; by 1912 it had 2,472 accounts with £182,352 savings, an average per account of
£73.77: see Percy Redfern, *New History of the CWS* (London, 1938), pp. 56 and 404; Thomas
Goodwin, 'Banking and Finance', *Cooperative Wholesale Societies' Annual 1914* (Manchester,
1914), pp. 165–88.

27   Again there were many specialist rivals in London.

on a longer term basis than bankers.[28] Unlike some provincial cities, Oxford had no merchant bank or overseas bank branch, but several hundred were an hour away in London and one local shop specialised in money-changing. This looks nearer to workable competition than a tight oligopoly in financial services. Local bank managers perhaps showed some gentlemanly distaste for aggressively poaching on each other's turf,[29] but they advertised competitively and Gilletts attracted small traders' accounts from national chains by offering longer term loans with less onerous security requirements (though usually requiring a life policy).[30] Since 1886 most Oxford banks had London head offices colluding to restrict credit interest to 1.5% (rather than the customary 1%) below bank rate, but this was negotiable in the provinces and for large accounts; and small savers sensibly used alternatives paying higher rates but offering more limited services.[31]

It did not require America's anti-branching laws and interstate banking bans to preserve this workable level of bank competition: the 1920 UK gentleman's agreement to ban large commercial bank mergers (or an outright legal ban on banks acquiring rivals with more than, say, £200,000 capital) would have sufficed (if implemented seven years earlier, perhaps with guarantees of clearing house access for new entrants). Was America's banking system already more competitive before these policy omissions? A similar American university city – New Haven, Connecticut (the home of Yale but with twice Oxford's population before 1914) – suggests caution before so concluding. It was home to only five 'national'[32] banks (one with as many as two offices)[33] and there were seven state banks in the tiny state of Connecticut (not all in New Haven),[34] plus a branch of White Weld (NY City Bank's

---

28   In 1906, British insurance company non-mortgage loans constituted 16.9% of their investment portfolios, compared with 10.7% in the USA and 6.7% in Germany, though mortgage loans (difficult to compare because part of a wider market everywhere) were favoured by German insurers.

29   Capie and Collins report occasional refusals to make competing loan rate offers before 1914: Capie and Collins, 'Industrial Lending', p. 40.

30   Audrey Taylor, *Gilletts: Bankers at Banbury and Oxford* (Oxford, 1964), pp. 195–7.

31   Brian Griffiths, 'The Development of Restrictive Practices in the UK Monetary System', *Manchester School* 41 (1973), 3–18. The reduction to 2% below bank rate in 1918 indicates a strengthening of monopoly powers following wartime mergers. Sheppard suggests that in 1913 the commercial banks had only 55% of the market in cashable assets (with savings banks, building societies and insurance companies being significant competitors): Sheppard, *Growth and Role*, p. 18. Gilletts ignored the London cartel rate and offered a minimum of 2.5% interest: Taylor, *Gilletts*, p. 198.

32   In British English these banks were 'local', though with less freedom to issue notes than British legacy issuers. The term 'national' in American English reflects not their scope but the fact that their dollar bills were printed by their federal supervisor (the Comptroller of the Currency) and backed by US Treasury securities.

33   Comptroller, *Annual Report 1913*, p. 408.

34   Comptroller, *Annual Report 1913*, p. 726.

retail security subsidiary)[35] and a fringe of quasi-banks and other financial service providers.[36] New Haven's mainly unit-banks were not obviously more competitive than Oxford's (there were fewer banks and offices per capita), though they were more exclusively rooted in the local community than any except Oxford's private banks. Yet, even with their correspondents 1½ hours away in New York (and, in two cases, six days away in London) and client referrals to trust companies and stockbrokers, they did not self-evidently offer a superior service to Oxford's branch banks, linking with their groups' more cosmopolitan and diverse in-house range of services.[37]

There is a persistent strand in the literature stressing the conservatism of British banks, but Capie and Mills show no increase in conservatism before 1914 as measured by return volatility.[38] However, one area where even their defenders concede banks were conservative was in lending to new businesses, where the lending rules imposed in national chains were perhaps unnecessarily restrictive.[39] Yet there were still exceptions to banker conservatism in Oxford. Its banks congregated in the city centre around Carfax until the suburban branch expansion of the 1920s, but Gilletts had already opened a branch in the Cowley Road where William Morris (a local motorcycle, garage and omnibus entrepreneur) was a client. He first caught the shrewd eye of the banker Arthur Gillett in 1904. After being dragged into bankruptcy by a feckless undergraduate partner, Morris had later honourably compensated partnership creditors for their losses of £500, though under no legal obligation to do so. In 1912, the resilient and entrepreneurial Morris was converting the disused Temple Cowley grammar school into a car factory, a challenge to Henry Ford's greenfield Manchester assembly plant (Morris would eventually overtake Ford as Europe's largest automobile manufacturer). Convinced he was worthy of trust, Gillett backed Morris's new enterprise both with loans (from the bank) and equity (on his personal account), supplementing funds that Morris had obtained from Lord Macclesfield (an enthusiastic automobilist): enough (with customer deposits, trade credit and his own resources) to assemble from bought-in parts his first 250 cars (Ford was assembling over a thousand in Manchester). It was symptomatic of the way British banking was going that in 1920 it was only with some difficulty that Gillett (by then a local director in a corporate managerial hierarchy which had acquired his bank, no

35 Vincent Carosso, *Investment Banking in America: A History* (Cambridge, MA, 1970), p. 103.

36 I have not been able to consult a contemporary local directory, but the *Ninth Annual Report of the Commissioner of Labor 1893* (Washington, DC, 1894), p. 44, showed six savings and loans in New Haven county.

37 For the merits and demerits of branch banking, see Jakob Riesser, *The Great German Banks and their Concentration* (Washington, DC, 1911), pp. 689–96.

38 Forrest Capie and Terence Mills, 'British Bank Conservatism in the Late 19th Century', *Explorations in Economic History* 32 (1995), 409–20.

39 Capie and Collins, 'Industrial Lending'.

longer a private banker) persuaded Barclays' head office to extend generous overdraft accommodation for Morris, helping his (now substantially larger) enterprise survive the post-war recession without the receivership which Midland Bank and Eagle Insurance creditors inflicted on his British arch-rival, Austin.[40] Morris Motors was so successful that, hardly using his overdraft, Morris was soon depositing millions with Barclays (and, expressing strong distaste for merchant bankers' excessive fees, insisting that Barclays handle his 1926 IPO);[41] he also became a major philanthropic supporter of Oxford University and medical charities. It would be absurd to claim that Gillett's serendipitous commercial banking support for Morris at these crucial junctures was the only reason Oxford (where BMW still make the Mini and the graduate social science college Morris founded is named after him)[42] now has twice its 1913 population, while New Haven's population has not grown, but it certainly helped.[43]

Bank lending: international yardsticks

All analysts agree that British banks before 1914 increased the proportion of their balance sheets in liquid investments to high levels, and by more than bankers abroad, but the a priori characterisation of this as 'conservative' is misleading.[44] British banks took fractional reserve banking to extreme limits, with much lower capital relative to their balance sheet totals than banks overseas.[45] Other things being equal, that would have condemned them to

40　Morris files in Barclays archives, Wythenshawe, Manchester; Philip Andrews and Elisabeth Brunner, *Life of Lord Nuffield* (Oxford, 1955), pp. 105–6; Roy Church, *Herbert Austin* (London, 1979), pp. 58–68.

41　The prospectus issue, underwritten at zero cost and little risk by Morris himself (apparently looking to diversify his personal holdings, not to raise expansion capital), was oversubscribed, with institutions gaining five of the largest ten allotments: see London Guildhall Library, LSE archives, MS 18001, File 133 253 B, 22 December 1926.

42　Nuffield College, Lord Nuffield being the title he chose when elevated to the peerage.

43　Lamoreaux bemoans the eclipse of New England's bankers stimulating such new industries – its bankers had become more conservative by 1900: Naomi Lamoreaux, *Insider Lending* (New York, 1994), pp. 155–6. Alfred Sloan of General Motors was born in New Haven but notably pursued his career in New York and Detroit.

44　Michael Collins and Mae Baker, *Commercial Banks and Industrial Finance in England and Wales, 1860–1913* (Oxford, 2003); Braggion, Dwarkasing and Moore, *Economic Impact*, pp. 23–5; Lucy Newton, 'British Retail Banking in the Twentieth Century: Decline and Renaissance in Industrial Lending', *Business in Britain in the Twentieth Century: Decline and Renaissance?*, ed. Richard Coopey and Peter Lyth (Oxford, 2009), pp. 189–206.

45　Michie, 'Banks and Securities Markets', p. 52, though published accounts understated true capital reserves in British banks by around 20%: see Mark Billings and Forrest Capie, 'Capital in British Banking 1920–1970', *Business History* 49 (2007), 139–62.

higher failure rates than overseas banks with stronger capital resources. In fact, the outcome was the reverse: by 1913 UK bank bankruptcies were already rare and small and that situation was maintained for many more decades, while American and German banks (despite their greater capital backing) collapsed like flies. Insistence on large liquid reserves (a valuable mainstay of short-term lending on the London money market) was thus arguably not a symptom of conservatism, but, on the contrary, a corollary of adventurously and *safely* pushing fractional reserve banking to its extreme limit, thus facilitating faster balance sheet growth.

If British banks nonetheless committed fewer funds to (relatively illiquid) direct business lending than foreign banks the criticism would stick. In fact, even *after* prudently providing higher liquidity reserves, British banks slightly led those of other countries in the two main forms of direct lending to business (bill discounts/acceptance credits and advances/overdrafts/loans).[46] Table 3.1 shows that Germany and France were not in this sense more 'bank-orientated' economies than Britain, though their commercial banks did almost as much lending as British (or American) banks. Mortgages (which provided some business funds) are largely absent from this table, especially where they came from specialist institutions mainly providing property finance,[47] and we cannot in most countries separate business from personal loans, but in other respects Table 3.1 possibly understates the slight British lead in bank finance for business. The data are confined to the domestic commercial banking sector, but Britain also had many merchant banks (also discounting bills and providing longer-term finance) and overseas banks headquartered or operating in London were larger than similar sectors abroad, yet excluded. Unlike banks in some other commercial centres (notably in highly protectionist New York) – where laws prevented foreign engagement in deposit-taking and other banking activity – overseas banks in London (though they concentrated on serving the needs of overseas clients in the London money markets) were free to take deposits as well as lend locally and many did so; they actually had more assets than the UK domestic banks included in the table.[48] British-headquartered businesses – which then both

46 Sylla made similar points about the size of Anglo-Saxon banking on the deposit side: Richard Sylla, 'Wall Street Transitions 1880–1920: From National to World Financial Centre', *Financial Centres and International Capital Flows in the Nineteenth and Twentieth Centuries*, ed. Youssef Cassis and Laure Quennoëlle-Corre (Oxford, 2011), pp. 161–78. Generally the telegraph had reduced usage of discounting and increased that of overdrafts.

47 Such as British building societies, American savings and loans, German *Hypothekenbanken* and the French *Crédit Foncier*.

48 The *Economist Banking Number* (as cited in Forrest Capie and Alan Webber, *Monetary History of the United Kingdom, 1870–1982*, vol. 1: *Data, Sources* (London, 1985), p. 254) in 1914 reported their assets as 157% of those of the domestic commercial banks shown in Table 3.1. Jones reports thirty-one 'British overseas' banks in London with 1,387 overseas

Table 3.1. Commercial Banks, their interest rates, and their lending
(in billion dollars) relative to GDP (various countries 1913)

	UK	USA	Germany	France[1]		Italy
GDP	11.76	39.52	11.54	9.57		4.74
Number of banks	72	24,015	362	(a) 10	(b) 600+	95+
Loans/advances/overdrafts	2.653	11.801	1.773	(a) 0.631	(b) 1.500	1.305
Bills/acceptances	1.205	n/a[2]	1.432	(a) 0.936	(b) 1.300	n/a[3]
Total lending (non-mortgage)	3.858	11.801	3.205	(a) 1.567	(b) 2.800	1.305
Lending/GDP (%)	33	30	28	(a) 16	(b) 29	28
Policy interest rate (%)[4]	4.77	5.00	5.88	4.00		5.62

National currencies have been converted to dollars at gold standard rates (£1 = $4.86, 1 mark = $0.237, 1 franc or lira = $0.193); at purchasing power parity the pound was probably worth rather more and the dollar rather less relative to Continental European currencies.

1   For France the 'a' data relate only to the six leading commercial banks and four major investment banks. I have been unable to trace any data for the hundreds of provincial banks (League of Nations, *Memorandum on Commercial Banks 1913–1929* (Geneva, 1931), p. 124), though they clearly played a large role in French business finance: the figures marked 'b' are unsupported conjectures.

2   The US bill market was small and the certificate of deposit market much better developed. The previous line certainly includes CDs and appears to include bills and acceptances also (though presumably not the bills of exchange then commonly used in US interbank dealings).

3   I assume these are included in the above line.

4   Note that actual lending rates could vary considerably above or below this. Riccardo De Bonis, Fabio Farabullini, Miria Rocchelli, Alessandro Salvio and Andrea Silvestrini, *A Quantitative Look at the Italian Banking System: Evidence from a New Dataset Since 1861*, Ministry of Economy and Finance Working Paper 9 (Rome, 2013), table 5, shows short-term rates in 1913 Italy of 6.1% for short-term loans and 4.5% for long-term loans; for the variety in the USA see Comptroller, *Annual Report 1913*, pp. 35–6. The figures here are very similar to the yields at market prices on government loans (see the *Economist 1913*, *passim*).

Sources: See Appendix to this chapter.

exported and imported more, and invested more abroad than rivals – then typically kept their current account with one local banker,[49] buying trade finance and specialist advice from these other banks only when their international business required it or prices looked attractive.[50]

Even the low number of UK banks in line 2 of Table 3.1 would stand out less, if we took account of this more cosmopolitan range of competitors, not to speak of the thousands of building societies, savings banks, financial and investment trusts, insurers, friendly societies and other quasi-banks that are excluded from the UK data.[51] However, not even counting every commercial bank globally could conceal the fact that the USA comfortably exceeded the rest of the world in its numbers of small, local banks. These were – given the distinctive and growing US political taste for banking intervention[52] – substantially regulated by federal and state civil servants,[53] rather than by professional management hierarchies with strong national or regional brand

branches in 1913: Geoffrey Jones, *British Multinational Banking, 1830–1990* (Oxford, 1995), appendix.

49   Braggion and Ongena, 'Century'.

50   Clearing banks had only recently entered the acceptance credit market which was dominated by UK merchant banks; seven of the latter had more than £45 million of acceptance credits outstanding in 1913: Stanley Chapman, *The Rise of Merchant Banking* (London, 1984), pp. 107 and 209.

51   In contrast to the 72 joint-stock banks and discount houses (classified by the League of Nations as 'commercial') in Table 3.1, the *Banker's Almanac 1913* lists 285 private and joint-stock banks operating in the UK, 70 discount houses, exchange agents and similar financiers, 73 merchant bankers, and many foreign and colonial bank head offices and branches. The *Stock Exchange Official Intelligence* listed 803 non-bank, non-insurance 'land, finance and investment' companies in 1914 of which 665 analysed by Essex-Crosby had £347 million ($1,686 million) subscribed share capital (44% alone of the bank accommodation shown in Table 3.1): Alan Essex-Crosby, 'Joint Stock Companies in Great Britain, 1884–1934' (M.Com. thesis, University of London, 1937). The Inland Revenue (including more unquoted firms and miscellaneous brokers) reported 12,080 corporate enterprises and 7,800 partnerships and sole proprietorships assessed for tax in the non-bank, non-insurance finance category in 1911/12, with aggregate profits higher than banks and insurance companies combined: George Worswick and David Tipping, *Profits in the British Economy 1909–1938* (Oxford, 1967), pp. 101, 103 and 106. These companies were significantly involved in business finance, using stock exchange, money market and private funds. In 1913, there were also 1,611 building societies, 2,497 industrial and provident societies and nearly 17,000 post offices with savings bank and basic money transmission facilities, but they were little involved in lending to general business (focusing instead on government, municipalities, utilities and housing).

52   The US partiality for inefficiently small banks was not shared by other North Americans: for Canadians' British tastes in banking, see Michael Bordo, Angela Redish and Hugh Rockoff, 'A Comparison of the United States and Canadian Banking Systems in the Twentieth Century: Stability v Efficiency?', *Anglo-American Financial Systems*, ed. Bordo and Sylla, pp. 11–40; Michael Bordo, Angela Redish and Hugh Rockoff, 'Why Didn't Canada Have a Banking Crisis in 2008 (or in 1930, or in 1907, or ...)?', *Economic History Review* 67 (2015), 218–43.

53   There was also some regulation by clearing houses and New York money centre correspondents.

identities and head-office branch inspection teams that were the norm in the rest of the world. The Japanese – generally making astute judgements on what to copy from the West – initially adopted US-style banking laws, but were shifting as rapidly as they could to the European model.[54] It is, then, difficult to argue that the UK had an esoteric, unaccommodating, restrictive, small or uncompetitive commercial banking sector. The indicative interest rate figures in the last line of Table 3.1 also suggest that loans and discounts were as cheap as they were plentiful in Britain; perhaps because labour productivity in the finance sector then led that in Germany or the USA.[55]

Stock exchanges provided further financial accommodation for business. The UK was not slightly ahead of other countries on this dimension but well ahead, with a ratio of quoted corporate securities to GDP approaching 190% at market, while corporate stocks and bonds in other industrial countries remained below 100% of GDP, though in all leading countries stock exchange securities comfortably exceeded the bank accommodation shown in Table 3.1.[56] Between 1884 and 1914, the value of securities of UK companies tradable on the London Stock Exchange (LSE) alone had more than quintupled, while provincial markets mainly catered to smaller, local firms.[57] This provided formidable competition for banks in longer-term business finance, though their relationship with stock exchanges was also complementary. This did not necessarily require that British commercial banks become 'universal' (i.e. more multi-product, including investment banking services), as was (and remained) legally permissible in the UK. Apart from their own extensive liquid reserves invested in stock exchange securities, bankers provided LSE brokers and jobbers with the funds required to hold their stock-in-trade, offered credit to their investors and extended bridging finance to issuing houses so they could hold IPO assets between purchase from vendors and transfer to subscribers or underwriters. Bankers often recommended that their larger joint-stock business customers make a stock exchange issue when they asked for longer-term bank

54 Leslie Hannah, 'The Development of Japanese Banking in the Twentieth Century: Reflections in Western Mirrors', *Bankhistorisches Archiv* 37 (2011), 120–36; Richard Smethurst, *From Foot Soldier to Finance Minister: Takahashi Korekiyo, Japan's Keynes* (Cambridge, MA, 2007).

55 Broadberry suggests that American productivity was behind the UK's in 1890 in financial services generally but ahead by 1910: Stephen Broadberry, *Market Services and the Productivity Race, 1850–2000: Britain in International Perspective* (Cambridge, 2006), p. 30. Hannah, confining his measure to the commercial banking sector, shows UK productivity consistently ahead of the USA and Germany before 1914: Leslie Hannah, 'Twentieth-Century Banking Productivity Comparisons' (forthcoming).

56 Leslie Hannah, *Rethinking Corporate Finance Fables: Did the US Lag Europe Before 1914?*, CIRJE Working Paper F-994 (2015), pp. 27–8 and 31. The ratio was 91% for the USA, 56% for France and 48% for Germany, though these three countries were closer together if railway bonds guaranteed by the German and French governments were added to corporate securities.

57 Essex-Crosby, 'Joint Stock Companies', pp. 200–203.

accommodation than was judged appropriate or when they wanted to liquidate accumulated borrowings. There was no legal bar to banks acting as full service issuers (and/or underwriters) for such clients' equity IPOs or bond issues, and they did so,[58] but more usually passed the business to other professionals: lawyers, stockbrokers, accountants and other intermediaries, many also bank clients, specialising in the issue market. The bank's name usually graced a company's IPO prospectus, but their participation was normally confined to receiving applications at branches and distributing the share or debenture certificates to successful applicants (routine, fee-based, large-scale clerical processing functions similar to their core business), deducting the traditional 1% commission for their own clients' subscriptions. Many banks also offered their retail clients the facility to buy any stock exchange securities within the branch, sharing the commission 50/50 with a stockbroker, and sometimes offering safe custody of securities and collection of dividends/coupons.[59] Banks were legally permitted to act as stockbrokers and some did make a market in their own (and occasionally other) shares, but stock exchange rules pointedly barred bankers from membership.[60] By encouraging their clients to issue debentures on the stock exchange for longer-term fixed-interest capital,[61] British banks thus *deliberately* shifted their longer-term business to stock exchanges, as did German and French commercial banks, but the latter engaged more in off-exchange share trading for customers and in sponsoring IPOs.[62] In the UK, thousands of financial and investment trusts, venture capitalists, ad hoc consortia and wealthy 'angel' investors were competitively offering development capital to banks' more ambitious business clients, often with a view eventually to assisting the more successful to make an IPO. The slightly higher ratio of UK bank lending to GDP (*after* this diversion) is, then, remarkable.

---

58   Commercial bankers providing such services included the London & Westminster for Allsopp's Brewery, Sir Samuel Scott Bart & Co. for Bass, Ratcliff & Gretton, and Barclays for Morris Motors. London merchant bankers such as Hambros, Rothschild, Morgan and Baring also sponsored IPOs, but stockbrokers were then the major company promoters and underwriters: Carsten Burhop, David Chambers and Brian Cheffins, 'Regulating IPOs: Evidence from Going Public in London, 1900–1913', *Explorations in Economic History* 51 (2014), 60–76 (p. 68).

59   William Reader, *A House in the City 1825–1975* (London, 1979), p. 109.

60   This did not prevent LSE brokers issuing and underwriting securities: the Stock Exchange Committee did not consider what we define as investment banking to constitute 'banking' under its rules.

61   Capie and Collins, 'Banks, Industry'.

62   Carsten Burhop, David Chambers and Brian Cheffins, *Law, Politics and the Rise and Fall of German Stock Market Development, 1870–1938*' (University of Cambridge Faculty of Law, Working Paper 283 (Cambridge, 2015); Pierre-Cyrille Hautcoeur, 'Le Marché Boursier et le Financement des Entreprises Françaises (1890–1939)' (Ph.D. thesis, Paris School of Economics, 1994). For a critical view of the moral hazard in French bankers' involvement in securities promotion to clients, see Marcel Labordère, 'The Mechanism of Foreign Investment in France and its Outcome, 1890–1914', *Economic Journal* 24 (1914), 525–42.

Conclusion

Is all this too rosy a picture? Undoubtedly it is: Edwardian England was not a perfect society, nor economy, and I suspect Francesca would have chided me for paying insufficient attention to what made *local* bankers better than national chains. Alternatively, maybe financial services were not only well developed in the UK before 1914, but perhaps *too* well developed? Problems with bank links to financiers emerged in the overcapitalisation boom at the end of the war, but had some pre-war roots.[63]

Economists have been increasingly raising concerns about *today's* financial markets,[64] their critical questioning driven by the obvious suspicion that innovative products sold by the finance sector before the global financial crisis plainly went too far. Yet modern levels of bank debt (relative to GDP) dwarf those shown in Table 3.1[65] and it is not easy to find equivalents before 1914 of today's more egregious financial sins: bankers selling products that enable governments to lie about deficits (as Goldman Sachs sold to Greece); people obtaining 'liar' loans (mortgages they could not repay being conveniently repackaged and concealed until after bonuses were paid to originators); insurance sold to people ineligible to benefit (much 'payment protection' insurance). There were also numerous misrepresentations and frauds before 1914, but they typically resulted from individual or small-group skulduggery, not – as recently – institutionalised kleptocracy, reinforced by corporate cultures and bonus schemes rewarding misrepresentation.[66] Moreover, the costs of liquidity assistance and recapitalising the Munster and Leinster Bank in 1886, Barings in 1890, or the Yorkshire Penny Bank in 1911 were trivial and substantially covered by the financial sector – anxious to preserve stability and reputation – rather than by taxpayers, though the government might have had to rescue the Banks of England or Ireland, had their liquidity assistance faltered or these (still entirely privately held) central banks failed.[67]

63   For example, David Higgins, Steven Toms and Igor Filatotchev, 'Ownership, Financial Strategy and Performance: The Lancashire Cotton Textile Industry, 1918–1938', *Business History* 57 (2015), 97–121.

64   For example, Luigi Zingales, *Does Finance Benefit Society?*, NBER Working Paper 20894 (Cambridge, MA, 2015); John Kay, *Other People's Money* (London, 2015).

65   Arcand, Berkes and Panizza find a non-monotone relationship between credit and GDP, but their tipping point at which more credit reduces growth is when credit to the private sector reaches 80–100% of GDP: Jean-Louis Arcand, Enrico Berkes and Ugo Panizza, *Too Much Finance?*, International Monetary Fund Working Paper WP/12/161 (Washington, DC, 2012). It is not easy to find empirical evidence supporting the view (popular among modern financial economists) that securities markets grew in the twentieth century faster than bank lending.

66   James Taylor, *Boardroom Scandal: The Criminalization of Company Fraud in Nineteenth-Century Britain* (Oxford, 2013).

67   The costs of the 1890 Baring lifeboat were quickly recovered, unlike the more long-drawn-out settlement of the Overend Gurney debts of 1866, which took decades. This illustrates the

The picture I have painted is of a workably competitive free market in finance that was destroyed by anticompetitive forces reasserting themselves under the 'Big Five' banks (and LSE restrictive practices) after 1914. This story is an echo for the finance sector of the more comprehensive modern reinterpretation of British economic growth in international perspective by Stephen Broadberry and Nicholas Crafts, reflecting the Thatcherite/Blairite consensus which was a backdrop to their writing.[68] It also has a similar knotty problem at its core. If competitive markets were really so good, how come the UK had an economic climacteric before 1914, while rivals forged ahead? It is hard to think of any real economy nearer to free market ideals than the UK economy then, though others were less competitive on some dimension (notably American tariff protection or German government ownership and regulation). That was well before all the cartels, tariffs, nationalisations and so on which Broadberry and Crafts see as eroding the UK market economy in the decades after 1914, and from which Britain only broke free after 1979. Explanations for this big hole in their model vary, though they note that UK institutions were not conducive to the levels of human capital formation which modernisation of the British economy required. Crafts was influenced in this direction by his work with Mark Thomas on revealed comparative advantage, which found a relatively low human capital content in British exports, though they omitted the finance sector, not to speak of distribution, transport and communications, which were human capital intensive and export orientated before 1914.[69]

---

advantages of decisive action by a lender of last resort rather than courtroom remedies (which arguably played too large a role in the 1866 and 2008 crises, while failing to impose criminal penalties).

68 Nicholas Crafts, 'British Relative Economic Decline Revisited: The Role of Competition', *Explorations in Economic History* 49 (2012), 17–29; Stephen Broadberry and Nicholas Crafts, 'Explaining Anglo-American Productivity Differences in the Mid-Twentieth Century', *Oxford Bulletin of Economics and Statistics* 52 (1990), 375–402; Stephen Broadberry and Nicholas Crafts, 'Britain's Productivity Gap in the 1930s: Some Neglected Factors', *Journal of Economic History* 52 (1992), 531–58; Stephen Broadberry and Nicholas Crafts 'Competition and Innovation in 1950s Britain', *Business History* 43 (2001), 97–118.

69 Nicholas Crafts and Mark Thomas, 'Comparative Advantage in UK Manufacturing Trade, 1910–1935', *Economic Journal* 96 (1986), 629–45. This article is confined to manufacturing, but one econometric result that they downplay (emphasising instead the low human capital content of British manufacturing exports) is that Britain had a comparative advantage in *capital*-intensive exports. This would be compatible with the view of finance expressed here: one might expect that outcome if finance was cheaper and more plentiful in the UK than in Germany and the USA. Moreover, if financial and other service exports were included in their equations and exports were measured in value-added rather than gross terms (so Britain's cotton exports were substantially American), it is possible that the low human capital content of British exports would disappear. For more positive assessments of British adoption of capital-intensive technologies, see Alexander Field, 'Land Abundance, Interest/Profit Rates, and Nineteenth-Century American and British Technology', *Journal of Economic History* 43 (1983), 405–31; Leslie Hannah, 'Corporations in the US and Europe', *Business History* 56 (2014), 865–99;

Another possible explanation of the British climacteric is that it was unrelated to the efficiency of business organisation. For example, current explanations of European slowdown relative to the USA find evidence that the age structure of the population is a major determinant: similar factors alone might explain any early British climacteric.[70] Moreover, in the modelling of Crafts and Mills, the UK's long-term trend growth around 2% persisted to 1914, with only a minor blip in 1899–1907, so there may, in fact, be rather little to explain.[71]

Might British finance, if quantitatively more than adequate, have lagged *qualitatively* behind that of Germany and the USA? One ghost stalking this discussion is a persistent view that banks (and stock markets) should have fostered more innovation and, if they had, the UK economy would have forged further ahead rather than merely maintaining its stately growth. Yet the influential intuition – championed by Whiggish historians like Schumpeter, Landes and Chandler among many others – that Germany had stronger innovation capabilities than Britain before 1914 is not firmly grounded. German inventors still lagged Britons in US patenting[72] and German banks may have been more

Pieter Woltjer, *The Great Escape: Technological Lock-In vs Appropriate Technology in Early Twentieth Century British Manufacturing*, GGDC Research Memorandum 141 (Groningen, 2013). It is noteworthy that, even today, the UK is a much larger net exporter of financial services than the USA: Thomas Philippon, 'Has the US Finance Industry Become Less Efficient? On The Theory and Measurement of Financial Intermediation', *American Economic Review* 105 (2015), 1408–38. For US evidence that finance was a high-skill sector (before 1933 and after 1980), see Thomas Philippon and Ariell Reshef, 'Wages and Human Capital in the US Finance Industry: 1909–2006', *Quarterly Journal of Economics* 127 (2012), 1551–609.

70   The proportion of the population aged over sixty was 26% higher in the UK than the USA, and 8% higher than in Germany: Wassily Woytinsky, *Die Welt in Zahlen*, vol. 4 (Berlin, 1926), p. 46. Modern US estimates suggest that a 10 percentage point increase in this ratio decreases GDP per capita by 5.7%: Nicole Maestas, Kathleen Mullen and David Powell, *The Effect of Population Aging on Economic Growth*, Rand Corporation Working Paper (Santa Monica, CA, 2014). Before mass retirement such effects might have been lower, but if older people were less healthy then the effects would have been larger.

71   Nicholas Crafts and Terence Mills, 'British Economic Fluctuations 1851–1913: A Perspective Based on Growth Theory', *Britain in the International Economy*, ed. Steve Broadberry and Nicholas Crafts (Cambridge, 1992), pp. 98–134. Apart from such manipulations, the data they and others use may be questioned. Charles Feinstein's estimates of Edwardian national income hardly differ from contemporary estimates by Stamp and Giffen and have been widely accepted, while the early estimates for Germany, the USA, France and Italy have been substantially revised. This is probably because Feinstein was exceptionally assiduous, but future revisions cannot be entirely ruled out.

72   New UK and German patents in the USA per million population (a conventional historical measure) rose from, respectively, 57 and 28 in 1890–92, to 66 for the UK and 60 for Germany in 1910–12 (author's calculation from data in John Cantwell, *Technological Innovation and Multinational Corporations* (Cambridge, MA, 1989), p. 23). Germany impresses not for its *superior* patenting prowess, but for *nearly* catching up from considerable backwardness in only two decades.

involved in reinforcing the position of established, large enterprises than in financing risk-taking innovators.[73] The superior merits of Germany's research universities (the best in the world), of its engineering apprenticeships and of its fine chemical, phosphate, electrical engineering, coal, piano, horse-breeding, machine-building and reinsurance industries are clear, but arguably depended more on technical than financial prowess. Yet technical prowess was concentrated in thirty firms, which accounted for more than half of German patents in the USA.[74] In many other areas – shipping, naval architecture, civil engineering and construction, automobiles, non-electrical machinery, cable networks, rubber, oil, non-ferrous metal mining and processing, electronics, high-tech armaments, cigarettes, branded, chilled and preserved food, manufactured gas and its chemical by-products, mass retailing, trade finance, investment trusts, exploration companies, special steels, electronics, nitrates, soda ash, explosives and rayon – British pre-1914 innovation capabilities and market shares appear to be a match for (indeed often superior to) Germany's. European markets for manufactures and services were reasonably open (in 1913 tariffs averaged only 4.6% of import values in Britain and 6.3% in Germany and transport costs had massively fallen)[75] so naturally European production (as in the modern EU) tended to concentrate in countries which produced most efficiently. This could hardly always be Britain or always Germany, any more than, in the USA, with interstate free trade, it could always be New England or always the Midwest. What requires explanation (in a European comparative context) is why – unlike today – so many pre-1914 large-scale and innovative industries in Germany did not do as well as (or better than) those in Britain. Business historians of Germany perhaps need to work harder explaining their

73   Richard Tilly, 'German Banking, 1850–1914: Development Assistance for the Strong', *Journal of European Economic History* 15 (1986), 113–51; Jeremy Edwards and Sheilagh Ogilvie, 'Universal Banks and German Industrialisation: a Reappraisal', *Economic History Review* 49 (1996), 427–46. Their equity investments also appear to be on a similar (small) scale to that of English banks: see Caroline Fohlin, 'The Balancing Act of German Universal Banks and English Deposit Banks, 1880–1913', *Business History* 43 (2001), 1–24. However, Lehmann and Streb suggest that banks and investors effectively evaluated the IPOs of 172 innovative firms on the Berlin Stock Exchange between 1892 and 1913: Sybille Lehmann and Jochen Streb, *The Berlin Stock Exchange in Imperial Germany: A Market for New Technology?*, CEPR Discussion Paper 10558 (London, 2015).

74   Harald Degner, 'Schumpeterian German Firms Before and After World War I: The Innovative Few and the Non-Innovative Many', *Zeitschrift für Unternehmensgeschichte* 54 (2009), 50–72. This may also be why Cantwell (*Technological Innovation*, p. 22) found that among the thirty largest European companies patenting in the USA, thirteen (concentrated in chemicals and electricals) were German, while ten (more evenly distributed) were British.

75   Stephen Broadberry, *The Productivity Race: British Manufacturing in International Perspective, 1850–1950* (Cambridge, 1997), pp. 140–1; Leslie Hannah, 'Logistics, Market Size and Giant Plants in the Early Twentieth Century: A Global View', *Journal of Economic History* 68 (2008), 46–79.

lags, matching the extensive literature on electrical equipment and dyestuffs explaining why there was no British AEG, Siemens, Bayer or Hoechst.

They might start by explaining why Reemtsma was behind Imperial Tobacco and BAT, why Deutsche Uberseeische Bank was behind Colonial Bank, why Borsig was behind the LNWR's locomotive manufacturing division, why Internationale Baugesellschaft was behind S. Pearson & Son, why Metallgesellschaft was behind Rio Tinto, why Deutsche Gold und Silber was behind Consolidated Goldfields, why Telefunken was behind Marconi, why Deutsche Solvay was behind Brunner Mond, why Calmon was behind Turner Brothers and Cape Asbestos, why Portland-Cementfabrik Germania was behind APCM and BPCM, why Vereinigte Glanzstoff was behind Courtaulds, why Opel was behind Morris, why Continental was behind Dunlop, why Schultheiss was behind Guinness, why Deutsche Linoleum was behind Williamson, why Henkel was behind Lever Brothers and Reckitt, why Wenderoth was behind Boots Pure Drug, and why Deutsche Erdöl and Vereinigte Deutsche Petroleum-Werke were behind Shell and Burmah.[76] There was a remarkable and sustained UK multinational lead: British enterprises in 1914 had more than three times as much foreign direct investment as their German rivals.[77] That was partly because many multinationals based on German patents or brands or substantially operating in the German market – such as Liebig, Van den Bergh, Deutsche Babcock, Imperial Continental Gas, Japhet & Co., Apollinaris & Johannis and Nobel-Dynamit-Trust – were headquartered in London rather than in Berlin.[78]

However, that theoretical hole is easier to fill than Crafts' British puzzle. Apart from the fact that Germany was still poorer than the UK and catching up,[79] it had more limited supplies of the financial services that were

76 'Behind' is a simple word concealing complexity, and all cases merit further discussion. Absolute size (by capital or output) is my main measure, though usually the British lead extended to world export shares, R & D, patenting, brand values, productivity and growth rates (though with some exceptions: Deutsche Gold und Silber had more patents; the LNWR did not export). There is an abundance of Whig misperceptions, including Chandler's amusingly counterfactual 'explanations' of why many German companies in these pairs were larger, when they were not: Leslie Hannah, 'Strategic Games, Scale and Efficiency, or Chandler Goes to Hollywood', *Business in Britain in the Twentieth Century*, ed. Coopey and Lyth, pp. 15–47.

77 Geoffrey Jones, *The Evolution of International Business: An Introduction* (London, 1996), p. 30.

78 These appear to exceed the much-celebrated reverse flow that included Mannesmann, benefiting from supportive bank interventions paralleling the support that Baker and Collins noted for distressed British industry, and Siemens, paralleling the Gilletts/Barclays relationship with Morris. On the two German cases, see Timothy Guinnane, 'Delegated Monitoring, Large and Small: German Banking 1800–1914', *Journal of Economic Literature* 40 (2002), 73–124 (pp. 111–14).

79 In manufacturing, German labour productivity had possibly already caught up with, or even overtaken, the UK (Albrecht Ritschl, 'The Anglo-German Industrial Productivity Puzzle,

conducive to rapid business development of firms with distinctive organisational, technical and marketing capabilities, particularly in the early stages
of advanced and capital-intensive technologies.[80] With limited economic
resources (some wastefully expended on overprotected agriculture and an
unnecessary arms race), Germany could hardly do as well as or better than
the UK on as wide a front as the USA: then larger, richer, more financially
developed, more protected (by distance and tariffs) and less militarised. Of
course, no country led in everything and both the UK and USA could surely
have done more to invigorate their apprenticeship training or strengthen their
research universities to German levels.[81]

Yet, arguably the last thing that Britain – then naturally at the leading edge
of so many contemporary technologies – needed was to emulate relatively
underdeveloped German finance and business services rather than those of
the richer USA. Many more educated young Germans flocked to London
to participate in its business opportunities than Englishmen travelled in
the reverse direction.[82] The enthusiastic participations of Deutsche Bank
and Crédit Lyonnais in London's banking market suggest an appreciation
of the merits of deregulated, competitive markets was not confined to the
Anglosphere.[83] Even Georg Siemens, founding director of Deutsche Bank and
its first chairman until 1900 – though his bank benefited from the privileged
intermediary position German restrictive corporate legislation conferred on it
– was in little doubt that British liberalism was preferable to German restric-
tionism in financial matters.[84] From time to time critics have nonetheless
recommended that Britain could have done better by suppressing or

1895–1935: A Restatement and a Possible Resolution', *Journal of Economic History* 68 (2008),
535–65), though in other sectors German productivity markedly lagged. Allen's backward
extrapolations suggest lower German capital productivity, driven by accumulating more capital
to finance (Anglo-American) frontier manufactured technologies more advanced than its own
lower wages required: Robert Allen, 'Technology and the Great Divergence: Global Economic
Development Since 1820', *Explorations in Economic History* 49 (2012), 1–16.

80   Diego Comin and Ramana Nanda, *Financial Development and Technology Diffusion*,
Harvard Business School Working Paper 15-36 (Cambridge, MA, 2014). Their use of the bank
deposits/GDP ratio as a proxy for 'angel' investing (that they identify as critical from US case
studies) is implausibly heroic (though shows Germany lagging), but more relevant indicators,
such as those in n. 51 above, would likely (in view of Germany's discouragement of informal
equity markets) show an even clearer British lead.

81   The USA (and, less markedly, Britain) lagged Germany in 1900–14 Nobel prizes.

82   As revealed by the numbers reciprocally interned as enemy aliens in August 1914.

83   Kathleen Burk and Manfred Pohl, *Deutsche Bank in London* (Munich, 1998).

84   Georg Siemens' speech to the Reichstag on 21 January 1885 (Georg Siemens, *Stenographische Berichte des Deutsches Reichstags* (Berlin, 1885) and many subsequent speeches
complaining of the 1896 restrictive legislation. Riesser's *Great German Banks* was a later plea
by a Darmstädter Bank director against further threatened regulation.

channelling some financial markets on the German model.[85] At a time when the financial sector has massively expanded without bringing commensurate improvements in economic performance, yet facilitated enormous increases in inequality, it is tempting to apply modern remedial prescriptions to the past. Yet Morris without Barclays, Brunner Mond without its early regional bank support and provincial IPO, and Shell and Marconi without bankers assisting their LSE junior market debuts may all have existed in some form, but would probably have grown more slowly. Governments may now benefit the economy by compelling the financial sector to cover its hidden costs and restricting its propensity to pay bonuses for value destruction, but before 1914 the case that financial repression would have boosted growth in the British economy needs to be more critically evaluated, in the face of a good deal of evidence to the contrary.

85 Undervaluing competitive assortment, Shannon extols the virtues of restricted corporate registration in Germany: Herbert Shannon, 'The Limited Companies of 1866–1883', *Economic History Review* 4 (1933), 290–316. On the basis of unconvincing yardsticks, Burhop, Chambers and Cheffins suggest there would have been gains from restricting the LSE to its official list, suppressing the more entrepreneurial junior ('special settlement') market: Burhop, Chambers and Cheffins, 'Regulating IPOs'. During and after the war, British businessmen admired German banks (for their alleged discrimination against non-German suppliers), coveting similar restrictions on British banks' overseas loans, though overseas borrowers are unlikely to have shared these anticompetitive enthusiasms.

Appendix: Sources for Table 3.1

Line 1. USA and UK from *MeasuringWorth*, http://www.measuringworth.
com; France and Germany from the Groningen GGDC website, http://www.
rug.nl/ggdc (both accessed 15 March 2015); Italy from Alberto Baffigi, *Italian
National Accounts, 1861–2011*, Bank of Italy Economic History Working
Papers 18 (Rome, 2011).

Line 2. The UK data include three discount houses, eight London private
(clearing/retail) banks and sixty-one joint-stock banks, but exclude private
country banks, such as Gilletts' in Oxford. Sheppard (*Growth and Role*,
pp. 184–5) suggests these and other commercial bank omissions would add
only a little over 1% to the lending figures shown, though other financial
institutions (including building societies and insurance companies) would
add much more. In the USA there were an estimated 29,254 banks, but the
figure here excludes 1,978 savings banks and 3,261 non-reporting banks (e.g.
J. P. Morgan & Co.). The Comptroller (*Annual Report 1913*, p. 46) estimated
that the deposits of non-reporters were only 2.6% of the reporting total.
The German data include only joint-stock (AG) banks, but state, savings,
mortgage, co-operative and private banks were collectively more important
in Germany. In 1913, 160 AG banks with more than 1 million marks capital
(accounting for 92% of the capital in the total of 362 AG banks) were supple-
mented by 132 GmbH banks (though in 1907 they had less than 1.6% of the
deposits of AG banks), as well as 1,221 private banks (of unreported size),
44 state land banks, 3,133 savings banks, 17,564 co-operative banks, 46
Zentralkassen and 13 postbanks; all these together had more assets than the
joint-stock banks though their lending to business was of lesser importance:
Deutsche Bundesbank, *Deutsches Geld- und Bankwesen in Zahlen, 1876–1975*
(Frankfurt, 1976), pp. 17, 67; League of Nations, *Memorandum*, pp. 130–1).
The number for Italy is for joint-stock banks; there were many hundreds of
co-operative, savings banks, etc., accounting for nearly two-thirds of the
lending shown in lower lines.

Lines 3–4. League of Nations, *Memorandum*, pp. 116, 139, 280–94, 332.
'Participations' (which often include investments in other banks) and 'investments' (usually held for near-cash, short-term investments and including
many government bonds) are excluded. To the (unknown) extent that they
differentially involved support for the business sector (e.g. subscriptions to
corporate bonds and equities) this may result in underestimation. Generally,
loans to households and government are included but interbank loans are
excluded. Most of the credit was short term everywhere (with overdrafts
dominating in Britain and Italy, though rare in the USA). In countries with
poorly developed corporate bond markets (notably Germany and Italy), loans

may have been more frequently rolled over, but the source is generally silent on this. For the UK I have arbitrarily allocated the undifferentiated small total of lending reported for eight London private retail banks, as to 40% discounts and 60% advances. For the USA the League of Nations reported a 1914 figure, but I have substituted 1913 to align it with the other countries, following the League by deducting savings banks to make the data more comparable to commercial banks elsewhere (Comptroller, *Annual Report 1913*, p. 37). Most of the loans of these omitted institutions were for mortgage purposes, and many similar loans are also omitted from the data for other countries. For Italy, De Bonis *et al.*, *Quantitative Look* (appendix data converted at €1 = 1936.27 lira), covers special credit institutions and co-operative banks (which peaked at 23% of the total loans of the Italian banking system in 1910) omitted by the League of Nations and other previous studies. In 1913, commercial (joint-stock) banks (including banks of issue) accounted for 37% of the loans, savings banks and *monti de pietà* 29%, co-operative, rural and artisans' banks 21% and special credit institutions (which specialised in longer-term loans) 13% (I am grateful to Riccardo de Bonis of the Bank of Italy for clarification of the methodology: email to the author, 23 October 2014).

Line 5. Line 3 + line 4

Line 6. Line 5 / line 1 x 100

Line 7. Central bank policy rates from Mark Flandreau and Frederic Zumer, *The Making of Global Finance, 1880–1913* (Paris, 2004), p. 126, except for the USA, where the lowest rate in 1914 after the FRB was created is used: Susan Carter, Scott S. Gartner, Michael R. Haines, Alan L. Olmstead, Richard Sutch and Gavin Wright, eds., *Historical Statistics of the United States*, vol. 3 (New York, 2006), p. 624.

4

Large-Scale Retailing, Mass-Market Strategies and the Blurring of Class Demarcations in Interwar Britain

PETER SCOTT AND JAMES T. WALKER

Introduction

Since the War and particularly during the last ten years there has been a revolution in the chief factors governing retail trade. The balance of spending power has moved swiftly from one class to another, improved social services and increased wages have brought millions of people into the orbit of the retailer's influence whose standard of living was formerly so low that except for foodstuffs they were of little importance ... 'Fashion' is now the keynote of appeal and knows no barriers either of class, age, or sex. Mass production of many fashion articles at extremely moderate prices has been developed to meet the ever-widening market for these goods and new forms of distribution to handle them.[1]

Francesca's later work focused on how consumer goods with fashion and status connotations were made available to progressively wider sections of the population; the resulting impacts on class differentials in lifestyles and consumption patterns; and the mediation of these processes between producers, retailers and consumers.[2] This chapter explores these themes in the context of the expansion of mass retailers in Britain during the 1920s and 1930s.

1 Harrods Company Archives, London, HS 9/1/17, Frank Chitham, 'London department stores: Their organisation and the effect of competition on their present position and future prospects', report, 22 June 1938 (hereafter Harrods Archives, Chitham report).
2 See, for example, Francesca Carnevali, 'Fashioning Luxury for Factory Girls: American Jewelry, 1860–1914', *Business History Review* 85 (2011), 295–317; Francesca Carnevali and Lucy Newton, 'Pianos for the People: From Producer to Consumer in Britain, 1851–1914', *Enterprise and Society* 14 (2013), 37–70.

The above quotation by Frank Chitham (a director of Harrods) sums up the profound changes in the relationship between the leaders of the retail trade and the mass of the British people over the quarter century after 1914. On the eve of the First World War working-class families had remained sharply segregated from the rest of society, not only in their work and housing, but in their access to such mundane 'public' spaces as shops and places of refreshment. This segregation was sometimes overt, such as the intimidating presence of the floor-walker at the entrance to the department store – one of whose principal tasks was to keep out 'undesirables'. More commonly it was invisible, but no less effective, operating through such subtle screening mechanisms as the need to negotiate any purchase with the sales clerk and without being able to physically view all goods stocked, or knowing their prices. Even the outward appearance of a 'middle class' emporium was usually enough to signal which sections of society were, and were not, welcome.

Meanwhile the relationship between the working classes and those shopkeepers who supplied them was, to say the least, problematic. Working-class households often had irregular incomes and relied on local shopkeepers to extend them credit during periods of hardship. However, this often led to them becoming tied to particular stores, who might not necessarily provide the best value for money. Moreover, shopkeepers were organised into a powerful political lobby, capitalising on their numerical strength as one of the largest sections of the middle class – a power they consistently used in ways detrimental to the interests of their working-class customers. Shopkeepers pressed for 'economy' in government – which generally translated into blocking or limiting measures to improve conditions for the working-classes, such as state education, council housing, or social welfare provision.[3] Their trade associations also sought to suppress price competition through retail price maintenance, and to oppose rival retail formats, including both traditional channels – such as street traders and fairs – together with more recent innovations such as the co-operative societies and the early multiples.[4]

Furthermore, Victorian and Edwardian retailers (with the exception of the Co-op and a few, generally large, stores) were notorious for poor staff conditions, including the 'living in' system (where shop staff were treated as domestic servants, receiving accommodation and food as part of their wages); systems of arbitrary 'fines' from wages for the most minor infractions of their numerous rules; and very long hours. Meanwhile even modest attempts at reform, such as the 1909 Shops Bill – which sought to limit shop

---

3   Michael J. Winstanley, *The Shopkeeper's World 1830–1914* (Manchester, 1983), pp. 28–30, 79–88.
4   Winstanley, *Shopkeeper's World*, pp. 28–30, 79–88; Stanley Chapman, *Jesse Boot of Boots the Chemists* (London, 1974), pp. 103–19.

assistants' working hours to sixty per week – met with vigorous opposition from their trade bodies.[5]

In contrast, the twenty years between the end of the First World War and the start of the Second witnessed a radical, though incomplete, revolution in the social segmentation and 'exclusiveness' of those retailers commanding the dominant pitches on Britain's high streets. Few remained exclusively middle class in their customer base and some principally targeted working-class families. Demand-side factors played a significant role in this transformation. The interwar years witnessed more rapid working-class income growth (for those lucky enough to be in employment). Real wages rose by 1.21% per annum over the period 1913 to 1938, while wage differentials between unskilled and more highly skilled manual workers narrowed.[6] Smaller families and the expansion of social welfare provision served to further temper the perceived insecurity of some sections of the working class – especially in the Midlands and southern Britain.

However, as this chapter will show, there was also an important 'supply-side' dimension to this process. Large-scale retailers introduced a number of innovations which effectively boosted working-class living standards. These included providing goods at lower prices (through trading margins for volume and restructuring supply chains to reduce up-stream production and inventory costs); making prices more transparent via policies of open display and clear ticketing; and adding a leisure and social value to working-class shopping by developing stores as public spaces with cheap or free services, such as cafes, libraries and exhibitions. Moreover, they were leading actors in an initiative that had both supply- and demand-side impacts on working-class living standards – the 'industrial welfare' movement. This chapter examines these innovations, drawing on the archives of a number of major retailers, including Marks & Spencer, Woolworths, Boots and leading department stores.

The interwar expansion of mass retailing

Up to 1914 most major multiple retailers – such as Freeman, Hardy & Willis; Singer; and Lipton's – had focused on selling a narrow product range. Vertical integration, standardisation and scale economies in production and retailing enabled them to undercut smaller shopkeepers and rival brands, within their very limited product range.[7] However, there were other approaches, such as

---

5 Winstanley, *Shopkeeper's World*, pp. 46, 71–3.
6 George R. Boyer, 'Living Standards, 1860–1939', *The Cambridge Economic History of Modern Britain*, vol. 2: *Economic Maturity, 1860–1939*, ed. Roderick Floud and Paul Johnson (Cambridge, 2004), pp. 280–313 (pp. 284–7).
7 Winstanley, *Shopkeeper's World*, p. 36.

Table 4.1. The proportion of total retail sales undertaken by large-scale
retailers, 1900–39

Year	1910	1920	1925	1930	1935	1939
Multiples	6.0–7.5	7.0–10.0	9.5–11.5	12.0–14.0	14.0–17.0	18.0–19.5
Food and household goods	6.5–9.0	8.5–11.0	10.5–12.0	12.5–14.0	14.0–16.0	16.5–18.0
Confectionery, stationery, tobacco	2.5–4.0	3.5–5.0	4.5–5.5	6.0–7.0	7.5–9.5	9.5–11.5
Clothing and footwear	6.0–8.0	7.0–10.0	11.5–14.0	15.0–17.0	18.5–21.0	24.0–27.0
Other goods	3.5–5.0	5.0–6.5	8.0–10.0	12.5–15.0	16.5–19.0	21.0–24.0
Co-operatives	7.0–8.0	7.5–9.0	7.5–8.5	8.5–10.0	8.5–10.5	10.0–11.5
Department stores	1.5–3.0	3.0–4.0	3.0–4.0	3.5–5.0	4.0–5.5	4.5–5.5
Total	14.5–18.5	17.5–23.0	20.0–24.0	24.0–29.0	26.5–33.0	32.5–36.5

Source: James B. Jefferys, *Retail Trading in Britain 1850–1950* (Cambridge, 1954), pp. 72–3.

the 'Penny Bazaars', that offered a broad product range, but for very low-value
goods, and one or two firms, such as Boots, that offered a large selection of
merchandise to a wider customer base. The interwar years witnessed a strong
trend among the most rapidly growing multiples towards multi-product
retailing; some movement away from just price appeal – with the development
of strong retail branding, services and more leisure-orientated retail environments – and an increasing focus on centrally located shopping pitches.

Table 4.1 shows the growth of multiple retailing by broad product class,
together with the share of multiples, co-operatives and department stores
in all retail sales. In 1939 large-scale retailers accounted for an estimated
32.5–36.5% of all retail sales, compared with 14.5–18.5% in 1910. They
were much more important for urban 'high street' retailing and in certain
subsectors, such as the clothing and footwear trades – where they comprised
45.0–50.0% of national retail sales in 1939 (boosted by the department stores'
strong focus on this sector).[8]

The co-operative movement mainly built on its successful pre-1914 sales
formula. Membership of co-operative societies rose from just over 3 million in
1914 to 4.5 million in 1920 and 6.5 million in 1938. Yet much of this was due to
geographical extension into areas where they had hitherto been weakly represented (particularly southern Britain and the Midlands), while innovations in

8   James B. Jefferys, *Retail Trading in Britain 1850–1950* (Cambridge, 1954), p. 74.

their product scope and retailing methods were generally gradual and evolutionary. They made some inroads into non-grocery lines, with the development of town centre department stores and a variety of line-specialised non-grocery businesses (such as funeral directors, opticians, coal dealers and pharmacies), in an effort to serve the full range of their members' shopping needs.[9] However, food remained their dominant line, accounting for three-quarters of total sales in the 1930s (compared with around 80% before 1914). Diversification into other areas was hampered by the Co-op's territorial structure – comprising retail societies with local monopolies over co-operative trading.[10]

Nevertheless, the co-operative movement retained a strong effective price advantage for its core market of household essentials (when the dividend, or 'divi' – the trading surplus distributed back to members – is factored in). An efficient Co-operative Wholesale Society (CWS) – and a separate Wholesale Society for Scotland – achieved purchasing economies that enabled even the small retail societies to compete with the multiple chains. Meanwhile the dividend was seen as a key attraction, providing a form of automatic saving that could be used to fund bulkier purchases not easily fitted into the weekly budgeting cycle.[11] Co-operatives had traditionally eschewed credit, thus limiting the access of lower-income families, who typically had irregular incomes. However, the interwar years witnessed growing use of retail credit by Co-ops, including 'clubs' (both 'draw clubs' which were rotating credit vehicles and 'mutuality clubs' which were more straightforward retail credit) and hire-purchase (HP) facilities.[12]

However, it was principally the multiple traders, and to a lesser extent the department stores, that spearheaded *new* initiatives to create a broad 'mass market', encompassing both the working and lower middle classes within the same store's offering. The methods used to achieve this, and their implications for working-class living standards and welfare, are discussed below.

Breaking down class segmentation

One of the key factors behind the reduction in retail class segmentation was the development of new semi-self-service retail systems that offered the freedom to browse and select goods without the intermediation of the sales assistant. The

9 Nicole Robertson, *The Co-operative Movement and Communities in Britain 1914–1960* (Aldershot, 2010), pp. 24, 31.
10 Jefferys, *Retail Trading*, pp. 55–8, 85–6.
11 Royal Pharmaceutical Society Library and Archives, IRA 1996.417, 'Survey of retail organisation and trends', O. W. Roskill, unpublished report, 5 July 1939 (hereafter RPS Library, Roskill report), pp. 224–5.
12 Robertson, *Co-operative Movement*, pp. 38–9.

transition from traditional counter-service department stores to new 'walk-round' stores, and the accompanying switch in policy from policing customers to filter out those with no specific intention to purchase, to providing a more relaxed, leisure-orientated, shopping environment, is often attributed to the opening of Selfridges in 1909. However, while Gordon Selfridge played a key role in demonstrating that the American department store model would work in Britain (even for a high-end London store), the uniqueness of his innovation has been exaggerated. In the north of England – where higher working-class wages and a smaller proportion of middle-class households made serving the mass market attractive at an earlier date – a few pioneering stores, such as Fenwick's of Newcastle and Binns of Sunderland, had begun to introduce 'silent sales assistants' from around the turn of the century.[13]

Selfridges' spectacular success led to rapid diffusion of the 'walk-round' department store format. Shopwalkers and sales assistants were now told to maintain a discreet distance and wait for customers to approach them. As the staff rules for Frasers of Glasgow noted: 'Some customers come in "just to look around." ... It should be remembered at all times that Customers are the shop's guests ...' Thus a suitable greeting was 'Good morning, madam', rather than 'Is there anything you require?' – which implied an obligation to purchase.[14]

However, changing the internal character of the store was not sufficient, of itself, to draw in working-class customers; people needed to be told they were welcome. Multiple retailers had typically developed to serve lower-income groups and therefore faced the challenge of creating a broad market appeal as an upward, rather than downward, expansion of their customer base. Boots was an early pioneer, developing a series of departmentalised stores during the Edwardian era that offered some of the features of traditional department stores, while openly welcoming customers of all classes.[15] For example, a March 1910 *Daily Mail* Boots advert, shown in Figure 4.1, makes an explicit appeal to 'the Classes & the Masses'.

Boots sold fast-moving goods[16] that already enjoyed a substantial working-class market. Retailers of consumer durables and high-ticket semi-durables (such as men's suits) faced a harder challenge, as before the 1920s few working-class people would, for example, consider buying their furniture

13   Bill Lancaster, *The Department Store: A Social History* (London, 1995), p. 69; Susan F. Lomax, 'The View from the Shop: Window Display, the Shopper and the Formulation of Theory', *Cultures of Selling: Perspectives on Consumption and Society Since 1700*, ed. John Benson and Laura Ugolini (Aldershot, 2006), pp. 265–92 (p. 280).

14   Glasgow University Archive Service, Fraser & Son, HF/25/7/1, regulations, 1920s, cited in Susan F. Lomax, 'The Department Store and the Creation of the Spectacle, 1880–1940' (Ph.D. thesis, University of Essex, 2005), pp. 64–5.

15   Boots plc Archives, Beeston (hereafter Boots Archives), CA15 9827, advert, n.d., c.1905.

16   Frequently purchased, low-cost consumer products.

Figure 4.1. Boots' appeal to the classes and the masses

Source: Boots advert, *The Daily Mail*, 25 March 1910. We are indebted to the Boots Archivist, Sophie Clapp, for providing this illustration.

new. Multiples had made limited inroads into this sector by 1914, though their importance was to be transformed over the following twenty-five years, with furniture becoming one of the sectors where multiple and other large-scale retailers enjoyed the strongest market share by 1939.[17]

The creation of a substantial working-class market in new suites of furniture owes much to London furniture entrepreneur Benjamin Drage, who launched an innovative new way of marketing furniture to a mass public in 1922. Large display adverts appeared in national newspapers ranging from *The Times* to the tabloids, under the general title, 'The Drage Way of furnishing out-of-income'. These showed a conversation between 'Mr Drage'

17   Peter Scott, 'Mr Drage, Mr Everyman, and the Creation of a Mass Market for Domestic Furniture in Interwar Britain', *Economic History Review* 62 (2009), 802–27 (pp. 806–9); Jefferys, *Retail Trading*, p. 425.

and 'Mr (sometimes Mrs, Reverend, Captain, etc.) Everyman'. The scripts were constantly varied, giving the adverts a 'viral' appeal. However, each followed the same basic plot. The would-be purchaser needed furniture owing to various circumstances (such as marriage), but had limited cash. After expressing delight with Drage's furniture, they broached the subject of credit and received a reply along the lines of: 'That rests entirely with you. What can you conveniently pay now? We always try to agree with any reasonable suggestion.'[18] The customer invariably suggested a deposit of at least 10% and monthly payments of around 2.5% (implying a three-year repayment period). Mr Everyman was also assured that no references would be required and that the furniture would be delivered in plain vans (removing the reputational risk associated with HP, at a time when it still carried a strong social stigma in working-class communities).[19]

The advertisements sought to remove customers' fears of a negative reception. In one, Mr Everyman states: 'elsewhere we were treated almost as intruders. Here we were welcomed like old friends.'[20] An inclusive policy was asserted: 'All Classes Furnish at Drage's ... All receive the same cordial welcome, the same courteous treatment, and the same generous terms.'[21] Drage's business formula of liberal HP terms, secrecy, guarantees of generous treatment in the event of falling on hard times during the HP contract, clear pricing, and free delivery and carpet laying, initially proved very successful, but was soon widely copied by larger rivals such as Smart Brothers and Times Furnishing Co. Drage thus succeeded in establishing a new model for mass furniture retailing, but it was his emulators who were the long-term beneficiaries.[22]

Variety stores proved particularly successful in developing a strong working-class market, while still being of considerable attraction to all income groups. A key element of their appeal was the use of open display techniques, as illustrated in Figure 4.2. Making all goods available for inspection without reference to a sales assistant, and with clearly marked prices, removed the dread of being asked for a higher payment than expected – something which extended even to the lower middle classes. As with the transformation of department store display, an American firm, Woolworths (which, like Selfridges, arrived in Britain in 1909) is often credited as the key innovator and certainly exerted a very powerful demonstration effect on its competitors. While the Victorian 'Penny Bazaars' had used open display – drawing on their

---

18 'The Drage Way', *The Times*, 18 September 1922, p. 5.
19 See Peter Scott, 'The Twilight World of Interwar Hire Purchase', *Past & Present* 177 (2002), 195–225.
20 'You've Given a New Meaning to Credit Furnishing, Mr Drage', *The Times*, 21 May 1924, p. 7.
21 Geffrye Museum, London, Drages Ltd, 'Mr & Mrs Everyman talk things over with Mr Drage', brochure, n.d. (mid–late 1920s).
22 Scott, 'Mr Drage', pp. 817–19.

Figure 4.2. Open merchandise display at Marks & Spencer in 1930

Reproduced courtesy of Marks & Spencer Company Archive, Leeds

roots in market trading – Woolworths applied this to spacious modern stores, selling better-quality goods.

Stores also used internal and external shop design to project retail brands that identified the store at a glance and appealed to their entire target market. Some opted for plainer fittings in order not to scare off working-class customers (who associated grand stores with high prices and social exclusivity). For example, while the Debenhams group retained the traditional appearance of their more up-market stores, their 'C' (popular provincial) stores very profitably 'splashed whitewash messages across their windows and replaced carpets with lino and low-cost fittings ... glass cases replaced wooden counters'.[23] A similar policy was advocated, unsuccessfully, by a W. H. Smith executive who urged the firm's conservative partners to stop using fittings, 'too ornate and expensive in appearance ... Our shops perpetuate the popular idea now no longer true that "Smiths are dear." People are afraid to enter them and cannot discover their mistake.'[24]

23   Maurice Corina, *Fine Silks and Oak Counters. Debenhams 1778–1978* (London, 1978), pp. 116–17.
24   W. H. Smith Archives, University of Reading (hereafter W. H. Smith Archives), memorandum from G. A. E. Marshall to partners, 21 February 1930.

Yet there were limits to how plain a store should be, at a time when middle-class values of dress and taste were being projected to the working class via the popular press, the BBC, cinema and other media. For example, Britain's largest chain of men's outfitters, Montague Burton, opted for stores with the inward appearance of traditional bespoke retailers to target a market ranging from manual labourers to white-collar workers.[25]

Lowering prices to the consumer

Despite a trend towards adding a significant element of service for some multiple retailers – such as men's outerwear chains – multiples continued to focus principally on price appeal and value for money. This was exemplified by the variety chain stores, which were estimated to have grown from under 3% of total multiple store sales in 1920 to almost 20% by 1938.[26] Retail consultant O. W. Roskill attributed this to a combination of their buying policy (discussed below) and their superior sales efficiency – employing systems that simultaneously maximised stock-turn and minimised inventory costs.[27] Weekly 'checking list' systems for recording sales provided a perpetual inventory of stock, while target sales per foot of counter space rules removed slow-selling items. Lines (or particular sizes and colours within lines) that did not meet minimum sales targets were ruthlessly discarded. This was also applied on a seasonal basis, while stock was even varied over the week to reflect the fact that most working-class family shopping was done on Friday evenings and Saturdays.[28] Meanwhile purchasing directly from the manufacturer eliminated the extra inventory costs of wholesale supply, allowed greater control over product quality, and lowered the manufacturer's inventory costs by providing a more stable stream of orders.[29]

These policies were also adopted by other multi-product multiples, often drawing on American practice. American retail systems were imported to Britain through inward foreign direct investment (as with Woolworths, or Boots – which came under the ownership of US-based United Drug Co. from 1920 to 1933) or research trips to the USA by British retailers. For example, Simon Marks responded to Woolworths' competitive threat via a 1924 research visit, where he learned the importance of statistics-driven retail

25 Katrina Honeyman, 'Style Monotony and the Business of Fashion: The Marketing of Menswear in Inter-War England', *Textile History* 34 (2003), 171–91 (pp. 180–3).

26 Jefferys, *Retail Trading*, pp. 69–70.

27 RPS Library, Roskill report, p. 28.

28 RPS Library, Roskill report, pp. 28–9.

29 Richard S. Tedlow, *New and Improved. The Story of Mass Marketing in America* (Oxford, 1990), pp. 209–13.

management using accounting machines to rapidly process stock-turn data in order to optimise stock composition.[30]

Retailing efficiency was also boosted by the development of larger, central, stores that generated economies of scale – through a higher ratio of selling space to total floor-space, more efficient labour utilisation and greater customer throughput. The potential gains are illustrated by Marks & Spencer (M&S), which restricted its stores to central sites in towns of significant size (the 234 stores developed by 1938 having almost exhausted the locations considered suitable). A programme of store openings and extensions saw average floor-space per store rise from 2,897 to 9,427 square feet from 1926 to 1938, while real (1930) takings per square foot rose from £3.08 to £9.88.[31] This 'superstore' strategy was facilitated by a progressive concentration on clothing and textiles – items people were happy to travel into town to purchase. Conversely some leading multiples that focused mainly on convenience items, such as Woolworths and Boots, found it profitable to develop stores with much smaller catchment areas, as this added to turnover and profits (at the cost of depressing aggregate productivity to a figure well below that for their larger, central, stores).

Multiples also gained important cost advantages through transforming their relationships with suppliers. Independent retailers typically purchased goods through wholesalers and had little direct contact with manufacturers apart from the commercial traveller's visit. In a few sectors, such as radio, manufacturers introduced direct supply to authorised dealerships during the 1930s.[32] Yet neither arrangement gave the retailer any real scope to negotiate purchase prices.

The first generation of multiples had typically gained their competitive advantage through integrating production and distribution of a small number of standardised product lines. Yet even before 1914 a few were already developing integrated manufacture and distribution of a more complex range of products. For example the 1890s witnessed the birth of the wholesale bespoke system, where retailers provided 'measured' suits at ready-made prices, by sending customers' measurements to their factory for production and delivery within a few days. However, this system is estimated to have accounted for 10% or less of men's ready-made clothing sales at the turn of the century and became a major channel of supply only after the First World

---

30   Simon Marks, undated typescript, cited in Israel Sieff, *Memoirs* (London, 1970), p. 138.
31   Peter Scott and James Walker, 'Barriers to "Industrialisation" in Interwar British Retailing: The Case of Marks & Spencer', *Business History* 59 (2017; published online 4 May 2016), http://www.tandfonline.com/doi/abs/10.1080/00076791.2016.1156088?journalCode=fbsh20, accessed 14 December 2016. Figures for turnover are for year ended 31 December and those for square footage are for 31 March of the following year. Prices are shown in decimal form.
32   Peter Scott, 'The Determinants of Competitive Success in the Interwar British Radio Industry', *Economic History Review* 65 (2012), 1303–25 (p. 1320).

War.[33] Boots was one of a very few retailers before 1914 producing broad ranges of own-brand goods.[34]

The interwar period witnessed an expansion in integrated manufacture and distribution for certain sectors of the retail market, particularly men's outerwear, bread and flour, confectionery, and wallpaper and paint.[35] However, in 1938 only 4% of all consumer goods were estimated to have been sold by integrated producers/retailers. The major change in distribution channels arising from the expansion of large-scale retailers was cutting out the wholesaler, with some 53% of 1938 consumer expenditure involving goods that went direct from manufacturer or importer to retailer.[36] This was often combined with the development of much closer, interventionist, relationships with suppliers, where the retailer not only negotiated on price but influenced design, production methods and, in some cases, took control of product branding.

Woolworths had already developed close, co-operative, relationships with some of its suppliers by the time it opened its first British store in Liverpool in 1909. Price negotiation was assisted by its formula of only two fixed price points, 3d and 6d (the 1930 value of which would be equivalent to 72p and £1.43 in 2015 prices).[37] Woolworths enjoyed rapid growth in Britain; by 1939 it had 768 stores and sales of £39.5 million, making it Britain's largest retail brand.[38] In common with M&S, Woolworths carried over 90% of British-made goods during the 1930s and despite its broad range of merchandise, its sheer size made it the leading retailer in several product classes.[39]

Woolworths, M&S and the smaller British Home Stores chain, pursued broadly similar buying strategies. They focused on lines where they could offer substantially better value for money, through cutting out the wholesaler and developing long-term co-operative relationships with manufacturers. Suppliers were offered bulk sales in return for meeting their price point (typically substantially lower than the standard price for goods of equivalent quality and style).[40] The differences in costs achieved just by removing the wholesaler and persuading the manufacturer to accept a lower margin

33 Eric M. Sigsworth, *Montague Burton: The Tailor of Taste* (Manchester, 1990), pp. 34–5; Honeyman, 'Style Monotony', p. 173.
34 Chapman, *Jesse Boot*, pp. 91–5.
35 Jefferys, *Retail Trading*, p. 68.
36 Jefferys, *Retail Trading*, p. 48. Jefferys includes goods sold by the co-operative movement and channelled via the Co-operative Wholesale Societies under this heading.
37 Lawrence H. Officer and Samuel H. Williamson, 'Five Ways to Compute the Relative Value of a UK Pound Amount, 1270 to Present', *MeasuringWorth*, 2017, https://www.measuringworth.com/ukcompare/, accessed 24 January 2017.
38 Source: Paul Seaton Collection of material for F. W. Woolworth Ltd, accounts for financial years to 31 December 1930 and 31 December 1939.
39 'F. W. Woolworth & Co.', *The Times*, 28 January 1933, p. 18, col. F.
40 Marks & Spencer Company Archive, Leeds (hereafter M&S Archives), K5/1, *Weekly Bulletin*, 21 April 1928, 'Foundations of good merchandising – (3)'.

Table 4.2. An example of cost savings on canned fruit when sold by a major variety store

	A: Variety store (pence)	B: Independent store (pence)
Manufacturing costs		
Fruit	0.75	0.75
Canning, labour and overheads	3.00	3.00
Total	3.75	3.75
Margins and distribution costs		
Manufacturer's profit	0.75	1.25
Wholesaler's margin	n/a	1.25
Price paid by retailer	4.50	6.25
Retailer's margin	1.50	1.25
Retail price	6.00	7.50

Source: Royal Pharmaceutical Library and Archives, London, IRA 1996.417, 'Survey of retail organisation and trends', O. W. Roskill, unpublished report, 5 July 1939, pp. 24–5.

on each sale are illustrated by the example of canned fruit shown in Table 4.2, provided by retail consultant O. W. Roskill and said to be based on a prominent variety chain. Similarly in hosiery (where M&S focused its expansion into clothing/textiles) manufacturers selling through wholesalers were said to receive margins of only 6% from wholesalers who then added margins of 15–20% – providing both the manufacturer and retailer with a clear incentive to eliminate the middleman.[41]

Yet retailers' control over supply chains did not always lead to a transformation in production methods. For example, the mass furniture retail chains insisted on using their own branding (sometimes even creating the impression that they manufactured their furniture directly). However, weak scale economies in furniture manufacturing (accentuated by retailers' desire to offer a variegated range of designs, plus frequent style changes) reduced opportunities for lowering costs through interventions in their suppliers' production methods. Instead the furniture chains often commissioned the same designs from several manufacturers (encompassing both large and small firms), switching between contractors on the basis of price and seeking to lower costs through squeezing manufacturers' margins.[42]

41 Stanley Chapman, *Hosiery and Knitwear: Four Centuries of Small-Scale Industry in Britain* (Oxford, 2002), pp. 190–1.
42 Scott, 'Mr Drage'.

By contrast, the variety chains tasked their buyers not only to negotiate prices with manufacturers and ensure that quality standards were maintained, but to assist them in making the transition from batch to mass production. As a 1928 M&S weekly bulletin informed its managers:

> The problem of buying finally resolves itself into the relationship between mass production and mass distribution ... for it is in their interest to produce, even on the basis of a lower margin of profit, a larger quantity of a restricted number of lines as against small quantities of a large number of varieties and patterns.[43]

The key obstacle was opposition from trade associations of independent retailers and manufacturers, who often worked in concert to boycott retailers selling at below manufacturer's fixed retail prices (and firms that supplied them). Resale Price Maintenance (RPM) – both by individual manufacturers and trade associations – grew from representing 3% or less of all consumer expenditure in 1900 to almost 30% by 1938.[44] It was most prevalent in sectors characterised by strong manufacturers' brands and convenience purchases, or high-value durables requiring after-sales service, such as radios, white goods and cars. These were among the sectors where independents were most strongly represented during the late 1930s.

Protecting suppliers from trade boycotts was a prime motivation behind M&S launching their 'St Michael' home brand of clothing from 1928. That year also saw Woolworths respond to a grocery trade boycott by launching their own home brand (despite a preference to sell well-known manufacturer brands, wherever possible).[45] Retailer brands also enabled prestigious manufacturers to segment their retail markets, by supplying variety chains with products functionally identical to their manufacturer brand, but without their brand name. For example, Ever Ready supplied M&S with batteries identical to their 'Winner Brand' (retailing at a price-maintained 11s) except for the printing on the cover, but for sale at less than half its retail price.[46]

Large multiples, together with the co-operative movement, became increasingly hostile to RPM over the interwar period, though manufacturers often sided with the independent retailers – partly because controlling their brands' price points helped them to retain control over supply chains, in the face of

43 M&S Archives, K5/1, *Weekly Bulletin*, 15 May 1928, 'Foundations of merchandising V'.
44 Jefferys, *Retail Trading*, p. 54.
45 Woolworths Archive, University of Reading (hereafter Woolworths Archive), Executive Committee minute book no. 1, p. 131, 28 June 1928; Paul Bookbinder, *Simon Marks: Retail Revolutionary* (London, 1993), p. 99.
46 Keith Geddes and Gordon Bussey, *The Setmakers: A History of the Radio and Television Industry* (London, 1991), p. 199.

growing supply chain co-ordination by large-scale retailers.[47] This, in turn, led some large retailers to establish their own, retailer-led, supply chains to challenge price-maintained brands. For example, the Co-op marketed a wide range of own-brand products by the 1930s, including complex consumer durables. This involved both direct production in CWS factories (such as their 'Dudley' brand vacuum cleaners, electric washing machines, toasters and hairdryers) and production contracted out to manufacturers, such as their famous 'Defiant' brand radios, produced for CWS by Plessey.[48] Sainsbury's also extended its range of own grocery brands as a reaction to RPM, thereby undercutting competitors' prices. By 1937/8 own brands constituted almost all Sainsbury's grocery sales and they were dealing with only six suppliers that supported RPM.[49]

M&S adopted a particularly ambitious approach to restructuring its supply chains, embarking on systematic R&D to either lower the costs and/or improve the quality of its merchandise. This strategy focused primarily on their textiles and clothing lines, laying the foundations of their post-war R&D-based competitive advantage.[50] New textile technologies offered considerable scope for cost-reducing product innovation. Moreover, they found that women's clothing and textile goods often had very elastic demand. Price reductions might sometimes increase sales by as much as eight- or tenfold; thus offering considerable scope for mass production.[51] Following their establishment in 1935 of a textile laboratory, in 1936 they added a Merchandise Development Department (to test for product characteristics such as colour fastness and shrinkage) and a Design Department to monitor fashion trends.[52]

These innovations helped to establish M&S as the most important British retailer for this class of clothing and played an important role in extending middle-class women's fashion to the working-class market, similar to that played by the Leeds-based men's outerwear chains, such as Montague Burton and Price's Fifty Shilling Tailors, in making the fitted suit affordable to all classes and thus reducing men's visual markers of class distinction.[53]

---

47 Gareth Shaw, Andrew Alexander, John Benson and Deborah Hodson, 'The Evolving Culture of Retailer Regulation and the Failure of the "Balfour Bill" in Interwar Britain', *Environment and Planning A* 32 (2000), 1977–89 (p. 1982).

48 John F. Wilson, Anthony Webster and Rachel Vorberg-Rugh, *Building Co-operation: A Business History of The Co-operative Group, 1863–2013* (Oxford, 2013), p. 191–6; Geddes and Bussey, *Setmakers*, p. 178.

49 Bridget Williams, *The Best Butter in the World: A History of Sainsbury's* (London, 1994), p. 86.

50 Sieff, *Memoirs*, pp. 145–7.

51 Sieff, *Memoirs*, pp. 145–55. This is supported by implied productivity growth estimates for the hosiery sector in Chapman, *Hosiery and Knitwear*, pp. 166–7 and 239–40.

52 M&S Archives, E7/24, Annual report of Joint Secretary & Chief Accountant, 1937; Sieff, *Memoirs*, pp. 156–7.

53 Honeyman, 'Style Monotony', pp. 172–3.

Collectively, these retailers fostered the emergence of a mass high-street fashion market prior to the Second World War.

Independent retailers increasingly fell back on political solutions to these new challenges, relying on their continued numerical strength and active political role (especially at local level). New organisations, such as the Union of Small Traders and Shopkeepers, were formed to lobby against the growth of multiple and co-operative trading. However, these efforts proved fruitless. Britain's dominant 'liberal-conservative' socio-legal system had developed to serve what was primarily a financial and mercantile economic elite, and thus sought to avoid state 'interference' in private property and commerce.[54] Thus, while many Conservative politicians were happy to extol the virtues of small retailers, there was little real enthusiasm for regulation. For example Tory MP Captain Harold Balfour's 1937 bill to limit new multiple and Co-operative stores (through a restrictive licensing system), generated little Parliamentary support and failed in its second reading.[55]

The considerable productivity impacts of the innovations discussed above are sometimes obscured by simplistic estimates of interwar retail productivity growth, based on dividing aggregate retail sales by the number of workers in the distribution sector.[56] Such measures are dominated by a very 'long-tail' of small-scale independent retailers, whose ranks had been considerably swelled by mass unemployment.[57] During the 1930s many people turned to retailing – generally on a very small-scale basis, as a means of subsistence.[58] Roskill estimated that in 1939, despite the reduction in unemployment from its peak levels of the early 1930s, there were still around 375,000–400,000 of these small family shops in existence, probably outnumbering 'professional' independent shopkeepers.[59]

Measuring the full extent to which mass retailers lowered purchase costs for the consumer is problematic, as one major element – the lower prices at which they purchased their merchandise – cannot be quantified. However, the cost savings gained through lower retailer price mark-ups and operating expenses can be assessed. Table 4.3 provides a comparison of available data for retailers that shared the common characteristic that their largest single category of merchandise constituted clothing and/or household textiles. The

54   Nigel Harris, *Competition and the Corporate Society: British Conservatives, the State and Industry, 1945–1964* (London, 1972), p. 25.

55   Shaw *et al.*, 'Evolving Culture', pp. 1983–5.

56   Stephen Broadberry, *Market Services and the Productivity Race, 1850–2000: Britain in International Perspective* (Cambridge, 2006), pp. 20–9, 138–9, 374.

57   Peter Scott and James Walker, 'The British "Failure" That Never Was? The Anglo-American "Productivity Gap" in Large Scale Interwar Retailing – Evidence from the Department Store Sector', *Economic History Review* 65 (2012), 277–303 (p. 280).

58   Jefferys, *Retail Trading*, p. 46.

59   RPS Library, Roskill report, p. 36.

Table 4.3. A comparison of productivity and efficiency for small and large-scale retailers that traded principally in drapery-related goods, 1933/4 financial year (or nearest available date)

| | Gross margin | Expenses | | | Net margin | Net sales per employee (£) | |
		Labour	Other	Total		All	Sales
Drapers with net sales:							
Under £5,000	27.65	18.56	7.91	26.47	1.18	650	716
£5,000–10,000	26.72	13.93	9.32	23.25	3.47	774	960
£10,000–25,000	27.59	13.34	9.82	23.16	4.43	776	1021
£25,000–50,000	27.61	14.01	10.07	24.08	3.53	849	1126
£50,000–100,000	28.13	15.83	8.97	24.80	3.33	773	1145
Over £100,000	28.99	13.30	10.79	24.09	4.91	884	1438
Marks & Spencer	26.18	7.29	9.21	16.50	9.68	1064	n/a
Co-op (drapery)	27.69	n/a	n/a	17.84	9.85	n.a	1369
Dept. stores	30.14	13.18	10.86	24.04	6.10	n/a	1828

Notes: Data for drapery and department stores are for year ended 31 January 1934. Sales per selling employee for department stores are based on a larger sample of around 130 stores. Data for M&S are for year ended 31 March 1934, except for net sales per employee, which are for the year ending 31 December. 1933. Co-op drapery data refer to 1932 and are based on a 1932 survey of one hundred co-operative societies.

Sources: Drapery retailers: British Library of Political and Economic Science Archives COLL MISC 0330 (hereafter BLPES, 0330), Arnold Plant and R. F. Fowler, 'Operating costs of drapers and allied trades for the year ending 31st January 1934 (January 1935)'. Department stores: sales per selling employee data, BLPES, 0330, Incorporated Association of Retail Distributors and Drapers Chamber of Commerce, Report Prepared by the Economics and Statistics Section, Bank of England, on Sales, Stocks, Transactions and Staff in Department Stores and Drapery Establishments for the Year Ended January 31st 1934 (March 1934), p. 20. Other department store data: BLPES 0330, Arnold Plant and R. F. Fowler, 'Operating cost of department stores for the year ended January 31st, 1934 (June 1935)', p. 4. Marks & Spencer: Marks & Spencer Company Archive, Leeds, A05/413c, A05/414/f–h, Profit and loss accounts for years ended 31 March 1934–38. Co-op: A. M. Carr-Saunders, P. Sargant Florence and Robert Peers, Consumers' Cooperation in Great Britain, rev. edn (London, 1942), pp. 367–77.

first category is independent stores and small multiples that were members of the Drapers' Chamber of Trade. Some 181 establishments were surveyed for the year ending 31 January 1934, with aggregate sales of £7.535 million, or £41,631 per establishment. These are compared with M&S (the largest retailer in this sector, with aggregate turnover of £10,138,000, or £56,322 per store, around 58% of which represented clothing and textiles); a large sample of Co-op drapery stores (for 1932); and some 112 department stores, with average net sales per store of £445,155.

The table shows no great differences in gross margin (price mark-up). Instead the major differences are in expenses ratios, with M&S and the Co-op having much lower expenses, relative to net sales, than both the drapers and the department stores. This enabled them to achieve much higher net profit margins. However, the most striking differences between large and small stores are in sales per employee. Net sales per selling employee rose rapidly from £716 for the smallest class of draper to £1,438 for drapers with net sales over £100,000. The Co-ops outperformed all but the largest class of drapers, while department stores achieved particularly high sales per member of staff. Data on sales per selling employee are not available for M&S, though their sales per total employee were some 20.4% higher than the largest class of drapers shown in the table.

The high net margins of M&S and the Co-op might be interpreted as reflecting a policy of taking much of their efficiency gains in higher profits, rather than passing on the savings to the consumer. However, the Co-op distributed its surpluses back to members, in the form of the 'divi', while M&S ploughed back profits into a vigorous programme of store extensions and associated investment – enabling it to further reduce gross margins to only 23.80% by the year ending 31 March 1939, while increasing sales per employee to £1,470 by 31 December 1938.

Shops as working-class social centres

Frank Chitham of Harrods' commentary on the interwar democratisation of retailing – which opened this chapter – noted that one of the key competitive threats from the variety chains was their ability to foster a leisure appeal encompassing all classes:

> There will probably be more motor cars outside Woolworth's or Marks and Spencer stores than any other shop in the locality. The appeal of these stores is practically a universal one, it is not confined to any one class of person, and is not based on price alone – it goes far deeper and wider than that … [These stores] are an overwhelming attraction to children who insist on their parents taking them there, and they revel in the freedom of these

places – where else can they spend their sixpence to such advantage? ...
At the weekend these places have become a kind of social centre, particularly in the outer suburbs and country and seaside towns. Visiting them is
to many people a form of inexpensive recreation, a mild excitement and
has become to countless thousands a favourite way of spending time and
money.[60]

As Paul Johnson noted, Victorian workers were viewed almost as a species
apart, not on account of their low incomes per se, but for lifestyles that bore
little similarity to those of higher income groups. Large-scale retailers played
a major role in blurring the sharp demarcations in working- and middle-class
lifestyles. Before 1914 the range of urban commercial buildings available to
working-class women, children, or families was extremely limited, while
those available to men were generally venues for drink or sport. The development of the variety chains and 'popular' department stores widened the
scope of affordable commercial family entertainment, giving working-class
people access to a wide range of 'public' urban buildings. This reinforced the
social integration created by the availability of cheap, fashionable clothing,
discussed earlier, which markedly diminished the visible distinctions in
appearance that hitherto sharply demarcated the working-classes from the
rest of society. Large-scale retailers thus collectively played a significant role
in the working-classes becoming gradually accepted as part of the broad
British 'public', a process arguably more important than the extension of the
franchise in bringing manual workers and their families within the boundaries
of what their middle-class counterparts would conceive of as 'citizenship'.[61]

This broadening in the scope of the British 'public' also had a gender
dimension. In the Victorian era even middle-class women were highly
restricted in the range of leisure facilities they could patronise, while the
absence of women's conveniences, either on public thoroughfares or in
commercial buildings (other than hotels) proved a substantial handicap to a
day out. The development of stores with not only toilets, but a range of other
leisure facilities, such as hairdressers, cafes and freedom to browse without
obligation to purchase, is often attributed to Gordon Selfridge. Again,
Selfridge played a key role in repositioning the department store as both a
respectable, safe, leisure venue for women and a provider of services and
entertainment, but was not the sole originator.[62]

60 Harrods Archives, Chitham report.
61 Citizenship is here used in the general sense of the term, rather than in terms of people
expressing their citizenship through consumer activism. For discussion of this separate
phenomenon of 'consumer citizenship', see Martin Daunton and Matthew Hilton, eds, *The
Politics of Consumption: Material Culture and Citizenship in Europe and America* (Oxford,
2001).
62 Lancaster, *Department Store*, p. 80.

Boot's earlier pioneering contribution has been neglected – partly on account of their stores serving a lower (though still broad) class spectrum than that of the department stores. Jesse Boot's wife, Florence, was instrumental in developing their 'No. 2 Department', selling stationery, books, artists' materials, picture frames, silverware and fancy goods – products of considerable appeal to women. This move was associated with the development of new large, imposing, departmentalised stores, with a range of customer services, including moderately priced cafes (by contemporary standards) and 'Boots' Booklovers' Libraries', which, by the end of 1903, were available in almost half their stores.[63]

Boots were hosting in-store exhibitions several years before Selfridges began to do so, while also promoting their larger stores as leisure venues. For example, a 1904 advert for their Manchester (St Ann Street) branch invited:

> Everyone ... to visit our NEW SPACIOUS ART GALLERIES which have been recently ENLARGED & EXTENDED to meet the growing demands of a discriminating public ... We exhibit a Splendid Collection of ORIGINALS BY BEST BRITISH ARTISTS.[64]

The advert also mentioned that Boots had a range of modestly priced reproductions for sale. Boots specifically appealed to women. Another 1904 advert for the same store advised the public that 'The showroom in itself is well worth a visit. It is delightful, bright, and artistically decorated ... Ladies are welcome at any time to while away an hour there and rest. Retiring rooms and passenger lifts are provided.'[65]

However, Selfridge was more ambitious in the range of spectacular exhibitions and live entertainments he laid on, reflecting his greater imperative to pull in the crowds to a single, massive, centrally located store. His example was widely copied during the interwar years, particularly by the 'popular' department stores – that drew principally on a lower-middle and working-class customer base. Some of their publicity stunts have passed into local folklore, such as the spectacle of Anita Kittner (a young Swedish woman) diving some 63 feet from the top of the escalator hall at Bentall's of Kingston into a small pool of water.[66] Cut-price sales were another occasion for spectacle. For example, Jimmy Driscoll, manager of Kennards of Croydon (in the Debenhams group) and a notable impresario of crowd-pulling publicity stunts, introduced 'blue pencil' days, where he would lead a column of shoppers through the store, slashing prices with a blue pencil as he went.[67]

---

63   Chapman, *Jesse Boot*, pp. 73–88.
64   Boots advertisement, *Manchester Guardian*, 15 December 1904, p. 4.
65   Boots advertisement, *Manchester Guardian*, 24 November 1904, p. 5.
66   Adrian Bingham, *Gender, Modernity, and the Popular Press in Interwar Britain* (Oxford, 2004), pp. 147–67.
67   Corina, *Fine Silks and Oak Counters*, pp. 117–18.

Stores also often copied Selfridge's example by hosting exhibitions on their upper floors. Many had some merchandising objective – such as displaying the contents of a modern house in a realistic setting so that people could see a co-ordinated display of furnishings.[68] While multiples typically targeted a primarily female buying public, those serving male customers also sometimes devised entertainment strategies to draw in customers. For example, Montague Burton often leased the upper floors of his stores to billiard hall operators. Burton even integrated into this sector during the 1930s, with the acquisition of Bright Billiard Halls Ltd.[69]

Variety stores had a more universal leisure appeal, offering a huge array of attractively displayed, easily affordable goods. As Roskill noted:

> A shopper with some time to spare will ... often prefer to go to a Woolworth's to buy a tube of proprietary toothpaste because she can spend a further twenty minutes looking round at all the other varieties of merchandise in the store. Part of the success of the variety chains is, incidentally, due to the fact that many shoppers of this type will, on the spur of the moment, buy something else as well.[70]

This appeal was boosted by the provision of self-service cafes in some of the larger Woolworths. These were not particularly profitable in themselves, but were of immense attraction to customers – as they provided one of the very few town-centre venues for cheap indoor catering. Cafeteria facilities were emphasised in the promotion of new stores; a 1932 advert for Woolworths' new Oxford Street store emphasised its cafe's price appeal – with the slogans 'PUREST FOOD', 'QUICK, CLEAN SERVICE', 'NO TIPS' and 'Nothing over 6^D'.[71]

Woolworths and M&S managed to achieve the difficult feat of appealing strongly to their core working-class market, while at the same time not alienating higher income groups. These were drawn in by the attraction of 'pick & mix' (bulk chocolate assortments, that could be selected in any combination and were sold by weight) to their children and by their relatively plush fittings and displays – compared, for example, to a modern 'Pound Store'. As a W. H. Smith executive wrote to the firm's partners in 1929 (in a vain attempt to get them to change their exclusive ways), 'This is an age of cheapness, and all classes – even the Queen herself – have patronised Woolworths.'[72]

---

68   See Peter Scott, *The Making of the British Home: The Suburban Semi and Family Life Between the Wars* (Oxford, 2013), pp. 152–74.
69   Sigsworth, *Montague Burton*, p. 48.
70   RPS Library, Roskill report, pp. 61–2.
71   Woolworths virtual museum, http://museum.woolworths.co.uk/1932advert.htm, accessed 25 March 2008.
72   W. H. Smith Archives, 156/1, memorandum from P. R. Chappell to Partners of W. H. Smith, 28 June 1929.

Staff welfare policies

As noted earlier, retailing was one of the sectors most condemned for poor working conditions before 1914, partly on account of the treatment of the juveniles and young women that made up a large proportion of its workforce. Yet by 1939 no sector of the British economy, apart from perhaps chocolate confectionery, was more strongly associated with the industrial welfare movement. The key innovators were, again, leading multiple retailers and department stores. The co-operative movement's staff welfare policies attracted less public attention, though it had been an early exemplar of good practice and was widely recognised as such by well-informed interwar retail commentators.[73] Meanwhile some retailers with important manufacturing interests, such as Boots and Montague Burton, also acted as pioneers of industrial welfare in manufacturing.

Boots was, again, an early innovator. Jesse Boot had initiated tentative, ad hoc, moves towards developing a welfare policy from the 1890s and in 1914 Boots employed four professional industrial-welfare workers (at a time when there were estimated to be only sixty in all British firms). Some new Edwardian department stores, particularly Selfridges, had challenged the exploitative working arrangements that characterised the Victorian department store. In common with American department stores, which typically adopted a similar stance at this time, policy was influenced by a number of mutually reinforcing considerations. Store proprietors appreciated that rising aggregate purchasing power would boost their own sales and offering good pay and conditions to their mainly female staff would help avoid any backlash by an increasingly politicised female customer base.[74] Moreover, this policy served to 'legitimise' department and other large retailers in the eyes of the general public, at a time when they were coming under attack from small retailers' trade associations, both nationally and locally. Following Selfridges' example, there was a rapid move after the First World War from bound apprenticeships to a system of 'voluntary service' in which both employee and employer were regarded as free to terminate their contract without any implication of bad faith. This in turn fostered a much more meritocratic and competitive job market for store employees.[75]

Those firms that had begun to develop chains of department stores were particularly active in welfare initiatives. Lewis's of Liverpool appointed a Welfare Supervisor in each of its stores from 1921, established its first pension

---

73 Harrods Archives, Chitham report.
74 Vicki Howard, *From Main Street to Mall: The Rise and Fall of the American Department Store* (Philadelphia, PA, 2015), pp. 47–50.
75 Lomax, 'Department Store', p. 193.

scheme in 1928, and encouraged staff sports and social organisations.[76] A more radical approach was developed by John Spedan Lewis, who broke with the autocratic business style of his father (the firm's founder, John Lewis) by experimenting with industrial welfare and staff consultation from around the end of the First World War in their Peter Jones store. In 1920 he started distributing preference shares to the staff, who were renamed 'Partners'. Following the death of John Lewis in 1928, John Spedan Lewis constituted the Partnership on a formal basis in 1929, encompassing all their stores – as a trust that would distribute its profits to the staff. This marked the start of what became one of the most successful and influential British examples of 'industrial democracy'.[77]

However, there were limits to the general adoption of staff welfare policies among department stores. As late as 1938 Frank Chitham noted that the London County Council School of Retail Distribution only managed to get a full class of students in their employers' time for one of the fifteen years since it was opened, as department stores generally did not consider they could spare juniors for retail education. He contrasted this attitude with the Co-operative societies, 'who insist that every selling employee must attend classes, and in the societies time, for general and trade education. ... [They consequently] reach a higher standard of selling ability than ... the average West End Store.' Chitham saw training, together with their greater security of tenure, as the reason behind the Co-op's lower staff turnover and ability to pay higher wages than the trade unions had negotiated with any department store.[78]

Among the multiple retailers, Marks & Spencer's contribution to what was then known as 'industrial welfare' was probably the most advanced, not only in its range of services but in the rigorous ways it subjected policy innovations to empirical testing – using key labour performance indicators such as staff retention and absenteeism. M&S developed its formal welfare organisation later than some of its competitors, after the firm had achieved its broader project of transformation from a 'Penny Bazaar' to an American-style high-price-limit variety chain. In 1932 investigations were commenced to compare the firm's wages and working hours to those of other retailers.[79] These led to the establishment of a Welfare Department and a medical service in 1933, plus a dental service from 1934. A pension scheme for senior male staff was

76 Asa Briggs, *Friends of the People: The Centenary History of Lewis's* (London, 1956), p. 165.
77 Peter Cox, *Spedan's Partnership: The Story of John Lewis and Waitrose* (Cambridge, 2010), pp. 59–79.
78 Harrods Archives, Chitham report.
79 'The Experience of Marks & Spencer Ltd in Caring for 18,000 Employees Proves that Staff Welfare is a Business Investment', *Chain and Multiple Store*, 10 December 1938, 190–3.

introduced in 1936, membership of which was progressively widened, while the Marks & Spencer Benevolent Trust provided retirement benefits for those outside the scheme. By the beginning of 1939 Marks & Spencer's welfare activities also included ophthalmic services, convalescent homes, access to specialist medical consultants, subsidised holiday camps, a holiday savings fund, long-service payments and wedding gifts.[80] Working hours had also been reduced, to an average of around forty-four per week by the beginning of 1939.[81]

By 1938 M&S were spending around £100,000 annually on welfare (or £6.50 per member of staff), in order to provide almost £250,000 worth of services.[82] Meanwhile, labour turnover (the ratio of persons leaving to normal staff, excluding staff reductions) had been reduced from 39.52% in 1933 to 24.26% in 1937, by which time the firm claimed that its absenteeism rates were lower than any published figures for British firms employing similar classes of worker.[83] Furthermore, from 1932 to 1937 the average term of employment of salesgirls had increased from 1.25 years to 5 years (regarded as very satisfactory, in an era when women typically left work on marriage).[84]

Marks & Spencer's demonstration effect may have encouraged Woolworths – probably Britain's largest retail employer, with 38,520 female and 2,803 male store employees in 1939 – to look seriously at expanding its welfare policy.[85] In contrast to its American parent, Woolworths UK had a good reputation for pay and conditions (though it shared the American parent's vehemently anti-union stance).[86] The British Woolworths operated on an overtly paternalistic basis, with a clear understanding that managers accepted considerable responsibility for the health and well-being of their employees and that staff

80 M&S Archives, A05 413 D, M&S, Annual Report of the Joint Secretary and Chief Accountant, 1938, p. 46.
81 M&S Archives, A05 413 D, M&S, Annual Report of the Joint Secretary and Chief Accountant, 1938, p. 50; AGM, Chairman's speech, 10 May 1939.
82 M&S Archives, Chairman's speech, 1 June 1938. Employment figure is for permanent staff at 31 December 1938: M&S Archives, A05/413E, Marks & Spencer Ltd, Annual Report of the Chief Accountant, 1939.
83 M&S Archives, E7/24, Annual report of Joint Secretary & Chief Accountant, 1937; E7/24, J. A. Berger, Confidential report to the directors on the conduct of the administration for the year 1934 (19 January 1935).
84 M&S Archives, E7/24, J. A. Berger, Confidential report to the directors on the conduct of the administration for the year 1934 (19 January 1935); 'The Experience of Marks & Spencer Ltd in Caring for 18,000 Employees Proves that Staff Welfare is a Business Investment', *Chain and Multiple Store*, 10 December 1938, 190–3 (p. 193).
85 Woolworths Archive, Buyers Committee minute book no. 1, p. 258, 9 August 1940.
86 Mark G. Dixon, 'Stephenson, William Laurence (1880–1963), Chain Store Chairman', *Dictionary of Business Biography*, vol. 5, ed. David Jeremy (London, 1986), pp. 303–8; Robert Hendrickson, *The Grand Emporiums: The Illustrated History of America's Great Department Stores* (New York, 1979), p. 119.

were expected to show high standards of loyalty to both the company and each other.[87] From around 1936 policy became more formalised, wages being increased and welfare facilities extended in an effort to improve staff turnover and morale.[88] In January 1938 Woolworths' chairman, W. L. Stephenson, informed shareholders that sales assistants' working hours were now limited to forty-eight per week (with the exception of seasonal trade, when they were paid overtime) and that £60,000 had been distributed as cash Christmas presents to the female staff in 1937. Meanwhile, their holiday with pay scheme had been extended, providing one week's paid holiday for employees with six months' service, and two weeks for those with twelve months' continuous service.[89] By this time Woolworths was also in discussions with M&S to see if they could agree an earlier Saturday closing time.[90]

Boots also continued as a leader in industrial welfare during this period. Jesse Boot's son, John (who became Boots' chief executive in 1933) was an outspoken advocate for improved shop workers' conditions.[91] By 1938 Boots were spending around £6 annually on welfare expenses per member of staff: including pension funds, canteen subsidies and various benevolent funds, together with an elaborate health service at Nottingham for their manufac-turing and wholesale staff.[92] John Boot also pushed through the introduction of a five-day, 42½-hour working week at their new Beeston factory during the 1930s – when the 48-hour week was still standard for industrial workers.[93]

Some line-specialised multiples also embraced industrial welfare. Montague Burton was a welfare pioneer in both clothes retailing and manufacture – a sector notorious for 'sweat-shop' wages and conditions. Burton's paid more than trades union wage rates and by 1925 their new purpose-built Hudson Road factory in Leeds had a welfare superintendent, a nurse to provide first aid, dining facilities, a holiday savings club and a sick club – providing benefits akin to those of a friendly society. They also provided social and sporting facilities (managed by an elected sports council). By 1935 a formal Welfare Department had been established, to manage both these facilities and more recently introduced medical and leisure services. In common with M&S, Boots

87 Barbara Walsh, *When the Shopping Was Good: Woolworths and the Irish Main Street* (Dublin, 2011), p. 25.
88 Woolworths Archive, Executive Committee minute book no. 4, p. 82, Annual Executive Meeting, 21–23 January 1936.
89 'F. W. Woolworth & Co.', *The Times*, 22 January 1938, p. 16, Col. A.
90 M&S Archives, E7/24, Annual report of Joint Secretary & Chief Accountant, 1937. The outcome of these negotiations is not known.
91 'The Annual Report of the Boots Pure Drug Co. Ltd', *The Retail Chemist*, July 1936, 218–20.
92 Boots Archives, Boots Pure Drug Co. & Associated Companies – Statistical record for year to 31 March 1938 (1938).
93 Chapman, *Jesse Boot*, pp. 169–94; J. E. Greenwood, *A Cap For Boots* (London, 1977), p. 57.

and Woolworths, Burton's justified these policies in terms of their impacts on labour productivity.[94]

Retailer initiatives in these areas were important not only in boosting the living standards of their own workers, but in their wider demonstration effect. Advocates of industrial welfare could point to some of the best-known and rapidly growing British companies as exemplars of best practice. These firms thus contributed to a broader trend, among at least a section of British employers, towards viewing staff pay and conditions as an investment, as well as a cost.

Conclusion

Francesca's research on the Victorian jewellery and piano sectors illuminated processes whereby manufacturers and distributors diffused 'luxury' products to successively lower-income households, via strategies that simultaneously emulated high-end products while segmenting the popular and elite markets.[95] Here we examined a later episode in the history of retail democratisation, which also incorporates elements of market segmentation based on goods of superficially similar appearance but differing quality (as in men's outerwear and women's clothing), together with the creation of genuinely 'mass markets' for a wide variety of – mainly fast-moving – consumer goods.

We identify how this process was led by a (mainly) new breed of mass, popular, retailers who – in contrast to an increasingly parasitic independent retailer class – often appreciated that they had common cause with the working classes in initiatives to provide better value for money and raise living standards. This involved a number of interrelated policies. Major retailers reduced the costs of the goods they purchased – through cutting out the wholesaler, bulk buying, encouraging mass production of standardised goods and, in some cases, taking control of product design, R&D and branding. Their operating expenses were also cut, through efficiency gains from firm and store-level economies of scale, new supply-chain relationships and statistically driven stock control systems that both increased stock-turn and reduced inventory costs.

Moreover, through policies of open display, clear price ticketing and advertising that signalled they were open to all classes, they extended their market to a broad social spectrum, including working-class families. Some retailers, generally those running large, multi-product stores, also reduced market

94   Sigsworth, *Montague Burton*, pp. 64–8.
95   Francesca Carnevali, 'Luxury for the Masses', *Entreprises et Histoire* 46 (2007), 56–70; Carnevali, 'Fashioning Luxury'; Carnevali and Newton, 'Pianos for the People'.

segmentation by creating new social and leisure spaces which people of all classes could enter with confidence and that offered a variety of services, the most fundamental of which was the freedom to browse. Finally, large-scale retailers, in common with some leading consumer goods manufacturers, were at the forefront of campaigns to improve employee welfare, via better pay, welfare services and shorter hours.

It is important not to exaggerate the reduction in class differentials during the interwar years. Working-class households were still sharply divided from higher-income sections of society not only through major barriers in areas such as access to secondary and higher education, but by such trivial things as being able to afford the cost of a meal at a restaurant (or feeling confident enough to negotiate the social rituals surrounding restaurant dining). Nevertheless, the interwar period had witnessed a major decrease in the differences in dress, lifestyle and access to urban 'public' buildings that had so sharply demarcated the working classes even from the clerical class in 1914, and mass retailers had played no small role in this transformation.

5

'Made in England': Making and Selling the Piano, 1851–1914

LUCY NEWTON (WITH FRANCESCA CARNEVALI)[1]

Introduction

This chapter considers the production and sale of household goods during the Second Industrial Revolution; how their production was organised and how manufacturers responded to consumer tastes in an entrepreneurial manner in order to profit, and to add to the economic growth of Great Britain.[2] It was a project started by Francesca, who was inspired to examine the production of goods for the home due to their general neglect by scholars in favour of the history of staple and capital goods. In terms of industrial production, our understanding of the dynamics of economic growth during the period of the Second Industrial Revolution is largely confined to the contribution of staple goods such as textiles and food, or capital goods such as ships, iron and steel and coal, although work has been done on pottery.[3] There was, Francesca felt, an element of bias against goods that were considered to be of prime

1   I would like to dedicate this paper to Francesca Carnevali, with whom I worked on the British consumer goods project and our more specific research into the piano. She appears as co-author, as sections in this chapter are written by her. I would also like to thank the staff of the Surrey History Centre, Woking (SHC); the Guildhall Library, London; the British Library Newspaper Collection (BLNC); Harrods Company Archive, London (HCA); University of Glasgow Archive, Glasgow; City Archives, London (WCA); Hackney Archives, London; Victoria and Albert Museum Archives, London; Dr Leigh Shaw-Taylor and the Cambridge Group for the History of Population and Social Structure, Cambridge; and the Victoria and Albert Museum National Art Library, London, for their help during the research for this project.
2   Robert Solow, 'A Contribution to the Theory of Economic Growth', *The Quarterly Journal of Economics* 70 (1956), 65–94; Robert E. Lucas Jr., 'On the Mechanics of Economic Development', *Journal of Monetary Economics* 22 (1988), 3–42; Joel Mokyr, *The Gifts of Athena: Historical Origins of the Knowledge Economy* (Princeton, NJ, 2002).
3   Andrew Popp, *Business Structure, Business Culture and the Industrial District: The Potteries, c.1850–1914* (Aldershot, 2001).

importance to the home and therefore perceived to be of prime importance to women.[4] Both of us shared a suspicion that more importance was placed upon the 'large', 'important' and 'weightier' (i.e. less frivolous) products made of iron and steel – engines, machinery and rails – that had traditionally been seen as part of the male preserve. Francesca wished to redress this imbalance by outlining the importance of household goods to the manufacturing sector as a whole. She also wished to highlight the importance of the interaction between the consumer and the producer in shaping changes in the manufacture of such goods. She further sought to build upon her previous work on industrial districts, given that the making of household goods often took place in specific towns and cities, carried out by skilled and specialised labour.

That is not to say that consumer goods have been ignored. They have been considered for their artistic merit and for their functional purpose. The history of retailing is well documented, taking into account the sale of household goods. The world of nineteenth-century consumption has been amply illustrated by a rich literature on the cultural relationship between consumers and the objects they purchased, or aspired to own. This literature has provided us with extensive information about the goods purchased by the Victorians and Edwardians, but entirely from the consumers' point of view.[5]

Alternatively, economic historians have mainly considered the consumption of these goods as a variable responding to changes in production.[6] The supply-side orthodoxy has been challenged by the work of historians of the eighteenth century such as Berg and de Vries, and by those of the modern period such as Tedlow and Jones, Forty, Loeb and Oldenziel.[7] Our research into the production and sale of consumer goods began with the piano and considered its marketing and sale, and how producers interacted with consumers through these

---

4   Indeed Cohen has emphasised that, in fact, the Victorian home and its decoration was just as much, if not more so, the preserve of men as well as women: Deborah Cohen, *Household Gods: The British and Their Possessions* (New Haven and London, 2006), pp. 89–104.

5   John Benson, *The Rise of Consumer Society in Britain, 1880–1980* (New York, 1994); Cohen, *Household Gods*; Lizabeth Cohen, *A Consumer's Republic: The Politics of Mass Consumption in Postwar America* (New York, 2003); Matthew Hilton, *Consumerism in 20th-Century Britain: The Search for a Historical Movement* (Cambridge, 2003); Matthew Hilton, *Smoking in British Popular Culture, 1800–2000* (Manchester, 2000).

6   John Brewer and Roy Porter, *Consumption and the World of Goods* (London and New York, 1993).

7   Maxine Berg, 'From Imitation to Invention: Creating Commodities in Eighteenth-Century Britain', *Economic History Review*, 55 (2002), 1–30; Jan de Vries, *The Industrious Revolution: Consumer Behavior and the Household Economy* (Cambridge, 2008); Adrian Forty, *Objects of Desire: Design and Society 1750–1980* (London, 1986); Lori Anne Loeb, *Consuming Angels: Advertising and Victorian Women* (Oxford, 1994); Adri Albert de la Bruhèze and Ruth Oldenziel, *Manufacturing Technology, Manufacturing Consumers: The Making of Dutch Consumer Society* (Amsterdam, 2009); Richard S. Tedlow and Geoffrey Jones, eds, *The Rise and Fall of Mass Marketing* (London, 1993).

intermediaries.[8] All of this work highlights that such production is inextricably linked to changes in consumers' demands and considers the creative process that leads entrepreneurs to make decisions about their resources.[9]

But there is still more work to be done on the production and sale of consumer goods in Great Britain. Although most of these categories of goods were not new – they had been available in the eighteenth century[10] – what marked the period that followed the Great Exhibition of 1851 was their growing availability and affordability, a proliferation of variants and a quickening of the fashion cycle. The fashioning of 'style-goods' for broadening sections of society allowed manufacturers to expand the size of their business, but only if they were able to sustain a strong connection with consumers and their changing desires. Despite the existence of 'fashion intermediaries' and the development of sophisticated ways of obtaining knowledge about consumers,[11] nobody ultimately knew whether a certain line of pottery, or wallpaper, or indeed piano, would sell. Thus, decisions about how to organise labour, structure firms and invest in machinery, as well as sales methods, were powerfully dominated by how much producers understood about what their customers wanted.[12] In short, this dilemma constitutes the challenge of how to match supply with demand. In this process, entrepreneurial activity played a central role in devising strategies to cope with the problem of scarce or ambiguous information and limited market power.[13]

How did manufacturers of consumer goods achieve flexibility in production to successfully respond to changes in consumer demand? Did their operation in industrial clusters, with a skilled labour force, help or hinder their success? Ideally, during times of rapidly growing consumer demand and structural change, entrepreneurial creativity would allow manufacturing firms to innovate and reorganise their activities, and recombine human capital, skills and technology. Were consumer goods producers entrepreneurial in this way?

---

8   Francesca Carnevali and Lucy Newton, 'Pianos for the People: From Producer to Consumer in Britain, 1851–1914', *Enterprise and Society*, 14 (2013), 37–70.
9   Joseph Schumpeter, *Capitalism, Socialism and Democracy* (New York, 1942), especially pp. 79–85; Richard E. Caves, *Creative Industries: Contracts Between Art and Commerce* (Cambridge, MA, 2002).
10   Maxine Berg, 'Consumption in Eighteenth- and Early Nineteenth-Century Britain', *The Cambridge Economic History of Modern Britain*, vol. 1, *Industrialisation, 1700–1860*, ed. Roderick Floud and Paul Johnson, (Cambridge, 2004), pp. 357–87; Berg, 'From Imitation to Invention'.
11   Gerben Bakker, *Entertainment Industrialised: The Emergence of the International Film Industry* (Cambridge, 2008); Regina L. Blaszczyk, *Imagining Consumers: Design and Innovation from Wedgwood to Corning* (Baltimore, 1999); de la Bruhèze and Oldenziel, *Manufacturing Technology, Manufacturing Consumers*.
12   A fascinating strand of research would be into products that failed to sell. This would allow us to consider times when producers 'got it wrong', or rather, misread consumer taste and demand. And why they did so.
13   Schumpeter, *Capitalism, Socialism and Democracy*, pp. 79–85.

In an attempt to answer such questions, this chapter continues to examine the piano, the consumer good that Francesca and I decided to use as our 'pilot' project.[14] Having considered in detail the marketing and sale of the piano, and how piano producers interacted with consumers through these intermediaries,[15] this chapter will add to this aspect of our work through new material. But its main focus will be to build upon our previous research by considering in more detail the production of the piano, an area that was less developed in our initial work. Here the attention is on the industrial cluster in which piano makers located; the firms that made pianos; and the sharing of knowledge at both firm and district level. The aim is to examine more closely how piano makers organised production to be flexible and to successfully respond to consumer demand. Thus, the chapter builds on our research on consumer goods but also Francesca's research regarding industrial districts, shared knowledge, co-operation and social networks – thus the chapter extends a number of themes in Francesca's work and makes possible a dialogue with several other chapters in this volume.

First, research into the area of consumer goods more broadly will be examined – the sources and methodology used to research these products – before considering the context of the consumer goods manufacturer in the nineteenth and early twentieth century. The chapter will then consider the manufacturer of the piano, in terms of the scale and location of its production, with a particular focus on the knowledge existing at the firm and district level that was so crucial in the manufacture of this musical instrument.

The production of consumer goods: sources and methodology

One way to match supply with demand was through custom and batch production. Indeed, this type of production of household goods played a central role in the growth of the American economy during the Second Industrial Revolution,[16] but we know very little about the production of these goods in Britain. Most economic historians of this period have focused on the beginning of Britain's relative economic decline; as such this historiography has studied in depth Britain's main exports, such as textiles, coal, and iron

---

14   The piano is one of the larger items for the home yet was chosen for our pilot project as it was a product mainly manufactured (or certainly put together) by one firm, making the analysis of its production and sale slightly easier than those goods which passed through the hands of a variety of makers/firms. Piano makers also tended to cluster in an area of north London where we both had once lived, bringing a personal interest to their manufacture.

15   Carnevali and Newton, 'Pianos for the People'.

16   Phil Scranton, *Endless Novelty: Specialty Production and American Industrialisation, 1865–1925* (Princeton, NJ, 2000), pp. 10–17.

and steel. By focusing on decline and concentrating almost exclusively on the supply of staple and capital goods this literature has skewed our understanding of this period. However, the production of household goods made up a sizeable proportion of Britain's total manufacturing output, and data from the 1907 Census of Production reveal that the production of these goods accounted for 8% of net output of total manufacturing. If finished manufactured goods alone are considered, the share of household goods goes up to 12%.[17]

Many of these producers of household goods clustered in specific areas, and these clusters were to be found throughout the British Isles, from cut glass on the east coast of Ireland, to carpets and linoleum in Scotland, to cutlery in South Yorkshire, stained glass and metal goods in the Midlands, to musical instruments in London, linoleum in Lancashire, wallpaper in the south and north-west of England, and pottery in Staffordshire. Such industrial clusters allowed small-scale and batch production. This allowed flexibility in manufacture, allowing firms to change production of their goods to suit the market and shifting consumer tastes.

One of the reasons why the production of household goods might have been neglected, for example by Broadberry in his seminal work on productivity,[18] is that, unlike for the USA, official output and employment data for the nineteenth century are unavailable, as the first Census of Production started only in 1907, and the early Board of Trade reports present data that are too aggregated (glass with bricks, cutlery with other metal goods, carpets with textiles).

The aim of our research into consumer durables has been to avoid the limitations imposed by official statistics (or lack of them), by using different types of sources. This may be described as a 'bottom-up' approach to research through the consultation of a variety of dispersed and disparate sources. This can be illustrated through our research into piano production. Surviving company records are scare and tend to be for larger companies in the sector. Most records that survived the mergers and consolidation of firms in the UK piano-manufacturing industry were lost in a fire at Chappell's headquarters in 1964.[19] Most other piano-making firms were very small scale and therefore have left no records behind. They can be found listed in trade directories, which confirm their location but little else of detail concerning their operation remains. Trade journals also form a valuable source of information. House

---

17   These figures are likely to be an underestimate as the 1907 Census did not include small establishments, those employing fewer than ten people, which is where many of these goods would have been made.

18   Stephen Broadberry, *The Productivity Race: British Manufacturing in International Perspective, 1850–1990* (Cambridge, 1997); Stephen Broadberry, *Market Services and the Productivity Race, 1850–2000: Britain in International Perspective* (Cambridge, 2006).

19   Lucy Newton and Francesca Carnevali, 'Researching Consumer Durables in the Nineteenth Century: The Case of the Piano', *Business Archives: Sources and History* 101 (2010), 17–29 (p. 21).

of Commons Parliamentary Papers for trade are available but figures tend to relate to musical instruments in general rather than pianos in particular. They also provide figures for exports and imports of pianos rather than total production by British companies. There are a few retailers and brand names of producers that were founded in the nineteenth century and still exist today. But no pianos have been made in the UK since 2012. And small retailers do not make their records available to researchers. Department stores' archives give a partial view of the retailing side of pianos, as do catalogues for mail-order firms, such as Army & Navy. Newspaper advertisements exist for second-hand pianos. Some trade catalogues for piano producers and retailers survive, as do exhibition catalogues, such as those for the Ideal Home Exhibitions of the early twentieth century. The consumer dimension may be viewed from the perspective of periodicals for the 'home' such as *Hearth and Home*, *The Alexandra Magazine*, *The Englishwoman's Domestic Magazine* and *The Furnisher and Decorator*. Wills available online on The National Archives A2A database have also provided information for the inheritance of pianos within families. Yet these sources are very widely dispersed and often very patchy in their coverage. As a result, research into the production and consumption of household goods is problematic and time-consuming. It is understandable that research in this sector has been limited before now, but our research into pianos demonstrates that such studies yield worthwhile results.

The production of consumer goods: the economic and social context

What of the context in which household goods were produced? The second half of the nineteenth century saw both rapid structural change and the second industrial and consumer revolutions. From the Great Exhibition of 1851 to the First World War, firms were provided with opportunities through growing incomes and the expansion of the middle class; rapid urbanisation and the growth of suburbs; diminishing transport costs as the railway network expanded; telephones and faster communications and electrification. International exhibitions had a tremendous impact on both consumers and producers. The Great Exhibition of 1851, held in the Crystal Palace in Hyde Park, London, was the first international exhibition of consumer goods in the UK and is taken as the starting point of this research.[20] Exhibitions intensified the challenge of competition as firms were exposed to imitation and the public were exposed to foreign aesthetics and products to a far greater extent

---

20   Dionysius Lardner, *The Great Exhibition and London in 1851* (London, 1852); Trevor May, *Great Exhibitions* (Oxford, 2010); David Wainwright, *The Piano Makers* (London, 1975), pp. 104–5.

than ever before. In addition, the new department stores, the 'Penny Bazaars', the new shopping arcades, the Co-operative emporia, the expansion of mail-order catalogues and the provision of hire-purchase agreements created new approaches to selling. All these retail opportunities gave the skilled working classes and middle classes places to spend their money.[21]

Producers responded to demand generated through rising incomes, increased leisure time and the growth of the suburbs. Retailers extended the number of outlets for consumer goods. Consumers responded to their exposure to a greater variety of consumer goods gained from viewing them at exhibitions and a growing array of retail outlets. As a result, during the second half of the nineteenth century, British consumers filled their homes with an increasing range of consumer goods. These included: carpets, rugs, linoleum, furniture made of wood and papier mâché, drapes, pianos, toys, toilets and baths, tiles, metal ornaments in all shapes and sizes, cutlery, glasses for drinking and stained glass for windows, china and pottery, wallpaper, oilcloth, light fittings, and even stuffed animals. Looking through the mail-order catalogues of the time gives some idea of the wealth of objects that the Victorians, and later the Edwardians, could purchase.[22]

To summarise, in the UK the period from 1850 saw producers turn items that in the past had been luxuries, available to a relatively small sector of society, into affordable goods for the homes of a growing middle class and an affluent working class. Increasingly complex and differentiated demand, driven by notions of fashion and style, led to changes in technology, and the use of human capital. For this period, and in relation to these types of products, this is not a story of lowering costs as a result of mass production. Rather, production focused on the recombination of custom and batch methods of production (specialty production) together with technology.[23] Household furniture, china and glass, are all examples of batch manufacturing where aggregated advance orders determined the size of lots. Producers showed wholesalers or retailers a range of samples, but could also adapt these to suit specific purchasers' designs. Production was entirely dominated by the unpredictability of demand and large inventories could turn into costly mistakes.

In order to illustrate more fully the production side of household goods, the piano will be taken as a case study in the following sections. The research on pianos has shown how these demand-driven strategies induced a process

21   John K. Walton, 'Towns and Consumerism', *The Cambridge Urban History of Britain*, vol. 3: *1840–1950*, ed. Martin Daunton (Cambridge, 2000), pp. 715–44.

22   For example see Army & Navy Co-operative Society, *Yesterday's Shopping: The Army & Navy Co-operative Society 1907 Issue of 'Rules of the Society and Price List of Articles Sold at the Stores'*, facsimile edn (Newton Abbot, 1969).

23   Michael J. Piore and Charles F. Sabel, *The Second Industrial Divide: Possibilities for Prosperity* (New York, 1984); Scranton, *Endless Novelty*.

of creative destruction, whereby piano manufacturers modified production methods and technology, labour, skills and capital were recombined. First, piano makers' responses to consumer demand will be considered, outlining and adding to our previous work in this area.

The organisation of piano production: what of the consumer?

The piano is able to communicate the subtlest universal truths by means of wood, metal and vibrating air.[24]

For the Victorians the piano had multiple associations and meanings. It was a musical instrument that provided a social focus for gatherings of family and friends; it was linked with the arts and grand concerts; and its possession by consumers suggested musical skills and artistic merits. It was also expensive and thus ownership implied prosperity. In the British drawing-room or parlour, contemporary arbiters of taste considered the piano an essential item.[25] The piano was presented in the public rooms of the Victorian home where household goods were displayed as symbols of success.[26] Thus, by 1910 piano ownership was well established among the middle classes. Ehrlich estimated that by the early twentieth century 'perhaps one Englishman in 360 purchased a new piano every year, a proportion at least three times higher than in 1851 and exceeded only in the USA where it was about 1:260. In Germany the ratio was 1:1000, and in France 1:1,600.'[27]

The signals transmitted by the possession of the piano – worth, social status – linked to the social aspiration of the consumer, and in particular social aspiration in competition with others. One author articulated this bluntly as follows: 'A large proportion of sales of musical instruments, both pianos and organs, is made through a feeling of jealousy of one neighbour by another.'[28] This element of competition between neighbours meant that

24 Quotation by Kenneth Miller, in Herb Galewitz, ed., *Music: A Book of Quotations* (New York, 2001), p. 34.
25 Mrs Haweis was a regular contributor to *The Lady's Realm*, and her books included *The Art of Beauty* (London, 1878), *The Art of Dress* (London, 1879), *The Art of Decoration* (London, 1881), *Beautiful Houses: Being a Description of Certain Well-Known Artistic Houses* (London, 1882), *Rus in Urbe: or Flowers that Thrive in London Gardens and Smoky Towns* (London, 1886) and *The Art of Housekeeping: A Bridal Garland* (London, 1889). Mrs Panton's advice manuals were intended for those with modest incomes (about £200 a year) and included *Homes of Taste: Economical Hints* (London, 1890).
26 Judith Flanders, *The Victorian House* (New York and London, 2003), p. xxix.
27 Cyril Ehrlich, *The Piano: A History* (Oxford, 1990).
28 BLNC, *Piano, Organ and Music Trades Journal*, 13, no. 149 (January 1895) (New Series no. 117), 4.

many consumers also wanted a non-standardised product, one that was different from their neighbour's. Those with the means were able to exchange an existing piano for an 'improved' or more fashionable, newer model. And the piano manufacturers provided them with an ample range of instruments to choose from, differentiated by different shapes, sizes and designs:

> The eclectic range of motifs applied to these modern instruments – motifs whose origin ranged from the ancient past to the imperial present – represented one of the most distinctive elements of Victorian design.[29]

The late-Victorian period saw a fashion for ornamentation that was influenced by styles discovered through foreign travel or international exhibitions. For example, the end of the nineteenth century witnessed a particular penchant for Japanese crafts. In response, Broadwoods produced a Japanese-style upright piano.[30]

Thus, piano makers could expand the range of types of pianos they made to suit a variety of tastes, with designs and ornamentation responding to changes in fashion in interior decoration.[31] In the 1880s, an article in *The Pianoforte Dealers' Guide* discussed adaptability of English piano manufacturing firms as 'having already accomplished much that their customers desire'. In the face of competition from foreign manufacturers British makers were, according to dealers, 'now laudably striving to get up cases of improved design, and in keeping with present homes tastes'.[32] Comments such as these in the trade press illustrate the dynamic dialogue between consumer, retailers and manufacturers.

Many innovations were designed to suit differing consumer needs in terms of cost and size. Cheaper pianos meant that they were affordable to more people and smaller pianos meant that the instrument could fit in the parlour of an ordinary house. At the end of the nineteenth and beginning of the twentieth century, more people began to live in flats in London and provincial cities. In response Broadwoods developed the 'Bijou Pianoforte', 3 feet 8 inches in height and 4 feet 5 inches wide:[33]

> Customers who live in residential flats with artistically furnished rooms of a small size have often-times raised an objection that pianofortes of

---

29 Michael Snodin and John Styles, *Design and the Decorative Arts: Britain 1500–1900* (London, 2001), p. 355.

30 Wainwright, *The Piano Makers*, p. 113.

31 Robert William Edis, *Decoration & Furniture of Town Houses: a Series of Cantor Lectures Delivered before the Society of Arts, 1880* (New York, 1881), p. 20; J. H. Elder-Duncan, J. H., *The House Beautiful and Useful: Being Practical Suggestions on Furnishing and Decoration* (New York, 1907), p. 153.

32 BLNC, *The Pianoforte Dealers' Guide*, 1, no. 5 (25 September 1882), 183.

33 Wainwright, *The Piano Makers*, p. 112.

good tone occupy too much space. The extreme portability of this class of piano [the Bijou Pianoforte] has rendered it in request, not only by purchasers living in residential flats ... but by military officers on foreign service constantly moving from one station to another, to whom every extra inch in height or extra pound in weight is of consideration.[34]

Producers thus adapted to consumer requirements and consequently the product could be modified to suit a range of needs and tastes. This process shows the importance of understanding how consumer demand can drive technological and production changes. The technologies used to make goods such as the piano were largely well established by 1850, but manufacturers continued to make small but significant changes in styles, size, technology and production methods.[35]

Given that the piano was loaded with such symbolic meaning, it was vital for producers to meet the needs of the buyer in terms of style, cost and cultural and social representation. But producers usually did not exist close to the consumer. As a result it was the retailer and dealer that acted as 'fashion intermediaries', negotiating and transmitting the messages and tastes of the consumer to the manufacturer.[36] The role of the dealer was discussed in the trade journals where, for example, *The Piano, Organ and Music Trades Journal* opined that: 'The public is fickle ... and dealers have to be fickle as well to accommodate ever-changing public taste.'[37] It was in the interests of dealers to translate and transmit the shifting demands of consumers to producers.

By the end of the nineteenth century non-specialist retailers also entered into the selling of pianos. For most of the nineteenth century pianos had been purchased at specialist music dealers, which were usually small retail outlets staffed by those with a deep knowledge of the musical instruments that they sold. From the 1890s direct competition came from department stores; Harrods in London opened its piano department in 1895.[38] Whiteleys, another London department store, sold pianos from the late nineteenth century,[39] as did Army & Navy, both through its department store in London and also its mail-order catalogue.[40]

---

34 Wainwright, *The Piano Makers*, p. 112.

35 Examining contemporary trade journals linked to the piano industry reveals lists of the latest patents taken out relating to piano manufacturing technology. For example, BLNC, *The Piano, Organ and Music Trades Journal*, 8, no. 102 (January 1891), 19.

36 Blaszczyk, *Imagining Consumers*, pp. 9–10.

37 BLNC, *Piano, Organ and Music Trades Journal*, 17, no. 210 (February 1900) (New Series no. 178), 632.

38 HCA, *Harrod's Stores Catalogue 1895*, p. 1537, Pianoforte and Musical Instrument Dept.

39 WCA, William Whiteley Ltd., Department Store Archive.

40 Army & Navy, *Yesterday's Shopping*.

Department stores provided ample space to view instruments on display and ample choice for the consumer. In 1994, *The Harrodian Gazette* recalled the first sale of a piano by Harrods one hundred years previously in their 'Salon'. In its heyday the Salon stocked six hundred pianos (compared to one hundred today) and if you wandered through the department you would have seen staff wearing black frock-coats, striped trousers and black shoes.[41]

Of course the piano was also an object to be heard. Manufacturers and retailers realised the value of potential consumers being able to listen to any musical instrument that they might purchase and so they invested in concert halls. A trade journal commented:

> The English maker (and the German here) is firmly convinced of the value of concert work as a means of pushing his piano, and most of the leading houses have salons, where recitals and concerts of greater or less presentations are constantly given.[42]

In London there was Steinway Hall, Brinsmead Concert Hall, Broadwood Recital Hall and Bechstein Hall (now Wigmore Hall), all venues built by piano makers in which their instruments were played.[43] Thomas Patey Chappell, of the piano-making firm Chappell and Company, financed the building of St James's Hall, a concert hall in Regent Street, London in 1858. St James's Hall was demolished in 1893 to make way for the Piccadilly Hotel but in that year Chappells obtained the lease of the Queen's Hall in Langham Place, London and transferred their concerts to this location.[44] Harrods held concerts in its piano department and weekly recitals by famous musicians.[45]

The piano was therefore a very particular type of household good. It was a musical instrument, purchased for entertainment, but also one that for the consumer was not only relatively expensive but also had symbolic and aspirational social meaning. For the retailer it was a specialist product that required specialist selling. For the producer it was an instrument that required adaptation to consumer tastes, but also one that took specialist skills to make. The next section considers in further detail the manufacturing process; the specialist skills and knowledge required to make the piano; and the districts in which piano makers clustered and knowledge accumulated.

41 HCA, '100 not out!', *The Harrodian Gazette*, Summer 1994.
42 BLNC, *Piano, Organ and Musical Trades Journal*, 17, no. 216 (August 1900) (New Series no. 183), 791.
43 BLNC, *Piano, Organ and Musical Trades Journal*, 17, no. 216 (August 1900) (New Series no. 183), 791; Julia MacRae, *Wigmore Hall: The Story of a Concert Hall* (London, 2011), http://wigmore-hall.org.uk/about-us/history/41-the-history-of-a-concert-hall/file, accessed 14 December 2016.
44 Wainwright, *The Piano Makers*, pp. 105–6 and 111.
45 HCA, *The Harrodian Gazette*, 3 October 1938.

The organisation of piano production:
industrial clusters and knowledge

Many producers of household goods clustered in specific areas, and the piano was no exception. Francesca provided eloquent arguments for 'the importance of clusters of small firms in industrial districts and of regional economies in making flexible specialisation a viable, modern alternative to mass production'.[46] This section therefore expands on our previous work on pianos to consider in more detail the clusters in which piano makers located. The aim is to analyse further the organisation of production – the location of the skills and knowledge required to make the piano – and how this impacted upon the flexibility of the manufacture of this musical instrument.

Here we will take Marshall's original definition of the industrial district/ cluster: the tendency to 'concentrate particular industries in special locali- ties'.[47] Marshall described regions in which the business/industrial structure was made up of small-scale, localised firms. In this environment, economies of scale were relatively low and thus firms remained relatively small. Trade within the district often entailed long-term contracts and a high level of commitment between actors. The movement of finance to lubricate production took place efficiently at the level of the industrial district, with local business people and investors committing to the long-term economic health of their region.[48]

The industrial district is made distinct by the nature of its labour, according to Marshall. This labour is localised, specialised and flexible. Owners and workers inhabit the same space, live in the same communities and benefit from shared experience and knowledge: 'The mysteries of the trade become no mysteries; but are as it were in the air.'[49] Skilled labour and experienced management hold this knowledge, an asset that allows firms to be innovative and maintain competitiveness in the market.[50] Knowledge of various types – tacit, technological, cultural, codifiable, etc. – may be based at the level of the

46   Francesca Carnevali, 'Golden Opportunities: Jewelry Making in Birmingham Between Mass Production and Specialty', *Enterprise and Society*, 4 (2003), 272–98 (p. 273).

47   Alfred Marshall, *Industry and Trade* (London, 1919), IV.X.14.

48   Lucy Newton, 'Networks and Clusters: Capital Networks in the Sheffield Region, 1850–1885', *Industrial Clusters and Regional Business Networks in England, 1750–1970*, ed. John F. Wilson and Andrew Popp (Ashgate, 2003), pp. 130–54.

49   Marshall, *Industry and Trade*, IV.X.7. For further studies on industrial clusters see Piore and Sabel, *The Second Industrial Divide*; Udo H. Staber, Norbert V. Schaefer and Basu Sharma, eds, *Business Networks: Prospects for Regional Development* (Berlin, 1996); Charles F. Sabel and Jonathan Zeitlin, *World of Possibilities: Flexibility and Mass Production in Western Industrialization* (Cambridge and New York, 1997).

50   Robert M. Grant, 'Toward a Knowledge-Based Theory of the Firm', *Strategic Management Journal* 17 (1996), 109–22.

firm, the district, country or trading block. At the firm level, those analysing knowledge have argued that it can provide competitive advantage. What has been called the 'knowledge-based view' of the firm asserts that 'a firm's competitive advantage lies in the ability to collect, accumulate, integrate, disseminate, and exploit knowledge ... which is essential to the development of technological capabilities'.[51]

To be of use to the firm, this knowledge needs to be shared and utilised effectively. This can take place within industrial districts. Tacit knowledge is based upon the idea that more is known than can be written down on paper.[52] Obtaining such knowledge needs personal experience and practice, and others already possessing such knowledge often facilitate the learning process. This has been described as the 'learning by doing' approach.[53] In the case of manufacturing, this leads to tacit knowledge often being directly related to specific industries and specific districts or clusters. Tacit knowledge can, consequently, provide competitive advantages to small firms operating in clusters. It can also provide competitive advantage to a group of firms operating in the same cluster that chose to co-operate, perhaps by 'co-operating in sharing, for example, machinery, the training of workers, and information about processes and customers, small firms can reduce these costs'.[54] This is especially the case where knowledge is difficult to transfer.

Knowledge was vital for the production of the piano. It was/is a specialised musical instrument that required a specialist skill set to make. It was not a good that was mass-produced in the nineteenth century. Even once machines and the assembling of parts were introduced to speed up production and to reduce costs, there remained a very clear skills element in the production of a piano. Specialist knowledge was/is also required to play the piano and to read music, and specialist knowledge was needed to maintain the instrument, for example via tuning. Knowledge was required to improve the piano, in terms of design and technology and, as outlined above, to keep pace with changes in consumer tastes.

Piano production formed an industrial cluster in the classic definition by Marshall. London was the focus for production, initially central London in the late eighteenth century (Soho) and then north London in the nineteenth

---

51   Shaker A. Zahra, Donald O. Neubaum and Bárbara Larrañeta, 'Knowledge Sharing and Technological Capabilities: The Moderating Role of Family Involvement', *Journal of Business Research* 60 (2007), 1070–9 (p. 1070).
52   Michael Polanyi, *The Tacit Dimension* (Chicago, 1966), p. 4.
53   Kenneth J. Arrow, 'The Economic Implications of Learning by Doing', *The Review of Economic Studies* 29 (1962), 155–73.
54   Francesca Carnevali, '"Crooks, Thieves and Receivers": Transaction Costs in Nineteenth-Century Industrial Birmingham', *Economic History Review*, 57 (2004), 533–50 (p. 534). See also Peter Maskell, 'Towards a Knowledge-Based Theory of the Geographical Cluster', *Industrial and Corporate Change*, 10 (2001), 921–43.

Figure 5.1. *D'Almaine's Pianoforte Manufactory* (Thomas Hosmer Shepherd, c.1835)

Source: Museum of London

century (Camden and Kentish Town), as firms pursued cheaper rents and more space.[55] London had the advantage of access to coastal shipping, via the River Thames; to the Regent's Canal; to the docks, and onwards to a global market; and the railheads of King's Cross, Euston and St Pancras (from north London).[56] This industrial cluster allowed access to a pool of skilled labour and access to materials but, importantly, the key source of demand from the country's capital. In a history of Camden the following description amply illustrates this industrial cluster in north London:

> The district's staple industry, however, was piano manufacture, having been drawn north from Fitzrovia by the ease of transporting timber by canal. It

55   There were some small piano makers outside the capital but Pohlmann & Sons in Halifax was the sole firm of significant size and only employed forty people by 1890: West Yorkshire Archive Service, Pohlmann and Sons, Halifax, piano manufacturers, Catalogue, A2A.

56   Jack Whitehead, 'Piano Manufacture in Camden Town', *Local Local History* ([London], 2012), http://www.locallocalhistory.co.uk/industrial-history/piano/page1-m.htm, accessed 14 December 2016.

was often said that every street in north London contained a piano works, and in many parts of Camden Town this was literally true; Bayham Place was a notable piano-making enclave.[57]

Once such a cluster formed, it was perpetuated by the further clustering of makers of piano parts: piano key makers; piano pin makers; sellers of key leads; hammer coverers; piano hammer and damper cloth makers; incisors, who cut the fretted wooden fronts; truss carvers; gilders; marquetry workers; French polishers; veneer, timber and ivory suppliers; makers of piano castors; candle-sconce makers; piano-back makers. All were essential suppliers to the main piano makers. Dolge summarises: 'Perhaps no other class of manufacturing depends more largely on auxiliary industries, each of itself of considerable magnitude, than the piano industry.'[58]

Thus, in 1850, piano manufacture was still a craft-based industry. It did not enjoy economies of scale and employed little machinery.[59] This can be seen clearly in Figure 5.1, in which thirteen workmen stand working with hand tools at benches around the edges of a medium-sized room with large windows, piano frames stand in the middle, waiting for the addition of parts for full construction.

Tomlinson's *Cyclopaedia of Useful Arts & Manufactures* (1853) lists the job descriptions of various skills within the piano trade: 'In the manufacture of a piano there are, in fact, upwards of 40 different classes of operatives employed, each of whom, with his assistants, is exclusively engaged in his own peculiar branch of the manufacture.' Descriptions are included about the beam-maker, bent side maker, bottom-maker, bracer, brass stud-maker, bridge-maker, canvas-frame-maker, carver, case-maker, check-maker, damper-lifter-maker, finisher, French polisher, fronter, gilder, hammer-leatherer, hammer-maker, key-maker, leg block-maker, lyre-maker, marker-off, metallic brace-maker, metallic plate-maker, music-smith, notch-maker, plinther, regulator of action, regulator of tones, rougher-up, sawyer, scraper, sounding-board-maker, spun-string-maker, steel arch-maker, stringer, top-maker, transverse bar-maker, tuner and turner.[60]

57   David Hayes, 'A History of Camden Town 1895–1914', *The Camden Town Group in Context*, ed. Helena Bonett, Ysanne Holt, Jennifer Mundy (London, 2012), https://www.tate.org.uk/art/research-publications/camden-town-group/david-hayes-a-history-of-camden-town-1895-1914-r1104374, accessed 14 December 2016.

58   Alfred Dolge, *Pianos and Their Makers: A Comprehensive History of the Development of the Piano* (Covina, CA, 1911), p. 115.

59   For a description of these technological developments, see Ehrlich, *The Piano*; Edwin M. Good, *Giraffes, Black Dragons, and Other Pianos: A Technological History from Cristofori to the Modern Concert Grand* (Stanford, CA, 2001); James Parakilas, *Piano Roles: Three Hundred Years of Life with the Piano* (New Haven, CT, 1999); Arthur Loesser, *Men, Women, and Pianos: A Social History* (1954; New York, 1991).

60   Charles Tomlinson, ed., *Cyclopaedia of Useful Arts & Manufactures* (London, 1853).

Table 5.1 Estimates of piano production, 1850–1930, thousands

Year	Britain	France	Germany	USA	Japan	Russia	Total
1850	23	10		10			43
1870	25	21	15	24			85
1890	50	20	70	72			212
1910	75	25	120	370		10	600
1930	50	21	20	120	2		213

Source: Cyril Ehrlich, *The Piano: A History* (Oxford, 1990), p. 222

This gives some indication of the number of trades, and the specific skills that would have been needed for each, which were involved in the manufacture of a piano. At the firm level, knowledge of piano production was swiftly transmitted: 'When shops were small, nearly everyone working in them eventually learned the entire "art, Trade and Mystery" of making pianos.'[61] This echoes Marshall's writing of the mysteries of trade in an industrial district being 'in the air'. This knowledge of piano-making, accumulated at firm level, was transmitted at district level as workers served apprenticeships and then often went on to establish their own firms (see below).

Thus, for example, a Broadwood grand could pass through the hands of forty different workmen.[62] Costs tended to be high and productivity low. Consequently, turnover was low but large profit margins could be achieved as retail prices at mid-century remained relatively high.[63] As well as a lack of machinery, the industry was also characterised by a lack of standardisation in production. A large firm would produce a range of different types of piano and even smaller firms could differentiate their finished products in terms of ornamentation, type of wood, etc. A contemporary estimated that Broadwoods could only produce about seven pianos per workman per annum, little different from the productivity of a small firm.[64]

Despite such division of labour, the number of pianos produced increased significantly between 1850 and 1914, as can be seen in Table 5.1. Germany and America led the way in producing greater numbers of pianos more cheaply but of a decent quality. From the 1880s, imports from these countries into the UK forced British manufacturers to do the same and the fragmented structure of the trade

---

61 Parakilas, *Piano Roles*, p. 37.
62 Lardner, *The Great Exhibition*.
63 Ehrlich, *The Piano*, p. 34.
64 Also, before construction could begin, wood had to be left to season before it could be utilised: Ehrlich, *The Piano*, pp. 36–8.

allowed innovation to take place. Manufacturers assembled pre-manufactured parts, rather than buying and seasoning wood then building the piano from scratch. The number of companies supplying these parts (and supplying them on credit), typically located in the existing cluster of piano producers, increased. In addition, mass production of precast iron frames and mass-produced, standardised but good-quality actions simplified the production process. Thus, the system of 'buying out' parts of the piano allowed manufacturers to purchase parts that were cheaper but also better than those that could have been produced in their workshops. Suppliers could also add the advantage of economies of scale to production and price upon sale to purchasers. Mechanisation of production was increasing, with the USA leading the way as a result of its shortage of skilled labour but abundance of wood. Machines were introduced, for example in woodworking, hammer covering and winding strings.[65]

The firm and piano production: co-operation, knowledge and families

What of the firms themselves? How did piano makers gain advantage from the industrial cluster in which they operated? How did they structure themselves? And how did they survive? Firms producing and selling pianos needed to keep pace with such changing environments and develop, what would be termed today, dynamic capabilities in order to allocate resources in order to create new products to meet the demands of customers.[66] They needed to behave entrepreneurially to survive in such markets. But in terms of production, flexible specialisation was required, as outlined above, as opposed to cost-saving full-scale mass production.

In the UK, piano producers were dominated by large numbers of small firms, or even solo piano makers; a few medium-sized enterprises; and a very small number of large-scale producers that enjoyed longevity. A survey of Kelly's trade directories for London reveals 178 entries under 'pianoforte makers' in 1851. The number of piano makers in London thereafter remained stable until 1914 at around two hundred and most of these were small-scale enterprises.[67] Broadwood & Sons (one of London's largest employers)

65 Ehrlich, *The Piano*, p. 81; Good, *Giraffes, Black Dragons, and other Pianos*, pp. 199, 211–13, 230.
66 Francesco Chirico and Mattias Nordqvist, 'Dynamic Capabilities and Trans-generational Value Creation in Family Firms: The Role of Organizational Culture', *International Small Business Journal* 28 (2010), 487–504.
67 *Kelly's Post Office Directory of London*. Directories were surveyed between 1851 and 1914. The directory only clearly differentiates which firms were operating solely as dealers in the 1914 directory, when forty-four dealers are included in the list of entries. This still left 212 enterprises that were solely makers of pianofortes.

produced 7–10% of UK pianos in this period,[68] and represented the exception in piano production.[69] There was a high entry and exit rate among small piano makers as they were badly hit by any recession. New entrants, however, often previously having been workers in existing factories, were ready to risk establishing a piano-making enterprise on their own due to the potential profits that could be made. Also, from the 1870s, larger producers would contract out their work to such smaller makers.[70]

One characteristic of an industrial cluster already mentioned was that, despite competition, there was often co-operation between firms. A trigger for such co-operation was adversity and, in the case of piano manufacturing, this often came in the form of fire. Many piano manufacturers experienced fires due to the amount of wood, glue and varnish present in their factories. But fellow manufacturers, despite being competitors, would often help when such disasters struck. In 1812 the factory in Oxford Street of Robert Wornum burnt down but the greater proportion of their finished stock was saved, in part by their neighbours and other volunteers.[71] In 1807 a fire at the Clementi piano factory caused an estimated capital loss of £40,000, of which the insurance companies paid out only £15,000. Broadwoods came to the aid of Clementi by helping him to fulfil orders, and Broadwood's workmen collected enough money among themselves to re-equip Clementi's men with the tools of their trade.[72] The fire was announced in *The Times* thus:

> FIRE. Clementi and Co. having unfortunately had their premises, in Tottenham-court-road, destroyed by fire, beg to inform the public, that through the generous exertions of their neighbours and friends, they have saved their grand and square piano-forte cases, and also a principal part of their dry manufactured and unmanufactured stock.[73]

In 1856 Hopkinson's was struck by a fire, after which both the firms of Broadwoods and Collard provided help to bring them back up to production.[74] As the chance of being struck by fire was high (there are many more

---

68   David Wainwright, 'Broadwood, Henry Fowler (1811–1893), Piano Manufacturer', *Dictionary of National Business Biography*, vol. 1: A–C, ed. Jeremy David (London, 1984), pp. 458–9.

69   It may be expected that large firms tend to be mass-producers of lower-quality goods. Yet in the case of pianos, large firms were also the high-end, quality producers. The same was true in the pottery industry: see Popp, *Business Structure*.

70   Ehrlich, *The Piano*, pp. 143–5.

71   'To the Public – Dreadful Fire!', *The Times*, 13 October 1812, p. 2.

72   Robert Palmieri, ed., *The Piano: An Encyclopedia* (Abingdon, 2014), pp. 71, 83–4.

73   *The Times*, 24 March 1807, p. 1, cited in David Rowland, 'Clementi's Music Business', *The Music Trade in Georgian England*, ed. Michael Kassler (Aldershot, 2011), pp. 125–57.

74   Barrie Heaton, 'A History of John Hopkinson, Piano Manufacturer', *Association of Blind Piano Tuners* (n.l., 2007), http://www.piano-tuners.org/history/hopkinson/, accessed 14 December 2016.

examples), this meant that help was all the more likely to be offered as any piano maker, large or small, could have had production ceased by such an event. It was therefore in the interests of all to help those afflicted.

These examples demonstrate that co-operation between firms existed in the industrial cluster of piano manufacturers. Knowledge was also a vital element in piano production that existed within the cluster. It is possible to see the classic industrial cluster whereby the production of a piano in the nineteenth century required specialist, often tacit, knowledge and the support of ancillary trades that likewise required knowledge and skill. But it was not only at the district level that knowledge was important. At firm level, tacit knowledge could be passed down through generations when the family firm was used as a vehicle for such knowledge transfer. The skills-based production methods that dominated piano production before 1914, combined with the particular specialist nature of producing a musical instrument, meant that family firms played an important role in piano production throughout this period.

The knowledge-based view of the firm argues that the firm is the holder of skills, experience and knowledge – the primary holder of the 'mysteries'.[75] The setting of the family firm has been viewed as a positive environment in which to create and share knowledge 'due to the high level of emotional involvement of family members and the socially intense interactions fueled by trust between family members and with external parties'.[76] Once knowledge is shared within the family and accumulated over time it changes from being merely individual knowledge but rather 'becomes part of the collective wisdom of the firm'.[77] Informal knowledge sharing in the setting of a family firm can be a competitive advantage.[78] Knowledge levels may also increase when more generational levels of the family are involved with the firm.[79] Ideally, new generations would be integrated into the family firm and knowledge trans-ferred from one generation to the next.[80] Such cross-generational sharing of knowledge has been found to be 'richer' than knowledge sharing across the same generation.[81] New generations can also bring fresh advantages to the

75   Christian Knudsen, 'The Competence Perspective: A Historical View', *Towards a Competence Theory of the Firm*, ed. Nicolai Foss and Christian Knudsen (Abingdon, 2006), pp. 13–37.

76   Chirico and Nordqvist, 'Dynamic Capabilities', p. 490.

77   Francesco Chirico, 'The Creation, Sharing and Transfer of Knowledge in Family Business', *Journal of Small Business and Entrepreneurship* 21 (2008), 413–33 (p. 417).

78   Michael D. Ensley and Allison W. Pearson, 'An Exploratory Comparison of the Behavioral Dynamics of Top Management Teams in Family and Nonfamily New Ventures: Cohesion, Conflict, Potency, and Consensus', *Entrepreneurship Theory and Practice* 29 (2005), 267–84.

79   Zahra *et al.*, 'Knowledge Sharing', pp. 1071, 1073.

80   Katiuska Cabrera-Suárez, Petra De Saá-Pérez and Desiderio García-Almeida, 'The Succession Process from a Resource- and Knowledge-Based View of the Family Firm', *Family Business Review* 14 (2001), 37–46.

81   Kelin F. Gersick, John A. Davis, Marion M. Hampton and Ivan Lansberg, *Generation to Generation: Life Cycles of the Family Business* (Boston, MA, 1997).

firm – fresh knowledge and/or fresh perspectives.[82] Subsequent generations in family firms are also shown to demonstrate a strong commitment to the firm and a strong appetite to ensure its success, and therefore are likely to strengthen the desire to share knowledge.[83]

On the other hand, family firms may hinder effective management of their knowledge, for example through conflict and family jealousy[84] or through a key individual family member not fully sharing knowledge and experience with other family members. In particular, founders' of family firms may be reluctant to pass down knowledge to the next generation,[85] which may lead to inertia within the firm. Moreover, subsequent generations may be unwilling to learn from their leaders.[86] Conflicts within families generate tensions, reduce trust and take time and energy away from successfully running the business. They also inhibit knowledge sharing.[87]

Specialist knowledge was crucial in the manufacture of pianos and such knowledge was often maintained in family firms and passed down from one generation to the next. Many firms in piano production were family-based enterprises. Nex has written of the importance of family firms in the production of musical instruments:

> Instrument makers were craftspeople and artisans who, like furniture makers or clock makers, had to source their raw materials, find or train skilled workers, deal with their finances, and sell their finished products. In addition, they were positioned within their own family structures both in terms of their professional and private lives.[88]

Broadwood & Sons is probably the most well-documented example of a family piano-manufacturing firm, although there are many others.[89] The firm

---

82 Wendy C. Handler, 'The Succession Experience of the Next Generation', *Family Business Review* 5 (1992), 283–307.

83 John P. Meyer and Natalie J. Allen, 'A Three-Component Conceptualization of Organizational Commitment', *Human Resource Management Review* 1 (1991), 61–89.

84 Jim Grote, 'Conflicting Generations: A New Theory of Family Business Rivalry', *Family Business Review* 16 (2003), 113–24.

85 Ivan Lansberg, *Succeeding Generations: Realizing the Dream of Families in Business* (Boston, MA, 1999).

86 Grote, 'Conflicting Generations'.

87 Francesco Chirico and Carlo Salvato, 'Knowledge Integration and Dynamic Organizational Adaptation in Family Firms', *Family Business Review* 21 (2008), 169–81.

88 Jennifer Susan Nex, 'The Business of Musical-Instrument Making in Early Industrial London' (Ph.D. thesis, Goldsmiths' College, University of London, 2013), p. 40.

89 The following sections on Broadwoods have been completed from the following sources: *Pierce Piano Atlas*, 12th edn (Albuquerque, NM, 2008); John Broadwood & Sons Ltd, 'History of John Broadwood & Sons Ltd Piano Manufacturer', *John Broadwood & Sons* (Whitby, n.d.), http://www.broadwood.co.uk/history.html, accessed 14 December 2016; Wainwright, 'Broadwood, Henry Fowler'; George Dodd, 'Piano-manufacture', *British Manufacturers*, series

had its origins in 1728. John Broadwood, founder of the company, had worked as an apprentice for the famous harpsichord maker Shudi from 1761. He then married Shudi's daughter, Barbara, in 1769 whereupon the harpsichord firm changed its name to Shudi & Broadwood. In 1771, Shudi stepped down from the business and handed over the running of the firm to his son Burkat and his son-in-law John Broadwood. When Shudi died in 1773, he left the firm to Burkat and John, with John becoming the effective head of the firm. By 1783 the firm was producing more pianos than harpsichords and was at the forefront of innovations in the instrument. Broadwoods patented improvements, such as to the brass underdamper that made the square piano much more stable, and to the English double action. The firm introduced the 'divided bridge' on the grand piano in 1788, which improved the bass tone. In the 1790s additional keys were added to the keyboard, increasing it from 5, to 5½, then to 6 octaves.

In 1795 James Shudi, John's son, entered the company. In 1808 another son, Thomas, joined the firm, and the name changed to John Broadwood & Sons. John Broadwood retired in 1811, aged seventy-nine, and died a year later. His sons, James Shudi Broadwood and Thomas Broadwood (then aged forty and twenty-five respectively), took over the running of the company, which expanded and prospered. The company had smoothly passed through three generations but there is, however, no detail on what happened to Shudi's son Burkat. He may have chosen to step away from the company, and let John, who was clearly a successful businessman, take the reigns. John Broadwood had clearly developed his skills and knowledge of keyboard manufacture as an apprentice under Shudi. In their turn, John's sons ran the company successfully and the presumption is that they had developed expertise in the business from their involvement in the family firm. Dolge describes the qualifications of John's son, James:

> Bought up in that house in Great Poulteney Street, where his grandfather had build harpsichords for kings and nobility, where Mozart, Handel and Haydn had practiced, and where his father had built his pianos under the advice and according to the demands of Muzio Clementi and other masters of the piano, James S. Broadwood was eminently qualified to add to the glory of the house, as a piano maker and a business man.[90]

4 (London, 1845), pp. 387–408; David Wainwright, *Broadwood by Appointment: A History* (Shrewsbury, 1982); Alastair Laurence, 'The Evolution of the Grand Piano, 1785–1998' (D.Phil. thesis, University of York, 1998), held at the SHC, Archive of John Broadwood & Sons, 2185/jb/83/51; SHC, 'John Broadwood and Sons Piano Manufacturers', *Surrey History Centre* (Woking, 2016), https://www.surreycc.gov.uk/heritage-culture-and-recreation/archives-and-history/surrey-history-centre/surrey-history-centre-help-for-researchers/archives-and-history-research-guides/john-broadwood-and-sons-piano-manufacturers, accessed 14 December 2016.
90　Dolge, *Pianos and Their Makers*, p. 245. Likewise, Thomas Chappell was taken out of school at the age of fifteen in 1834 to join the family firm 'to study it from the stock room upwards': Wainwright, *The Piano Makers*, p. 107.

This description eloquently illustrates the knowledge, experience and expertise that could be successfully passed down from father to son-in-law to son, both at home and in the family business.

Evidence of success and expansion under James Shudi Broadwood and Thomas Broadwood came in the form of a change to the location of production. In 1823 the firm leased a site in Horseferry Road, Westminster, belonging to the Grosvenor estate, upon which they constructed a purpose-built piano factory. The company continued to innovate. It introduced metal bars to the grand piano and a metal stringplate to the square, giving greater power and volume. In 1836, Henry Fowler, son of James Shudi, joined the business. James Shudi would have been sixty-four by this date, and potentially looking to hand over the reigns of the business but the move to the fourth generation of the family did not fare so well.

By 1840, Broadwoods was one of the twelve largest employers in London and was a pioneer of production methods. At its peak it manufactured 2,500 instruments a year and exported throughout the world. Henry Fowler became a partner in 1836, a senior working partner in 1861 and was in charge for over thirty years. He oversaw recovery from a fire at the Horseferry Road site in 1856 which burnt down the factory. It was rebuilt by using personal funds from Henry Fowler, showing his commitment to the company. Although he was an active leader of the firm, Henry Fowler was conservative in business: he did not agree, for example, that the firm should pay for advertising and believed it to be 'unnecessary and vulgar'.[91] Such attitudes suggest resistance to change and managerial inertia. The firm recovered from the fire but in the long term, sales declined during Henry Fowler's tenure in charge. He refused to switch to the new technology, such as to the single-cast iron frame and overstringing being used by the majority of other manufacturers. Conservatism in the design of the Broadwood grand in the second half of the nineteenth century was also down to Henry Fowler, who had complete control of design and manufacturing.

The firm reached a crisis point following Henry Fowler's death in 1893 and was wound up in 1901. One of Henry Fowler's sons married the sister of C. E. Heath, a City insurance financier and, through Heath, the firm received an injection of City funds and was reformed as a limited company. Members of the family continued to be involved in the running of the firm, as directors and as employees, but acrimonious disputes had raged for years as strong personalities vied for power. Henry Fowler's grandson, Captain Evelyn Broadwood, was chairman from 1931, and remained actively engaged in the firm until his death in 1975.

The progression of Broadwoods to fourth- and fifth-generation family control demonstrates the negative side of family firms. Broadwoods, once

---

91   SHC, Archive of John Broadwood & Sons, Catalogue.

such an innovative company, lost this entrepreneurial drive under Henry Fowler, despite his personal and financial commitment to the firm. Thus, Broadwoods became dominated by one, paternal, source of power and control, but also one that was conservative in nature.

Ownership structure did not help. After Henry Fowler joined the company in 1836 partnership rules had changed such that any partner was allowed to introduce his son as a new partner, without paying a premium into the firm. Thus, partners took a stake in Broadwoods without putting any capital into it nor contributing to its running, yet still taking resources away from the company. These were: Thomas junior, who joined the company in 1841 with a 10% stake; Walter Stewart Broadwood who took a stake in the company in 1843; George Thomas Rose and Frederick Rose joined in 1857; George Daniel Rose in 1883; and W. C. Dobbs, grandson of Henry Fowler, joined in 1893.

In the example of Broadwoods, it is evident that there was a long history of success in the family firm and knowledge was passed down through the generations. Even as late as 1893, James Henry Shudi Broadwood, inventor of the barless steel frame, became a partner in the firm and bought in his expertise. However, after many generations, problems involving ownership structure, a decline in the innovative nature of the company, a lack of entrepreneurial vitality and problems of foreign competition, meant that Broadwoods was unable to continue to flourish. Nonetheless, in terms of its size, longevity and overall success in the UK piano industry, Broadwoods remains unparalleled.

It should also be emphasised that knowledge in piano-making was passed down by other means than family involvement. John Broadwood served an apprenticeship under Burkat Shudi, harpsichord manufacturer, before he became part of the family. George Wilkinson was apprenticed to Francis Broderip, former partner in the piano manufacturer Longman & Broderip, before then going on to establish Wilkinson and Co., piano manufacturers. Frederick William Collard worked for Longman, Lukey & Broderip and also Clementi, before establishing a piano manufacturing company with his brother in 1831. Thus, apprenticeships within piano-making firms remained a vital source of knowledge transfer within and outside family firms, and within the industrial cluster.

Knowledge was also enhanced when firm survival rates were high. How long did a piano-manufacturing firm last? Although entry and exit rates were high, survival rates were good and worth the risk given the potential profits that could be made. From a survey of over 327 piano firms by Ehrlich taken from 1850 onwards, as shown in Table 5.2, 43% lasted from 1 to 20 years, 30% lasted from 21 to 40 years and only 10% survived over 40 years. There would have been some very small-scale producers that went in and out of business very quickly, which may have been omitted from this survey as its starting point is those firms that lasted at least a year, but the survival rates from this sample look relatively healthy, given the poor prognosis for modern

Table 5.2. Survival rates of piano-making firms

Survival in years	Number of piano makers	Percentage
1–10	55	17
11 20	86	26
21–30	59	18
31–40	39	12
41–50	32	10
51–60	18	6
61–70	8	2
71–80	8	2
81–90	6	2
91–100	4	2
100+	1	3
		100

Source: Cyril Ehrlich, *The Piano: A History* (Oxford, 1990), Appendix 1, pp. 203–21.

small firms. There were also some very healthy exceptions – Broadwoods lasted over two hundred years and Brinsmeads for over a century – but most firms did not 'live' for so long.

Overall, piano-making firms benefited from operating in an industrial cluster. They found support in adversity, such as loss of operation through fire; a pool of skilled labour; a wealth of related industries to support production; and the sharing of knowledge through skilled labour, apprenticeships and within relatively long-lived family firms. The family firm itself could be both a positive and negative influence on entrepreneurial activity. In the case of Broadwoods, knowledge sharing was extremely successful for the first three generations of the firm but thereafter, organisation as a family firm appears to have inhibited growth and innovation. Such a cluster of manufacturers and auxiliary trades, such a concentration of skills and knowledge, built over decades, permitted flexible, specialised production. This system of production condensed in this particular geographical area provided a viable alternative to mass production, given the nature of the product and the distinct and changing nature of consumer demand for this symbolic household item.

Conclusion

This chapter has considered the production of consumer goods, outlining why these goods deserve our attention, the methods by which they may be researched, given source constraints, and the particular context for their production in the period 1850–1914. In particular, the manufacturer of the piano has been considered to illustrate the nature of production via flexible specialisation to meet changing consumer tastes and demands, and how this production took place in a knowledge-intensive district and in knowledge-intensive, often family-based, firms. The piano was, and remains, a musical instrument about which members of the public had limited information but which was loaded with social significance. It was a highly specialised good, requiring expertise by makers and retailers.

The chapter shows that, during the heyday of the piano, north London was the centre of UK production, forming a well-functioning industrial cluster. Within this cluster, where skills and knowledge in piano production were vital, family firms thrived. Piano manufacturers innovated in terms of production and design, behaving in an entrepreneurial manner. Evidence shows that they adapted to consumer demands and were able to do so given the specific way in which they organised production.

This work was inspired by, and in parts written by, Francesca. The attempt by both of us has been to illuminate an area that has been overlooked by historians, due to the problematic nature of primary source material, as well as a previous preoccupation with the manufacture of staple and capital goods and Britain's industrial decline. Just because research is problematic does not mean that we should not try to discover more. In the same vein, just because these goods were made for the home, they should not be deemed as frivolous, or gendered. It is to be hoped that research in this area will progress and that the example set by Francesca to investigate from an alternative and original viewpoint, and to illuminate the less scrutinised, will continue.

PART III

MAKING PEOPLE MATTER: EMERGING APPROACHES IN ECONOMIC HISTORY

6

Twentieth-Century British History:
Perspectives, Trajectories and
Some Thoughts on a Revised Textbook

MATTHEW HILTON

Introduction

In 2007, Francesca Carnevali and Julie-Marie Strange published *20th Century Britain: Economic, Cultural and Social Change*. A textbook for undergraduate history students, the volume was the second edition of a work first put together by Paul Johnson in 1994.[1] It is possible that were Francesca still with us, she would now be turning her attention to creating a third edition. In this chapter I want to speculate on what such an updated textbook might now look like, taking into consideration not only new directions in the field of modern British history, but also what we as teachers feel our students want to, and should, know. For reference, the table of contents of both editions appear at the end of this chapter.

In what follows I do not intend in any way to provide a definitive account of twentieth-century British historiography since 2007. The task would be enormous and the footnotes themselves would run to tens of thousands of words. Indeed, the sheer scale and specialist nature of much of what has been published is, in any case, worthy of consideration in itself. But I offer the following observations to continue a more general conversation about the current state of twentieth-century British history. This is a conversation which lies at the heart of what the University of Birmingham's Centre for Modern British Studies is trying to achieve, and this chapter emerges as much

---

1   Francesca Carnevali and Julie-Marie Strange, eds, *20th Century Britain: Economic, Cultural and Social Change* (Harlow, 2007); Paul Johnson, ed., *20th Century Britain: Economic, Social and Cultural Change* (Harlow, 1994). I am extremely grateful to Julie-Marie for her helpful comments on an earlier version of this chapter.

from my Birmingham colleagues' reflections on the subject as my own.[2] It is also one which would have been enriched by Francesca's presence, expertise and characteristically forceful interventions. Moreover, textbooks are there to be updated regularly and they have an opportunity to reflect our – and our students' – concerns in the present. There are many criteria that can be used to organise a textbook and decisions to make as to whether chapters should be arranged by period, theme or subject. But I want to add too an additional criteria that the chapters should consider ongoing issues in public debate. The traditions of economic and social history from which the two editions of the textbook emerged were very much keen to engage with the world in the present as much as the past. In order to better encourage history students I have deliberately let the choices and possibilities reflected below take into account the sort of questions they might be asking both in and beyond the academic seminar room.

Narratives and the absence of a 'big picture'

Less than two years before Francesca and Julie-Marie published their textbook, Geoff Eley had made some important observations about the state of historical research more generally. In *A Crooked Line*, he concluded generously that after all the battles associated with the culture wars, the nature of class as a category of analysis (and consequently the relationship of economic history to social and cultural history), and the challenges of postmodern theory, history had come to be practised by a new generation of scholars that was empirically rich, analytically sophisticated and attuned to the necessity of approaching a subject that drew on the economic, social, cultural and political context.[3] Historical subjects might be narrowly conceived or framed, but they were being richly executed with an eye to context, evidence and theory.

In many ways, a textbook that divides the history of a century of just one country into twenty-two digestible chunks goes against such an apparently synthetic moment. But it actually points to another issue behind Eley's optimistic intervention. That is, for all the excellent work that has been produced over the last decade or so, the study of twentieth-century British

2 See Modern British Studies (MBS), *Working Paper No. 1* (Birmingham, 2014), https://mbsbham.wordpress.com/working-papers/working-paper-no-1/, accessed 14 December 2016, plus the blog posts in response to the 'Rethinking Modern British Studies' conference held in Birmingham in July 2015: https://mbsbham.wordpress.com/rethinking-modern-british-studies-blogs-and-responses, accessed 14 December 2016.
3 Geoff Eley, *A Crooked Line From Cultural History to the History of Society* (Ann Arbor, MI, 2005).

history continues to be marked by a degree of detailed specialisation that is suggestive of both disciplinary strength and intellectual fragmentation. Textbooks such as Francesca and Julie-Marie's are therefore important mechanisms to bring together diverse literatures but two issues still stand out. First, if one were to imagine a Venn diagram of the guides to further reading that appear at the end of each chapter, one might be taken aback by the very few books that could reside at the intersection of any two sets of literature. Moreover, one might wonder if any books at all could occupy the intersection of all twenty-two chapters. This relates to a second issue as to whether twentieth-century British history lacks the sort of seminal works that might preoccupy all historians of the period. I do not wish to inflate such a concern into one about the lack of grand narratives, but I do think the field is marked by an absence of key reference points to which all historians might seek to contribute, or at least the absence is more apparent in comparison with other centuries and time periods. What it means for such a textbook is that the most difficult chapter of all to write is the introduction, for all that Eley's intervention might have given us cause to think otherwise.

Many have speculated as to what these reference points might be. Empire might be one suggestion, though it has so far served a better function for nineteenth-century historians. Social democracy and market cultures might be another, though few have sought to understand the reasons for both its rise and fall in a manner which might parallel Hobsbawm's global short twentieth century.[4] 'Decline' is another still, though as a concept it has remained resolutely within the provenance of economic historians, albeit often those such as Jim Tomlinson who are prepared to take the debate beyond the pages of the *Economic History Review*.[5] Yet despite these attempts – and others to be discussed in what follows – the field has remained marked by what an optimist might describe as pluralism and a pessimist as fragmentation. In one sense, this would actually make it easier to put together such a textbook today. But in another, the problem of the introduction remains.[6]

The New Oxford History of England series reflects many of these issues. Ross McKibbin's *Class and Cultures*, covering the period 1914–1951, was an impressive attempt to write a history of almost one half of the century that

4 See the round-table discussion in *Twentieth Century British History* in 2010, especially the essays by Susan Pedersen, 'Money, Space and Time: Reflections on Graduate Education', *Twentieth Century British History* 21 (2010), 382–96; and James Vernon, 'The Local, the Imperial and the Global: Repositioning Twentieth-Century Britain and the Brief Life of its Social Democracy', *Twentieth Century British History* 21 (2010), 404–18.

5 Jim Tomlinson, 'Thrice Denied: "Declinism" as a Recurrent Theme in British History in the Long Twentieth Century', *Twentieth Century British History* 20 (2009), 227–51.

6 Perhaps this was acknowledged by the editors. In 1994, Johnson, *20th Century Britain*, put together an eighteen-page introduction. In contrast, that by Carnevali and Strange in *20th Century Britain* in 2007 ran to just four – albeit succinct and incisive – pages.

embraced an attention to the economic, the social and the cultural. But while McKibbin is the sort of historian particularly attuned to the political dimensions of popular culture, it was remarkable that the more formal sphere of political activity had to be reserved for a second volume. Here, his *Parties and People* does not have the same ambition or scale as *Classes and Cultures* and having to wait from 1998 to 2010 hardly helped the two to be read in tandem.[7] For the post-war period, Brian Harrison has weighed in with two enormous volumes: *Seeking a Role* covers the two decades after McKibbin, and *Finding a Role* takes us to the downfall of Thatcher. They are an incredible pair of works, the detail and range extraordinary. But neither volume really draws strength from an existing literature and Harrison prefers instead to refer to a considerable, if often idiosyncratic, set of primary sources. These are volumes very much to be read with the indexes at hand. They do not offer significant reinterpretations as such, and the narrative remains conventionally shaped by events in the political sphere.[8]

In the absence of synthetic works that offer powerful new analytical frameworks and interpretations, the field – still incredibly popular to students, scholars and the wider public – has given rise to a peculiar publishing phenomenon. Well-remunerated authors are slowly working their way through the post-Second World War years, one decade – or even half-decade – at a time. Peter Hennessy appears to have ground to a halt before the excitement of the 1960s and has returned to the types of monograph with which he made his name. The enthusiasm of the others, however, is unabated. David Kynaston has the edge on Dominic Sandbrook for a focus on explanation as well as entertainment, but the relative merits of each of their series is not really the point. Rather it is that in the absence of challenging overarching frameworks being offered by those with a longer time-span in mind, the field is being carved up by a number of highly readable interventions. But these remain less concerned with uncovering the real drivers of change or with offering the type of overview that might be the subject of the introduction to a third edition of a textbook on twentieth-century Britain.

Established topics: strengths and weaknesses

All of this, of course, is not to say that there have not been some significant books and articles published since 2007 which could easily be used to update the text. In many areas the selection of chapters needs no substantial rethink. The history of sexuality, for instance, continues to thrive. But whereas an

---

7 Ross McKibbin, *Classes and Cultures: England, 1918–1951* (Oxford, 1998); Ross McKibbin, *Parties and People: England, 1914–1951* (Oxford, 2010).
8 Brian Harrison, *Seeking a Role: The United Kingdom, 1951–1970* (Oxford, 2009); Brian Harrison, *Finding a Role? The United Kingdom, 1970–1990* (Oxford, 2010).

earlier body of literature focused on what have been perceived to be deviant sexualities, important new works have explored also the meaning of sex and attitudes to sexuality within the mainstream. Stephen Brooke, for instance, uses a long history of the Labour Party and the left to examine changing lifestyles and regulations over the entire century.[9] From a different perspective, Kate Fisher and Simon Szreter have examined the meaning of sex for ordinary people, importantly uncovering an everyday sexuality that has for so long been unarticulated or else expressed only privately.[10]

The financial crisis of the last few years has ushered in a wider debate about a whole range of issues associated with economic and social justice. In 2007, chapters on poverty and social exclusion (Julie Rugg) and education and opportunity (Katherine Watson) appeared as products of well-established literatures in social history. These subjects have a renewed resonance in our present-day austere times and it is difficult to see how students would not also like to see these chapters included once more. The nature of public debate about inequality has revived an issue long the central concern of economic and social historians. Inequality is a thematic subject that lends itself to the century overviews provided at the beginning of the 2007 volume and which recent work is addressing directly.[11] Indeed, Piketty's influential yet accessible historical overview of inequality offers an interesting bridge between mainstream economics and historical studies, relaunching the hope of a deeper dialogue between the two disciplines.[12] The same might be said for Catherine Schenk's introduction to the international economy.[13] The ongoing consequences of the financial crisis, it seems, has focused public debate on the sorts of issues that have been the preoccupations of economic and social historians for many decades.

Max Jones' chapter on war and national identity was a new departure for the textbook in 2007. In this decade of anniversaries it would be difficult to argue that such a chapter ought not to be included once more. The year 2014 saw a publishing phenomenon and it is all set to continue as each anniversary of the battles of First World War is marked by a mini-publishing industry. Indeed, it is unlikely that the chapter on the war and 'its aftermath' (Jon Lawrence in 1994; Julian Greaves in 2007) could be excluded from a third edition, given the 'deluge' – to borrow a phrase – of books with titles such as 'The Aftermath' which will undoubtedly begin to appear in two to three years

9   Stephen Brooke, *Sexual Politics: Sexuality, Family Planning, and the British Left from the 1880s to the Present Day* (Oxford, 2011).
10   Simon Szreter and Kate Fisher, *Sex Before the Sexual Revolution: Intimate Life in England 1918–1963* (Cambridge, 2010).
11   Pat Thane, ed., *Unequal Britain: Equalities in Britain Since 1945* (London, 2010).
12   Thomas Piketty, *Capital in the Twenty-First Century* (Cambridge, MA, 2014).
13   Catherine Schenk, 'Britain's Changing Position in the International Economy', *20th Century Britain. Economic, Cultural and Social Change*, ed. Francesca Carnevali and Julie-Marie Strange (Harlow, 2007), pp. 58–78.

time. But what such a chapter might do today is to take stock of what the 2014 anniversary has done for the field of modern British history as a whole. How many historians have turned their attention to the subject and, more pragmatically, how much funding was disbursed by the Arts and Humanities Research Council to scholars who were prepared to link their work to anniversary-related themes?

Much of this work has been important and fascinating, but one wonders too where such energies might otherwise have been deployed. Likewise, military history has thrived during these years, both within and beyond the academy. Some of the best of this work is very good indeed, and tells us about broader questions associated with twentieth-century Britain. But much else is of a rather internalist nature and it is not at all obvious that any textbook ought to devote a chapter to it, notwithstanding the number of practitioners it has attracted.

One chapter in the 2007 edition stands out in particular for its represent-ativeness of historical trends. Stephen Brooke was commissioned to write on both class *and* gender. This would have been unthinkable a decade earlier and, indeed, Pat Thane had been commissioned to write a chapter specifically on women's history in the 1994 edition. Reflecting the flourishing of women's history up to 2007 and the turn to gender, Francesca and Julie-Marie wrote that a point had been reached within the historiography that 'the analysis of women as a separate category is not, perhaps, the most fruitful approach to under-standing the differences between the male and female experiences'. Moreover, they felt that to separate out a treatment of femininity and masculinity was still not possible since they believed critical analyses of masculinity to be 'still in their inception'.[14] This latter claim could hardly be made today, given the huge amount of work that has now appeared on masculinity, not least Julie-Marie's own recently published *Fatherhood and the British Working Class*.[15]

But it is the former claim about the importance of the category of gender that is interesting in today's climate. While the analytical significance of gender as a relational category now appears beyond dispute, it is the interest in women's history that remains strong and which might even justify a return to a chapter focused on just women. There is a revived interest in feminism among a younger generation of students that might stimulate a demand for such a chapter. Indeed, second-wave feminism itself has become the subject of research for a new generation of scholars.[16] Mixed with this too is a currently

---

14   Carnevali and Strange, *20th Century Britain*, p. 2.
15   Julie-Marie Strange, *Fatherhood and the British Working Class, 1865–1914* (Cambridge, 2015).
16   See for instance, Jeska Rees, 'A Look Back at Anger: The Women's Liberation Movement in 1978', *Women's History Review* 19 (2010), 337–56; Eve Setch, 'The Face of Metropolitan Feminism: The London Women's Liberation Workshop, 1969–1979', *Twentieth Century British History* 13 (2002), 171–90.

heightened sense of the gender inequalities within Higher Education itself. While this is far from an issue specific to the discipline of History, the Royal Historical Society's recent report on Gender Equality and Historians in UK Higher Education will focus minds on issues that women in particular have to face as well as on achievement too easily assumed to have come about.[17] Reflecting the immediate popularity of the Women's Equality Party in Britain, with 60,000 members upon its official launch in October 2015, there is a case to be made for a reinvigorated radicalism to influence a separate essay on women's history, for all that an attention to gender might permeate so many other pages of the book.

The coupling of class with gender is also questionable now. In returning to the 1994 collection it is surprising to find that there was no discrete chapter on the subject then. That it had been paired with another category in 2007 was perhaps understandable given the turn away from it over the intervening years. But as within women's history, class is back on the agenda. The twentieth-century working classes have become a popular subject of study, if not yet quite to the same extent as their nineteenth-century forebears were in previous decades.[18] Again, this is evidence of a stimulating field that attests also to how social historians have the potential to make their work resonate with broader public debate, for instance with the likes of Owen Jones' *Chavs*.[19] What the best of this new work is doing is, on the one hand, problematising traditional notions of class-based identities. Work on domestic service, for instance, destabilises the image of the male proletarian and broadens the meaning of a working-class identity.[20] On the other hand, it is this changing meaning of class identity that has come under greater scrutiny. Scholars such as Mike Savage, Jon Lawrence and Florence Sutcliffe-Braithwaite have revisited the field notes and surveys of various anthropologists and social scientists, from Mass-Observation onwards, to examine how class remained an important identifier but one in which its finer meanings, symbols and nuances changed subtly over time.[21]

17   Royal Historical Society, *Gender Equality and Historians in UK Higher Education* (London, 2015), http://royalhistsoc.org/rhs-report-gender-equality-historians-higher-education/, accessed 14 December 2016.

18   Ben Jones, *The Working Class in Mid Twentieth-Century England: Community, Identity and Social Memory* (Manchester, 2012).

19   Owen Jones, *Chavs: The Demonization of the Working Class* (London, 2012).

20   Lucy Delap, *Knowing Their Place: Domestic Service in Twentieth-Century Britain* (Oxford, 2011); Carolyn Steedman, *Labours Lost: Domestic Service and the Making of Modern England* (Cambridge, 2009).

21   Mike Savage, *Identities and Social Change in Britain Since 1940: The Politics of Method* (Oxford, 2010); Florence Sutcliffe-Braithwaite, '"Class" in the Development of British Labour Party Ideology, 1983–1997', *Archiv für Sozialgeschichte* 53 (2013), 327–62; Jon Lawrence, 'Social-Science Encounters and the Negotiation of Difference in Early 1960s England', *History Workshop Journal* 77 (2014), 215–39.

If subjects such as class and gender are experiencing a revival, it is not always clear where other specialisms are heading. The 1994 edition featured articles on sport (Tony Mason), cinema (Andrew Davies) and youth culture (John Street). In the 2007 edition Penny Tinkler took over on youth culture but sport and cinema were dropped and Julie-Marie heroically tackled a vast literature on 'leisure' on its own. This was a remarkable decision given the proliferation of subfields within the history of leisure and popular culture. But perhaps it too reflected a sense that the fields had lost their critical edge or resonance with wider debates. By 2007, long gone were discussions of, say, the 'cultures of consolation' or of the role of popular culture in the remaking of the working class. Excellent work continued – and continues – to be produced, but each specialism has generated its own internal debates.

Sports history in particular has followed a trajectory similar to military history. So while a fledgling literature in another country might, for example, connect a study of football with questions about, say, nationalism, only a very few and the very best continue to use sport as a means to explore the bigger issues in modern British history.[22] Similar questions might also be asked of specialist fields such as cinema and television studies. The *Historical Journal of Film, Radio and Television* continues to thrive but whether it does so alongside other trends within modern British history or according to its own agendas and debates is not so apparent. The omission of separate chapters on these subjects in 2007 was arguably justifiable, and could continue to be so in any third edition.

The same argument might also be made about consumption. In both volumes the subject was taken as an economic and social act by an increasingly affluent population ever more exposed to a world of goods. This is a subject that is far from exhausted. What our current experience of austerity might do, however, is focus attention on those aspects of consumer society that relate to a wider political economy. More recent work in the field has moved away from analysing how goods were purchased, used and recycled, and moved towards the peripheries of mainstream consumer society. Thus, for instance, we have learned more about purchasing as an ethical and political act or as an aspect of citizenship, more about consumption as a right, particularly in relation to utilities and public services, and more about the limits of markets, their regulation and their alternatives.[23] In the present,

22   For example, Richard Mills, 'Fighters, Footballers and Nation Builders: Wartime Football in the Serb-Held Territories of the Former Yugoslavia, 1991–1996', *Sport in Society* 16 (2013), 945–72.

23   Peter Gurney, *Wanting and Having: Popular Politics and Liberal Consumerism in England, 1830–70* (Manchester, 2015); Frank Trentmann, *Free Trade Nation: Commerce, Consumption, and Civil Society in Modern Britain* (Oxford, 2008); Lawrence Black, *Redefining British Politics: Culture, Consumerism and Participation, 1954–70* (Basingstoke, 2010); Mark Roodhouse, *Black Market Britain: 1939–1955* (Oxford, 2013).

challenges from the environment, notions of redistributive justice and issues about who has access to material culture have coloured our discussions of the affluent society, and such concerns are shaping the historical literature too.

Likewise, our present-day situation must surely inflect the chapter on religion. Such was the dominance of the secularisation thesis that it was appropriate for the 2007 edition to feature only a revised version of that which had appeared in 1994. The debate by that time had been reinvigorated by Callum Brown's provocative *The Death of Christian Britain*, but any chapter now might be less inclined to give the starring role to Christianity and its secularisation.[24] Indeed, over a longer time frame, secularisation might prove to be the exceptional moment and other faiths would need their place in such an overview. The influence of faith-based institutions beyond the immediate belief systems of their adherents has also come under greater scrutiny. The importance of faith in stimulating the voluntary sector has been crucial, as Frank Prochaska has demonstrated, while the relevance of religious interventions in questions such as poverty at home and abroad has remained as pertinent as ever.[25]

Where there is a case for a more general rethink of the chapters is on subjects such as citizenship and national identity. Citizenship was dealt with in a reasonably conventional manner: in relation to suffrage by Martin Pugh and in regard to taxation and welfare by Martin Daunton. These remain important topics but the whole issue of citizenship might be framed as a subject in its own right. The twentieth century was, by and large, a democratic century in Britain, but questions of participation go well beyond the ballot box. Inclusion and exclusion might be recast and examined in terms of voice: who speaks and who gets to be heard are aspects of citizenship that traverse the social, economic, political and cultural realms.[26] Likewise, national identity as a subject is particularly prone to the concerns of the day. In 2007, it was a subject coupled with war. Any new edition is likely, following the agenda being pursued by the early career researchers of the Four Nations History Network, to be concerned not only with devolution but with how those writing separately on either England, Ireland, Scotland and Wales can do so in conversation with one another.[27]

24 Callum Brown, *The Death of Christian Britain: Understanding Secularisation, 1800–2000* (London, 2009). For a more nuanced treatment of the same subject see Hugh McLeod, *The Religious Crisis of the 1960s* (Oxford, 2007).
25 Hilary M. Carey, *God's Empire: Religion and Colonialism in the British World, c.1801–1908* (Cambridge, 2011); Liza Filby, *God and Mrs Thatcher: The Battle for Britain's Soul* (London, 2015); Frank Prochaska, *Christianity and Social Service in Modern Britain* (Oxford, 2006).
26 These themes are explained in MBS, *Working Paper No. 1*.
27 See https://fournationshistory.wordpress.com, accessed 14 December 2016.

New directions

The real challenge of any such textbook is to identify the new chapters that might be selected to better reflect current trends in historical writing and student interests. As a book focused on 'economic, cultural and social change' (note the different order from the 'economic, social and cultural change' of the 1994 subtitle), the political realm was not tackled directly. Aspects of it – such as managing the economy (Jim Tomlinson) – were included but political history as such was beyond the remit of the book. It would be difficult to argue for its exclusion today. However inappropriate a phrase, the 'new political history' that has been attached to a whole variety of works has shown that politics does not take place in sites and institutions separated from the economic, social and cultural realms. Whether discussing the changing nature of public debate, the visual communication strategies of politics, or the discussion of politics in the media so much new work has enriched our understanding of how politics takes place in Westminster and Whitehall but also how it has expanded politics beyond these formal institutions.

There have been many influences at work here that have opened up new avenues of research. The very nature of 'governance' has been productively explored, demonstrating the extent to which 'the state' incorporates a whole host of institutions concerned with governing subjects that do not fall within a traditional understanding of the state apparatus.[28] At one level, this development is a product of the Foucauldian-inspired analyses of how everyday aspects of ordinary lives have been governed within liberal democracies, as seen in the works of Nikolas Rose, for instance.[29] But on another level, it has come through the rich and innovative empirical investigation of conventional historical subjects, be it the wartime state, the post-war consensus, the expansion of official statistics, or the development of systems of personal identification.[30] On another level still, a number of historians have taken their cue from a growing transnational historical literature that focuses on the interplay between official and unofficial forms of expertise in the development of global governance, particularly in realms such as public health, standards of living, diet and disease.[31] Much of the work referenced here could form the

28   Patrick Joyce, *The State of Freedom: A Social History of the British State Since 1800* (Cambridge, 2013).

29   Nikolas Rose and Peter Miller, *Governing the Present: Administering Economic, Social and Personal Life* (Cambridge, 2008).

30   David Edgerton, *Britain's War Machine: Weapons, Resources and Experts in the Second World War* (London, 2011); Edward Higgs, *Identifying the English: A History of Personal Identification, 1500 to the Present* (London, 2011); Glen O'Hara, *Governing Post-War Britain: The Paradoxes of Progress, 1951–1973* (London, 2012).

31   Matthew Connelly, *Fatal Misconception: The Struggle to Control World Population* (Cambridge, 2008); James Vernon, *Hunger: A Modern History* (Cambridge, 2007); Matthew

basis of new chapters in any textbook, but the whole subject of governance and its relationship to everyday life, subjectivity and citizenship would make for a very different type of thematic exploration of economic, social and cultural change.

Additionally, the types of institutions involved in a wider notion of governance might provide the focus for another chapter. Charities and the voluntary sector have long been the preoccupation of historians of the nineteenth century, especially those interested in the mixed economy of welfare and the origins of the social democratic state. But studies are emerging too of the important role played by voluntary groups in the interwar period where their role cannot be reduced to the mere auxiliaries of a more important formal political sphere.[32] And in the post-Second World War period, despite the expansion of welfare regimes, charities and the voluntary sector have continued to have a role.[33] Certainly, their welfare role altered significantly and the rise of the modern NGO in particular has blurred the boundaries existing between new social movements, pressure groups and voluntary life. In the 1994 edition Paul Byrne tackled the question of pressure groups (although Chris Wrigley did write of the trade unions in 2007, a topic curiously missing in the earlier edition). This was dropped for 2007, but there is a case now for the introduction of possibly two new chapters: one focusing on the continuing role of charities and the voluntary sector; the other summarising the important new work being done on new social movements, whether concerned with peace, gender, race, sexuality, the environment and human rights and possibly their connections to older movements of the left.[34]

A complementary if rather different area of focus has been on the interior lives of individuals and the development of subjectivities within the domestic and most intimate of personal spheres. While a focus on governance has given rise to a literature that explores the institutions and ideas that seek to

Hilton, *Prosperity for All: Consumer Activism in an Era of Globalisation* (Ithaca, NY, 2009); Nick Cullather, *The Hungry World: America's Cold War Battle Against Poverty in Asia* (Cambridge, 2010).

32   Helen McCarthy, *The British People and the League of Nations: Democracy, Citizenship and Internationalism, c.1918–1945* (Manchester, 2011).

33   Kate Bradley, *Poverty, Philanthropy and the State: Charities and the Working Classes in London 1918–1979* (Manchester, 2009); Alex Mold and Virginia Berridge, *Voluntary Action and Illegal Drugs: Health and Society in Britain Since the 1960s* (London, 2010).

34   An indicative list would include Lucy Robinson, *Gay Men and the Left in Post-War Britain: How the Personal Got Political* (Manchester, 2007); Anandi Ramamurthy, *Black Star: Britain's Asian Youth Movements* (London, 2013); Christopher Moores, 'The Progressive Professionals: The National Council for Civil Liberties and the Politics of Activism in the 1960s', *Twentieth Century British History* 20 (2009), 538–60; Holger Nehring, *Politics of Security: The British and West German Protests Against Nuclear Weapons and the Early Cold War, 1945–1970* (Oxford, 2013); Daisy Payling, '"Socialist Republic of South Yorkshire": Grassroots Activism and Left-Wing Solidarity in 1980s Sheffield', *Twentieth Century British History* 25 (2014), 602–27.

categorise and understand modern subjectivity, others have focused on those subjects themselves and how they have lived their lives and understood the possibilities of their own formation. Work on the history of psychology has been particularly fruitful in this regard exploring the psychological subject as both object and agent in the creation of modern selfhood, from childhood onwards.[35] So has the history of emotions, Thomas Dixon's *Weeping Britannia* setting a standard for future work for which there is clearly a growing demand.[36]

But cultural historians in particular have sought to delve further into the notion of modern subjectivity. Of course, there is a long tradition in this vein, as in Carolyn Steedman's *Landscape for a Good Woman*, but new work on the interior lives of individuals has become a popular type of historical publishing. For historians of modern Britain, selfhood is being innovatively explored through detailed analyses of diaries, personal relationships (whether conventional or otherwise), or through biographies of those who have sought to constantly – if not consistently – reinvent themselves.[37] One other consequence of such a detailed focus on ordinary life has been a reinvigoration of the study of the domestic sphere. Family relationships, hidden secrets and bonds of emotional attachment even when geographically separated have provided compelling material for new studies of the importance of the domestic sphere to modern identity.[38] Indeed, even family history and genealogy are now being explored for their potential to unsettle narratives, chronologies and identities.[39]

The chronology offered in the 2007 textbook is conventional, however, in that Francesca and Julie-Marie divide the chapters pre- and post-1945. What is worthy of note is that they did not commission many chapters to focus on specific decades. Christopher Price wrote of the depression which inevitably privileged the 1930s as a key moment and Michael Oliver examined

---

35   Matthew Thomson, *Psychological Subjects: Identity, Culture, and Health in Twentieth-Century Britain* (Oxford, 2006); Matthew Thomson, *Lost Freedom: The Landscape of the Child and the British Post-War Settlement* (Oxford, 2013).

36   Thomas Dixon, *Weeping Britannia: Portrait of a Nation in Tears* (Oxford, 2015). See the high number of blog posts written in response to the 'Rethinking Modern British Studies' conference that deal with the history of emotions: https://mbsbham.wordpress.com/rethinking-modern-british-studies-blogs-and-responses, accessed 14 December 2016.

37   Seth Koven, *The Match Girl and the Heiress* (Princeton, NJ, 2014); Joe Moran, 'Private Lives, Public Histories: The Diary in Twentieth-Century Britain', *Journal of British Studies*, 54 (2015), 138–62; Matt Houlbrook, *Prince of Tricksters: The Incredible True Story of Netley Lucas, Gentleman Crook* (Chicago, 2016).

38   Deborah Cohen, *Family Secrets: Living with Shame from the Victorians to the Present Day* (London, 2013); Elizabeth Buettner, *Empire Families: Britons and Late Imperial India* (Oxford, 2004).

39   Tanya Evans, 'Secrets and Lies: The Radical Potential of Family History', *History Workshop Journal* 71 (2011), 49–73; Alison Light, *Common People: The History of an English Family* (London, 2014).

'the retreat of the state' which focused on the 1980s and 1990s. But no essay was commissioned to deal with the 1960s 'cultural revolution'. If the editors believed the subject to be a little well-worn, the specialisation of much of the literature might have made it a subject that could appeal, and be taught, to students. Indeed, new work continues to valorise what is still an emotionally and politically charged moment.[40] In any such textbook today further opportunities might be considered. The notion of the 'interwar', for instance, has come under challenge. Rather than existing between two more important events, the two decades have been taken as the point of focus in their own right. Here, London in particular has been made the basis for a kind of microhistory that both reflects the most accomplished writing and research in social and cultural history yet also the absence of those political agendas that drove many of its pioneers.[41]

Two decades in particular have attracted much recent interest and might warrant separate treatment. In contrast to the cultural revolution of the 1960s, the 1970s are being posited as just as revolutionary, if for global, transnational and political economic reasons. The decade is being described as an era of global shocks associated with the oil crisis, the rise of new political language associated with human rights and the global South as well as the ushering in of what Mark Mazower has described as the 'real New International Economic Order' that paved the way for the neo-liberal world order more commonly associated with the post-Uruguay Round of trade negotiations.[42] The decade has come under scrutiny by British historians keen to understand both the glam and the drab, the flourishing of radical social and political experimentalism alongside the breakdown of the post-war affluent consensus.[43] For related reasons, the 1980s have been seen as pivotal. Of course, Thatcher and Thatcherism have dominated much of the discussion. But the social and cultural significance of a more individualist economics and politics has also being explored. The question is whether the rhetorically novel Thatcher political experiment affected everyday life in quite such radically transformative ways.[44]

40 Frank Mort, *Capital Affairs: London and the Making of the Permissive Society* (New Haven, CT, 2010).
41 Judith Walkowitz, *Nights Out: Life in Cosmopolitan London* (New Haven, CT, 2012).
42 Niall Ferguson, Charles S. Maier, Erez Manela and Daniel J. Sargent, eds, *The Shock of the Global: The 1970s in Perspective* (Cambridge, 2010); Mark Mazower, *Governing the World: The History of an Idea* (London, 2012); Samuel Moyn, *The Last Utopia: Human Rights in History* (Cambridge, 2010).
43 Lawrence Black, Hugh Pemberton and Pat Thane, *Reassessing 1970s Britain* (Manchester, 2013).
44 Richard Vinen, *Thatcher's Britain: The Politics and Social Upheaval of the Thatcher Era* (London, 2009); Ben Jackson and Robert Saunders, eds, *Making Thatcher's Britain* (Cambridge, 2012).

Finally, it is without doubt that empire, race and decolonisation would now feature far more prominently in 2007. The 'imperial turn' was recognised as the most significant trend in North American-based British historical scholarship at the end of the 1990s.[45] Arguably, work now conducted from within British universities is similarly inflected. Such topics were not absent from the 2007 edition, but it is likely that any updated version would break down and expand the topics covered in Panikos Panayi's then quite conventional treatment of 'immigration, multiculturalism and racism'.[46] Imperialism as a subject has become something of relevance to the study of metropole as well as colony, a trend which has a certain irony since Catherine Hall and others have long argued the same for the nineteenth century.[47] But the acknowledgement of the all-pervasive influence of empire in the twentieth century has been most poignantly marked by the publication of the hundredth work in John McKenzie's series with Manchester University Press on 'popular imperialism'. It is a milestone which indicates which side the majority of the profession has taken in McKenzie's debate with Bernard Porter on the influence of empire at home.

Not only have recent works demonstrated the persistence of empire on the flows of ideas, individuals and institutions, but they have shown how, in a sense, British history, even after decolonisation, cannot be understood without reference to empire and cannot be examined solely from within the boundaries of an island.[48] There has been a flurry of examinations of racialised thinking and representation in all aspects of popular culture, a particular vibrant field being on film and television.[49] But the influence of multiculturalism goes beyond the representation of race. Even 'going for an Indian' has become the subject of serious scrutiny amid an appreciation of how much 'the afterlife of empire' continues to permeate everyday life.[50] Such is the depth and detail of scholarship now that Panayi himself may well wish

45 Peter Stansky *et al.*, 'NACBS Report on the State and Future of British Studies in North America (1999)', *North American Conference on British Studies* (n.l., 1999), http://www.nacbs. org/archive/nacbs-report-on-the-state-and-future-of-british-studies, accessed 15 December 2016.
46 Panikos Panayi, 'Immigration, Multiculturalism and Racism', *20th Century Britain. Economic, Cultural and Social Change*, ed. Francesca Carnevali and Julie-Marie Strange (Harlow, 2007), pp. 247–61.
47 Catherine Hall, *Civilising Subjects: Metropole and Colony in the English Imagination, 1830–1867* (Chicago, 2002).
48 Jordanna Bailkin, *The Afterlife of Empire* (Berkeley, CA, 2012); Bill Schwarz, *Memories of Empire*, vol. 1: *The White Man's World* (Oxford, 2011); Andrew Thompson, ed., *Britain's Experience of Empire in the Twentieth Century* (Oxford, 2012).
49 See, for instance, the following two works which deal with broadcasting: Gavin Schaffer, *The Vision of a Nation: Making Multiculturalism on British Television, 1960–80* (Basingstoke and New York, 2014); Simon Potter, *Broadcasting Empire: The BBC and the British World, 1922–1970* (Oxford, 2012).
50 Elizabeth Buettner, '"Going for an Indian": South Asian Restaurants and the Limits of Multiculturalism in Britain', *Journal of Modern History*, 80 (2008), 865–901.

to replace his own chapter on all aspects of immigration with one perhaps focused solely on food.[51]

One irony of the focus on empire is a kind of renewed parochialism in British history. It is as though all paths lead to the colony and Britain's relationship with Europe is overlooked (not so in the 2007 volume with an essay by Neil Rollings).[52] Yet new work is also emerging which explores other forms of global responsibility, often the product of imperial legacies, but also the consequence of rights-based activism and third-world solidarity emerging throughout Western Europe. The work appearing on humanitarianism, for instance, especially by a generation of early career researchers, is impressive for its explorations of the tensions between internationalism and imperialism and for its abilities to draw out longer continuities that straddle the traditional dividing line of 1945.[53]

Building bridges

Cases could easily be made for the inclusion of other discrete topics as well. But the greater challenge still is to provide an overall coherence to these too-often disparate subjects and themes. Significantly, the fragmentation of the field itself has become an important and frequent subject of discussion. The aim of a number of historians has been to provide the types of framework and narratives that could become the common points of debate for historians of all persuasions working on the period.

Some of these frameworks have been discussed above. Empire and the legacies of imperialism are likely to remain key points of discussion since it is unlikely there will be any let up in the range of high-quality works continuing to appear. Bill Schwarz's *The White Man's World*, for instance, is but the first part of a trilogy of the *Memories of Empire* that will demonstrate far from being a moment of rupture, decolonisation continued to have ongoing consequences for British identities, and in ways in which go beyond the obvious impact and effects of immigration. Similarly, Stuart Hall's much-anticipated memoirs will be likely to offer a rich history of the interplay of race, empire

51 Panikos Panayi, *Spicing Up Britain: The Multicultural History of British Food* (London, 2010).
52 Pedersen, 'Money, Space and Time'.
53 Emily Baughan, '"Every citizen of empire implored to Save the Children!" Empire, Internationalism and the Save the Children Fund in Inter-War Britain', *Historical Research* 86 (2013), 116–37; Anna Bocking-Welch, 'Imperial Legacies and Internationalist Discourses: British Involvement in the United Nations Freedom from Hunger Campaign, 1960–70', *Journal of Imperial and Commonwealth History* 40 (2012), 879–96; Andrew Jones, 'The Disasters Emergency Committee (DEC) and the Humanitarian Industry in Britain, 1963–85', *Twentieth Century British History*, 26 (2015), 573–601.

and identity over many decades through the life of one of Britain's key intellectuals of the twentieth century.[54]

Likewise, work inspired by the new political history or the governmentality debates will continue to produce excellent work that will demonstrate the ever shifting terrain of the political over the course of the twentieth century. It remains to be seen, though, whether such a technopolitical turn can connect the necessary focus on the changing institutional arenas of politics with the traditional questions of agency, selfhood and identity formation that have exercised the minds of social and cultural historians. Too often, it seems, the analysis of governmentality has required a focus on expertise and professionalism that is in many ways reminiscent of the 'rise of professional society' that Harold Perkin outlined as long ago as 1989.[55]

James Vernon has admirably attempted his own synthesis of British history, focusing more on the nineteenth century but with obvious implications for the twentieth. Modernity is the central theme and the complexities of governing strangers its principal characteristic. But his selection for the drivers of change are, perhaps, a little surprising. Not wanting to assign primary agency to such traditional categories as individuals, 'society' or 'the economy', he instead turns to a depersonalised set of demographic factors: population growth, urbanisation and mobility. People as individuals, rather than as abstracted masses, make a return later in the book with an optimistic – and possibly fortuitous – 'dialectical' agency, but on the whole his drivers of change might not in themselves stimulate the type of engagement about the nature of modern Britain that he has rightly called for.[56]

One fruitful avenue to explore is the contribution history can make to wider interdisciplinary discussions of the nature of neo-liberalism and its roots. These austere times have revived a debate about the economy, finance and inequality that provide an opportunity for economic history to become fully reintegrated with the other subspecialisms of modern British history and in ways which fill the explanatory gaps that arguably characterise both certain types of cultural history and the new political history. In these respects what is perhaps most remarkable about Thomas Piketty's *Capital* has nothing to do with its intrinsic merits. Rather, it is that it took an economist to use historical data to revive a public debate about the nature and causes of inequality. Surely, this is the bread and butter of our craft as professional historians? But we arguably no longer have the same lead in wider disciplinary and public debates about subjects such as class formation, social exclusion, economic justice and capitalist development in the ways that

54   Stuart Hall, *Familiar Stranger: A Life Between Two Islands*, ed. Bill Schwarz (Durham, NC, forthcoming).

55   Harold Perkin, *The Rise of Professional Society: England Since 1880* (London, 1989).

56   James Vernon, *Distant Strangers: How Britain Became Modern* (Berkeley, CA, 2014).

an earlier generation of economic and social historians did in the 1950s and 1960s. The turn to culture by social historians and the influence of postmodernism diluted the pressure to explain causal change and, alongside economic history's increasing quantification, the analytical distance between the economic and the social widened.

Piketty's intervention reminds us that inequality needs to be examined as a historical process. What the developments in modern historiography can do is show the full extent to which inequality can be experienced: socially, culturally, politically and psychologically. Piketty himself is rather weak on the causes as opposed to the manifestation of inequality, providing a challenge to economic history to articulate the nature of capitalist development in modern Britain in tandem with an attention to its consequences for actual people. The chapters that drew on issues of economic and social exclusion in the 2007 edition of *20th Century Britain* were written from a corner of the library far removed from where the chapters on the international economy were written. Piketty and the discussion around his volume at least now provides a debating space where the two might come into contact with one another.

Indeed, what the present-day politics of austerity has done is raise a spectre of neo-liberalism which all too often – particularly in political science – appears as a thing in itself that is used to explain everything – yet nothing – that is happening in the modern world. It is lazy thinking to ill-define a vague, shadowy and conspiratorial enemy. What historians can do is set out how the neo-liberal economy or the neo-liberal state or the neo-liberal world order or the neo-liberal state of mind came about, and thus challenge what it means and what can rightly be ceded to the term's explanatory power. Whether the term itself actually works as the chief descriptor of our present-day situation is not the most important matter. Rather, it is an acknowledgement that there are bigger issues out there which constantly need to be addressed.

Rather than seeing neo-liberalism as the point at which all paths meet, modern British historians might see it as the latest stage in a history of liberalism marked by other – at times more laissez-faire, at times more social democratic – characteristics. How the liberal state, market and economy have developed in modern Britain – be it through the power of economic actors, the deliberate intervention of politicians or intellectuals, or the self-perpetuating logic of the institutional infrastructure which governs and regulate the economy – are now questions that seem to resonate once more with those scholars otherwise concerned with, say, the minutiae of everyday life or the nature of modern selfhood (itself created and recreated by actors using the limited tools and resources available). The debates about neo-liberalism, for all that they might not accurately characterise our present and how we arrived at it, at least create an agenda in which the historian can see once again how both structure and agency are pertinent to their chosen specialist subject.

Such attention to the broader processes that shape modern life might also take their cue from the recent trends in transnational history. One of its chief contributions has been to examine forms of interaction around the world that are not influenced by the traditional sites of power. This is not to go so far as to argue – as an early body of globalisation theorists did – that all power has become so decentralised that networks can be shaped from any point within the metaphorical web. The new security state and the financial crisis put paid to any such anti-hierarchical ideas. But it is to recognise that the modern world is subject to flows of people, ideas, institutions and capital that do not always follow a path from London, Moscow or Washington outwards. All countries and states become nodal points in the distribution of power, some larger than others. But the consequence is that any national history must be seen as a nodal point through which transnational flows pass through. A twentieth-century British history therefore would be one with very porous boundaries.

Of course, historians of the international economy have long recognised the fact. But that their work might now be used alongside studies of the flows of people and ideas, in addition to capital and finance, might influence all the chapters of a revised textbook which recognises that British history can never be understood in isolation. Again, historians of empire have long argued for an attention to both metropole and colony, and an updated set of chapters might approach their subjects not as 'Britain and …' but as more thematic explorations of phenomena that are rightly accepted as not peculiarly British and of which Britain is only one part of a bigger story.

Finally, the economy itself would be properly acknowledged as a site of both production *and* consumption. Francesca's last project, 'Made in Britain', co-designed with Lucy Newton, offers another reminder of the interconnected nature of historical change and the importance of economic prosperity to the development of modern Britain. The creation of the affluent society, the experience of it, and the persistent inequities of access to it, must surely be a key theme of any introduction. But affluence had to be manufactured and its products sold, before it could be consumed. This attention to the materiality of modern life, how it was created and how it was used, as well as the opportunities that access to and exclusion from new objects had for the development of modern individual and communal identities, was a defining feature of twentieth-century Britain. Francesca knew that objects such as jewellery mattered – in both senses of the term – just as so many other commodities do too. Understanding how they were produced tells us about the changing nature of the organisation of the economy and who the winners and losers were in changing modes of production. But this was never in isolation from how they were sold or how the meanings of such objects might be imagined for both personhood and social relations which helped drive demand in the first place. Undoubtedly, then, the world of goods, understood as economic, social, cultural – and political – history, offers a type of analysis that connects so many aspects of modern British history.

Francesca knew that this was a type of economic history that spoke to other developments in the broader field, just as her work on other subjects had a political edge and motivation that spoke to wider agendas to which all historians could contribute. For all that scholars of twentieth-century Britain might be practising a type of history praised by Eley in 2005, their ongoing specialisation means we have not yet arrived at quite the moment of synthesis that would make it an easy task to write an introduction to any imagined third edition. But I do think the field of twentieth-century British history is operating within a space created by public debate that could allow common agendas to emerge that would see the need for both economic analysis and cultural critique, and for the two to be conducted in tandem. This might also require the addition of the 'political' to the subtitle of Francesca and Julie-Marie's book. But in doing so this would reflect not only the enriched nature of the field since 2007, but its much greater potential to set out an introductory framework attuned to certain key dominant and interconnected narratives for twentieth-century British history which also resonate with the world we live in today.

Appendix

Francesca Carnevali and Julie-Marie Strange, eds, *20th Century Britain: Economic, Cultural and Social Change* (Harlow: Pearson, 2007)

1. Introduction *Francesca Carnevali and Julie-Marie Strange*

PART ONE: THE LONG TWENTIETH CENTURY

2. The British economy   *Nicholas Crafts*
3. Modernity and modernism   *Harry Cocks*
4. Class and gender   *Stephen Brooke*
5. Britain's changing position in the international economy
    Catherine R. Schenk
6. War and national identity since 1914   *Max Jones*

PART TWO: THEMES PRE-1945

7. Suffrage and citizenship   *Martin Pugh*
8. Motoring and modernity   *Sean O'Connell*
9. The First World War and its aftermath   *Julian Greaves*
10. Depression and recovery   *Christopher Price*
11. Consumption, consumer credit and the diffusion of consumer durables
    Peter Scott
12. The role of the state: Taxation, citizenship and welfare reforms
    Martin Daunton
13. Leisure   *Julie-Marie Strange*
14. Youth   *Penny Tinkler*

PART THREE: THEMES POST-1945

15. Managing the economy, managing the people   *Jim Tomlinson*
16. Immigration, multiculturalism and racism   *Panikos Panayi*
17. The retreat of the state in the 1980s and 1990s   *Michael J. Oliver*
18. Trade unions: Rise and decline   *Chris Wrigley*
19. Sexuality   *Rebecca Jennings*
20. Poverty and social exclusion   *Julie Rugg*
21. Religion and 'secularization'   *John Wolffe*
22. Britain and Europe   *Neil Rollings*
23. Education and opportunity   *Katherine Watson*

Paul Johnson, ed., *20th Century Britain: Economic, Social and Cultural* (Harlow: Longman, 1994)

1. Introduction: Britain, 1900–1990   *Paul Johnson*

    PART ONE: 1900–1914

2. Britain in the World Economy   *Maurice Kirby*
3. Regions and Industries in Britain   *Clive H. Lee*
4. Edwardian Britain: Empire, Income and Political Discontent
    Peter Wardley
5. Poverty and Social Reforms   *E. P. Hennock*
6. The Social, Economic and Political Status of Women   *Pat Thane*
7. Sport and Recreation   *Tony Mason*
8. Nationality and Ethnicity   *David Feldman*

    PART TWO: 1914–1939

9. The First World War and its Aftermath   *Jon Lawrence*
10. The Onset of Depression   *Dudley Baines*
11. Recovery from Depression   *Dudley Baines*
12. Unemployment and the Dole in Interwar Britain   *Bernard Harris*
13. Attitudes to War   *Martin Ceadel*
14. The New Consumerism   *Sue Bowden*
15. Cinema and Broadcasting   *Andrew Davies*

    PART THREE: 1939–1990S

16. The War Economy   *Peter Howlett*
17. Austerity and Boom   *Catherine R. Schenk*
18. The 'Golden Age', 1955–1973   *Peter Howlett*
19. Crisis and Turnaround? 1973–1993   *Leslie Hannah*
20. Postwar Welfare   *Rodney Lowe*
21. Education and Social Mobility   *Michael Sanderson*
22. Women since 1945   *Pat Thane*
23. Immigration and 'Race Relations' in Postwar British Society
    Tony Kushner
24. Religion and 'Secularization'   *John Wolffe*
25. Pressure Groups and Popular Campaigns   *Paul Byrne*
26. Youth Culture   *John Street*
27. The Role of the State in Twentieth-Century Britain   *Paul Johnson*

7

From Social Capital to Social Assemblage

KENNETH LIPARTITO

Introduction

'Ha, ha! What a fool Honesty is! and Trust, his sworn brother, a very simple gentleman!' So says Autolycus in Shakespeare's *The Winter's Tale*. The devious peddler, named for a mythological trickster, has just taken advantage of some naive shepherds, and Shakespeare alerts us to the multiple and ironic meanings of trust. Derived from the Old Norse *traust*, trust has as its primary denotation confidence in a person, thing or attribute, with the related meaning of strong, as in a strong faith or bond. But placing faith in someone also brings risk, a risk of betrayal as trust is used to quietly advance self-interest. Trust as misplaced faith seems to enter the language in Shakespeare's era, a time when the English economy ran on credit. In a credit economy, trust could be a sign of failure, as in this quotation from Dr Johnson: 'my master lived on trust at an alehouse.'[1] Historians have a tendency to use trust only in its simplest and most gentlemanly or gentlewomanly form, meaning a well-placed confidence in others. But those who know trust know that it is often not to be trusted.

The positive side of trust dominates discussions in the literature on social capital. A network of affective relationships, spatial connections, shared identities and common values, social capital is often seen as encouraging trust, and thereby lubricating the wheels of industry, commerce and finance. If humans were angels, they could always trust each other and so deal at arm's length. Since they are not, they need mechanisms to either monitor and discipline bad behaviour, or encourage and cement trust. Business organisation can provide these mechanisms but, following the argument of Ronald Coase, corporations, and formal organisation more broadly, signify

---

[1] Samuel Johnson, *Idler*, no. 26, p. 8, quoted in *The Compact Edition of the Oxford English Dictionary* (Oxford, 1971), p. 432.

the failure of the market and the need to internalise transactions. Firms are thus the bastard child of our own fallen natures. Social capital, on the other hand, puts us on the road to redemption. When present in sufficient quantity, it takes us back to decentralised economic relationships among individuals or small firms, working on the basis of trust.

While many neoclassical economists look to trust and social capital as ways to bring the market back in, and push the corporation and the state back out, many business historians see trust and social capital as the allies of small firms and a more democratic organisation of production. They share the neoclassical economists' suspicion of the large, hierarchical firms, though not because they relish the utopian dream of pure and unfettered markets. Their utopia is one of decentralised, co-operative relations among business owners, workers and consumers, without the heavy hand of hierarchical management.

Given the multiple connotations of the word trust, perhaps we should step back and question both of these visions. If social capital encourages people to have confidence in each other, then it also creates the possibility of deceit and betrayal. The other side of trust is what today we might call affinity fraud. If there is no confidence, then there is no con game. I submit that we have placed too much trust in trust, and assumed that it can simply be conjured up, with the right mix of social capital, to solve transactions and co-ordination problems.

Francesca's writings engaged these issues, and in doing so traced the arc of social capital theory from the neoclassical to the new (for economic and business historians) cultural. She passed through microhistory on the way, but always sought to use the techniques of social and cultural history to understand the economics of organisation, notably trade associations. Sociability and self-interest, she concluded, could work together, though not without tension between the narrowly economic interests of actors and their deep need for inclusion in social groups and networks of peers. Cheating and dissembling, and ruinous competition, were always standing just outside the door of the trade association. Inside, actors found ways to bring parties together and stave off these destructive forces. The ways of association were simultaneously material, social and cultural. Nothing about the process was inevitable, all was contingent and, not surprisingly, what might be successful at one moment could fall apart at another. Her history of social capital was complex, compared with the simplicity of neoclassical theory. But then as she herself said, why make things simple when they can be complicated?[2] And as we shall see, embracing complexity and tension adds value to our understanding.

2   The exact quote from Jacques Revel is 'Why make things simple when one can make them complicated?': Francesca Carnevali, 'Social Capital and Trade Associations in America, c.1860–1914: A Microhistory Approach', *Economic History Review* 64 (2011), 905–28 (p. 905).

The critique

Trust and social capital are part of a wider literature that engages the role of social and cultural institutions in the economy. This literature takes a variety of forms. Mark Granovetter's identification of the embeddedness of economic action shows that we cannot assume markets operate of their own accord, by a purely internal logic removed from other social relations. Instead, markets depend on the social context of the actor. Douglass North's multiple works on institutions make the case that economic outcomes depend on the basic institutional matrix of a society, including its cultural values. Avner Greif has demonstrated how religious and ethnic ties can provide for trust, sanction and control of cheating in the absence of formal state and legal mechanisms. Robert Putnam has differentiated between the productive places that have abundant social capital to encourage exchange and co-operation, and failed societies that are poor in it.[3]

Despite differences, all of these works at base posit a strong, clear relationship between the social (including in some cases the cultural) and the economic. At their best, they connect the one to the other without either economic or social reductionism. Actors can pursue their self-interest, but not every social goal, value, or interaction is simply self-interest by another name.[4] In this way they acknowledge that individuals are born into and live through a social reality and cultural matrix they themselves do not create. But they do not so over-socialise people as to negate their ability to act with

---

3 Mark Granovetter, 'Economic Action and Social Structure: The Problem of Embeddedness', *American Journal of Sociology* 91 (1985), 481–510; Douglass C. North, John Joseph Wallis and Barry R. Weingast, *A Conceptual Framework for Interpreting Recorded Human History*, NBER Working Paper 12795 (Cambridge, MA, 2006), p. 20. North developed his position in a number of works, including 'Institutions, Ideology, and Economic Performance', *Cato Journal* 11 (1992), 477–88; 'Institutions', *Journal of Economic Perspectives*, 5 (1991), 97–112; 'Institutions and Economic Theory', *American Economist* 36 (1992), 3–6; *Understanding the Process of Economic Change* (Princeton, NJ, 2010); *Institutions, Institutional Change and Economic Performance* (New York, 1990). Douglass C. North, John Wallis and Barry Weingast, *Violence and Social Orders: Conceptual Frameworks for Interpreting Recorded Human History* (Cambridge, 2009); Avner Greif, *Institutions and the Path to the Modern Economy: Lessons from Medieval Trade* (Cambridge, 2006); Robert Putnam, *Bowling Alone: The Collapse and Revival of American Community* (New York, 2000); Robert Putnam, Robert Leonardi and Raffaella Y. Nonetti, *Making Democracy Work: Civic Traditions in Modern Italy* (Princeton, NJ, 1994).

4   This is a criticism that can be made of neo-institutionalists such as Douglass North, who see institutions as arising endogenously from the logic of self-interest: see Martin Daunton, 'Rationality and Institutions: Reflections on Douglass North', *Structural Change and Economic Dynamics*, 21 (2010), 147–56; Francesco Boldizzoni, *The Poverty of Clio: Resurrecting Economic History* (Princeton, NJ, 2011). A less reductive approach to institutions is found in Daron Acemoglu and James Robinson, *Why Nations Fail: The Origins of Power, Prosperity and Poverty* (New York, 2012).

self-interest. Both the social and the economic have their place, but neither dominates the relationship. Rational action does not take place in a vacuum; it depends on a variety of social conditions and resources to move forward, resources such as trust or networks of relationships that reduce search and transactions costs.

This balanced model of social and economic relationships has largely prevailed in the literature on trust and social capital. But it relies on a number of strong assumptions. It takes social relations as pre-existing, non-economic features or conditions that in one way or another impinge on economic behaviour and outcomes. It also tries to measure and assess this social landscape to see how it promotes (or inhibits) economic activity, assuming that the relationships between the social and economic are stable. The overall thrust of the literature is that some social contexts, some social resources, are better able to promote economic activity, better in the sense of enhancing growth, productivity, efficiency and innovation. As the name implies, social capital is taken as a factor of production and, as such, it can be measured for its contribution to economic outcomes.

If we take such claims seriously, then we are saying that the social landscape is a realm of human interaction separate from the economy, one with its own rules and meanings. If this were not the case, then theories of social capital would add little value to standard economic models based on individual self-interest, returning us once again to those earlier formulations of purely rational institutions, or to economic reductionism. So social capital is a form of capital, exerting control over resources, as when friendships or family provide the entrée to jobs or allow favoured access to credit. But it is also distinct from these other economic resources, following its own rules of operation, and coming into being by its own processes.[5]

What is it, though, that connects the distinctly social (and cultural) realm to the distinctly economic realm, if one cannot be assimilated into, or made endogenous to the other? Here is where trust serves as a crucial linchpin. Trust can be equally a matter of social and affective relationships and economic ones, a player in both spaces. At the individual level, trust enters to reduce the costs of exchange and promote growth, by making it easier for parties to co-operate, learn, and share ideas and practices.[6] At the macrosocial level it permits collective action by overcoming free-rider problems and encouraging

---

5   Dario Gaggio, 'Do Historians Need Social Capital?', *Social History* 29 (2004), 499–513; Pierre Bourdieu, 'The Forms of Capital', *Handbook of Theory and Research in the Sociology of Education*, ed. John G. Richardson (New York, 1986), pp. 241–58. Bourdieu's definition is much different from that of Robert Putnam. For Putnam, social capital is a pre-existing arrangement of society that encourages and supports certain types of behaviour.
6   The trust effect has to be separated out from standard human capital theory, whereby education or other attainments mean higher skills and greater productivity. But this distinction is precisely what was intended by the term social capital.

broad civic participation on issues of common concern. But trust, let's recall, is also a fickle friend. It may facilitate fraud, the sort of affinity fraud that comes from people who think they know and can trust a familiar face. From Autolycus to Bernie Madoff, rogues have used trust to separate fools from their money. Seen this way, trust is hardly the redemptive magic that makes transactions costs disappear. Nor does it suggest an alternative to the ruthless market – the optimistic view implied in the more utopian discussions of social capital. One might argue that invoking trust only pushes the question back a step. How do people sort out real trust from trust that is merely a lure to reel in the gullible?

In the face of these complications, some economists have grown distrustful of trust.[7] As Timothy Guinnane argues, trust is an unnecessary concept, one that, following the principles of Occam's Razor, should be excised from theory. What we call social capital is merely a very good system of monitoring and evaluating actors, and exchanging the needed information to catch out bad behaviour. What we call trust is simply the successful outcome of this process.[8] This stripped-down view, however, leaves open the question of how such well-functioning mechanisms can be developed, since they are not imposed from above by a sovereign power, but grow organically out of human interactions. We might think of trust as operating in the context of newness and uncertainty, providing the basis by which people interact to gradually create information-monitoring systems. Where we initially lack such mechanisms, we depend on trust; a hazardous reliance to be sure, but better than nothing. Those on the outside of trust networks face uncertainty and unknowns and, yes, exclusion and disadvantages, compared with the insiders. Surveillance and sanction are not the opposite of, or alternative to, trust, but the mechanisms that build on it.

Whether we speak of bonds of trust or an information-monitoring system, we still have to ask, how do these arrangements come into being, and what makes them work? The interactions cannot be purely instrumental, for then they would merely be another form of economic rationality. This would reduce social institutions to their functional contributions to the self-interested logic

---

7 For a sceptical view of social institutions, see Sheilagh Ogilvie, *Institutions and European Trade: Merchant Guilds, 1000–1800* (Cambridge, 2011). She rightly points out that institutions often exert power in the economy. Some people are kept out, denied an opportunity to participate in exchange. Embeddedness can easily come to mean favouring insiders at the expense of outsiders, monopolising markets, fixing prices, reducing completion, and merging the state and business into a form of crony capitalism. All this is true of course of the 'dark side' of social capital, but Ogilvie assumes that some sort of pure, disembedded market would be possible.

8 Timothy Guinnane, *Trust: A Concept Too Many*, Economic Growth Center Discussion Paper 907 (New Haven, CT, 2005), notes that one does not really need cultural concepts such as trust if there is a clear information and enforcement system in operation.

of economic action.[9] The argument that social institutions matter, however, is predicated on the idea that they constitute a separate realm of action, a part of human experience that complements the economic but cannot be reduced to it. Invoking social institutions should add value to what we already know about economic behaviour and not be reduced to economic behaviour by another name.

To preserve the autonomy of the social, it is common to claim that ethnicity, religion and family are by their very nature trust-inducing. Families, for example, can serve as platforms for extensive economic engagements because they are believed to be cohesive bodies defined by relations of trust, affection and affinity. Yet immediately the thoughtful historian detects an untested supposition. Ethnic groups and families are treated as primordial, presumably operating in the same fashion regardless of time or place.[10] Only someone who has very limited experience with family life could assume that families always naturally operate to inculcate trust and reduce conflict.

Avner Greif, for example, has argued that religious and ethnic ties in early modern societies instilled trust and enforced rules against cheats and frauds in economic exchange at a time when markets were weak and states unable to regulate transactions.[11] Greif is implicitly identifying a micro-causal mechanism that works on individual interests and behaviour. He simply takes for granted that co-religionists or members of the same ethnic group will trust each other, presumably because they are connected by some set of social or religious bonds that cannot be violated by way of self-interested behaviour. But treating social institutions as primordial leaves them with no history, offers no scope for human agency, no possibility of conflicts and contests over meanings or resources. As Francesca Trivellato notes, rather than 'assum[ing] that blood ties and putative likeness ... forged bonds of trust that gave trading diasporas significant competitive advantages', relations are established over time, both within and across religious and ethnic groups.[12]

Institutions and culture thus are not preset frameworks that encourage

---

9   The danger of the latter is that we end up simply assuming the right sort of connections and organisations will naturally arise out of the individual self-interest of members. See Daunton, 'Rationality and Institutions'; Ben Fine, *New and Improved: Economics' Contribution to Business History*, SOAS Department of Economics Working Paper 93 (London, n.d.).

10   Fine, *New and Improved*, p. 8. North agrees that markets are embedded, but he sees this framework as operating to make (or prevent) free markets, an ideal and universal type: North *et al.*, *A Conceptual Framework*, p. 37.

11   Greif, *Institutions and the Path to the Modern Economy*. Rationality itself is often unexamined. It is possible for self-interested behaviour to generate self-reinforcing beliefs that may not be rational in the sense of testable in the real world.

12   Francesca Trivellato, *The Familiarity of Strangers: The Sephardic Diaspora, Livorno, and Cross-Cultural Trade in the Early Modern Period* (New Haven, CT, 2009), pp. 3–4. For a similar approach see also Ghislaine Lydon, *On Trans-Saharan Trails: Islamic Law, Trade Networks, and Cross-Cultural Exchange in Nineteenth-Century Western Africa* (Cambridge, 2009), pp. 349–52.

efficient exchange. Markets, social institutions and culture are interwoven in ways that vary significantly depending on the particular history and experience of a people.[13] The same social arrangements that might seem to facilitate economic exchange in one context, may work against it in another. Predictions about the links between particular institutional forms and particular economic outcomes are often weak and inconsistent, evidence that ties of blood, family, religion and familiarity are not unproblematic or primordial.[14] Sometimes religious ties or cultural affinities encourage exchange, sometimes they do not. It is a problem that goes back at least as far as Weber's claims about the relationship between Protestantism and capitalism, claims that seemed to hold up until Asian and Catholic cultures produced equally good capitalists.

The alternative

I would like to suggest a different way to understand the relationship between the economic and the social. Rather than embedding the first into the second, we can treat them both as parts of a larger socio-economic assemblage. The term assemblage derives from the writings of philosophers Gilles Deleuze and Félix Guattari. It is very close, perhaps for all practical purposes the same, as the concept of an actor network developed by Bruno Latour.[15] Both invite us into a new social ontology. Rather than starting with pre-existing categories and divisions, between the economic and social, between humans and nature, between objective and subjective realities, they instead ask us to examine all the possible 'actants', to use Latour's term, that make up the social (and economic) world. People, institutions, economic exchanges, products, nature, art, technology, language, symbols, expressions all come into play. The social and economic world is constructed of many parts brought together in contingent ways, brought together and maintained by constant work and labour on the part of multiple actors, who must continually contend against other actors to hold their place. The important thing to remember is that the actors are not only human beings and that the actions, or effects, are not either material or expressive, but frequently both.

---

13 Claude Markovits, *The Global World of Indian Merchants, 1750–1947* (Cambridge, 2000).
14 One way to explain this variation is by an evolutionary approach. A particular mixture of social relations, politics, culture and economic incentives could set up either an efficient, growth-producing future path, or an inefficient, rent-seeking one. Once a society starts down a particular institutional path, the effects are self-reinforcing, negating the efficacy of rational individual behaviour. The evolutionary approach thus takes into account time, but it does so in an extremely limited way – usually the key inflection point at the beginning that sets places on their particular path.
15 Graham Harman, *Prince of Networks: Bruno Latour and Metaphysics* (Melbourne, 2009).

Thus there is no need to reduce a social institution to its economic functions, but also no need to rely on mediating concepts such as trust to explain how the social or cultural link to economic matters. Assemblages invariably connect material objects and expressive or symbolic processes. Indeed, material objects may operate 'materially' – oil in the ground as a monetarily significant resource – or may play a largely expressive role – oil as the symbol of the national patrimony. Expressive components can be based in material things but symbols can also mobilise and organise material resources in ways that have real consequences.[16] To give one present-day example, the German government's repression of any hint of inflation is as much a symbolic as a material act. It cannot be understood without considering the symbolic resonances carried over from the great German inflation of the 1920s.

The key features of an assemblage are first, that the distinctive parts – markets, technologies, human beings, communities, organisations – come together in distinctive ways, though they retain their separate existence.[17] There are no 'essential' parts or compositions, meaning that we do not proceed by building up larger structures from more fundamental ones – markets from individual self-interest, individual self-interest from non-reducible human nature. Nothing can be reduced to anything else or explained as a surface manifestation of an underlying reality. The markets, or rather each market, is a thing itself, a distinctive assemblage, whose parts can be examined and interactions studied. Those parts may well include self-interested beings (perfectly possible objects), but equally important and no less fundamental are cultural expressions, social relationships, technologies, political and legal structures. What matters is how these ontologically distinct objects assemble and interact to create new things – in this case a particular market in a particular place in time. Assemblages thus work rigorously against gener- alisations – the market, the state. Nothing is subsumed into a whole, and different parts can fall away or be broken off and moved elsewhere.[18] This is

16 Gilles Deleuze and Félix Guattari, *A Thousand Plateaus: Capitalism and Schizophrenia* (London, 1988) – their ideas are scattered throughout this distinctly non-linear book. More useful renditions of the assemblage idea and related concepts are found in Manuel DeLanda, *A New Philosophy of Society: Assemblage Theory and Social Complexity* (London, 2006); Bruno Latour, *Reassembling the Social: An Introduction to Actor-Network-Theory* (Oxford, 2005); Paul Leonardi, 'Theoretical Foundations for the Study of Sociomateriality', *Information and Organization* 23 (2013), 59–76; Frank Trentmann, 'Materiality in the Future of History', *Journal of British Studies* 48 (2009), 283–307.

17 Some of these parts, such as community or organisation, may themselves be seen as smaller assemblages, and any assemblage may itself be a part of a larger one – cities within nations, nations within transnational systems.

18 In Deleuze and Guattari's language, the distinction is between relations of interiority among the parts and relations of exteriority. In the former, we conceptualise organisms, or functional institutions, whereby the individual parts are defined by how they fit into the whole organism. The definition of the part, in other words, is in part its function. In the latter, as with

one reason that institutions or cultural configurations might work perfectly well to promote exchange or encourage economic interaction in one context while in another they may not. Much depends on the particular configuration of the parts and their interactions.

Assemblages thus preserve one feature that concepts such as social capital, embeddedness and trust seek to convey – how collectivities can have consequences beyond the sum of their parts. But they dispense with the belief that these relationships are stable and measurable. Instead, they are emergent. Emergence implies a more radical unpredictability from the separate elements. We cannot say that every time self-interest plus ethnic group affiliation come together we will see a system of exchange that disciplines adverse behaviour and controls fraud – as though there was something essential in that coming together that made for a new synthesis. We may see the emergence of such a pattern depending on how the various parts are interacting, but the continual labour that is required to maintain the network of interaction may also fail, break down, become exposed to contending forces and actors. So, contrary to microeconomics analysis, there is such a thing as society. But contrary to macrosocial analysis, societies are not functional organisms. The individual parts retain their identities and potential for detaching themselves to move elsewhere. This contingency makes assemblages ripe for historical treatment, particularly microhistorical treatment. To understand assemblages and what they are doing depends heavily on genealogy, on peeling back the layers of interactions to show how the parts came together in a particular place and time, what keeps them working together, or what causes them to fall apart.

The Providence jewellers

I suggest that we can understand Francesca's work on the Providence jewellers through assemblage theory.[19] She argues that the jewellery makers in that city formed an organisation, the New England Manufacturing Jewelers and Silversmiths' Association, to provide collective solutions to a variety of industry problems: unruly labour, unscrupulous design copying, ruinous price competition, risky lending, and disruptive bankruptcies that dumped inventory on to the market at low prices. The Association had few formal powers. Trade association contracts and agreements were not enforceable in American law,

---

assemblages, the parts are perfectly well defined outside of the assemblage, but they interact and contribute to emergent results when they come together. The paradigmatic example is horse, rider, spear. Each exists independently of the other and can be deployed for other purposes. But bring them together and you have a formidable weapon. By contrast, the organic metaphor treats parts like the limbs of a body. Cut off an arm and is it an arm any more?

19   Carnevali, 'Social Capital and Trade Associations'.

and in fact could be signs of anti-trust violations. Enforcement thus depended on sharing information and taking collective action, notably by members who agreed to shun and deny important social and business contacts to those who violated the rules of fair trade. For a long time, these arrangements worked, though eventually they gave way, resulting in the classic pattern of larger, more integrated firms replacing smaller, specialised producers. Thinking in terms of assemblages can help us understand this story.

The Association had two principal components. One was its economic or material side, which included mechanisms for monitoring the industry and disciplining recalcitrant actors. But just as important was its social and cultural side. The Association constituted a 'fabric of social interaction and networks' which included systems of 'beliefs, of values and representations'.[20] It thus acted on members' economic behaviour, but also shaped their perceptions and understandings of markets, competition and labour. Indeed, it acted on their conception of their selves.

Standard theories of economic embeddedness or social capital are inadequate to account for these features and effects of the Association. The jewellers of Providence were not some primordial group with homogenous social and cultural features that were ready to serve economic functions. In fact, they seem to have been ethnically and religiously diverse. The Association was open to immigrant and Jewish as well as native and Christian members, and these members did not share a set of pre-existing community, family or social connections. Jewellery manufacturing was also a highly competitive business with quick entry and exit, so jewellery makers' individual short-term interests frequently ran against the public and collective interests of the trade. Finally, the Association was created deliberately, suggesting it was a rational rather than affective entity. Yet it originated not for functional reasons, as neo-institutional economics would tell us. It began as a social organisation, one that over time inculcated emotional and personal ties among its members. There was agency behind its history, but not the sort of agency reducible to rational self-interest. In fact, the Association was economically effective only because it was socially affective. The social and culture, indeed leisure-time, activities were precedent to the Association's material and economic functions, which became viable only because of social and cultural ties. At the same time, its social existence was meaningful because it connected to its economic purpose. The social and the economic features of the Association, one might say, shaped each other, and together did the work necessary to sustain the organisation and direct economic outcomes.

Rather than inculcating trust, the Association cracked the social network like a whip. Free-riders and cheaters who engaged in undesirable business

---

20   Carnevali, 'Social Capital and Trade Associations', p. 906.

practices were shunned by other members. They faced a loss of business and, perhaps more importantly, membership in social and community activities that yielded other business opportunities. This may seem like perfectly rational behaviour for an organisation bent on controlling competition, but it did not arise spontaneously. It depended crucially on how individuals understood their interests.

Looked at from a purely individual point of view, a jeweller had little incentive to punish those who violated the standards of practice set by the Association. Indeed, one of the problems that the organised jewellers were seeking to address was competitive behaviour – how to get members of the trade to 'act collectively ... in a macro-institutional environment that gave them an immediate incentive to behave individually'.[21] Disciplinary behaviour benefited the collective more than it did the individual who performed it, making it unlikely that individuals who were 'competing ceaselessly against each other' would undertake a collectively beneficial act for purely rational reasons.[22] As is often the case with cartels, the incentives of the members were to pursue individual interest rather than group interest, to cheat and to free-ride. Yet for a time the Association overcame such problems, with members acting on collective rather than individual interest.

Here is where the second part, the expressive part, of the assemblage came into play. The Association had strong cultural and symbolic features – meetings, dinners, songs, picnics, parades, rituals and emblems of membership. Social relationships derived in part from these expressive activities, the so-called 'trifles' of everyday life that were actually important 'actants' in the assemblage. They had force and agency precisely because they were *not* reducible to economics by another name. They did not conjure up trust to overcome self-interest and mitigate uncertainty. Instead, they shaped identities, giving members of the jewellery trade a new sense of who they were and what their interests consisted of. Rather than see expression and ritual as reflections of community, we can say that they were makers of community by the way they operated on the values of the members. This is a much more Bourdieusian view of social capital – as a part of one's identity and status. And it is also a social capital connected to power, in that these cultural resources would be put together with material ones to keep actors in line. Sanction had bite only because members of the Association placed value in membership and faced loss of status and identity if they were banned. Surveillance of behaviour was only possible because individual members watched the behaviour of other members of the trade with an eye towards the collective interest.

Assemblages are not a synthesis of parts, so self-interest among jewellers did not dissolve into communal goodwill. Likewise rituals and cultural forms

21 Carnevali, 'Social Capital and Trade Associations', p. 923.
22 Carnevali, 'Social Capital and Trade Associations', p. 910.

were not merely functional appendages to market relations. Self-interest and social relationships remained ontologically separate, but when they interacted they did so in ways that brought forth new qualities and led to emergent outcomes. Only because of the social relationships and social rituals did individual members come to think in terms of the collective interests of the trade, rather than their own particular competitive positions. Had those rituals really been simply trifles, covering up raw self-interest, they would not have had the power to shape consciousness so as to build group identity and group interest in ways that let sanction and surveillance operate. And likewise, the material penalties imposed by the Association mattered only because the social life mattered. Only because members had come to see each other as partners in trade, only because their social contacts were their business contacts and only because they derived status and position from being members in good standing (which status brought still more material opportunities) was it possible to make the penalties against cheaters and free-riders count. Indeed, it became much easier for the jewellers to store information and carry out enforcement once members shared a common identity. All that was required was the word of any one Association member, it did not matter who, and the full force of the group would be brought to bear against the miscreant.

The mistake would be to try to parse this process as either a simple enforcement mechanism determined by self-interest, on the one hand, or as a cultural ritual that overcame self-interest, on the other. The power of the assemblage was instead its harnessing of collective ritual and self-interest to redefine what proper interest was, and how one accordingly should act. Monitoring and enforcement were simply common-sense behaviour, doxa, once this identity emerged. To put it another way, once a family or ethnic group is defined by its patterns of trade, exchange, or economic activity, it makes perfect sense that members will behave in ways that support and extend those economic interests, since doing so also supports or extends the family. But there is no innate, necessary connection among the members that has to continue forever. Family fortunes, created by the economic value of family ties, can also dissipate as families fall into discord. Where we should look for explanations is not at the family or its economic activities, but at the way the two link.

Likewise, the rituals and cultural expressions of the Association were distinct from economic self-interest but at the same time they mobilised resources and directed economic behaviours. They were the reason that members were willing to act against those who violated group norms. The economic benefits that members received reinforced their commitment to the group. Self-interest not inflected by cultural meanings and performances would never have allowed for collective behaviour. But collective rituals and expressions of values not bound by self-interest would have been hollow and ineffective. Without both of these separate and distinct objects coming together, collective action would not have been possible. Indeed, the very distinctiveness and separation of the cultural from the material and economic domains of the Association were what made them so powerful when brought together.

While the Association formed an assemblage of interacting parts, it was not detached from other contexts. Assemblages are themselves embedded in still larger entities and environments. In this case, the connections that mattered were political, the politics of labour. The Providence jewellers acted collectively against unions by relying on deeply held, shared values about employer autonomy. This anti-union sentiment was widespread in early-twentieth-century America, but it cannot be explained by resort to generalisations – that US culture was simply 'anti-union'. Anti-unionism was as much a cause of employer organisation as a consequence. Quashing labour helped the jewellers express their identity, providing a rallying point for 'a collective political voice [to] shape the public sphere'.[23] The articulation of local organisational issues with national and even global political issues is part of the way that associative bonds are formed, as Dario Gaggio has shown.[24]

Why then did the New England Manufacturing Jewelers and Silversmiths' Association ultimately fail? This is where thinking in terms of an assemblage is much more powerful than thinking in terms of social capital or embeddedness. Assemblages are not transcendent totalities, and their history is not teleological. They do not have one, immanent, temporally revealed end point. Having created a system for collective action, the Association did not transform or transcend all other interests. The assemblage worked only as long as the parts interacted, against other contrary forces. Continual interactions among the members, their dinners, their social engagements, brought them together in a way that redefined their understanding of self-interest. They created a type of communal existence, one that neither depended on some long-standing prior set of social relationships, nor one that existed outside of the continual rubbing together in social life that the Association cultivated. We should expect, over time, that under new circumstances external factors may well wear down the parts and bring the interactions to a halt. The reasons may be entirely contingent.

The strength of writing the history this way is that it avoids essentialising culture – starting, for example, with the assumption that in American society, collective behaviour must be weak because law, values and social structure militated against trust and undercut the social capital needed for industrial co-operation. Likewise, the surprising success of association in the American

---

23   Carnevali, 'Social Capital and Trade Associations', p. 906.
24   Dario Gaggio, *In Gold We Trust: Social Capital and Economic Change in the Italian Jewelry Towns* (Princeton, NJ, 2007).

context throws light back on the history of jewellery manufacturing in Birmingham, England. There, the conventional wisdom holds, politics, the law and culture were favourable to industrial districts and collective actions. However, as Francesca showed us in her earlier study of jewellery making in Birmingham, collective action and collective identity there was no more natural, no less consciously created, than in supposedly laissez-faire America.[25] Associations in both places were actually local assemblages, traceable to the agency of humans and non-human elements that kept them together by continual effort and force.

The implications

We began with trust and we end with the conclusion that trust does not offer much help in understanding how agents undertake collective economic action. Trust is often invoked to explain how actors overcome the limitations imposed by imperfect information, opportunism and risk. But portmanteau concepts such as trust require us to suppress what Shakespeare told us long ago about the human capacity for deception and misrepresentation and about how the cunning exploit the gullible. Trust only begs the question: how do we know whom we can trust?

Social capital seeks to answer this question by identifying trust-enhancing social networks and institutions. Yet where, in one case, ties of affinity may work to encourage economic exchange, in another they may not. In one case, associations, networks and dense social interactions produce good behaviour; in other cases they promote closed cliques, organised crime and affinity fraud. For a time, it seems, the Providence jewellers trusted each other; yet rather than their long and continual social and economic interaction strengthening trust, it all broke down. Even as membership grew and the Association exerted more control over the trade, members still pursued their self-interest, cheated and cut corners, withheld full information, and acted against accepted norms and rules. Trust, in short, is no magical force to overcome self-interest. Instead, the way people behave – with solidarity, or against it – emerges from material and symbolic elements acting and interacting in an assemblage.

One of the most important legacies of Francesca's work on industrial districts is a strong case against teleology in economic history. Rather than starting from the end point – the eventual breakdown of the Providence district – and working backward to an explanation, she recognised that all economic structures are really temporal processes caught by the historians

---

25   Francesca Carnevali, '"Crooks, Thieves, and Receivers": Transaction Costs in Nineteenth-Century Industrial Birmingham', *Economic History Review* 57 (2004), 533–50.

in a frozen moment. That connections fray or behaviours are unstable is simply a reflection of the universal truth understood by all historians – time is the lever that moves all things. Efforts to find stable, enduring relationships between social structures or cultural systems and economic outcomes forget this fundamental lesson about process and time. Assemblages recall us to it by denying the positivist model of causality predicated on organic or functional relationships. Among the Providence jewellers, practices and rituals took place again and again, year in and year out. It was this interaction that made the Association more than merely a collection of cultural artefacts on the one hand, and material interests on the other. Seen as a collection, we would usually confine the first to the realm of cultural history and the second to economic history. Seen as an assemblage, we realise that it is the interaction of these disparate economic and cultural parts that made the Providence organisation effective, even against the conditions that should have stopped it from existing at all.

[Exit, pursued by a bear.]

8

Economic History and Microhistory

CHRIS WICKHAM

Introduction

Microhistory was perhaps the most significant original contribution by Italian historians to historiography since the Second World War. The main microhistorical texts were written between c.1975 and c.1995, with a particularly intense period of activity in the years around 1980. Many of its practitioners carried on writing in much the same vein afterwards, and many still do, but they now see this period as belonging in the (their) past; although the key principles of microhistory still seem fresh to me, it was their movement, so I guess they are right.

This chapter provides some reflections on microhistory, on its past as well as its (possible) future, with specific emphasis on the use of microhistory as a form of economic history. The chapter is divided in the following sections: first, an account of the origins and development of this microhistory is sketched, followed by an analysis of its aims and approach and of its limitations. The chapter continues with a study of the application of microhistory to economic history and concludes with some thoughts on possible future directions, including the use of microhistory to analyse the nature and logic of medieval economic organisation.

Origins and development

The intellectual focus of the movement was the Italian historical journal *Quaderni storici*, which published a number of explicitly microhistorical monographic issues between 1976 and 1987. As a whole, it was the work of a collectivity of left-wing historians, twenty or thirty in number, mostly early modernists, led – insofar as there were leaders – by Edoardo Grendi, Carlo Ginzburg and Giovanni Levi. The movement broadened out from *Quaderni storici* when the publishing house Einaudi (based in Turin, like many of the leading microhistorians) founded a monograph series called *Microstorie*, edited by Ginzburg and Levi and Simona Cerutti, which published longer microhistorical works, many of which became historical classics; this, too, ran until the mid-1990s. Microhistory was a highly self-conscious movement, and its activists wrote several accounts of it, including the first three historians mentioned above; of others, I would single out commentaries by Jacques Revel, and the recent backwards look by Osvaldo Raggio, another of the main participants.[1] From these self-analyses, the interested reader can reconstruct the main lines of the movement, although, unsurprisingly, the most significant demonstrations of its importance for historical understanding lie in the major empirical analyses which the microhistorians produced, such as Ginzburg's *Il formaggio e i vermi*, Levi's *L'eredità immateriale*, Raggio's *Faide e parentele. Lo stato genovese visto dalla Fontanabuona*, or Angelo Torre's *Il consumo di devozioni*.[2]

Microhistory: aims and approach

What actually was microhistory, though? That history writing very frequently – normally – operates on a very small scale, with great attention to detail and to narrative, is too obvious to discuss. But what the microhistorians tried to do, in their different and overlapping ways, was to *theorise* the small scale. In doing so, they opposed not simply traditional political history, but also, and perhaps above all, the grand and huge social-history syntheses, based increasingly on serial analyses, of the *Annales* school of the 1950s to 1970s. They advocated bottom-up approaches as opposed to top-down ones. They looked to anthropology for guides to how to create total analyses of small-scale societies, becoming, for example, among the first historians to use Clifford Geertz's 'thick description' as a guide to historical reconstruction. They

---

1   For example, Carlo Ginzburg, 'Microstoria: due o tre cose che so di lei', *Quaderni storici* 86 (1994), 511–39, translated as 'Microhistory: Two or Three Things That I Know About It', *Critical Inquiry*, 20 (1993), 10–35; Edoardo Grendi, 'Ripensare la microstoria?', *Quaderni storici* 86 (1994), 540–60; Jacques Revel, 'Microanalisi e costruzione del sociale', *Quaderni storici* 86 (1994), 561–75; Giovanni Levi, 'On Microhistory', *New Perspectives on Historical Writing*, ed. Peter Burke (Cambridge, 1991), 93–113; Osvaldo Raggio, 'Microstorie e microstorie', *Enciclopedia Treccani* (Rome, 2013), http://www.treccani.it/enciclopedia/microstoria-e-microstorie_%28altro%29/, accessed 15 December 2016; all of these cite other characterisations, by members of the movement and sympathetic observers.
2   Carlo Ginzburg, *Il formaggio e i vermi* (Turin, 1976), translated as *The Cheese and the Worms* (London, 1980); Giovanni Levi, *L'eredità immateriale* (Turin, 1985), translated as *Inheriting Power* (Chicago, 1988); Osvaldo Raggio, *Faide e parentele. Lo stato genovese visto dalla Fontanabuona* (Turin, 1990); Angelo Torre, *Il consumo di devozioni* (Venice, 1995).

stressed the variation in experience of different local social actors, and the absence of a unified context for social action on the ground, which allowed the most successful dealers to manipulate their environment, and maybe, by exploiting social contradictions, to effect real change (in this they differed from Geertz; the argument was closer to Pierre Bourdieu, but his work did not greatly influence them, as far as I can see). They stressed the problem of how to construct historical knowledge on the basis of clues in texts, which, Ginzburg convincingly argued, meant that history as a practice resembled medical diagnostics more than it did normative social science; but they rejected the deconstructive relativism for which Geertz at times argued.[3] And, above all, they theorised the issue of scale: the micro as a scale of analysis meant that individual experience could properly be focused on; millers and local charismatic preachers, and local family strategies, if handled with sufficient sophistication, could become as important as – more important than – the affairs of major political leaders; details of local symbolism and interaction could be apprehended in a way that classic big-picture *Annales* histories could never manage. And, using the other end of the microscope, traditional historical grand narratives, such as the 'rise of the modern state', could be tested to destruction; what *did* the Genoese state look like if it was seen from the experience of families and villages up in the Apennines in the Fontanabuona valley, as in the subtitle of Raggio's book?

Put as briefly and schematically as this, it may be that those readers who are more familiar with the Anglo-American cutting-edge social and cultural history of the last decades of the twentieth century will not find some of this approach so very surprising; bottom-up history, in particular, was very common by then and still is now (Edward Thompson was indeed a touchstone for the microhistorians), as have quasi-Geertzian analyses. What marked the microhistorians out, however, was the fact that they did all of these things at once, with very high-quality analysis; and that they articulated each monographic analysis with a constant social-scientific and literary-critical awareness, and a frequent preoccupation for how the scale of their micro-analyses articulated with the problematics of the grand narratives they were critiquing. To invoke two parallel examples from other countries: Natalie Davis's *The Return of Martin Guerre* (1983), with its constant probing of the inconsistent and incomplete historical sources for her micro-account of a highly atypical family crisis in a small Pyrenean village, Artigat, was indeed very similar to classic microhistory, and was in fact soon translated

---

3   Carlo Ginzburg, *Miti, emblemi, spie* (Turin, 1986), pp. 158–209, translated as *Clues, Myths and the Historical Method* (Baltimore, 1989), pp. 96–125 (but the original article dates from 1979); for the critique of Geertz (and of the use made of him by Robert Darnton), see Giovanni Levi, 'I pericoli del Geertzismo', *Quaderni storici* 58 (1985), 269–77, further developed in Levi, 'On Microhistory', pp. 98–105.

in the *Microstorie* series. But Emmanuel Le Roy Ladurie's *Montaillou*, which discusses another Pyrenean village in extreme detail, using parallels from anthropology, and which in 1975 marked the beginning in France of the break from *Annaliste* high-level synthesis, in just the years in which Grendi and the others were working microhistory out, is, however classic, not itself a microhistorical work. It is trusting of its inquisitorial evidence in a way that Ginzburg, who also used inquisition registers, was not, and it does not problematise its approaches, unlike every good piece of microhistory. Indeed, as a result, it has dated, in a way that *Il formaggio e i vermi*, and the other major microhistorical works, have not.[4]

Issues and limitations

My only problem with the microhistory school, to which I am otherwise intellectually close, lies in the question of comparison. If you know one village really well, and can use its specific experience to rethink the top-down assumptions of rise-of-the-state theory, then it might be worthwhile – I would argue that it is very important – to look at several other villages to see if they worked in the same way, and to use their collective, although of course different, experiences to replace the top-down models altogether. This was not an unknown démarche for microhistory, but it was not common. It did not fit well with the deep-rooted hostility of the leading microhistorical theorists to the big-history accounts they were reacting against. Davis's Artigat is only 50 kilometres away from Montaillou, but she only mentions it three times, and only once makes a comparative point. That was not, in her case, a result of polemic; her book is, in fact, too different for comparison to have been useful – she was, precisely, not trying to analyse a whole village, as Le Roy Ladurie was. But this is also part of the point about the microhistorical classics: they were all making different, often incommensurable, types of argument, linked together only by their wider theoretical engagement. That may also explain why the movement only lasted twenty years in its classic format: because the charisma of the major texts, so different as they are, resisted routinisation into a definable school of followers. And also because only a high-quality theoretical engagement, in the end, really distinguished these analyses from the kind of solid and dull localised history most of us write the rest of the time – one off day, that is to say, and one finds oneself simply adding 'una nuova tessera nel mosaico' ('a new piece in the jigsaw'), the stock phrase of lukewarm book reviews in Italian.

4   Natalie Zemon Davis, *The Return of Martin Guerre* (Cambridge, MA, 1983); Emmanuel Le Roy Ladurie, *Montaillou* (Paris, 1975), abridged and translated as *Montaillou* (London, 1978); see the sympathetic but critical review by Natalie Zemon Davis, 'Les conteurs de Montaillou', *Annales* 34 (1979), 61–73.

Microhistory and economic history

What can be done with microhistory now, then? Has its relevance faded, given that the *Annaliste* tradition it opposed has effectively (sadly) disappeared, and that the methods it pioneered are now much more common, indeed often standard – partly, indeed, because of the force of its example? That observation in itself shows that its individual approaches are indeed still relevant, because we follow them – it is non-microhistorians who have routinised them, that is to say. But I would argue that there is one area in which the subversive role of microhistory maintains, and maybe has increased, its potential: in economic history. In the last generation, the most systematic overarching theories have most often been in economic history. These do not replace the great *Annaliste thèses* in their contribution to empirical knowledge, for they are seldom based directly on empirical work by the authors (indeed, often enough, what their secondary or tertiary source-base actually is, is pretty obscure) – they tend to owe more to model-building in economics or social theory in general than they do to empirical engagement. They are also far too frequently focused on different versions of a hyper-modernist account of the 'triumph of the West' and of its inevitability. But their scale and ambition are notable; and they are also even more exposed than were the *Annalistes* to the balloon-pricking which a successful, and theoretically aware, microhistorical analysis can provide. Again, small-scale studies without that theoretical awareness are legion, and do not work to counter the overarching models if, indeed, they are trying to do so. But if one is aware of what one is doing, one can undermine these economic grand narratives quite effectively, and this seems to me an eminently positive, indeed necessary, step.

One example of this is Francesca Carnevali's work on jewellers, sadly incomplete as we know, but including, at least, one major article in which she took on precisely this task. Her article on 'Social Capital and Trade Associations in America, c.1860–1914' was explicitly in the subtitle 'a microhistory approach', and was headed with a quote from Jacques Revel.[5] It discussed the New England Manufacturing Jewelers and Silversmiths' Association in the late nineteenth century in Providence, which, it becomes clear across the article, functioned much like a medieval trade guild in its creation of internal mechanisms of trust and co-operation, including by inventing its own rituals, so as to combat what it saw as its external opponents, wholesalers ('jobbers') and trade unions. (Francesca intended this to develop into a comparative study, but never came back to the Birmingham end of her project from this standpoint.) The whole point of the article was to get at as much detail as possible about

---

5 Francesca Carnevali, 'Social Capital and Trade Associations in America, c.1860–1914: A Microhistory Approach', *Economic History Review* 64 (2011), 905–28. All the quotations in the next two pages come from this article.

the actual processes of trust creation, at least as expressed through a single source, the pages of the *Manufacturing Jeweler*, the Association's trade journal – a problematic source, on the level of those used by some of the microhistory classics, and one used with much the same deftness.

This work on trust of course fits in with specific versions of new institutional economics – including the more wide-ranging work of Robert Putnam and others on the establishment of social capital, whose insights Francesca already understood from the inside, given her work on Italy – and she duly cites them in her article. These versions already, by re-embedding economic activity in the social, undermine some of the more abstract overarching theories in the sector. But not all; as she notes, how trust and co-operation actually derive from associational activity – and, indeed, what the initial impetus for associational activity actually was, and whom this activity excludes – are not obvious, but are too often taken for granted. The development of social capital theory is a clear advance on some of the more schematic institutional and rational-choice analyses which preceded and frame it, but it is schematic in its own way; although there are certainly exceptions, it, too, often works by model-building rather than real empirical study, creating, once again, external impositions on the material.

Francesca's microstudy was therefore aimed at getting behind these abstract models and at giving 'agency back to agents', by focusing on the processual networks of relations 'in which actors define each other', through their 'specific cultural context': precisely, a microhistorical approach. The detailed history of the Association which she provides goes a long way to creating just that sense of agency. What did the *Manufacturing Jeweler* really care about, and how did that change? Who ran it, and how did their social origins and economic status change? How did the community embodied in the Association actually manage to combat the tendency of wholesalers to go bankrupt, or the influence of unions? What did jewellers think their dinners and outings actually achieved, in terms of community building? This last was perhaps the key issue, for it is very clear from the trade journal that jewellers really did believe they were creating a community, with mutual loyalty and shared values. It did not work 100% of the time to stop its individual members dealing with recognised dishonest wholesalers, for example, but it imposed informal sanctions on such members sufficiently often that the community was and remained protected. This was a highly competitive world, and these jewellers competed with each other too, but they did so in the framework of a 'larger moral order that they codified and expressed', through the creation of social bonds and a common cultural language. This microstudy was thus not, by any means, a simple piece of empirical research; it was a conscious intervention in the historiography of social capital which was designed to show how it was actually created on the ground, rather than in the heads of modern social scientists, just as were the works of Grendi or Levi in the 1980s. Francesca's microhistorical approach was a re-creation of real social relationships, which, if properly followed up, ideally in a comparative perspective, will enable social capital theory to be refigured from the ground up, and will further undermine the overarching certainties of the paradigms which frame it. That will be work for others to do, now, alas, but here is a starting point.

There are not that many examples of full-blown economic microhistories. There were some in the 1980s, it is true, like Franco Ramella's *Terra e telai*, about how family-based industrialisation worked in practice in a village in an Alpine valley in the nineteenth century, which undermines plenty of standard narratives, including ones written later. Francesca Trivellato's more recent work on early modern Livorno, *The Familiarity of Strangers*, is also in many ways a classic microhistorical text; she has related her conceptualisation of microhistory to global history very interestingly as well. In my medieval field, I would cite two recent examples: Jessica Goldberg's 2012 account of the personal relationships of Jewish merchants from Fustat (now part of Cairo) in the eleventh century, seen in particular through their letters; and Chris Dyer's 2012 reconstruction of the socio-economic world of a single Cotswold wool-merchant, John Heritage, around 1500, seen in particular through his account-book. Neither of these namecheck the microhistorians, but they are doing exactly the same sort of work: they are reassessing standard grand-narrative accounts by focusing on the micro scale, in as sophisticated a way as possible. Goldberg shows without difficulty how schematic – and incorrect – Avner Greif and other new institutional economic historians were to say that medieval Islamic trade networks, unlike those of Italy, were enforced by informal, not legal, means, which ultimately, because they could not easily be extended past a single community, undermined their force. Dyer does not critique current models to the same degree, not surprisingly given that they derive in large part from his own, less micro, work; but he shows how multifaceted, even contradictory, Heritage's economic activity was across his career, and how badly he fits into any of the standard categorisations of dealers in the commercial environment of his time.[6]

These two show how medieval economic history should be done: on the basis of complex, often inconsistent, sets of day-to-day documents, which indeed need to be treated statistically in part, but which are to a substantial degree irreducible to serial analysis – or, at least, which lose much of their usefulness if that is the only way they are treated. The micro is itself not the

---

6 Franco Ramella, *Terra e telai* (Turin, 1984); Francesca Trivellato, *The Familiarity of Strangers: The Sephardic Diaspora, Livorno, and Cross-Cultural Trade in the Early Modern Period* (New Haven, CT, 2009); Francesca Trivellato, 'Is There a Future for Italian Microhistory in the Age of Global History?', *Californian Italian Studies* 2 (2011), http://escholarship.org/uc/item/0z94n9hq, accessed 16 December 2016; Jessica Goldberg, *Trade and Institutions in the Medieval Mediterranean* (Cambridge, 2012), esp. pp. 12–17 and 148–56 for critiques of Greif, which make up only a small part of a substantial and much richer book; Christopher Dyer, *A Country Merchant, 1495–1520* (Oxford, 2012).

only way of dealing with the economy, and loses its critical force if this is the only field that a historian studies; but both these historians do indeed approach the macro as well. It is just that they do so on the interpretative basis which has been created by their microhistory and, by doing so, they offer us ways into the nuanced analysis of the way economies actually work which standard narratives often deny us.

Future perspectives: microhistory and the economic logic of medieval economic systems

There is another, final, point which needs to be made here. There has been very little work done on what the specific economic logics of medieval economic systems were. Most studies, indeed, actively deny such specificity. Apart from a pioneering and controversial monograph by Guy Bois on fourteenth-century Normandy (which was not, incidentally, any form of microstudy),[7] historians, when they theorise, tend to assume that the economic drivers of the medieval period were the same as those of the industrial world – just less efficient, and/ or blocked beyond a certain point of development. The grand overarching economic history narratives of recent years take the indivisibility of all economic systems for granted, indeed. I doubt this, very greatly, myself. If, however, we want to test it, to see whether it is possible to construct a model, or indeed more than one, for how medieval economies worked which is different from that of the industrial or industrialising world, we are going to need to look beyond serial data, which are so 'thin' as description. We are going, rather, to need to look at the motivations of highly localised economic actors, and at the detailed directions and framing of their economic choices; and we are going to need to look at how they dealt with their social and economic environments, how they thought they could achieve their aims, and how these aims could be thwarted. We are going to need, in short, to do microhistory – indeed, many microhistories, comparatively. Even though our aim might be to create as wide and overarching a model as those it replaces, we must do it on the basis of a detailed attention to the choices and values of individual actors; for otherwise we will be making assumptions as arbitrary as those currently on offer in the discipline. This is a direction to which studies like those of Goldberg and Dyer point us, and it is a crucial one. As, in the very different problematic of the nineteenth century, studies like Francesca's on Providence jewellers point us. Microhistory, in this respect, has not gone away, and will not go away; it may be historiographically located in the recent past, but it marks the future of the discipline too.

---

7 Guy Bois, *Crise du féodalisme* (Paris, 1976), translated as *The Crisis of Feudalism* (Cambridge, 1984).

9

Europe's Difference and Comparative History: Searching for European Capitalism

ANDREA COLLI

In a recent article published in a special issue of the journal *Business History*, Mats Larsson and I explored the contribution to be made by the comparative method in social science research.[1] As an example, or, better, a sort of 'test', we analysed a particular research topic from a comparative and longitudinal perspective, namely the governance of family firms in Italy and Sweden, with reference to two main dimensions: a) corporate finance and the structure of domestic financial markets, and b) the institutional determinants of the persistent eradication of family capitalism. For better or worse, the article provides an example of comparative analysis, of a largely qualitative nature, examining the same topic across different geographic, cultural and institutional settings while also taking into account the long-term horizon of the economic development of the two countries. In that article, our argument was, in sum, that solid historical research had to stand equally on two legs, one being the long-term orientation (highlighting structural transformations) and the other, a comparative perspective that could instead highlight idiosyncratic features.

This basic research methodology is well known to business historians, and is in some ways instinctive, or innate, in some colleagues, as was certainly true in the case of Francesca Carnevali. Francesca devoted a significant part of her research to longitudinal comparative analysis, as for instance in the book *Europe's Advantage*, in which she explored the relationships between banks and small firms in four large European economies in the twentieth century.[2] Francesca, in essence, ran a comparative analysis of the alternatives for industry financing in different countries characterised by different banking

1   Andrea Colli and Mats Larsson, 'Family Business and Business History: An Example of Comparative Research', *Business History* 56 (2014), 37–53.
2   Francesca Carnevali, *Europe's Advantage: Banks and Small Firms in Britain, France, Germany, and Italy Since 1918* (Oxford, 2005).

and corporate finance systems. In running this exercise she was thus able to understand better the dynamics of the British decline in manufacturing, as well as the way in which a specific banking system is able to positively, or negatively, influence the development of small firms and industrial districts.

In the above-mentioned *Business History* article, Mats Larsson and I concluded by stressing how, through an extensive use of cross-national comparisons, it would be easier to 'understand not only the development in specific companies but also the differences between national business systems'.[3] Indeed, the vast domain of governance and ownership structures, and, more generally, of the notion of 'varieties of capitalism', is an important arena for comparative analysis, as has been shown in multiple research fields ranging from organisation studies to sociology, political science and others.[4] The comparative analysis of capitalist business systems has resulted in a better understanding of the structural features of each of them, of their similarities and differences. Of course, a central focus in this framework falls on the basic building block of capitalist societies – the corporation. In this chapter, I will thus discuss a specific topic, that is the existence, nature and structure of the 'European Corporation', framing the analysis in the same comparative perspective. This exercise will thus allow us to identify and discuss similarities and/or differences and to better define the contours of the research topic itself.

The European Corporation: a history of a 'chomping-at-the-bit' topic[5]

The study of the 'European Corporation'[6] has experienced renewed interest in recent years, among both scholars and practitioners. As anticipated in the Introduction to this volume, part of this renewed interest derives from the

3   Colli and Larsson, 'Family Business', p. 49.
4   Seminal comparative research (published almost simultaneously) on different capitalist business systems includes Peter Hall and David Soskice, *Varieties of Capitalism: The Institutional Foundations of Comparative Advantage* (Oxford, 2001); Richard Whitley, *Divergent Capitalisms: The Social Structuring and Change of Business Systems* (Oxford, 1999); Neil Fligstein, *The Architecture of Markets: An Economic Sociology of Twenty-First-Century Capitalist Societies* (Princeton, NJ, 2002).
5   In writing these paragraphs I derived much benefit from discussions over several years with many colleagues, including Harm Schroeter, Youssef Cassis, Abe de Jong and Michelangelo Vasta. However, here I must make particular mention of Franco Amatori, who some time ago started his own research on this topic. Together we wrote a chapter in a book edited by Harm Schroeter about the European Enterprise and, although we do not necessarily share the same views, I nonetheless have benefited from Franco's ideas, and from the exchange of opinions we had on this topic. Notwithstanding, this chapter reflects my own views, for which I take personal responsibility.
6   It is important to note that we consider here a 'European Corporation' to be one that has been founded, headquartered and have experienced its process of corporate consolidation in

perpetually vibrant debate on the 'varieties of capitalism', which vigorously stresses the presence of different models of capitalism, and capitalist enterprise, around the world. The differences in organisational, financial and ownership structures between (very broadly speaking) North American, Continental European and Asian corporations are actively analysed and investigated in several research domains, as for instance in strategy and management, organisation studies, finance and corporate governance, but also economic sociology and, of course, business and economic history. The main research question concerns, of course, not only the differences and similarities among capitalist archetypes, but – more importantly – the impact that a model of capitalism may have on the 'performance' of the corporate sector and, in consequence, on the 'wealth of the nation'.

As is widely known, capitalist archetypes are largely believed to be connected to cultural, psychological and spiritual attitudes. Varieties of capitalism reflect, in sum, a sort of capitalist *Weltanschauung*, to put it in philosophical terms, which is in turn related to the way in which processes of economic growth and development have taken place in the long run, interacting with the general values which imprint a society and the way in which its individual members behave, think and devise institutions, both formal and informal. It is worth noting that we are still waiting for a comparative history of the philosophical foundations of capitalism, explaining the historical influence of shared ideologies on values underpinning the economic behaviour of individuals, in different geographic contexts. Now that capitalism has (for the moment) consolidated its presence almost everywhere as *the* way of dealing with the issue of subsistence after the (relatively short in historical terms) confrontation with centrally planned economies, such a reflection about the philosophical foundations of the varieties of capitalism is even more needed than in the past.

It is not surprising, thinking retrospectively, that the history of the debate around the differences across capitalist environments dates back (irrespective of the subfield of social sciences involved) to the 1990s, a period characterised by the demise of ideologies (and of their equivalent in centrally co-ordinated and controlled economic organisations) in competition with capitalism, and with a general intensification in the globalisation process, as well as in the level of interaction and confrontation among countries and companies. As a decade, the 1990s were opened by the pamphlet *Capitalisme contre*

Europe. It has to consider itself as 'European', and this is reflected for instance in the composition of its top management. It is thus difficult to include among European corporations the subsidiaries of foreign companies located in Europe, even if they are of considerable size. On the other hand, it is easier to include companies historically headquartered in Europe, even if a high percentage of their production or sales is located abroad. In principle, however, a 'selective' definition of the European Corporation would apply to those companies headquartered in Europe, with the majority of their investments, operations and employment similarly located in Europe.

capitalisme, written by the French journalist Michel Albert, that documented the economic and social consequences of different ways of thinking about the relationships between the general economic organisation of a country (or area), and the prevailing social values.[7]

This way of examining capitalism attracted the attention and interest of many social scientists. The 1990s and the early years of the new millennium became characterised, as stressed above, by the spread of research about the variety of capitalist environments, and their nuances, in, as already noted, sociology, anthropology, political sciences and political economy (to mention but a few). Of course, this emphasis could not ignore the basic building block of capitalist economies – the business enterprise. In Albert's original discourse – which I mention here as an example of a general trend in the way of thinking about capitalism – companies were considered as but one (albeit very relevant) component of a more complex picture in which individual thinking and aggregate behaviours were included in the individuation of at least two archetypes: the Anglo-Saxon and the subsequently much-celebrated Rhenish model of capitalism. Soon, however, research interest turned to the ways in which the corporate economy was shaped and its constituent units organised. This emerging focus has, in turn, galvanised scholars already active in the study of organisations, management and strategy, finance, organisation, international management and, not least, business history.

The research that followed culminated in the identification of several archetypes of company operating within different capitalist environments, providing a quasi-anthropological distinction among 'species' and/or 'races'. The main structural features (ownership and governance characteristics, policies and strategies, organisational structures, attitudes towards competition, the role of capital and that of labour) have been scrutinised in depth, as has the influence exerted by the external environment by way of, for example, markets and consumer attitudes, legal systems and other institutional influences, and the impact of business–government relations.

The 1990s were, it must be remembered, the period when the collapse of the bastions of Communism was supposed to inaugurate a phase of new globalisation in which, as the American economist Lester C. Thurow wrote, competition for 'supremacy' was going to be 'head to head' in technologically advanced sectors.[8] This, however – Thurow continued – was a three-way game, and the three competitors were beyond any doubt the USA, Europe and Japan. Each of them had assets and liabilities, and among the assets were their respective corporate models, each characterised by strengths and weaknesses. The American archetype of big business was thus contrasted with

7   Michel Albert, *Capitalisme contre capitalisme* (Paris, 1991).
8   Lester C. Thurow, *Head to Head: The Coming Economic Battle Among Japan, Europe, and America* (New York, 1992).

a European model of large companies. This European model was, in its turn, successfully (at the time) challenged by the emergence of a much smaller (in geographical terms) yet flourishing economy characterised by the outstanding aggressiveness of its corporate sector – Japan. In 1983, according to Dunning and Pearce, forty-six of the largest top hundred corporations in the world were headquartered in the USA, thirty-three in Europe and ten in Japan.[9] In 1995, according to the Fortune Global 500, the USA had only twenty-four but the Japanese had around forty, with Europe's representation remaining stable with thirty-two.

Three national capitalistic models, in sum, dominated the world and competed through their respective corporate sectors, which in turn accounted for the largest shares of employment and of GDP formation. They were, of course, composed overwhelmingly (if not solely) of large companies in capital- and technology-intensive industries. These large companies, however, were not *exactly* the same. Yes, all of them were 'large', but the effect of size rendered the differences sharper and more clear-cut. The archetypes of companies, which emerged from these investigations, are well known. For instance, in the case of the USA, the lists were full of publicly listed companies run by professional managers and owned by a plethora of small shareholders, vertically integrated and organised on a divisional principle, financed through a vast array of instruments ranging from public to private equity, in which market-based relationships prevailed in the area of labour relations, and acting in an environment in which business–government relations were mainly characterised by attitudes towards regulation. Japanese corporate giants epitomised, for Western observers at least, the mystery of Asia, given their apparently peculiar ownership structures comprised of a dense web of cross-shareholdings, their hard-to-penetrate co-operative attitudes, the unique nature of the relationships between capital and labour, and the apparently neutral attitude of the government which, instead, aimed at a sort of 'soft' co-ordination (without planning) of industrial policies. European corporations, taken as a whole, embodied another model again, in which different constituencies were present. Governments were characterised by interventionist attitudes, while powerful and politicised unions stood before business owners, who themselves were not dispersed but characterised by strong identities, including famous and celebrated family names that could often be traced back for several generations.

It is worth noting that business historians played no small part in the generation of these archetypes, with the discipline's founding father, Alfred D. Chandler, being the first to introduce labels for these different historical models of big business. In the years leading up to the publication of his last

9   John H. Dunning and Robert D. Pearce, *The World's Largest Industrial Enterprises* (London, 1985).

major book, *Scale and Scope*, his writings became more and more oriented towards the identification of historical patterns of development in different models of capitalist enterprise. As is widely known, however, Chandler was not dealing with the European enterprise per se, but with a small selection of stylised models, in particular those of Germany and Britain, which fitted particularly well into his ('Whig', as it is called today) vision of Western economic and business history. Teleological or not, Chandler's perspective heavily emphasised the existence of different models of capitalism from the perspective of the historical evolution of big business.

In *Scale and Scope*,[10] Chandler used only Germany and the UK as comparators for the then successful and dominant American process of growth, convergence and leadership acquisition as it unfolded between the end of the nineteenth and the beginning of the twentieth century. There were many good reasons for his choice. This does not mean he was not aware of, or interested in, other cases: among his papers preserved at Harvard Business School, there are plenty of insights about European countries and Japan, including a detailed plan for a book never written in which other European countries were to be taken into consideration.[11] Overall, Chandler's primary impact at Harvard in the 1970s was through his collaboration in supervising the dissertations of a group of scholars assembled by Bruce Scott. All them analysed systematically the status and adaptation processes of big business – focusing on the diffusion of the M-form – in European countries such as the UK (Derek Channon), Germany (Heinz Thanheiser), France (Gareth Dyas) and Italy (Robert Pavan), all compared to the standard archetype that is the USA (Richard Rumelt).[12] Chandler not only had access to, but actually helped supervise this research, and remained in close contact with some of the group after they left Harvard Business School.

The framework they established had an 'ideal' follow-up some years after the publication of *Scale and Scope*, when a group of more-or-less stubborn 'Chandlerians' composed an impressive 'fresco' of the diffusion and adaptation of big business during the twentieth century in different geographical contexts, in a collection of essays evocatively titled *Big Business*

---

10   Alfred D. Chandler, *Scale and Scope: The Dynamics of Industrial Capitalism* (Cambridge, MA, 1990).

11   See Herman Daems, 'Strategic and Structural Responses of Large European Enterprises, 1950–1980', typescript project outline, Baker Library Historical Collections, Chandler Papers, Box 111, f. 3 II, n.d. (presumably end of 1984).

12   The project led to works including Derek F. Channon, *The Strategy and Structure of British Enterprise* (London, 1973); Gareth Dyas and Heinz Thanheiser, *The Emerging European Enterprise* (London, 1976); Robert J. Pavan, 'The Strategy and Structure of Italian Enterprise' (D.B.A. thesis, Harvard Business School, 1972; Richard P. Rumelt, *Strategy, Structure and Economic Performance* (Cambridge, MA, 1974).

and the Wealth of Nations (edited by Chandler himself, Franco Amatori and Takashi Hikino).[13]

Neither Chandler nor his followers, however, were directly and explicitly interested in the issue of 'European' capitalism, and in its micro-level manifestation; that is, the presence of a sort of trans-European corporate model. Their focus was either on the processes of diffusion and local adaptation of big business or on the organisational structures adopted. The sole, specific comparison made was between these national cases and the USA, implicitly and explicitly considered as *the main* comparator. Implicit here also was the underlying concept of performance, never exactly defined but largely referring to size, such as greatest market share or market capitalisation.

Other business historians tried to tackle the issue of European capitalism, but with mixed results. Youssef Cassis wrote a seminal book on the history of European big business which discussed national cases – basically, Germany, France and the UK – referring to some general categories (e.g. performance or survival), but in the end treating national experiences separately.[14] Similarly, Harm Schroeter edited an ambitious book in which the issue of the comparative is again present, but where a national or even regional focus still prevails.[15] Richard Whittington and Michael Mayer mixed business history, strategy and organisational approaches in analysing the top European corporations in the 1990s.[16] They were, however, more in search of alternative views about the adoption of multidivisional structures in Europe, explicitly referring to the above-mentioned research by the Scott group.

Business historians are not the only scholars who have failed to fully address the issue. Turning to other research fields in social sciences, management and even economics in search of help is not always useful. Research in political science, for instance, has produced such general categories as that of liberal market economies (LMEs) or co-ordinated market economies (CMEs) and even mixed market economies (MMEs).[17] Studies in corporate ownership and governance have remained heavily attached to the concept of Continental capitalism as different and distinct from the Anglo-Saxon concept, seldom differentiating between the Rhenish model (in which, apparently, Scandinavia

13   Alfred D. Chandler, Franco Amatori and Takashi Hikino, eds., *Big Business and the Wealth of Nations* (New York, 1997).

14   Youssef Cassis, *Big Business: The European Experience in the Twentieth Century* (Oxford, 1997).

15   Harm Schroeter, *The European Enterprise: Historical Investigation Into a Future Species* (Heidelberg, 2008).

16   Richard Whittington and Michael Mayer, *The European Corporation: Strategy, Structure and Social Science* (Oxford, 2000).

17   Hall and Soskice, *Varieties of Capitalism*.

is included) and a Latin version, basically coinciding with the capitalist practices in use in the Mediterranean area.[18]

In sum, a curious investigator interested in better understanding the existence of a sort of European capitalism, translated into a European corporate model, does not have an easy life. Business history helps through its comparative attitude, but only to a certain extent, as up to now it has been more interested in the (comparative) analysis of national cases. Others either insist on meta-categories or stick to the familiar taxonomy that distinguishes Anglo-Saxon (US), European and Asian (Japanese) models. Our curious investigator is thus stuck between perspectives that concentrate either too much on the particular or too much on the general.

To be specifically interested in Europe, indeed, piles difficulty on difficulty. European corporations may originate and terminate in European countries, but European countries are by no means a homogeneous entity. One can thus quite easily speak of American corporations in America, or Japanese corporations in Japan; but the 'European Corporation' is a much more generic concept. Europe has in fact been characterised by an extremely variegated patchwork of industrialisation processes, with a sharp variance in their intensity and timing. This has, for some countries, been interrupted for some decades, during which they adhered more or less forcefully to the realm of centrally planned economic regimes. This has, of course, affected the shape of corporations in different European contexts, their relations with the financial system and with the state, and the relationships between capital and labour, and even between capital and bureaucracies. The European version of capitalism is, to some extent, too broad a category, one in which differentiation plays a great if not fully known part, but where instances of homogeneity are nevertheless also present.

The first, non-trivial, issue thus concerns the geographic boundaries of any analysis. To which countries does the label 'European' apply? What are the borders of 'corporate Europe'? Following a consolidated attitude, one may be tempted to limit the analysis to the principal nations, such as the UK, France and Germany. However, it is clear that minor economies, such as those of Italy and Spain in the Mediterranean, or those of Denmark, Sweden, Finland and Norway in the Baltic, may offer important insights into a model of European capitalism.[19] Moreover, there is an interesting pattern of timing. Countries progressively access European capitalism once they complete their industrialisation, through a non-simultaneous process, and the effects may

18 Jeroen Weimer and Joost Pape, 'A Taxonomy of Systems of Corporate Governance' *Corporate Governance: An International Review* 7 (1999), 152–66.
19 See, for instance, Susanna Fellman, Martin Jes Iversen, Hans Sjogren and Lars Thue, eds, *Creating Nordic Capitalism: The Business History of a Competitive Periphery* (Basingstoke, 2008).

vary depending on the country. For example, Spain has struggled for decades with the attitude to modernisation of its version of capitalism, reaching full maturity probably only in the 1980s, a whole century after the UK, and at least half a century after Italy. As argued above, some countries actually remained outside the realm of European capitalism for decades, returning to it only recently. However, to leave Eastern Europe and the Balkans, Russia included, completely out of the picture seems to be at least questionable. Until 1945 many Eastern European countries, such as Hungary, the Czech Republic, Poland and some former Yugoslavian republics, were fully integrated into the general framework of the European economy, to which, since the early 1990s, they have returned. The analysis of the European Corporation thus makes little sense if limited to the main industrial countries. Our curious investigator, however, has to be aware of the fact that the more one moves away from the core of European capitalist development, the more variation and differentiation in industrialisation patterns are going to prevail, as was authoritatively noted many decades ago by the Jewish-Ukrainian historian Alexander Gerschenkron.[20]

In botany, the oak is probably the most diffused tree in the world, having adapted to almost every latitude and longitude. However, this terrific achievement has only been possible through proliferation of species, around six hundred, with more than one hundred found in Mexico alone. This mythological tree sacred to Zeus and Thor thus assumes a multiplicity of shapes in different contexts in order to survive. In the same way, Europe seems to be characterised by an abundance of varieties even more pronounced than elsewhere, being found in areas ranging from the Greek Mediterranean islands to the cold forests of the Baltic.[21] Out of that metaphor, we might argue that big business is characterised by a similar degree of diffusion, and a consequent amazing degree of adaptation and variance. Things are probably easier to determine in botanic genetics, since it is technically possible to discern the exact individuation of what is common and what is different. As far as 'European capitalism' or the 'European Corporation' are concerned, common traits and genes are much more confused.

Our curious investigator has thus to start a sort of personal research into the individuation of commonalities and differences, starting from some non-trivial questions which might include the following:

1. Is it possible to talk of a 'European Corporation', or do we have to admit that regional variations prevail over homogeneities, and that a European Corporation as such does not exist, being replaced by several European Corporations?

---

20   Alexander Gerschenkron, *Economic Backwardness in Historical Perspective* (Cambridge, MA, 1962).
21   William B. Logan, *Oak: The Frame of Civilization* (New York, 2005).

2. Once similarities are identified, are they really strong enough for a supranational archetype to be configured?

3. Are similarities (or differences) to be found only among large enterprises? European countries display a diverse 'corporate demography' including large, medium, small and very small enterprises. Are different dimensional categories part of the more general picture?

4. What happens when the unit of analysis also includes the industrial sector? In other words, are similarities among companies influenced by their productive specialisation? Do companies in, say, the steel industry tend to be more homogeneous in their structural features across Europe, than those in the service sector?

The research would probably benefit from a longitudinal perspective looking at the roots of present similarities and differences across Europe, which date back to the origin of the process of industrialisation and its progressive diffusion over the Continent.

In the following paragraphs, a number of critical issues related to the identification of some common traits among the European corporations will be put forward. The process will involve, as anticipated in the introduction, a great deal of comparative analysis, of both a cross-sectional and longitudinal nature. The main areas of investigation will concern the morphological traits and the behaviour of the European Corporation, its intrinsic characteristics and its key institutional determinants, which point towards increasing, or reducing, the degree of variance among corporate structures.

Morphology and behaviour

The first area to be investigated in search of homogeneities, similarities and differences concerns morphological and behavioural aspects.

Concentrated ownership
One of the basic features of the European corporate model of big business is commonly considered to be the presence of high levels of ownership concentration, compared with the high levels of ownership dispersion, which characterises the Anglo-Saxon model.[22] Is this really true? The traditional view is increasingly being challenged. While on the one side some criticism

---

22 This view is considered as the established wisdom, for instance, in the literature on corporate finance and corporate governance. See, for instance, Rafael La Porta, Florencio López de Silanes and Andrei Shleifer, 'Corporate Ownership Around the World', *Journal of Finance* 54 (1999), 471–517; Fabrizio Barca and Marco Becht, eds, *The Control of Corporate Europe* (Oxford, 2001); Mara Faccio and Jerry P. Lang, 'The Ultimate Ownership of Western European Corporations', *Journal of Financial Economics* 65 (2002), 365–95.

is concerned with the real dominance of the public company in the USA, other research stresses a precocious presence of diffused ownership in some of the major European countries, starting with the UK. Thus, while the most recent data seem to confirm the fact that, in the long run, the ownership of European corporations has been constantly characterised by high levels of concentration and a widespread use of control-enhancing mechanisms, allowing the main shareholders to keep a firm grip over corporate life,[23] it is also necessary to review the issue more closely and to acknowledge the differences among European countries in the degree of ownership diffusion. At the very least, one must take into serious consideration the fact that to speak of 'ownership concentration' is too generic a description. In the interwar period, for instance, the federative attitude of British capitalism had resulted in the creation of large firms from the merger of smaller entities.[24] In many of these a nucleus of dominant shareholders coexisted with a large population of minority shareholders. Directors were mainly appointed from among the central block of shareholders, with a reduced recourse to professional managers. This peculiar ownership structure, which was in-between concentrated and dispersed ownership, has been defined as 'proprietorial capitalism'.[25] Curiously, the definition of post-Second World War British capitalism as dominated by public companies has been challenged by the idea that an elite comprised of mutual and pension fund managers exerts a close, clubby control over the largest British firms in services and manufacturing.[26]

Ownership typologies: families, states and banks
Having explored the ownership concentration puzzle, the second pattern of research about morphological elements concerns the nature of the main shareholders.[27] In this area, differences seem to prevail over similarities. While personal and family-related forms of ownership seem to be a prevailing trait in the long run almost everywhere, the levels and intensity of state ownership, for instance, vary among countries and over time.

23   See, for instance, Jean-Nicolas Caprasse, Christophe Clerc and Marco Becht, *Report on the Proportionality Principle in the European Union* (Brussels and Paris, 2007), http://ec.europa.eu/internal_market/company/docs/shareholders/study/final_report_en.pdf (accessed 17 December 2016).
24   John Wilson, *British Business History 1720–1995* (Manchester, 1995).
25   John Quail, 'The Proprietorial Theory of the Firm', *Journal of Industrial History* 3 (2000), 1–28.
26   Richard Minns, *Pension Funds and British Capitalism* (London, 1980).
27   The topic is particularly analysed by scholars interested in the impact of the nature of ownership on a firm's value. See, for instance, Torben Pedersen and Steen Thomsen, 'Ownership Structure and Value of the Largest European Firms: The Importance of Owner Identity', *Journal of Management and Governance* 7 (2003), 27–55.

In general, cycles of nationalisation and privatisation, and direct interventions by governments, both show a high level of heterogeneity across
European countries, being the consequence of the differential impact of
external elements (for instance, economic crises) on national capitalisms.
Periods of state ownership alternate with phases of liberalisation, in ways
(and with modalities) that are very different from case to case.[28] Recent
research has shown, for example, how in different European countries the
market behaviour and strategies of privatised 'national champions' reflects
the way they were managed as state-owned firms.[29] This issue becomes even
more striking when countries previously adherent to planned economies are
taken into consideration, where the nature, and heritage, of the state intervention has been profoundly different from that of the so-called 'market
economies' (both co-ordinated, liberal and mixed).[30]

Another relevant typology of ownership in European economic history is
that related to ownership by banking and financial institutions. The spread
of the mixed- or universal-bank model, starting from the second half of
the nineteenth century, undoubtedly characterised the core of the industrialisation process for some Continental countries, starting of course from
Germany. In this case, however, one can only partially speak of 'homogeneities'. For other countries, such as the UK, the commercial bank contribution remained marginal thanks to the historical presence of specialised
financial institutions.[31] Elsewhere, the contribution of universal banks was
fundamental, but time-limited. In the case of Italy, for instance, mixed banks
based on the German model served as a key factor in boosting the process of
industrialisation.[32] The intrinsic instability of a system in which banks both
controlled and were controlled by their debtors led, in the post-First World
War era, at the outbreak of the world depression of the early 1930s, to a ban
on commercial banking in Italy for more than six decades. The impact of
this situation was, of course, relevant in influencing the corporate finance
alternatives for large firms in Italy, and therefore their corporate governance

28   Pier Angelo Toninelli (ed.) *The Rise and Fall of State-Owned Enterprise in the Western
World* (New York, 2008).
29   See Andrea Colli, Sergio Mariotti and Lucia Piscitello, 'Governments as Strategists in
Designing Global Players: The Case of European Utilities', *Journal of European Public Policy*
21 (2014), 407–508.
30   See, for instance, Saul Estrin, 'Privatization Impacts in Transition Economies', *The New
Palgrave Dictionary of Economics*, ed. Steven N. Durlauf and Lawrence E. Blume, 2nd edn
(London, 2008), http://www.dictionaryofeconomics.com/article?id=pde2008_P000342, accessed
14 January 2017.
31   Michael Collins and Mae Baker, *Commercial Banks and Industrial Finance in England and
Wales, 1860–1913* (Oxford, 2003), p. 45.
32   Gerschenkron, *Economic Backwardness*.

practices,[33] which remained sharply different from those in use in other European countries, such as Germany, that were characterised by the long-standing presence of banking share ownership.[34]

Collusion and co-operation: cartels and trusts

A third set of distinctive features lies in the domain of corporate behaviour, and concerns the supposed tendency of European companies to engage in co-operative and collusive practices, at least until the (even in this case, gradual) introduction and diffusion of a European version of anti-trust legislation. This is an institutional transformation of relatively recent origin, whose 'business history' has, to my knowledge, still to be written. The propensity towards collusion seems to be a very common strategy at least before the 1950s, involving European companies in every country and almost all sectors – including those characterised by medium capital intensity. Even in this case, however, differences need to be carefully assessed. There is a fundamental difference between cartelisation strategies set up in order to protect internal markets and others aiming at the penetration of international markets. The participation in international agreements and cartels is probably common to all large European companies, particularly those headquartered in relatively small domestic markets, while the use of cartels as instruments of protection of internal markets was a much more differentiated practice across European countries.[35] However, more comparative research would be necessary in order to establish if cartelisation has really been a common trait of European capitalism, as it seems, and if homogeneity (even in this field) or differences prevail.

Demography

A discourse about the converging, or diverging, features of the European Corporation cannot ignore the fact that European countries sharply differ today in terms of the average sizes of firms. In this regard, the content of a recent policy report by Bruegel, a European think-tank, is quite illuminating;[36] specifically, European capitalism appears to be characterised by an extreme non-homogeneous industrial demography. This, in turn, has

33 Franco Amatori and Andrea Colli, *Corporate Governance: The Italian Story*, Corporate Governance, Innovation and Economic Performance in the EU (CGEP) Project Paper (Brussels, 2001).

34 See, for instance, Marco Becht and Erik Böhmer, 'Ownership and Voting Power in Germany', *The Control of Corporate Europe*, ed. Fabrizio Barca and Marco Becht (Oxford, 2001), pp. 128–53.

35 For a general summary of this argument, and of the large bibliography on the topic, see Christopher Harding and Julian Joshua, *Regulating Cartels in Europe* (Oxford, 2010).

36 Loris Rubini, Klaus Desmet, Facundo Piguillemand and Aranzazu Crespo, *Breaking Down the Barriers to Firm Growth in Europe: the Fourth EFIGE Policy Report* (Brussels, 2012), p. 9.

been influenced by historical national patterns of industrialisation. The overwhelming diffusion of small and very small enterprises was in fact an historical characteristic of some countries (for example, the Mediterranean, namely Spain, Portugal, Italy and Greece) but far less so for others (for example, Scandinavia and Central Europe, including the UK), which has a durable impact over the morphology of national capitalistic models.

A great deal of research has been devoted (and not only by business historians) to understanding the patterns that led to these structural long-run differences in firm size.[37] However, since a comprehensive longitudinal comparison highlighting the origins of the structural differences in industrial demography among European countries has still to be written, it is probably important not to underestimate the impact of this variance on the morphological traits of the European Corporation, taken as a whole.

As noted above, these critical areas to be investigated in search of similarities and differences across European corporations concern characteristics of enterprises which are related to morphological aspects. Further prudence has to be deployed when looking at more intrinsic aspects, for instance those connected to governance and organisation.

Inside the box

Capital vs. labour: co-determination and paternalism

European capitalism is perceived as being fundamentally different from the Anglo-Saxon model (and also from the Asian-Japanese model) for the way in which relationships between capital and labour have historically taken place. In this area, how industrialisation processes developed across the Continent obviously played a relevant role. It was also an area in which some more common traits probably prevailed. The relative abundance of skilled labour and artisanal traditions, for instance, is a shared feature in almost all European countries, and this undoubtedly had an effect on the shape of capital and labour relationships in the long run. The millennial heritage of accumulated capabilities dating back to the Middle Ages played, undoubtedly, a great role in explaining the persistence of personalistic labour relations, based on individualised relationships instead of the institutional regulation

---

37   In the case of Italy, for example, studies have been devoted both to the understanding of the decline of big business and to the alleged persistence and eradication of small firms, looking for instance at entrepreneurial and institutional failures. See Franco Amatori, Matteo Bugamelli and Andrea Colli, 'Technology, Firm Size and Entrepreneurship', *The Oxford Handbook of the Italian Economy Since Unification*, ed. Gianni Toniolo (New York, 2013), pp. 455–84; Andrea Colli and Alberto Rinaldi, 'Institutions, Politics and the Corporate Economy', *Enterprise and Society* 16, 2015, 249–69.

of conflict. In greater detail, however, variations can be identified across different areas. For instance, the balance between paternalistic attitudes towards the workforce and the management of conflict through institutional arrangements is different between Northern and Southern Europe. Similarly, the diffusion of co-determination practices – another alleged feature of the European Corporation – characterises Germanic and Scandinavian corporate cultures,[38] but is largely extraneous to those in Southern Europe.[39]

Stakeholders, shareholders, governance
The stakeholder orientation of companies across Europe is another trait that appears to be widely accepted. Commentators have considered this a key feature that nicely depicts the embeddedness of European companies into the more general climate, which characterises European society and culture as a whole. The stakeholder orientation of Continental companies and their propensity towards stable continuity, derived from close relations with workers, suppliers, customers, shareholders, local interests and municipalities, is considered as definitely prevailing over the concept of 'arm's-length relationships' prevalent in the so-called 'Anglo-Saxon perspective'. The literature is quite abundant on this point, as it is on the part of business historians adopting comparative and longitudinal perspectives.[40] The sole European exception to the general inclination towards a 'stakeholder-driven' model seems, in this framework, to be the UK, which is considered to be fully embedded in the Anglo-Saxon behavioural code of exclusive shareholder orientation. It is, however, often forgotten that the shareholder orientation of Anglo-Saxon capitalism is relatively recent, at least in its present form. The emphasis on value for shareholders is a direct consequence of the restructuring process of US capitalism during the 1980s which, in its turn, was the logical consequence of the excessive diversification that occurred in large corporations during the previous decade. The transformation took place mainly thanks to de-conglomeration processes generated by corporate raiders. As far as the UK is concerned, the transformation in the nature of British capitalism, from a family–personal–proprietorial orientation to one in which the interests of shareholders and funds take precedence, dates back to the 1960s. By contrast, European corporations have until recently been

38 See, for instance, Reinhard H. Schmidt, 'Corporate Governance in Germany: An Economic Perspective', *The German Financial System*, ed. Jan P. Krahnen and Reinhard H. Schmidt (Oxford, 2004), pp. 386–424.
39 As one may expect, the analysis of labour relations and practices in Europe is quite a consolidated field of comparative analysis. One major work stressing the diversity in the structure of European industrial relations is that by Colin Crouch, *Industrial Relations and European State Traditions* (Oxford, 1994).
40 See for instance Mary O'Sullivan, *Contests for Corporate Control: Corporate Governance and Economic Performance in the United States and Germany* (Oxford, 2000).

operating largely outside all these dynamics – given also their minor degree of diversification – and free to focus on a broader constituency. Recent studies in the field of corporate finance and governance also stress how stakeholder orientation seems to remain an attractive behaviour for European companies.[41]

Organizational structures

Another consolidated stream of research in management and organisation studies looks at the comparative analysis of organisational structures and administrative architectures of large firms. This field of research has of course also inspired business historians who, following in the footsteps of Alfred Chandler, have been analysing the 'organisational idiosyncrasies' of European corporations. The bulk of available research is not easy to summarise, and would probably constitute enough good material for a book chapter in its own right. In essence, the starting point for our curious investigator should be, in chronological order:

1. Research as carried out by the Scott group at Harvard Business School in the early 1970s (as mentioned previously). The outcome was an understanding (limited to some of the main countries) that between the 1950s and the 1970s – the years of the consolidation and emergence of European corporate power – the prevailing organisational structures among the largest corporations in Europe were functional and/or largely based upon holdings and business groups. However, multidivisional structures were also being diffused, albeit to a lesser extent than one could predict given the overall degree of maturity of the European business system as a whole.

2. Subsequent research by Richard Whittington and Michael Mayer,[42] as already noted, was more or less on the same lines. The two management scholars, however, stressed the way in which the slow diffusion of multidivisional structures had characterised even the more recent history of European capitalism (even if their research is limited to France, UK and Germany), that is, the phase going from the 1980s to the beginning of the new millennium.

3. Nonetheless, business historians are developing a line of research picked up from the finance sector that looks more carefully at a specific organisational form, which has apparently seen long-term diffusion across Europe. This is one based on legally independent

41   Franklin Allen, Elena Carletti and Robert Marquez, *Stakeholder Capitalism, Corporate Governance and Firm Value*, Wharton Financial Institutions Center Working Paper #09–28 (Philadelphia, PA, 2009), http://ssrn.com/abstract=968141 or http://dx.doi.org/10.2139/ssrn.968141.

42   Whittington and Mayer, *The European Corporation*.

areas of activity and connected through equity linkages to a holding. If a homogeneous trait is to be found in the area of organisational structures, it has to do with the widespread – albeit not exclusively European – use of business groups, a form that in the long run tends to be adopted across all industries.[43]

Is there a European entrepreneur?

A further relevant area, which I only mention here as a potentially promising field for comparative research, is that concerning entrepreneurial typologies in the history of corporate Europe. As one might imagine, the variance here is connected to the (relatively) abstract (and maybe too loose) concept of entrepreneurship that is applied in the analysis. 'Extractive' entrepreneurship, for instance, is common to all European countries, but probably more diffused in some than in others according to the prevailing model of business–government relations, in its turn forged by the development of the corporate sector over time. As in the dynastic model, private Schumpeterian entrepreneurship has spread everywhere, but the degree of its diffusion is historically influenced by many elements, such as the dominant industrial demography. A significant contribution to this field of research will only come from a more careful and comparative study of biographies of entrepreneurs in each nation, a project which is, however, still currently in its infancy.

The exogenous determinants

A comparative analysis such as that described in this chapter cannot recoil from a serious consideration of the influence exerted by the external environment in shaping the existence of common traits among European enterprises. In this respect, the diversity of development patterns across European countries militates against the existence of factors able to influence the homogeneity of European corporations. There are, however, some which are worth considering in more detail.

Business and government: the political economy of European countries and the relationship with politics

The first (and probably most relevant) homogeneous trait concerns the aspects related to political economy and to business–government relations, already introduced above. The latter (which broadly speaking includes aspects

---

43 See for instance, Geoffrey Jones and Asli M. Colpan, 'Business Groups in Historical Perspectives', *The Oxford Handbook of Business Groups*, ed. Asli M. Colpan, Takashi Hikino and James R. Lincoln (Oxford 2010), pp. 67–92.

of political economy, industrial policy, business and politics) is probably
the one where the similarities across Europe and, equally, the differences
between the European model of capitalism and the Anglo-Saxon model, are
more evident. The varying degree of European governmental involvement in
business activities, running along a spectrum from loose industrial policies
tolerating or even inducing cartel agreements to direct intervention through
to the creation of state-owned enterprises, has been one distinctive characteristic of Europe and, in this perspective, also an element of (perhaps even
sharp) differentiation. Differences among European countries have, of course,
included the intensity and the degree of direct governmental involvement.
In this perspective, a suggestive correlation is that connecting the intensity
of state intervention to the 'timing' of industrialisation and to the relative
peripheral position of an economy.[44]

Consumption markets and consumer attitudes

Two important factors concern the comparative analysis of European
consumption markets and consumer attitudes, another area in which significant similarities are shared among European companies.

The first is related to the size of potential consumption markets, which is in
turn connected to the expected effects of average corporate size and outreach.
The limited dimensions of some domestic markets in Europe are evident.[45]
This characteristic appears to be particularly relevant even for the larger
countries in phases of trade closure, when the market horizon of companies
and entrepreneurs is increasingly restricted to domestic markets. This is quite
evident in the period from 1914 to 1945. However, at the same time the limited
dimensions of national markets play a relevant role in fostering the internationalisation process of some European corporations, precociously crossing
national borders to reach consumers in other countries. It is interesting to
note how both business historians dealing with multinationals, and international business scholars, have confidently handled the concept of 'European
multinationals'.[46]

The second concerns local consumer attitudes. The cultural fragmentation
of Europe into historically differentiated markets appears to conflict with the
standardisation of consumption. Of course, this is in principle something that
can affect – and actually did affect – the marketing policies of corporations.

---

44   An effective synthesis of these issues can be found in James Foreman-Peck and Giovanni
Federico, *European Industrial Policy: The Twentieth-Century Experience* (Oxford, 1999).
45   See, for instance, the exemplary essay by Harm G. Schroeter, 'Small European Nations:
Cooperative Capitalism in the Twentieth Century', *Big Business and the Wealth of Nations*, ed.
Alfred D. Chandler, Franco Amatori and Takashi Hikino (Cambridge, 1997), pp. 176–204.
46   See, for instance, Mira Wilkins, 'European and North American Multinationals,
1870–1914: Comparisons and Contrasts', *Business History* 30 (1988), 8–45; Lawrence Franko,
The European Multinationals (Stamford, CT, 1976).

At the same time, this should in theory encourage European transnational entrepreneurship to follow precocious policies of local adaptation, as stressed by the available (but scarce) research on European multinationals.[47]

Financial markets

A further area in which similarities seem to prevail over differences is that of financial markets, translated into the issue of corporate financing strategies as mentioned above. The main characteristic of the European model is commonly considered to be an overwhelming diffusion of intermediated finance over market finance. Recent research regarding British financial markets – but also concerned with Continental financial markets[48] – is partially reshaping this view. Recent empirical research, which stresses the high variance in the structure of financial markets across European countries, calls for a prudent evaluation of what has so far been considered a main source of homogeneity.[49] Instead, what probably deserves more attention in a comparative research perspective is the absence, or lower intensity, of variety among sources of finance, which differentiates the European model of corporate finance from the Anglo-Saxon and, in particular, the US model. As a whole, European financial markets have probably been less able, or eager, to create stable, differentiated and thus flexible markets for corporate finance.

Conclusion

The above discussion has identified areas in which similarities and differences across European countries can be fruitfully analysed in a comparative perspective. These areas are considered by current research in social sciences as those in which homogeneous traits prevail. Business history provides no exception to this view. The above analysis, however, shows that many elements of this view are taken for granted. Differences and variance seem instead to prevail over homogeneous traits. The result of the exercise undertaken in this chapter could ultimately be frustrating for the 'curious investigator'. It may be useless to search for a general archetype of the European Corporation, being better to stick with some more or less common typologies in which variance is still dominant. Whatever the answer, our curious investigator cannot avoid two final questions concerning the impact of macro-institutional events on the general environment of European capitalism.

The first is about the impact of the European Union, since its beginnings

47   Wilkins, 'European and North American Multinationals'.
48   Youssef Cassis, *Capitals of Capital* (Cambridge, 2010).
49   Michiel J. Bijlsma and Gijsbert T. J. Zwart, *The Changing Landscape of Financial Markets in Europe, the United States and Japan*, Bruegel Working Paper 2013/02 (Brussels, 2013).

in the mid-1950s. Did the progressive creation of a Continental market and the diffusion of common rules and regulations have an impact on existing similarities and differences? Research projects on this issue have, so far, generated inconclusive evidence (or, perhaps more accurately, very little evidence at all).[50]

The second question, even more ambitious, concerns the effect of the present era of globalisation. European corporations and European capitalism are in fact clearly involved in the more general trend of globalisation which has characterised the world economy since 1989, with complex and often unforeseeable impacts on the strategies and structures of large corporations.

---

50   See Andrea Colli, Abe De Jong, Martin Jes Iversen, eds, *Mapping European Corporations: Strategy, Structure, Ownership and Performance* (London, 2011).

PART IV

CONCLUSIONS

Editors' Conclusion

PAOLO DI MARTINO, PETER SCOTT AND ANDREW POPP

Francesca Carnevali left an impressive academic legacy; a body of work able to inspire the preceding chapters and more. In the introduction to this volume we identified four concepts or themes that tie together our various contributions: a problematisation of the notion of the market; a 'thickening' out of understandings of trust; an emphasis on the economy as a system of ordering in which processes of legitimation play out; and, finally and most fundamentally, an insistence that we recognise human economic actors as *people*, with all their fascinating flaws. Taking these themes forward promises to be very rewarding – but also challenging. It may well require that we do economic history differently. Thus, we believe Francesca's legacy also constitutes the foundations for a rich future research agenda in terms of our approaches, one that might be summarised under three broad headings: 'economic history as if people matter'; 'bottom-up (rather than top-down) methodology'; and a more eclectic, expansive approach to modelling and explaining historical phenomena. While all three are closely and inextricably interlinked, it is convenient to discuss them one by one.

The first, 'economic history as if people matter', essentially involves a departure from the approach to economic history that was particularly dominant during the early years of Francesca's career – based on explaining historical phenomena using simple 'black box' economic models, usually based on maximisation of some clear objective, such as profits, subject to various constraints. Both the objective, and the constraints on it, were generally viewed in narrowly economic terms, while any other factors – reflecting sociological, political, cultural, psychological, or even biological phenomena, were generally rejected, downplayed, or simply ignored. People in all their wilful, messy, irrational, obdurate, obstinate and messy reality were not welcome.

Britain had a long-established and well-respected tradition of quantitative economic history and historical economics, including the Cambridge Group's pioneering reconstruction of Britain's population history and the work of Charles Feinstein, R. C. O. Matthews, Phyllis Deane, W. A. Cole and others on British economic growth and historical growth accounting. However, the cliometrics movement, as imported from America, represented a new and markedly narrower paradigm. Processes that were path dependent, or otherwise unsuitable for analysis using the comparative static approach of basic neoclassical economics, were typically rejected – in common with the potential influence of non-economic factors, such as technology, institutions, political environments and legacies, population dynamics, or more complex human motivations than greed. The list of unacceptable approaches also often encompassed those economists who had sought to build historical processes into their modelling, such as Thorstein Veblen, Joseph Schumpeter, Paul Krugman and Paul David, together with those, like Oliver Williamson, who tried to develop more realistic models by relaxing standard neoclassical assumptions, such as perfect information or zero transactions costs. In other words, we were in danger of rejecting not only non-economic approaches to economic history phenomena, but also economic approaches based on the premise that 'history matters'.

Such an agenda risked reducing economic history to a subject that merely serves to corroborate what the 'true believers' already hold to be self-evident – that the market is always and everywhere an optimal resource allocation device and one perfectly capable of solving any problem that it might encounter (though neo-liberal financial historians, who were among the most devout and outspoken disciples of this philosophy, were strangely quiet in their advocacy of market-based solutions during the 2008 credit crunch). That we might not all mean the same thing when we speak of 'the market' has been even less debated, as is true also of the questions from where, and how, do markets arise. By diminishing or impoverishing our understanding of the humanity of economic actors we in fact also risk diminishing or impoverishing our understanding of the markets they create.

This impoverishment has probably not been without serious consequence. Little research has been undertaken into the relationship between the ascendancy of the neoclassical approach to economic history and the long-term decline of the subject, both in Britain and internationally – though it seems at least plausible that its development as a discipline that principally served to verify, rather than modify, the predictions of neoclassical economics did little to raise its profile in the eyes of students, other academics and, especially, the wider public. Much more seriously, the diminishment of the human element in economic history was part of a wider trend in politics, economics, business education and finance that is clearly implicated in the deeply flawed decisions that created the conditions for the crash of 2008.

Francesca's work persistently (and, from the perspective of some of the discipline's 'gatekeepers', frustratingly) sought to put the people back into economic and social history, and with those people came all the complexities of real human behaviour arising from factors such as opportunism, learning, status-seeking, subjective conceptions of value, affection, emotion, empathy, solidarity and so forth. People's individual and collective behaviours – driven by the bundle of complex and often conflicting motivations that constitute the messy reality of human nature – pervaded her work. They influenced national bank–industry relationships by special (and, sometimes, local) interest lobbying and regulatory influence/capture. They worked to patiently, almost silently, construct the social norms, business practices and formal institutions that governed the (relatively) smooth functioning of industrial districts; and they designed marketing and market segmentation strategies that enabled 'luxury' items to be produced more cheaply and made more readily available to lower-income sections of society, without undermining the elite markets for these goods.[1]

Identifying such activities as central to economic life and business practices not only modifies the predictions, and limits the relevance, of simple neoclassical models in explaining these phenomena, but it also shines a beacon on what historical research can teach us about how real people interact to develop effective, if not necessarily perfect, solutions to real problems (and how their behaviours can sometimes produce dysfunctional or, better, unintended or unexpected results). For example, returning to the credit crunch, it is not difficult, with hindsight to see how factors such as biased incentives (for example, credit-rating agencies receiving their commission from the firms whose products they were rating, or traders having bonus structures based on short-term, rather than long-term, gains) might accentuate systemic risk, especially in an environment of pervasive regulatory capture. And thinking beyond economic factors such as incentives, should we not also allow a role for pride or hubris?

The second key theme in Francesca's research might be described as a 'bottom-up' rather than 'top-down' methodology, a forensic approach to historical research.[2] Towards the end of her career this feature of all Francesca's research began to move towards an explicit engagement with microhistorical approaches, perhaps a natural outcome for such a humane scholar and one schooled in the Italian traditions. Microhistory is not now a new concept, its origins being conventionally traced back to the 1970s (and

---

1   Francesca Carnevali, *Europe's Advantage: Banks and Small Firms in Britain, France, Germany, and Italy Since 1918* (Oxford, 2005); Francesca Carnevali, '"Crooks, Thieves, and Receivers": Transaction Costs in Nineteenth-Century Industrial Birmingham', *Economic History Review* 57 (2004), 533–50; Francesca Carnevali, 'Luxury for the Masses', *Entreprises et Histoire* 46 (2007), 56–70; Francesca Carnevali and Lucy Newton, 'Pianos for the People: From Producer to Consumer in Britain, 1851–1914', *Enterprise and Society* 14 (2013), 37–70.
2   See, for example, Francesca Carnevali, 'Social Capital and Trade Associations in America, c.1860–1914: A Microhistory Approach', *Economic History Review* 64 (2011), 905–28.

arguably, being implicit in a number of much longer-established approaches to historical research) but is, it seems, experiencing something of a renaissance as a range of historians ask how it might help them work in an ever wider range of contexts, including economic and business history.[3] It has been defined as 'asking large questions in small places'[4] – an approach ideally suited for those who see historical processes as being driven by patterns 'on the ground' rather than by impersonal macroeconomic (or macropolitical, macrosocial, etc.) factors. In these concerns it is naturally aligned with more recent developments in history from below, including subaltern and post-colonial studies.

This approach in turn implies another strand of 'bottom-up' methodology: intensive immersion in and investigation of archival sources in order to minutely reconstruct the key players, events, institutions and interactions that established and developed the 'rules of game' in these small places. Francesca's research was underpinned by extensive local archival research on the key 'places' of her projects, such as the City of London and the jewellery manufacturing districts of Birmingham and Providence. Only by reconstructing the actions of the people who lived and worked there could she capture the processes of co-operation, conflict, lobbying, creativity and innovation that underpinned their success and created order, however temporary or unstable.

For many historians it may seem self-evident that historical work is built on the intensive study of archival sources, but this approach was by no means universal, or universally accepted, in economic history research around the turn of the century, or even currently. Some leading historical economists appeared to view their lack of engagement with archival sources almost as a badge of honour, preferring to apply their economic models to secondary quantitative data, supported by (sometimes rather selective) summaries of qualitative information from published secondary sources. As Lance E. Davis has noted, cliometricians often seemed to regard archival research as a waste of their time, given that the rewards tended to go 'to the chap with a model and a couple of stylised facts'.[5] Meanwhile in social history the growing influence of the cultural turn led both to the questioning of whether a forensic reconstruction of a discoverable past was possible and – in its crudest applications – to an approach that rendered historical work more akin to literary criticism.

Finally, and (obviously) closely linked to history based around people,

3   See Carlo Ginzburg, 'Microhistory: Two or Three Things That I Know About It', *Critical Inquiry*, 20 (1993), 10–35.
4   Charles Joyner, *Shared Traditions: Southern History and Folk Lore* (Urbana, IL, 1999), p. 1.
5   Lance E. Davis, interviewed by Samuel H. Williamson and John S. Lyons, in John S. Lyons, Louis P. Cain and Samuel H. Williamson, eds, *Reflections on the Cliometrics Revolution: Conversations with Economic Historians* (London, 2008), pp. 221–31 (p. 224).

and to their activities in the specific, concrete locales within which they acted, was Francesca's belief that 'economic' historians should employ a large and varied theoretical toolbox, incorporating – where appropriate – economics, sociology, psychology, marketing, political economy and all the other insights and perspectives offered by the social sciences. As discussed in chapter 2, Francesca thought long and hard about how best to conceptualise and explore the phenomena she investigated and was ever critical, even of her own work. Having rejected the standard economic sociology approach to explaining co-ordination and co-operation in industrial districts in favour of a Williamsonian transactions cost perspective,[6] she eventually came to the conclusion that this approach (as applied, often mechanistically, by some of Williamson's disciples) was also limited, by its rejection of social processes as factors tempering opportunism and fostering co-operation.[7]

Francesca's final, uncompleted, project, on 'small things' or 'luxury' consumer goods marked the culmination of this interdisciplinary project, bringing together the study of production, consumption and the mediation between the two (which might be usefully, if incompletely, be termed 'marketing'), in a multidisciplinary study that sought to apply the lens of microhistory to a range of key Victorian luxury goods with important status and social connotations. This was a hugely ambitious project. It encompassed sectors that were poorly covered by conventional sources, compared with classic 'industrial revolution' industries such as cotton, coal, steel, shipbuilding and heavy engineering, and posed a formidable research problem. Dealing with a vast range of 'non-essential' consumer goods, it necessarily had to consider such basic human motivations and emotions as desire, aspiration, taste and perhaps even envy. And as these goods were generally made by a vast plethora of small firms and workshops, it was also necessarily a very 'bottom-up' endeavour. Moreover, dealing as it did with the fundamental question of how 'value' is created through the process of assigning status, aesthetic and other subjective characteristics to tangible objects, the project was an ideal candidate for Francesca's flexible, interdisciplinary, approach. This agenda – of examining production, consumption and distribution/marketing in relation to each other, in order to explore how the productive process creates value, from the subjective perception of the consumer (whose objective expenditure then reflects that value) – is, arguably, her most ambitious research legacy. It is one on which we very much hope others will wish to build.

---

6   Francesca Carnevali, '"Malefactors and Honourable Men": The Making of Commercial Honesty in Nineteenth-Century Industrial Birmingham', *Industrial Clusters and Regional Business Networks in England, 1750–1970*, ed. John F. Wilson and Andrew Popp (Aldershot, 2003), pp. 192–207; Carnevali, 'Crooks, Thieves, and Receivers'.
7   Carnevali, 'Social Capital and Trade Associations'.

Building on Francesca's research agenda

There are strong grounds for optimism that the key approaches of Francesca's work are gaining ground relative to methodologies that either seek to reduce economic history to simple neoclassical models or view historical research as a purely intellectual exercise, where the past is unknowable and thus a blank canvas on which to impose the researcher's concepts and values. The younger generations of economic, social and business historians are, generally, showing greater openness to alternative perspectives and greater respect for classic social scientists who have illuminated our understanding of human civilisation, whether their roots lie in the disciplines of economics, sociology, other social sciences, or – as was common with some great thinkers of the past – a less specific, broad, social science tradition.

For example, a survey of the last two annual reviews of periodical literature in the *Economic History Review*, for articles on the period 1850–1945 (where Francesca's later work was concentrated), indicates a range of interesting new research topics and approaches to the interconnections between production and consumption, including work on how exhibitions were used to combine popular entertainment with product and place promotion; the economic and social impacts of novel consumer products; changing notions of 'crafts-manship' in musical instrument making; and attempts by the wartime state to shift consumer preferences and reconfigure networks of production, distribution and consumption.[8] The reviews also highlight substantial new work on the social and institutional processes co-ordinating local systems of production, in agricultural and industrial communities; the role of regional branches of national social/voluntary institutions in creating networks between members of all social classes; alternative institutional arrange-ments for fostering co-ordination and co-operation between communities of firms; and institutional mechanisms to temper opportunism or encourage desired behaviours within firms (such as internal labour markets) and within households.

As a discipline, economic history was born into a world of 'trade and industry' that was largely dominated by 'producer goods' – coal, steel, shipbuilding, semi-manufactured textiles, shipping and (mainly producer-based) financial services. The late nineteenth century saw the start of a long transition away from the dominance of such goods in favour of consumer products whose value is based on complex and subjective characteristics – branded fast-moving goods, clothing and other 'fashion' items, consumer durables, and (arguably the most subjective, on account of their complexity

8 See Amanda Wilkinson, 'Review of Periodical Literature Published in 2014: (v) 1850–1945', *Economic History Review* 69 (2016), 341–51; Tim Crook and Aashish Velkar, 'Review of Periodical Literature Published in 2013', *Economic History Review* 68 (2015), 326–39.

and intangibility) consumer financial and other services. It is these goods which increasingly determine people's perceptions of status, welfare and living standards, and tracing their evolution, from the roots of 'popular' luxury in the late nineteenth century to its ubiquitous status by the end of the twentieth century, is likely to become a major, if not the major, research issue for economic history.

We hope that through this volume we and our contributors have managed not only to celebrate and build on Francesca's academic legacy, but to highlight what she rightly saw as exciting and formidable research agendas that might better capture the real drivers of economic development and change, and thereby help to rejuvenate a discipline that was once seen as potentially offering new insights into problems of global poverty, economic depression, crises and uneven development. If economic history is to have any chance of once again reaching the status it enjoyed in the 1960s and 1970s, as a popular subject represented in departments, and undergraduate programmes, in many leading universities, it needs to ask important questions and answer them with a distinctive voice. Putting people at the centre of the analysis, focusing on their behaviours at the micro level, and drawing on insights from across the social sciences, may provide us with the means to identify those questions and find that voice.

Appendix

Francesca Carnevali: Full List of Publications

Articles

Carnevali, Francesca, 'Between Markets and Networks: Regional Banks in Italy', *Business History* 38 (1996), 83–100

Carnevali, Francesca, 'A Review of Italian Business History from 1991 to 1997', *Business History* 40 (1998), 80–94

Carnevali, Francesca and Peter Scott, 'The Treasury as a Venture Capitalist: DATAC Industrial Finance and the Macmillan Gap, 1945–60', *Financial History Review* 6 (1999), 47–65

Carnevali, Francesca, 'State Enterprise and Italy's 'Economic Miracle': The Ente Nazionale Idrocarburi, 1945–1962', *Enterprise and Society* 1 (2000), 249–78

Carnevali, Francesca, 'Did They Have it So Good? Small Firms and British Monetary Policy in the 1950s', *Journal of Industrial History* 5 (2002), 15–35

Carnevali, Francesca, 'Golden Opportunities: Jewellery Making in Birmingham Between Mass Production and Specialty', *Enterprise and Society* 4 (2003), 272–98

Carnevali, Francesca, '"Crooks, Thieves, and Receivers": Transaction Costs in Nineteenth-Century Industrial Birmingham', *Economic History Review* 57 (2004), 533–50

Carnevali, Francesca, 'Luxury for the Masses', *Entreprises et Histoire* 46 (2007), 56–70

Carnevali, Francesca, 'Fashioning Luxury for Factory Girls: American Jewelry, 1860–1914', *Business History Review* 85 (2011), 295–317

Carnevali, Francesca, 'Social Capital and Trade Associations in America, c.1860–1914: A Microhistory Approach', *Economic History Review* 64 (2011), 905–28

Carnevali, Francesca and Lucy Newton, 'Pianos for the People: From Producer to Consumer in Britain, 1851–1914', *Enterprise and Society* 14 (2013), 37–70

Books

Carnevali, Francesca, and Giulio Sapelli, *Uno sviluppo fra politica e strategia: ENI (1953–1985)* (Milan, 1992)

Carnevali, Francesca, *Europe's Advantage: Banks and Small Firms in Britain, France, Germany, and Italy Since 1918* (Oxford, 2005)

Contributions to edited volumes

Carnevali, Francesca, and Leslie Hannah, 'The Effects of Banking Cartels and Credit Rationing on UK Industrial Structure and Economic Performance Since World War Two', *Anglo-American Financial Systems: Institutions and Markets in the Twentieth Century*, ed. Michael Bordo and Richard Sylla (Homewood, IL, 1995), pp. 65–88

Carnevali, Francesca, '"Malefactors and Honourable Men": The Making of Commercial Honesty in Nineteenth-Century Industrial Birmingham', *Industrial Clusters and Regional Business Networks in England, 1750–1970*, ed. John F. Wilson and Andrew Popp (Aldershot, 2003), pp. 192–207

Carnevali, Francesca, and Jennifer Aston, 'Victorian Capitalists and Middle-Class Formation: Reflections on Asa Briggs' Birmingham', *The Age of Asa: Lord Briggs, Public Life and History in Britain Since 1945*, ed. Miles Taylor (Basingstoke, 2015), pp. 79–89

Edited books

Carnevali, Francesca, and Giulio Sapelli, eds, *L'impresa. Storia e culture* (Rome-Bari, 1994)

Carnevali, Francesca, and Julie-Marie Strange, eds, *20th Century Britain: Economic, Cultural and Social Change* (Harlow, 2007)

Bibliography

Acemoglu, Daron, and James Robinson, *Why Nations Fail: The Origins of Power, Prosperity and Poverty* (New York, 2012)

Ackrill, Margaret, and Leslie Hannah, *Barclays: The Business of Banking 1690–1996* (Cambridge, 2001)

Albareto, Giorgio, 'Concorrenza e politica bancaria', *Stabilità e sviluppo negli anni cinquanta*, vol. 3: *Politica bancaria e struttura del sistema finanziario*, ed. Franco Cotula (Rome-Bari, 1999), pp. 198–206

Albert, Michel, *Capitalisme contre capitalisme* (Paris, 1991)

Allen, Franklin, Elena Carletti and Robert Marquez, *Stakeholder Capitalism, Corporate Governance and Firm Value*, Wharton Financial Institutions Center Working Paper #09–28 (Philadelphia, PA, 2009), http://ssrn.com/abstract=968141 or http://dx.doi.org/10.2139/ssrn.968141

Allen, Robert, 'Technology and the Great Divergence: Global Economic Development Since 1820', *Explorations in Economic History* 49 (2012), 1–16

Amato, Giuliano, ed., *Il governo dell'industria in Italia* (Bologna, 1972)

Amatori, Franco, 'Entrepreneurial Typologies in the History of Industrial Italy: Reconsiderations', *Business History Review* 85 (2011), 151–80

Amatori, Franco, Matteo Bugamelli and Andrea Colli, 'Technology, Firm Size and Entrepreneurship', *The Oxford Handbook of the Italian Economy since Unification*, ed. Gianni Toniolo (New York, 2013), pp. 455–84

Amatori, Franco, and Andrea Colli, *Corporate Governance: The Italian Story*, Corporate Governance, Innovation and Economic Performance in the EU (CGEP) Project Paper (Brussels, 2001)

Anderson, Gregory, *Victorian Clerks* (Manchester, 1976)

Andrews, Philip, and Elisabeth Brunner, *Life of Lord Nuffield* (Oxford, 1955)

'The Annual Report of the Boots Pure Drug Co. Ltd', *The Retail Chemist*, July 1936, 218–20

Arcand, Jean-Louis, Enrico Berkes and Ugo Panizza, *Too Much Finance?*, International Monetary Fund Working Paper WP/12/161 (Washington, DC, 2012)

Army & Navy Co-operative Society, *Yesterday's Shopping: The Army & Navy Co-operative Society 1907 Issue of 'Rules of the Society and Price List of Articles Sold at the Stores'*, facsimile edn (Newton Abbot, 1969)

Arrow, Kenneth J., 'The Economic Implications of Learning by Doing', *The Review of Economic Studies* 29 (1962), 155–73

Asso, Pier Francesco, and Gabriella Raitano, 'Trasformazione e sviluppo del credito mobiliare negli anni del governatorato Menichella', *Stabilità e sviluppo negli anni cinquanta*, vol. 3: *Politica bancaria e struttura del sistema finanziario*, ed. Franco Cotula (Rome-Bari, 1999), pp. 309–589

Associazione Bancaria Italiana (ABI), *La legislazione italiana sul credito speciale all'industria e al commercio* (Rome, 1963)

Baccini, Alberto, *Artigiancassa. Da Istituto di Credito Speciale a banca per le imprese artigiane* (Florence, 2002)

Baffigi, Alberto, *Italian National Accounts, 1861–2011*, Bank of Italy Economic History Working Papers 18 (Rome, 2011)

Bailkin, Jordanna, *The Afterlife of Empire* (Berkeley, CA, 2012)

Baker, Bruce E. and Barbara Hahn, *The Cotton Kings: Capitalism and Corruption in Turn-of-the-Century New York and New Orleans* (Oxford, 2016)

Baker, Mae, and Michael Collins, 'English Industrial Distress Before 1914 and the Response of the Banks', *European Review of Economic History* 3 (1999), 1–24

Bakker, Gerben, *Entertainment Industrialised: The Emergence of the International Film Industry* (Cambridge, 2008)

Balderstone, Laura, Graeme J. Milne and Rachel Mulhearn, 'Memory and Place on the Liverpool Waterfront in the Mid-Twentieth Century', *Urban History* 41 (2014), 478–96

Banca d'Italia, *Relazione Annuale* (Rome, 1948)

———, *Relazione Annuale* (Rome, 1952)

Banfi, Rodolfo, 'Gli Istituti di Credito Speciale e il sistema del credito agevolato', *Rivista Bancaria – Minerva Bancaria* 1981/1–2 (1981), 30–67

Barberis, Corrado, 'L'Artigianato in Italia', *L'artigianato in Italia e nella Comunità Economica Europea*, ed. Corrado Barberis, Gabriella Harvey and Olga Tavone (Milan, 1980), pp. 7–82

Barca, Fabrizio, and Marco Becht, eds, *The Control of Corporate Europe* (Oxford, 2001)

Barca, Luciano, and Gianni Manghetti, *L'Italia della banche* (Rome, 1976)

Battilossi, Stefano, 'L'eredità della banca Mista. Sistema creditizio, finanziamento industriale e ruolo strategico di Mediobanca 1946–1956', *L'Italia Contemporanea* 185 (1991), 625–54

Baughan, Emily, '"Every citizen of empire implored to Save the Children!" Empire, Internationalism and the Save the Children Fund in Inter-War Britain', *Historical Research* 86 (2013), 116–37

Becattini, Giacomo, *Distretti industriali e made in Italy. Le basi socioculturali del nostro sviluppo economico* (Turin, 1998)

Becattini, Giacomo, Marco Bellandi, Gabi Dei Ottati and Fabio Sforzi, eds, *From Industrial Districts to Local Development* (Cheltenham, 2003)

Becht, Marco, and Erik Böhmer, 'Ownership and Voting Power in Germany', *The Control of Corporate Europe*, ed. Fabrizio Barca and Marco Becht (Oxford, 2001), pp. 128–53

Benson, John, *The Rise of Consumer Society in Britain, 1880–1980* (New York, 1994)

Berg, Maxine, 'Consumption in Eighteenth- and Early Nineteenth-Century Britain', *The Cambridge Economic History of Modern Britain*, vol. 1: *Industrialisation, 1700–1860*, ed. Roderick Floud and Paul Johnson, (Cambridge, 2004), pp. 357–87

———, 'From Imitation to Invention: Creating Commodities in Eighteenth-Century Britain', *Economic History Review* 55 (2002), 1–30

Berger, Allen N., and Gregory F. Udell, 'Relationship Lending and Lines of Credit in Small Firm Finance', *The Journal of Business* 68 (1995), 351–81

———, 'Small Business Credit Availability and Relationship Lending: The Importance of Bank Organisational Structure', *The Economic Journal* 112 (2002), 32–53

Best, Michael H., *The New Competition: Institutions of Industrial Restructuring* (Cambridge, 1990)

Beunza, Daniel, Iain Hardie and Donald MacKenzie, 'The Price is a Social Thing: Towards a Material Sociology of Arbitrage', *Organization Studies* 27 (2006), 721–45

Bijlsma, Michiel J., and Gijsbert T. J. Zwart, *The Changing Landscape of Financial Markets in Europe, the United States and Japan*, Bruegel Working Paper 2013/02 (Brussels, 2013)

Billings, Mark, and Forrest Capie, 'Capital in British Banking 1920–1970', *Business History* 49 (2007), 139–62

———, 'Evidence on Competition in English Commercial Banking, 1920–1970', *Financial History Review* 11 (2004), 69–103

———, 'Financial Crisis, Contagion, and the British Banking System Between the World Wars', *Business History* 53 (2011), 193–215

———, 'Profitability in English Banking in the Twentieth Century', *European Review of Economic History* 5 (2001), 367–401

Bingham, Adrian, *Gender, Modernity, and the Popular Press in Interwar Britain* (Oxford, 2004)

Black, Lawrence, *Redefining British Politics: Culture, Consumerism and Participation, 1954–70* (Basingstoke, 2010)

Black, Lawrence, Hugh Pemberton and Pat Thane, *Reassessing 1970s Britain* (Manchester, 2013)

Blaszczyk, Regina L., *Imagining Consumers: Design and Innovation from Wedgwood to Corning* (Baltimore, 1999)

Bocking-Welch, Anna, 'Imperial Legacies and Internationalist Discourses: British Involvement in the United Nations Freedom from Hunger Campaign, 1960–70', *Journal of Imperial and Commonwealth History* 40 (2012), 879–96

Bois, Guy, *Crise du féodalisme* (Paris, 1976)

Boldizzoni, Francesco, *The Poverty of Clio: Resurrecting Economic History* (Princeton, NJ, 2011)

Bonelli, Franco, 'Il capitalismo italiano: linee generali di interpretazione', *Storia d'Italia*, vol. 1: *Dal feudalesimo al capitalismo*, ed. Ruggero Romano and Corrado Vivanti (Turin, 1978), pp. 1195–255

Bookbinder, Paul, *Simon Marks: Retail Revolutionary* (London, 1993)

Bordo, Michael, Angela Redish and Hugh Rockoff, 'A Comparison of the United States and Canadian Banking Systems in the Twentieth Century: Stability v Efficiency?', *Anglo-American Financial Systems: Institutions and Markets in the Twentieth Century*, ed. Michael Bordo and Richard Sylla (Homewood, IL, 1995), pp. 11–40

———, 'Why Didn't Canada Have a Banking Crisis in 2008 (or in 1930, or in 1907, or ...)?', *Economic History Review* 67 (2015), 218–43

Bourdieu, Pierre, 'The Forms of Capital', *Handbook of Theory and Research in the Sociology of Education*, ed. John G. Richardson (New York, 1986), pp. 241–58

Boyer, George R., 'Living Standards, 1860–1939', *The Cambridge Economic History of Modern Britain*, vol. 2: *Economic Maturity, 1860–1939*, ed. Roderick Floud and Paul Johnson (Cambridge, 2004), pp. 280–313

Bradley, Kate, *Poverty, Philanthropy and the State: Charities and the Working Classes in London 1918–1979* (Manchester, 2009)

Braggion, Fabio, Narly Dwarkasing and Lyndon Moore, *The Economic Impact of a Banking Oligopoly: Britain at the Turn of the 20th Century*, University of Melbourne Working Paper (Melbourne, 2015)

Braggion, Fabio and Steven Ongena, 'A Century of Firm–Bank Relationship', unpublished paper (2014)

Brewer, John, and Roy Porter, *Consumption and the World of Goods* (London and New York, 1993)

Briggs, Asa, *Friends of the People: The Centenary History of Lewis's* (London, 1956)

Brinton, Mary, and Victor Nee, eds, *The New Institutionalism in Sociology* (New York, 1998)

Broadberry, Stephen, *Market Services and the Productivity Race, 1850–2000: Britain in International Perspective* (Cambridge, 2006)

———, *The Productivity Race: British Manufacturing in International Perspective, 1850–1950* (Cambridge, 1997)

Broadberry, Stephen, and Nicholas Crafts, 'Britain's Productivity Gap in the 1930s: Some Neglected Factors', *Journal of Economic History* 52 (1992), 531–58

———, 'Competition and Innovation in 1950s Britain', *Business History* 43 (2001), 97–118

———, 'Explaining Anglo-American Productivity Differences in the

Mid-Twentieth Century', *Oxford Bulletin of Economics and Statistics* 52 (1990), 375–402

Brooke, Stephen, *Sexual Politics: Sexuality, Family Planning, and the British Left from the 1880s to the Present Day* (Oxford, 2011)

Brown, Callum, *The Death of Christian Britain: Understanding Secularisation, 1800–2000* (London, 2009)

Brusco, Sebastiano, 'The Emilian Model: Productive Decentralization and Social Integration', *Cambridge Journal of Economics* 6 (1982), 167–84

Brusco, Sebastiano, and Mario Pezzini, 'Small-Scale Enterprise in the Ideology of the Italian Left', *Industrial Districts and Inter-Firm Cooperation in Italy*, ed. Frank Pyke and Werner Sengenberger (Geneva, 1990), pp. 142–59

Buettner, Elizabeth, *Empire Families: Britons and Late Imperial India* (Oxford, 2004)

———, '"Going for an Indian": South Asian Restaurants and the Limits of Multiculturalism in Britain', *Journal of Modern History* 80 (2008), 865–901

Burhop, Carsten, David Chambers and Brian Cheffins, *Law, Politics and the Rise and Fall of German Stock Market Development, 1870–1938*, University of Cambridge Faculty of Law Working Paper 283 (Cambridge, 2015)

———, 'Regulating IPOs: Evidence from Going Public in London, 1900–1913', *Explorations in Economic History* 51 (2014), 60–76

Burk, Kathleen, and Manfred Pohl, *Deutsche Bank in London* (Munich, 1998)

Burke, Peter, 'Performing History: The Importance of Occasions', *Rethinking History* 9 (2005), 35–52

Cabrera-Suárez, Katiuska, Petra De Saá-Pérez and Desiderio García-Almeida, 'The Succession Process from a Resource- and Knowledge-Based View of the Family Firm', *Family Business Review* 14 (2001), 37–46

Cafagna, Luciano, *Dualismo e sviluppo nella storia d'Italia* (Venice, 1989)

Cafiero, Salvatore, *Storia dell'intervento straordinario nel Mezzogiorno (1950–1993)* (Manduria-Bari-Rome, 2000)

Cain, Peter, and Anthony Hopkins, 'Gentlemanly Capitalism and the British Expansion Overseas II: New Imperialism, 1850–1945', *Economic History Review* 40 (1987), 1–26

Calomiris, Charles, and Stephen Haber, *Fragile by Design* (Princeton, NJ, 2014)

Cameron, Rondo, Olga Crisp, Hugh T. Patrick and Richard Tilly, *Banking in the Early Stages of Industrialization: A Study in Comparative Economic History* (New York, 1967)

Camp, Richard L., *The Papal Ideology of Social Reform* (Leiden, 1969)

Cantwell, John, *Technological Innovation and Multinational Corporations* (Cambridge, MA, 1989)

Capie, Forrest, 'Commercial Banking in Britain', *Banking, Currency and Finance in Europe Between the Wars*, ed. Charles H. Feinstein (Oxford, 1995), pp. 395–413

———, 'Review of: *Europe's Advantage: Banks and Small Firms in Britain,*

France, Germany, and Italy Since 1918', *Business History Review* 80 (2006), 610–12

Capie, Forrest, and Michael Collins, 'Banks, Industry and Finance, 1880–1914', *Business History* 41 (1999), 37–62

——, *Have the Banks Failed British Industry? An Historical Survey of Bank/ Industry Relations in Britain, 1870–1990* (London, 1992)

——, 'Industrial Lending by English Commercial Banks, 1860s–1914: Why Did Banks Refuse Loans?', *Business History* 38 (1996), 26–44

Capie, Forrest, and Terence Mills, 'British Bank Conservatism in the Late 19th Century', *Explorations in Economic History* 32 (1995), 409–20

Capie, Forrest, and Alan Webber, *Monetary History of the United Kingdom, 1870–1982*, vol. 1: *Data, Sources* (London, 1985)

Caprasse, Jean-Nicolas, Christophe Clerc and Marco Becht, *Report on the Proportionality Principle in the European Union* (Brussels and Paris, 2007), http://ec.europa.eu/internal_market/company/docs/shareholders/study/ final_report_en.pdf (accessed 17 December 2016)

Carey, Hilary M., *God's Empire: Religion and Colonialism in the British World, c.1801–1908* (Cambridge, 2011)

Carli, Guido, 'Le origini del Mediocredito Centrale', *Credito Popolare* 1984/6 (1984), 261–7

Carnevali, Francesca, 'Between Markets and Networks: Regional Banks in Italy', *Business History* 38 (1996), 83–100

——, 'British and Italian Banks and Small Firms: A Study of the Midlands and Piedmont, 1945–1973' (Ph.D. thesis, London School of Economics, 1997)

——, '"Crooks, Thieves, and Receivers": Transaction Costs in Nineteenth-Century Industrial Birmingham', *Economic History Review* 57 (2004), 533–50

——, 'Did They Have it So Good? Small Firms and British Monetary Policy in the 1950s', *Journal of Industrial History* 5 (2002), 15–35

——, *Europe's Advantage: Banks and Small Firms in Britain, France, Germany, and Italy Since 1918* (Oxford, 2005)

——, 'Fashioning Luxury for Factory Girls: American Jewelry, 1860–1914', *Business History Review* 85 (2011), 295–317

——, 'Golden Opportunities: Jewellery Making in Birmingham Between Mass Production and Specialty', *Enterprise and Society* 4 (2003), 272–98

——, 'Luxury for the Masses', *Entreprises et Histoire* 46 (2007), 56–70

——, '"Malefactors and Honourable Men": The Making of Commercial Honesty in Nineteenth-Century Industrial Birmingham', *Industrial Clusters and Regional Business Networks in England, 1750–1970*, ed. John F. Wilson and Andrew Popp (Aldershot, 2003), pp. 192–207

——, 'A Review of Italian Business History from 1991 to 1997', *Business History* 40 (1998), 80–94

————, 'Social Capital and Trade Associations in America, c.1860–1914: A Microhistory Approach', *Economic History Review* 64 (2011), 905–28

————, 'State Enterprise and Italy's "Economic Miracle": The Ente Nazionale Idrocarburi, 1945–1962', *Enterprise and Society* 1 (2000), 249–78

Carnevali, Francesca, and Jennifer Aston, 'Victorian Capitalists and Middle-Class Formation: Reflections on Asa Briggs' Birmingham', *The Age of Asa: Lord Briggs, Public Life and History in Britain Since 1945*, ed. Miles Taylor (Basingstoke, 2015), pp. 79–89

Carnevali, Francesca, and Leslie Hannah, 'The Effects of Banking Cartels and Credit Rationing on UK Industrial Structure and Economic Performance Since World War Two', *Anglo-American Financial Systems: Institutions and Markets in the Twentieth Century*, ed. Michael Bordo and Richard Sylla (Homewood, IL, 1995), pp. 65–88

Carnevali, Francesca, and Lucy Newton, 'Pianos for the People: From Producer to Consumer in Britain, 1851–1914', *Enterprise and Society* 14 (2013), 37–70

Carnevali, Francesca, and Peter Scott, 'The Treasury as a Venture Capitalist: DATAC Industrial Finance and the Macmillan Gap, 1945–60', *Financial History Review* 6 (1999), 47–65

Carnevali, Francesca, and Julie-Marie Strange, eds, *20th Century Britain: Economic, Cultural and Social Change* (Harlow, 2007)

Carosso, Vincent, *Investment Banking in America: A History* (Cambridge, MA, 1970)

Carr-Saunders, A. M., P. Sargant Florence and Robert Peers, *Consumers' Cooperation in Great Britain*, rev. edn (London, 1942)

Carter, Susan, Scott S. Gartner, Michael R. Haines, Alan L. Olmstead, Richard Sutch and Gavin Wright, eds., *Historical Statistics of the United States*, vol. 3 (New York, 2006)

Cassese, Sabino, *È ancora attuale la Legge Bancaria del 1936? Stato, banche e imprese pubbliche dagli anni '30 agli anni '80* (Rome, 1987)

Cassis, Youssef, *Big Business: The European Experience in the Twentieth Century* (Oxford, 1997)

————, *Capitals of Capital* (Cambridge, 2010)

Caves, Richard E., *Creative Industries: Contracts Between Art and Commerce* (Cambridge, MA, 2002)

Chambers, David, 'The City and the Corporate Economy Since 1870', *The Cambridge Economic History of Modern Britain*, vol. 2: *1870 to the Present*, ed. Roderick Floud, Jane Humphries and Paul Johnson (Cambridge, 2014), pp. 255–78

Chandler, Alfred D., *Scale and Scope: The Dynamics of Industrial Capitalism* (Cambridge, MA, 1990)

Chandler, Alfred D., Franco Amatori and Takashi Hikino, eds, *Big Business and the Wealth of Nations* (New York, 1997)

Channon, Derek F., *The Strategy and Structure of British Enterprise* (London, 1973)

Chapman, Stanley, *Hosiery and Knitwear: Four Centuries of Small-Scale Industry in Britain* (Oxford, 2002)

——, *Jesse Boot of Boots the Chemists* (London, 1974)

——, *The Rise of Merchant Banking* (London, 1984)

Chirico, Francesco, 'The Creation, Sharing and Transfer of Knowledge in Family Business', *Journal of Small Business and Entrepreneurship* 21 (2008), 413–33

Chirico, Francesco, and Mattias Nordqvist, 'Dynamic Capabilities and Trans-generational Value Creation in Family Firms: The Role of Organizational Culture', *International Small Business Journal* 28 (2010), 487–504

Chirico, Francesco, and Carlo Salvato, 'Knowledge Integration and Dynamic Organizational Adaptation in Family Firms', *Family Business Review* 21 (2008), 169–81

Church, Roy, *Herbert Austin* (London, 1979)

Cohen, Deborah, *Family Secrets: Living with Shame from the Victorians to the Present Day* (London, 2013)

——, *Household Gods: The British and Their Possessions* (New Haven and London, 2006)

Cohen, Lizabeth, *A Consumer's Republic: The Politics of Mass Consumption in Postwar America* (New York, 2003)

Colli, Andrea, Abe De Jong and Martin Jes Iversen, eds, *Mapping European Corporations: Strategy, Structure, Ownership and Performance* (London, 2011)

Colli, Andrea, and Mats Larsson, 'Family Business and Business History: An Example of Comparative Research', *Business History* 56 (2014), 37–53

Colli, Andrea, Sergio Mariotti and Lucia Piscitello, 'Governments as Strategists in Designing Global Players: The Case of European Utilities', *Journal of European Public Policy* 21 (2014), 407–508

Colli, Andrea, and Alberto Rinaldi, 'Institutions, Politics and the Corporate Economy', *Enterprise and Society* 16 (2015), 249–69

Collins, Michael, *Money and Banking in the UK: A History* (London and New York, 1988)

Collins, Michael, and Mae Baker, *Commercial Banks and Industrial Finance in England and Wales, 1860–1913* (Oxford, 2003)

Comin, Diego, and Ramana Nanda, *Financial Development and Technology Diffusion*, Harvard Business School Working Paper 15-36 (Cambridge, MA, 2014)

Comptroller of the Currency, *Annual Report of the Comptroller of the Currency 1913* (Washington, DC, 1914)

Connelly, Matthew, *Fatal Misconception: The Struggle to Control World Population* (Cambridge, 2008)

Conti, Giuseppe, 'Le banche e il finanziamento industriale', *Storia d'Italia*, vol. 15: *L'industria*, ed. Franco Amatori, Duccio Bigazzi, Renato Giannetti and Luciano Segreto (Turin, 1999), pp. 441–504

Conti, Giuseppe, and Giovanni Ferri, 'Banche locali e sviluppo economico decentrato', *Storia del capitalismo italiano dal dopoguerra a oggi*, ed. Fabrizio Barca (Rome, 1997), pp. 429–65

Conti, Sergio, 'Industrialization in a Backward Region: The Italian Mezzogiorno' (Ph.D. thesis, University of London, 1979)

Corina, Maurice, *Fine Silks and Oak Counters. Debenhams 1778–1978* (London, 1978)

Cox, Peter, *Spedan's Partnership: The Story of John Lewis and Waitrose* (Cambridge, 2010)

Crafts, Nicholas, 'British Relative Economic Decline Revisited: The Role of Competition', *Explorations in Economic History* 49 (2012), 17–29

Crafts, Nicholas, and Terence Mills, 'British Economic Fluctuations 1851–1913: A Perspective Based on Growth Theory', *Britain in the International Economy*, ed. Steve Broadberry and Nicholas Crafts (Cambridge, 1992), pp. 98–134

Crafts, Nicholas, and Mark Thomas, 'Comparative Advantage in UK Manufacturing Trade, 1910–1935', *Economic Journal* 96 (1986), 629–45

Crook, Tim, and Aashish Velkar, 'Review of Periodical Literature Published in 2013', *Economic History Review* 68 (2015), 326–39

Crouch, Colin, *Industrial Relations and European State Traditions* (Oxford, 1994)

Cull, Robert, Lance E. Davis, Naomi R. Lamoreaux and Jean-Laurent Rosenthal, 'Historical Financing of Small- and Medium-Size Enterprises', *Journal of Banking and Finance* 30 (2006), 3017–42

Cullather, Nick, *The Hungry World: America's Cold War Battle Against Poverty in Asia* (Cambridge, 2010)

Daems, Herman, 'Strategic and Structural Responses of Large European Enterprises, 1950–1980', typescript project outline, Baker Library Historical Collections, Chandler Papers, Box 111, f. 3 II, n.d. (presumably end of 1984)

Daniels, George W., 'Cotton Trade with Liverpool Under the Embargo and Non-Intercourse Acts', *The American Historical Review* 21 (1916), 276–87

Daunton, Martin, '"Gentlemanly Capitalism" and British Industry 1820–1914', *Past & Present* 122 (1989), 119–58

———, 'Rationality and Institutions: Reflections on Douglass North', *Structural Change and Economic Dynamics* 21 (2010), 147–56

Daunton, Martin, and Matthew Hilton, eds, *The Politics of Consumption: Material Culture and Citizenship in Europe and America* (Oxford, 2001)

Davis, Natalie Zemon, 'Les conteurs de Montaillou', *Annales* 34 (1979), 61–73

———, 'The Reasons of Misrule: Youth Groups and Charivaris in Sixteenth-Century France', *Past & Present* 50 (1971), 41–75

———, *The Return of Martin Guerre* (Cambridge, MA, 1983)

De Bonis, Riccardo, Fabio Farabullini, Miria Rocchelli, Alessandro Salvio and Andrea Silvestrini, *A Quantitative Look at the Italian Banking System:*

Evidence from a New Dataset Since 1861, Ministry of Economy and Finance Working Paper 9 (Rome, 2013)

Degner, Harald, 'Schumpeterian German Firms Before and After World War I: The Innovative Few and the Non-Innovative Many', *Zeitschrift für Unternehmensgeschichte* 54 (2009), 50–72

de la Bruhèze, Adri Albert, and Ruth Oldenziel, eds, *Manufacturing Technology, Manufacturing Consumers: The Making of Dutch Consumer Society* (Amsterdam, 2009)

DeLanda, Manuel, *A New Philosophy of Society: Assemblage Theory and Social Complexity* (London, 2006)

Deleuze, Gilles, and Félix Guattari, *A Thousand Plateaus: Capitalism and Schizophrenia* (London, 1988)

De Long, Bradford, 'Did J. P. Morgan's Men Add Value: An Economist's Perspective on Financial Capitalism', *Inside the Business Enterprise*, ed. Peter Temin (New York, 1990), pp. 205–49

Democrazia Cristiana (DC), *Atti e documenti (1943–67)*, 2 vols (Rome, 1968)

Deutsche Bundesbank, *Deutsches Geld- und Bankwesen in Zahlen, 1876–1975* (Frankfurt, 1976)

de Vries, Jan, *The Industrious Revolution: Consumer Behavior and the Household Economy* (Cambridge, 2008)

Delap, Lucy, *Knowing Their Place: Domestic Service in Twentieth-Century Britain* (Oxford, 2011)

Di Martino, Paolo, and Michelangelo Vasta, 'Companies Insolvency and "the Nature of the Firm" in Italy, 1920s–1970s', *Economic History Review* 63 (2010), 137–64

Dixon, Mark G., 'Stephenson, William Laurence (1880–1963), Chain Store Chairman', *Dictionary of Business Biography*, vol. 5, ed. David Jeremy (London, 1986), pp. 303–8

Dixon, Thomas, *Weeping Britannia: Portrait of a Nation in Tears* (Oxford, 2015)

Dodd, George, 'Piano-manufacture', *British Manufacturers*, series 4 (London, 1845), pp. 387–408

Dolge, Alfred, *Pianos and Their Makers: A Comprehensive History of the Development of the Piano* (Covina, CA, 1911)

D'Onofrio, Pietro, and Roberto Pepe, 'Le strutture creditizie nel Mezzogiorno', Banca d'Italia, *Il sistema finanziario nel Mezzogiorno*, special issue of *Contributi all'analisi economica* (Rome, 1990), pp. 207–50

Dumbell, Stanley, 'Early Liverpool Cotton Imports and the Organisation of the Cotton Market in the Eighteenth Century', *The Economic Journal* 33 (1923), 362–73

Dunning, John H., and Robert D. Pearce, *The World's Largest Industrial Enterprises* (London, 1985)

Dyas, Gareth, and Heinz Thanheiser, *The Emerging European Enterprise* (London, 1976)

Dyer, Christopher, *A Country Merchant, 1495–1520* (Oxford, 2012)

Edelstein, Mark, *Overseas Investment in the Age of High Imperialism: The United Kingdom, 1850–1914* (London, 1982)

Edgerton, David, *Britain's War Machine: Weapons, Resources and Experts in the Second World War* (London, 2011)

Edis, Robert William, *Decoration & Furniture of Town Houses: a Series of Cantor Lectures Delivered before the Society of Arts, 1880* (New York, 1881)

Edwards, Jeremy, and Sheilagh Ogilvie, 'Universal Banks and German Industrialisation: A Reappraisal', *Economic History Review* 49 (1996), 427–46

Ehrlich, Cyril, *The Piano: A History* (Oxford, 1990)

Elbaum, Bernard, and William Lazonick, eds., *The Decline of the British Economy* (Oxford, 1986)

Elder-Duncan, John Hudson, *The House Beautiful and Useful: Being Practical Suggestions on Furnishing and Decoration* (New York, 1907)

Eley, Geoff, *A Crooked Line From Cultural History to the History of Society* (Ann Arbor, MI, 2005)

Ellison, Thomas, *The Cotton Trade of Great Britain, Including a History of the Liverpool Cotton Market and the Liverpool Cotton Brokers' Association* (London, 1886)

Ensley, Michael D., and Allison W. Pearson, 'An Exploratory Comparison of the Behavioral Dynamics of Top Management Teams in Family and Nonfamily New Ventures: Cohesion, Conflict, Potency, and Consensus', *Entrepreneurship Theory and Practice* 29 (2005), 267–84

Essex-Crosby, Alan, 'Joint Stock Companies in Great Britain, 1884–1934' (M.Com. thesis, University of London, 1937)

Estrin, Saul, 'Privatization Impacts in Transition Economies', *The New Palgrave Dictionary of Economics*, ed. Steven N. Durlauf and Lawrence E. Blume, 2nd edn (London, 2008), http://www.dictionaryofeconomics.com/article?id=pde2008_P000342, accessed 14 January 2017

Evans, Tanya, 'Secrets and Lies: The Radical Potential of Family History', *History Workshop Journal* 71 (2011), 49–73

'The Experience of Marks & Spencer Ltd in Caring for 18,000 Employees Proves that Staff Welfare is a Business Investment', *Chain and Multiple Store*, 10 December 1938, 190–3

Faccio, Mara, and Jerry P. Lang, 'The Ultimate Ownership of Western European Corporations', *Journal of Financial Economics* 65 (2002), 365–95

Federico, Giovanni, ed., *The Economic Development of Italy Since 1870* (Aldershot, 1994)

Federico, Giovanni, and Renato Giannetti, 'Italy: Stalling and Surpassing', *European Industrial Policy: The Twentieth-Century Experience,* ed. James Foreman-Peck and Giovanni Federico (Oxford, 1999), pp. 124–51

Federico, Giovanni, and Gianni Toniolo, 'Italy', *Patterns of European*

Industrialization: The Nineteenth Century, ed. Richard Sylla and Gianni Toniolo (London and New York, 1992), pp. 197–217

Fellman, Susanna, Martin Jes Iversen, Hans Sjogren and Lars Thue, eds, *Creating Nordic Capitalism: The Business History of a Competitive Periphery* (Basingstoke, 2008)

Ferguson, Niall, Charles S. Maier, Erez Manela and Daniel J. Sargent, eds, *The Shock of the Global: The 1970s in Perspective* (Cambridge, 2010)

Field, Alexander, 'Land Abundance, Interest/Profit Rates, and Nineteenth-Century American and British Technology', *Journal of Economic History* 43 (1983), 405–31

Filby, Liza, *God and Mrs Thatcher: The Battle for Britain's Soul* (London, 2015)

Fine, Ben, *New and Improved: Economics' Contribution to Business History*, SOAS Department of Economics Working Paper 93 (London, n.d.)

Flanders, Judith, *The Victorian House* (New York and London, 2003)

Flandreau, Mark, and Frederic Zumer, *The Making of Global Finance, 1880–1913* (Paris, 2004)

Fligstein, Neil, *The Architecture of Markets: An Economic Sociology of Twenty-First-Century Capitalist Societies* (Princeton, NJ, 2002)

Fohlin, Caroline, 'The Balancing Act of German Universal Banks and English Deposit Banks, 1880–1913', *Business History* 43 (2001), 1–24

Foreman-Peck, James, and Giovanni Federico, *European Industrial Policy: The Twentieth-Century Experience* (Oxford, 1999)

Forty, Adrian, *Objects of Desire: Design and Society 1750–1980* (London, 1986)

Franko, Lawrence, *The European Multinationals* (Stamford, CT, 1976)

Freeman, Mark, '"Splendid Display; Pompous Spectacle": Historical Pageants in Twentieth-Century Britain', *Social History* 38 (2013), 423–55

Gaggio, Dario, 'Do Historians Need Social Capital?', *Social History* 29 (2004), 499–513

———, *In Gold We Trust: Social Capital and Economic Change in the Italian Jewelry Towns* (Princeton, NJ, 2007)

Galewitz, Herb, ed., *Music: A Book of Quotations* (New York, 2001)

Garnett, Philip, Simon Mollan and Alexander Bentley, 'Complexity in History: Modelling the Organisational Demography of the British Banking Sector', *Business History* 57 (2015), 182–202

Geddes, Keith, and Gordon Bussey, *The Setmakers: A History of the Radio and Television Industry* (London, 1991)

Gerschenkron, Alexander, *Economic Backwardness in Historical Perspective* (Cambridge, MA, 1962)

Gersick, Kelin F., John A. Davis, Marion M. Hampton and Ivan Lansberg, *Generation to Generation: Life Cycles of the Family Business* (Boston, MA, 1997)

Gigliobianco, Alfredo, Giandomenico Piluso and Gianni Toniolo, 'Il rapporto banca–impresa in Italia negli anni Cinquanta', *Stabilità e sviluppo negli anni cinquanta*, vol. 3: *Politica bancaria e struttura del sistema finanziario*, ed. Franco Cotula (Rome-Bari, 1999), pp. 225–302

Ginzburg, Carlo, *Clues, Myths and the Historical Method* (Baltimore, 1989)

———, *Il formaggio e i vermi* (Turin, 1976)

———, 'Microhistory: Two or Three Things That I Know About It', *Critical Inquiry*, 20 (1993), 10–35

———, 'Microstoria: due o tre cose che so di lei', *Quaderni storici* 86 (1994), 511–39

———, *Miti, emblemi, spie* (Turin, 1986)

Glaisyer, Natasha, *The Culture of Commerce in England, 1660–1720* (Martlesham, 2006)

Goldberg, Jessica, *Trade and Institutions in the Medieval Mediterranean* (Cambridge, 2012)

Good, Edwin M., *Giraffes, Black Dragons, and Other Pianos: A Technological History from Cristofori to the Modern Concert Grand* (Stanford, CA, 2001)

Goodhart, Charles, *The Business of Banking, 1891–1914* (London, 1972)

Goodwin, Thomas, 'Banking and Finance', *Cooperative Wholesale Societies' Annual 1914* (Manchester, 1914)

Granovetter, Mark, 'Economic Action and Social Structure: The Problem of Embeddedness', *American Journal of Sociology* 91 (1985), 481–510

Grant, Robert M., 'Toward a Knowledge-Based Theory of the Firm', *Strategic Management Journal* 17 (1996), 109–22

Greenwald, Bruce, and Joseph Stiglitz, 'Information, Finance and Markets: The Architecture of Allocative Mechanisms', *Finance and the Enterprise*, ed. Vera Zamagni (San Diego, CA, 1993), pp. 1–36

Greenwood, J. E., *A Cap For Boots* (London, 1977)

Greif, Avner, *Institutions and the Path to the Modern Economy: Lessons from Medieval Trade* (Cambridge, 2006)

Grendi, Edoardo, 'Ripensare la microstoria?', *Quaderni storici* 86 (1994), 540–60

Griffiths, Brian, 'The Development of Restrictive Practices in the UK Monetary System', *Manchester School* 41 (1973), 3–18

Grossman, Richard, 'Rearranging Deck Chairs on the Titanic: English Banking Concentration and Efficiency, 1870–1914', *European Review of Economic History* 3 (1999), 325–49

Grossman, Richard, and Masami Imai, 'Contingent Capital and Bank Risk-Taking Among British Banks Before the First World War', *Economic History Review* 66 (2013), 132–55

Grote, Jim, 'Conflicting Generations: A New Theory of Family Business Rivalry', *Family Business Review* 16 (2003), 113–24

Gualandri, Elisabetta, 'The Restructuring of Banking Groups in Italy: Major Issues', *The Recent Evolution of Financial Systems*, ed. Jack R. S. Revell (Basingstoke, 1997), pp. 157–80

Gualtierotti, Piero, *L'impresa artigiana* (Milan, 1977)

Guinnane, Timothy, 'Delegated Monitoring, Large and Small: German Banking 1800–1914', *Journal of Economic Literature* 40 (2002), 73–124

———, *Trust: A Concept Too Many*, Yale University Economic Growth Center Discussion Paper 907 (New Haven, CT, 2005)

Gurney, Peter, *Wanting and Having: Popular Politics and Liberal Consumerism in England, 1830–70* (Manchester, 2015)

Hall, Catherine, *Civilising Subjects: Metropole and Colony in the English Imagination, 1830–1867* (Chicago, 2002)

Hall, Nigel, 'The Business Interests of Liverpool's Cotton Brokers, c.1800–1914', *Northern History* 41 (2004), 339–55

———, 'The Emergence of the Liverpool Raw Cotton Market, 1800–1850', *Northern History* 38 (2001), 65–81

Hall, Peter, and David Soskice, *Varieties of Capitalism: The Institutional Foundations of Comparative Advantage* (Oxford, 2001)

Hall, Stuart, *Familiar Stranger: A Life Between Two Islands*, ed. Bill Schwarz (Durham, NC, forthcoming)

Handler, Wendy C., 'The Succession Experience of the Next Generation', *Family Business Review* 5 (1992), 283–307

Hannah, Leslie, 'Corporations in the US and Europe', *Business History* 56 (2014), 865–99

———, 'The Development of Japanese Banking in the Twentieth Century: Reflections in Western Mirrors', *Bankhistorisches Archiv* 37 (2011), 120–36

———, 'J. P. Morgan in London and New York Before 1914', *Business History Review* 85 (2011), 113–50

———, 'Logistics, Market Size and Giant Plants in the Early Twentieth Century: A Global View', *Journal of Economic History* 68 (2008), 46–79

———, *Rethinking Corporate Finance Fables: Did the US Lag Europe Before 1914?*, CIRJE Working Paper F-994 (2015)

———, 'Strategic Games, Scale and Efficiency, or Chandler Goes to Hollywood', *Business in Britain in the Twentieth Century: Decline and Renaissance?*, ed. Richard Coopey and Peter Lyth (Oxford, 2009), pp. 15–47

———, 'Twentieth-Century Banking Productivity Comparisons', forthcoming

Harding, Christopher, and Julian Joshua, *Regulating Cartels in Europe* (Oxford, 2010)

Harman, Graham, *Prince of Networks: Bruno Latour and Metaphysics* (Melbourne, 2009)

Harris, Nigel, *Competition and the Corporate Society: British Conservatives, the State and Industry, 1945–1964* (London, 1972)

Harrison, Brian, *Finding a Role? The United Kingdom, 1970–1990* (Oxford, 2010)

———, *Seeking a Role: The United Kingdom, 1951–1970* (Oxford, 2009)

Hautcoeur, Pierre-Cyrille, 'Le Marché Boursier et le Financement des Entreprises Françaises (1890–1939)' (Ph.D. thesis, Paris School of Economics, 1994)

Hayes, David, 'A History of Camden Town 1895–1914', *The Camden Town Group in Context*, ed. Helena Bonett, Ysanne Holt, Jennifer Mundy (London, 2012), https://www.tate.org.uk/art/research-publications/camden-town-group/david-hayes-a-history-of-camden-town-1895-1914-r1104374, accessed 14 December 2016

Heaton, Barrie, 'A History of John Hopkinson, Piano Manufacturer', *Association of Blind Piano Tuners* (n.l., 2007), http://www.piano-tuners.org/history/hopkinson/, accessed 14 December 2016

Hendrickson, Robert, *The Grand Emporiums: The Illustrated History of America's Great Department Stores* (New York, 1979)

Higgins, David, Steven Toms and Igor Filatotchev, 'Ownership, Financial Strategy and Performance: The Lancashire Cotton Textile Industry, 1918–1938', *Business History* 57 (2015), 97–121

Higgs, Edward, *Identifying the English: A History of Personal Identification, 1500 to the Present* (London, 2011)

Hilton, Matthew, *Consumerism in 20th-Century Britain: The Search for a Historical Movement* (Cambridge, 2003)

———, *Prosperity for All: Consumer Activism in an Era of Globalisation* (Ithaca, NY, 2009)

———, *Smoking in British Popular Culture, 1800–2000* (Manchester, 2000)

Hobsbawm, Eric and Terence Ranger, eds, *The Invention of Tradition* (Cambridge, 1983)

Honeyman, Katrina, 'Style Monotony and the Business of Fashion: The Marketing of Menswear in Inter-War England', *Textile History* 34 (2003), 171–91

Houlbrook, Matt, *Prince of Tricksters: The Incredible True Story of Netley Lucas, Gentleman Crook* (Chicago, 2016)

Howard, Vicki, *From Main Street to Mall: The Rise and Fall of the American Department Store* (Philadelphia, PA, 2015)

Hyde, Francis E., Bradbury B. Parkinson and Sheila Marriner, 'The Cotton Broker and the Rise of the Liverpool Cotton Market', *Economic History Review* (new series) 8 (1955), 75–83

Hymes, Dell, 'Breakthrough Into Performance', *Folklore: Performance and Communication*, ed. Dan Ben-Amos and Kenneth Goldstein (The Hague, 1975), pp. 11–74

Jackson, Ben, and Robert Saunders, eds, *Making Thatcher's Britain* (Cambridge, 2012)

Jefferys, James B., *Retail Trading in Britain 1850–1950* (Cambridge, 1954)

John Broadwood & Sons Ltd, 'History of John Broadwood & Sons Ltd Piano Manufacturer', *John Broadwood & Sons* (Whitby, n.d.), http://www.broadwood.co.uk/history.html, accessed 14 December 2016

Johnson, Paul, ed., *20th Century Britain: Economic, Social and Cultural Change* (Harlow, 1994)

Jones, Andrew, 'The Disasters Emergency Committee (DEC) and the

Humanitarian Industry in Britain, 1963–85', *Twentieth Century British History*, 26 (2015), 573–601

Jones, Ben, *The Working Class in Mid Twentieth-Century England: Community, Identity and Social Memory* (Manchester, 2012)

Jones, Geoffrey, *British Multinational Banking, 1830–1990* (Oxford, 1995)

——, *The Evolution of International Business: An Introduction* (London, 1996)

Jones, Geoffrey, and Asli M. Colpan, 'Business Groups in Historical Perspectives', *The Oxford Handbook of Business Groups*, ed. Asli M. Colpan, Takashi Hikino and James R. Lincoln (Oxford, 2010), pp. 67–92

Jones, Owen, *Chavs: The Demonization of the Working Class* (London, 2012)

Joyce, Patrick, *The State of Freedom: A Social History of the British State Since 1800* (Cambridge, 2013)

Joyner, Charles, *Shared Traditions: Southern History and Folk Lore* (Urbana, IL, 1999)

Kay, John, *Other People's Money* (London, 2015)

Kennedy, William Paul, *Industrial Structure, Capital Markets and the Origins of British Economic Decline* (Cambridge, 1987)

Knudsen, Christian, 'The Competence Perspective: A Historical View', *Towards a Competence Theory of the Firm*, ed. Nicolai Foss and Christian Knudsen (Abingdon, 2006), pp. 13–37

Koven, Seth, *The Match Girl and the Heiress* (Princeton, NJ, 2014)

Labordère, Marcel, 'The Mechanism of Foreign Investment in France and its Outcome, 1890–1914', *Economic Journal* 24 (1914), 525–42

Lamoreaux, Naomi, *Insider Lending* (New York, 1994)

Lancaster, Bill, *The Department Store: A Social History* (London, 1995)

Lansberg, Ivan, *Succeeding Generations: Realizing the Dream of Families in Business* (Boston, MA, 1999)

La Porta, Rafael, Florencio López de Silanes and Andrei Shleifer, 'Corporate Ownership Around the World', *Journal of Finance* 54 (1999), 471–517

Lardner, Dionysius, *The Great Exhibition and London in 1851* (London, 1852)

Lastecoueres, Christophe, 'Review of: *Europe's Advantage: Banks and Small Firms in Britain, France, Germany, and Italy Since 1918*', *Financial History Review* 15 (2008), 98–100

Latour, Bruno, *Reassembling the Social: An Introduction to Actor-Network-Theory* (Oxford, 2005)

Laurence, Alastair, 'The Evolution of the Grand Piano, 1785–1998' (D.Phil. thesis, University of York, 1998)

Lavington, Ferdinand, 'The Social Importance of Banking', *Economic Journal* 21 (1911), 53–60

Lawrence, Jon, 'Social-Science Encounters and the Negotiation of Difference in Early 1960s England', *History Workshop Journal* 77 (2014), 215–39

League of Nations, *Memorandum on Commercial Banks 1913–1929* (Geneva, 1931)

Lehmann, Sybille, and Jochen Streb, *The Berlin Stock Exchange in Imperial Germany: A Market for New Technology?*, CEPR Discussion Paper 10558 (London, 2015)

Leonardi, Paul, 'Theoretical Foundations for the Study of Sociomateriality', *Information and Organization* 23 (2013), 59–76

Le Roy Ladurie, Emmanuel, *Montaillou* (Paris, 1975)

Levi, Giovanni, *L'eredità immateriale* (Turin, 1985)

———, 'On Microhistory', *New Perspectives on Historical Writing*, ed. Peter Burke (Cambridge, 1991), pp. 93–113

———, 'I pericoli del Geertzismo', *Quaderni storici* 58 (1985), 269–77

Light, Alison, *Common People: The History of an English Family* (London, 2014)

Lipartito, Kenneth, 'Culture and Practice of Business History', *Business and Economic History* 24 (1995), 1–41

Loeb, Lori Anne, *Consuming Angels: Advertising and Victorian Women* (Oxford, 1994)

Loesser, Arthur, *Men, Women, and Pianos: A Social History* (1954; New York, 1991)

Logan, William B., *Oak: The Frame of Civilization* (New York, 2005)

Lomax, Susan F., 'The Department Store and the Creation of the Spectacle, 1880–1940' (Ph.D. thesis, University of Essex, 2005)

———, 'The View from the Shop: Window Display, the Shopper and the Formulation of Theory', *Cultures of Selling: Perspectives on Consumption and Society Since 1700*, ed. John Benson and Laura Ugolini (Aldershot, 2006), pp. 265–92

Longoni, Giuseppe M., and Alberto Rinaldi, 'Industrial Policy and Artisan Firms (1930s–1970s)', *Forms of Enterprise in 20th Century Italy: Boundaries, Structures and Strategies*, ed. Andrea Colli and Michelangelo Vasta (Cheltenham and Northampton, MA, 2010), pp. 204–24

Lucas Jr, Robert E., 'On the Mechanics of Economic Development', *Journal of Monetary Economics* 22 (1988), 3–42

Lydon, Ghislaine, *On Trans-Saharan Trails: Islamic Law, Trade Networks, and Cross-Cultural Exchange in Nineteenth-Century Western Africa* (Cambridge, 2009)

Lyons, John S., Louis P. Cain and Samuel H. Williamson, eds, *Reflections on the Cliometrics Revolution: Conversations with Economic Historians* (London, 2008)

MacRae, Julia, *Wigmore Hall: The Story of a Concert Hall* (London, 2011), http://wigmore-hall.org.uk/about-us/history/41-the-history-of-a-concert-hall/file, accessed 14 December 2016

Mäenpää, Sari, 'Combining Business and Pleasure? Cotton Brokers in the Liverpool Business Community in the Late 19th Century', unpublished paper

Maestas, Nicole, Kathleen Mullen and David Powell, *The Effect of Population*

Aging on Economic Growth, Rand Corporation Working Paper (Santa Monica, CA, 2014)

Maraffi, Marco, 'L'organizzazione degli interessi in Italia, 1870–1980', *L'azione collettiva degli imprenditori italiani. Le organizzazioni di rappresentanza degli interessi industriali in prospettiva comparata*, ed. Alberto Martinelli (Milan, 1994), pp. 137–96

Markovits, Claude, *The Global World of Indian Merchants, 1750–1947* (Cambridge, 2000)

Marshall, Alfred, *Industry and Trade* (London, 1919)

Maskell, Peter, 'Towards a Knowledge-Based Theory of the Geographical Cluster', *Industrial and Corporate Change* 10 (2001), 921–43

Mattina, Liborio, *Gli industriali e la democrazia. La Confindustria nella formazione dell'Italia repubblicana* (Bologna, 1991)

May, Trevor, *Great Exhibitions* (Oxford, 2010)

Mazower, Mark, *Governing the World: The History of an Idea* (London, 2012)

McCarthy, Helen, *The British People and the League of Nations: Democracy, Citizenship and Internationalism, c.1918–1945* (Manchester, 2011)

McCloskey, Deirdre, *How to Be Human, Though an Economist* (Ann Arbor, MI, 2000)

McKibbin, Ross, *Classes and Cultures: England, 1918–1951* (Oxford, 1998)

——, *Parties and People: England, 1914–1951* (Oxford, 2010)

McLeod, Hugh, *The Religious Crisis of the 1960s* (Oxford, 2007)

Meyer, John P., and Natalie J. Allen, 'A Three-Component Conceptualization of Organizational Commitment', *Human Resource Management Review* 1 (1991), 61–89

Michie, Ranald, 'Banks and Securities Markets, 1870–1914', *The Origins of National Financial Systems: Alexander Gerschenkron Reconsidered*, ed. Douglas J. Forsyth and Daniel Verdier (London and New York, 2003), pp. 43–63

Mills, Richard, 'Fighters, Footballers and Nation Builders: Wartime Football in the Serb-Held Territories of the Former Yugoslavia, 1991–1996', *Sport in Society* 16 (2013), 945–72

Milne, Graeme, 'British Business and the Telephone, 1878–1911', *Business History* 49 (2007), 163–85

——, 'Business Districts, Office Culture and the First Generation of Telephone Use in Britain', *International Journal for the History of Engineering & Technology* 80 (2010), 199–213

Minns, Richard, *Pension Funds and British Capitalism* (London, 1980)

Modern British Studies, *Working Paper No. 1* (Birmingham, 2014), https://mbsbham.wordpress.com/working-papers/working-paper-no-1/, accessed 14 December 2016

Mokyr, Joel, *The Gifts of Athena: Historical Origins of the Knowledge Economy* (Princeton, NJ, 2002)

Mold, Alex, and Virginia Berridge, *Voluntary Action and Illegal Drugs: Health and Society in Britain Since the 1960s* (London, 2010)

Moores, Christopher, 'The Progressive Professionals: The National Council for Civil Liberties and the Politics of Activism in the 1960s', *Twentieth Century British History* 20 (2009), 538–60

Moran, Joe, 'Private Lives, Public Histories: The Diary in Twentieth-Century Britain', *Journal of British Studies* 54 (2015), 138–62

Mori, Giorgio, *Il capitalismo industriale in Italia. processo d'industrializzazione e storia d'Italia* (Rome, 1977)

Mort, Frank, *Capital Affairs: London and the Making of the Permissive Society* (New Haven, CT, 2010)

Moyn, Samuel, *The Last Utopia: Human Rights in History* (Cambridge, 2010)

Nehring, Holger, *Politics of Security: The British and West German Protests Against Nuclear Weapons and the Early Cold War, 1945–1970* (Oxford, 2013)

Newton, Lucy, 'British Retail Banking in the Twentieth Century: Decline and Renaissance in Industrial Lending', *Business in Britain in the Twentieth Century: Decline and Renaissance?*, ed. Richard Coopey and Peter Lyth (Oxford, 2009), pp. 189–206

———, 'Networks and Clusters: Capital Networks in the Sheffield Region, 1850–1885', *Industrial Clusters and Regional Business Networks in England, 1750–1970*, ed. John F. Wilson and Andrew Popp (Ashgate, 2003), pp. 130–54

Newton, Lucy, and Francesca Carnevali, 'Researching Consumer Durables in the Nineteenth Century: The Case of the Piano', *Business Archives: Sources and History* 101 (2010), 17–29

Nex, Jennifer Susan, 'The Business of Musical-Instrument Making in Early Industrial London' (Ph.D. thesis, Goldsmiths' College, University of London, 2013)

North, Douglass C., 'Institutions', *Journal of Economic Perspectives* 5 (1991), 97–112

———, 'Institutions and Economic Theory', *American Economist* 36 (1992), 3–6

———, 'Institutions, Ideology, and Economic Performance', *Cato Journal* 11 (1992), 477–88

———, *Institutions, Institutional Change and Economic Performance* (New York, 1990)

———, *Understanding the Process of Economic Change* (Princeton, NJ, 2010)

North, Douglass C., John Joseph Wallis and Barry R. Weingast, *A Conceptual Framework for Interpreting Recorded Human History*, NBER Working Paper 12795 (Cambridge, MA, 2006)

———, *Violence and Social Orders: Conceptual Frameworks for Interpreting Recorded Human History* (Cambridge, 2009)

Officer, Lawrence H., and Samuel H. Williamson, 'Five Ways to Compute the Relative Value of a UK Pound Amount, 1270 to Present', *MeasuringWorth*,

2017, https://www.measuringworth.com/ukcompare/, accessed 24 January 2017

Ogilvie, Sheilagh, *Institutions and European Trade: Merchant Guilds, 1000–1800* (Cambridge, 2011)

O'Hara, Glen, *Governing Post-War Britain: The Paradoxes of Progress, 1951–1973* (London, 2012)

Onida, Fabrizio, *Se il piccolo non cresce. Piccole e medie imprese italiane in affanno* (Bologna, 2004)

Orchard, Benjamin Guinness, *The Clerks of Liverpool* (Liverpool, 1871)

O'Sullivan, Mary, *Contests for Corporate Control: Corporate Governance and Economic Performance in the United States and Germany* (Oxford, 2000)

Ott, Julia C., '"The Free and Open People's Market": Political Ideology and Retail Brokerage at the New York Stock Exchange, 1913–1933', *The Journal of American History* (2009), 44–71

Owens, John, *The Cotton Broker* (London, 1921)

Palmieri, Robert, ed., *The Piano: An Encyclopedia* (Abingdon, 2014)

Panayi, Panikos, 'Immigration, Multiculturalism and Racism', *20th Century Britain: Economic, Cultural and Social Change*, ed. Francesca Carnevali and Julie-Marie Strange (Harlow, 2007), pp. 247–61

——, *Spicing Up Britain: The Multicultural History of British Food* (London, 2010)

Parakilas, James, *Piano Roles: Three Hundred Years of Life with the Piano* (New Haven, CT, 1999)

Partito Comunista Italiano (PCI), *La dichiarazione programmatica e le tesi dell'VIII Congresso del PCI* (Rome, 1957)

Pavan, Robert J., 'The Strategy and Structure of Italian Enterprise' (D.B.A. thesis, Harvard Business School, 1972)

Payling, Daisy, '"Socialist Republic of South Yorkshire": Grassroots Activism and Left-Wing Solidarity in 1980s Sheffield', *Twentieth Century British History* 25 (2014), 602–27

Pedersen, Susan, 'Money, Space and Time: Reflections on Graduate Education', *Twentieth Century British History* 21 (2010), 382–96

Pedersen, Torben, and Steen Thomsen, 'Ownership Structure and Value of the Largest European Firms: The Importance of Owner Identity', *Journal of Management and Governance* 7 (2003), 27–55

Peluffo, Paolo, and Vladimiro Giacché, *Storia del Mediocredito Centrale* (Rome-Bari, 1997)

Pergolesi, Simona, *Il credito agevolato alle imprese industriali. Le incentivazioni gestite dal Ministero dell'Industria, 1962–1984* (Milan, 1988)

Perkin, Harold, *The Rise of Professional Society: England Since 1880* (London, 1989)

Pesole, Dino, *L'artigianato nell'economia italiana. Dal dopoguerra a oggi* (Milan, 1997)

Philippon, Thomas, 'Has the US Finance Industry Become Less Efficient? On

The Theory and Measurement of Financial Intermediation', *American Economic Review* 105 (2015), 1408–38

Philippon, Thomas, and Ariell Reshef, 'Wages and Human Capital in the US Finance Industry: 1909–2006', *Quarterly Journal of Economics* 127 (2012), 1551–609

Pierce Piano Atlas, 12th edn (Albuquerque, NM, 2008)

Piketty, Thomas, *Capital in the Twenty-First Century* (Cambridge, MA, 2014)

Piluso, Giandomenico, 'From the Universal Bank to the Universal Bank: A Reappraisal', *Journal of Modern Italian Studies* 15 (2010), 84–103

Piore, Michael J., and Charles F. Sabel, *The Second Industrial Divide: Possibilities for Prosperity* (New York, 1984)

Polanyi, Michael, *The Tacit Dimension* (Chicago, 1966)

Pollard, Sidney, 'Capital Export, 1870–1914: Harmful or Beneficial?', *Economic History Review* 38 (1985), 489–514

Pontolillo, Vincenzo, 'Aspetti del sistema di credito speciale con particolare riferimento all'intervento dello Stato', Banca d'Italia *Bollettino*, 1971/1 (1971), 105–22

———, *Il sistema di credito speciale in Italia* (Bologna, 1980)

Popp, Andrew, 'The Broken Cotton Speculator', *History Workshop Journal* 78 (2014), 133–56

———, *Business Structure, Business Culture and the Industrial District: The Potteries, c.1850–1914* (Aldershot, 2001)

Popp, Andrew and Michael French, '"Practically the Uniform of the Tribe": Dress Codes Among Commercial Travelers', *Enterprise and Society* 11 (2010), 437–67

Porter, Michael E., *The Competitive Advantage of Nations* (London and New York, 1990)

Potter, Simon, *Broadcasting Empire: The BBC and the British World, 1922–1970* (Oxford, 2012)

Prochaska, Frank, *Christianity and Social Service in Modern Britain* (Oxford, 2006)

Putnam, Robert, *Bowling Alone: The Collapse and Revival of American Community* (New York, 2000)

Putnam, Robert, Robert Leonardi and Raffaella Y. Nonetti, *Making Democracy Work: Civic Traditions in Modern Italy* (Princeton, NJ, 1994)

Quail, John, 'The Proprietorial Theory of the Firm', *Journal of Industrial History* 3 (2000), 1–28

Raggio, Osvaldo, *Faide e parentele. Lo stato genovese visto dalla Fontanabuona* (Turin, 1990)

———, 'Microstoria e microstorie', *Enciclopedia Treccani* (Rome, 2013), http://www.treccani.it/enciclopedia/microstoria-e-microstorie_%28altro%29/, accessed 15 December 2016

Ramamurthy, Anandi, *Black Star: Britain's Asian Youth Movements* (London, 2013)

Ramella, Franco, *Terra e telai* (Turin, 1984)

Reader, William, *A House in the City 1825–1975* (London, 1979)

Redfern, Percy, *New History of the CWS* (London, 1938)

Rees, Jeska, 'A Look Back at Anger: The Women's Liberation Movement in 1978', *Women's History Review* 19 (2010), 337–56

Revel, Jaques, 'Microanalisi e costruzione del sociale', *Quaderni storici* 86 (1994), 561–75

Riesser, Jakob, *The Great German Banks and Their Concentration* (Washington, DC, 1911)

Ritschl, Albrecht, 'The Anglo-German Industrial Productivity Puzzle, 1895–1935: A Restatement and a Possible Resolution', *Journal of Economic History* 68 (2008), 535–65

Roberts, Richard, and David Kynaston, *The Lion Wakes: A Modern History of HSBC* (London, 2015)

Robertson, Nicole, *The Co-operative Movement and Communities in Britain 1914–1960* (Aldershot, 2010)

Robinson, Lucy, *Gay Men and the Left in Post-War Britain: How the Personal Got Political* (Manchester, 2007)

Roodhouse, Mark, *Black Market Britain: 1939–1955* (Oxford, 2013)

Rose, Nikolas, and Peter Miller, *Governing the Present: Administering Economic, Social and Personal Life* (Cambridge, 2008)

Ross, Duncan, 'Review of: *Europe's Advantage: Banks and Small Firms in Britain, France, Germany, and Italy Since 1918*', *Economic History Review* 59 (2006), 862–3

Rowland, David, 'Clementi's Music Business', *The Music Trade in Georgian England*, ed. Michael Kassler (Aldershot, 2011), pp. 125–57

Royal Historical Society, *Gender Equality and Historians in UK Higher Education* (London, 2015), http://royalhistsoc.org/rhs-report-gender-equality-historians-higher-education/, accessed 14 December 2016

Rubini, Loris, Klaus Desmet, Facundo Piguillemand and Aranzazu Crespo, *Breaking Down the Barriers to Firm Growth in Europe: The Fourth EFIGE Policy Report* (Brussels, 2012)

Rubinstein, William, *Capitalism, Culture, and Decline in Britain, 1750–1990* (London and New York, 1994)

Rumelt, Richard P., *Strategy, Structure and Economic Performance* (Cambridge, MA, 1974)

Sabel, Charles, and Jonathan Zeitlin, 'Historical Alternatives to Mass Production: Politics, Markets and Technology in Nineteenth-Century Industrialization', *Past & Present* 108 (1985), 133–76

——, *World of Possibilities: Flexibility and Mass Production in Western Industrialization* (Cambridge and New York, 1997)

Savage, Mike, *Identities and Social Change in Britain Since 1940: The Politics of Method* (Oxford, 2010)

Sayers, Richard S., *American Banking System* (Oxford, 1948)

Schaffer, Gavin, *The Vision of a Nation: Making Multiculturalism on British Television, 1960–80* (Basingstoke and New York, 2014)

Schenk, Catherine, 'Britain's Changing Position in the International Economy', *20th Century Britain: Economic, Cultural and Social Change*, ed. Francesca Carnevali and Julie-Marie Strange (Harlow, 2007), pp. 58–78

Schmidt, Reinhard H., 'Corporate Governance in Germany: An Economic Perspective', *The German Financial System*, ed. Jan P. Krahnen and Reinhard H. Schmidt (Oxford, 2004), pp. 386–424

Schroeter, Harm G., *The European Enterprise: Historical Investigation Into a Future Species* (Heidelberg, 2008)

———, 'Small European Nations: Cooperative Capitalism in the Twentieth Century', *Big Business and the Wealth of Nations*, ed. Alfred D. Chandler, Franco Amatori and Takashi Hikino (Cambridge, 1997), pp. 176–204

Schumpeter, Joseph, *Capitalism, Socialism and Democracy* (New York, 1942)

Schwartz, Anna, 'Stability, Efficiency and Credit Controls', *Anglo-American Financial Systems: Institutions and Markets in the Twentieth Century*, ed. Michael Bordo and Richard Sylla (Homewood, IL, 1995), pp. 94–100

Schwarz, Bill, *Memories of Empire*, vol. 1: *The White Man's World* (Oxford, 2011)

Scott, Peter, 'The Determinants of Competitive Success in the Interwar British Radio Industry', *Economic History Review* 65 (2012), 1303–25

———, *The Making of the British Home: The Suburban Semi and Family Life Between the Wars* (Oxford, 2013)

———, 'Mr Drage, Mr Everyman, and the Creation of a Mass Market for Domestic Furniture in Interwar Britain', *Economic History Review* 62 (2009), 802–27

———, 'The Twilight World of Interwar Hire Purchase', *Past & Present* 177 (2002), 195–225

Scott, Peter, and James Walker, 'Barriers to "Industrialisation" in Interwar British Retailing: The Case of Marks & Spencer', *Business History* 59 (2017; published online 4 May 2016), http://www.tandfonline.com/doi/abs/10.1080/00076791.2016.1156088?journalCode=fbsh20

———, 'The British "Failure" That Never Was? The Anglo-American "Productivity Gap" in Large Scale Interwar Retailing – Evidence from the Department Store Sector', *Economic History Review* 65 (2012), 277–303

Scranton, Phil, *Endless Novelty: Specialty Production and American Industrialisation, 1865–1925* (Princeton, NJ, 2000)

Setch, Eve, 'The Face of Metropolitan Feminism: The London Women's Liberation Workshop, 1969–1979', *Twentieth Century British History* 13 (2002), 171–90

Shannon, Herbert, 'The Limited Companies of 1866–1883', *Economic History Review* 4 (1933), 290–316

Sharples, Joseph and John Stonard, *Built on Commerce: Liverpool's Central Business District* (Swindon, 2008)

Shaw, Gareth, Andrew Alexander, John Benson and Deborah Hodson, 'The Evolving Culture of Retailer Regulation and the Failure of the "Balfour Bill" in Interwar Britain', *Environment and Planning A* 32 (2000), 1977–89

Sheppard, David, *The Growth and Role of UK Financial Institutions* (London, 1971)

Sieff, Israel, *Memoirs* (London, 1970)

Siemens, Georg, *Stenographische Berichte des Deutsches Reichstags* (Berlin, 1885)

Sigsworth, Eric M., *Montague Burton: The Tailor of Taste* (Manchester, 1990)

Smethurst, Richard, *From Foot Soldier to Finance Minister: Takahashi Korekiyo, Japan's Keynes* (Cambridge, MA, 2007)

Smith, Samuel, *My Life-Work* (London, 1902)

Snodin, Michael, and John Styles, *Design and the Decorative Arts: Britain 1500–1900* (London, 2001)

Solow, Robert, 'A Contribution to the Theory of Economic Growth', *The Quarterly Journal of Economics* 70 (1956), 65–94

Spadavecchia, Anna, 'Financing Industrial Districts in Italy, 1971–91: A Private Venture?', *Business History* 47 (2005), 569–93

Staber, Udo H., Norbert V. Schaefer and Basu Sharma, eds, *Business Networks: Prospects for Regional Development* (Berlin, 1996)

Peter Stansky *et al.*, 'NACBS Report on the State and Future of British Studies in North America (1999)', *North American Conference on British Studies* (n.l., 1999), http://www.nacbs.org/archive/nacbs-report-on-the-state-and-future-of-british-studies, accessed 15 December 2016

Steedman, Carolyn, *Labours Lost: Domestic Service and the Making of Modern England* (Cambridge, 2009)

Strange, Julie-Marie, *Fatherhood and the British Working Class, 1865–1914* (Cambridge, 2015)

Surrey History Centre, 'John Broadwood and Sons Piano Manufacturers', *Surrey History Centre* (Woking, 2016), https://www.surreycc.gov.uk/heritage-culture-and-recreation/archives-and-history/surrey-history-centre/surrey-history-centre-help-for-researchers/archives-and-history-research-guides/john-broadwood-and-sons-piano-manufacturers, accessed 14 December 2016

Sutcliffe-Braithwaite, Florence, '"Class" in the Development of British Labour Party Ideology, 1983–1997', *Archiv für Sozialgeschichte* 53 (2013), 327–62

Sylla, Richard, 'Wall Street Transitions 1880–1920: From National to World Financial Centre', *Financial Centres and International Capital Flows in the Nineteenth and Twentieth Centuries*, ed. Youssef Cassis and Laure Quennoëlle-Corre (Oxford, 2011), pp. 161–78

Szreter, Simon, and Kate Fisher, *Sex Before the Sexual Revolution: Intimate Life in England, 1918–1963* (Cambridge, 2010)

Taylor, Audrey, *Gilletts: Bankers at Banbury and Oxford* (Oxford, 1964)

Taylor, James, *Boardroom Scandal: The Criminalization of Company Fraud in Nineteenth-Century Britain* (Oxford, 2013)

Tedlow, Richard S., *New and Improved: The Story of Mass Marketing in America* (Oxford, 1990)

Tedlow, Richard S., and Geoffrey Jones, eds, *The Rise and Fall of Mass Marketing* (London, 1993)

Thane, Pat, ed., *Unequal Britain: Equalities in Britain Since 1945* (London, 2010)

Thompson, Andrew, ed., *Britain's Experience of Empire in the Twentieth Century* (Oxford, 2012)

Thompson, Edward Palmer, *Customs in Common: Studies in Traditional Popular Culture* (London, 1991)

——, 'The Moral Economy of the English Crowd in the Eighteenth Century', *Past & Present* 50 (1971), 76–136

Thomson, Matthew, *Lost Freedom: The Landscape of the Child and the British Post-War Settlement* (Oxford, 2013)

——, *Psychological Subjects: Identity, Culture, and Health in Twentieth-Century Britain* (Oxford, 2006)

Thurow, Lester C., *Head to Head: The Coming Economic Battle Among Japan, Europe, and America* (New York, 1992)

Tilly, Richard, 'German Banking, 1850–1914: Development Assistance for the Strong', *Journal of European Economic History* 15 (1986), 113–51

Togliatti, Palmiro, 'Ceto medio e Emilia rossa', *Critica Marxista* 2 (1964), 130–58

Tomlinson, Charles, ed., *Cyclopaedia of Useful Arts & Manufactures* (London, 1853)

Tomlinson, Jim, 'Thrice Denied: "Declinism" as a Recurrent Theme in British History in the Long Twentieth Century', *Twentieth Century British History* 20 (2009), 227–51

Toninelli, Pier Angelo, ed., *The Rise and Fall of State-Owned Enterprise in the Western World* (New York, 2008)

Toniolo, Gianni, *Osservazioni e discussioni durante le giornate sociali di Milano. Resoconto delle giornate sociali di Milano (7–9 febbraio 1907)* (Vatican City, 1951)

——, 'Il profilo economico', *La Banca d'Italia e il sistema bancario, 1919–1936*, ed. Giuseppe Guarino and Gianni Toniolo (Rome-Bari, 1993), pp. 5–101

Torre, Angelo, *Il consumo di devozioni* (Venice, 1995)

Trentmann, Frank, *Free Trade Nation: Commerce, Consumption, and Civil Society in Modern Britain* (Oxford, 2008)

——, 'Materiality in the Future of History', *Journal of British Studies* 48 (2009), 283–307

Trivellato, Francesca, *The Familiarity of Strangers: The Sephardic Diaspora,*

Livorno, and Cross-Cultural Trade in the Early Modern Period (New Haven, CT, 2009)

———, 'Is There a Future for Italian Microhistory in the Age of Global History?', *Californian Italian Studies* 2 (2011), http://escholarship.org/uc/item/0z94n9hq, accessed 16 December 2016

Vasta, Michelangelo, and Alberto Baccini, 'Banks and Industry in Italy, 1911–36: New Evidence Using the Interlocking Directorates Technique', *Financial History Review* 4 (1997), 139–59

Vernon, James, *Distant Strangers: How Britain Became Modern* (Berkeley, CA, 2014)

———, *Hunger: A Modern History* (Cambridge, 2007)

———, 'The Local, the Imperial and the Global: Repositioning Twentieth-Century Britain and the Brief Life of its Social Democracy', *Twentieth Century British History* 21 (2010), 404–18

Vinen, Richard, *Thatcher's Britain: The Politics and Social Upheaval of the Thatcher Era* (London, 2009)

Wainwright, David, *Broadwood by Appointment: A History* (Shrewsbury, 1982)

———, 'Broadwood, Henry Fowler (1811–1893), Piano Manufacturer', *Dictionary of National Business Biography*, vol. 1: *A–C*, ed. Jeremy David (London, 1984), pp. 458–9

———, *The Piano Makers* (London, 1975)

Walkowitz, Judith, *Nights Out: Life in Cosmopolitan London* (New Haven, CT, 2012)

Walsh, Barbara, *When the Shopping Was Good: Woolworths and the Irish Main Street* (Dublin, 2011)

Walton, John K., 'Towns and Consumerism', *The Cambridge Urban History of Britain*, vol. 3: *1840–1950*, ed. Martin Daunton (Cambridge, 2000), pp. 715–44

Weimer, Jeroen, and Joost Pape, 'A Taxonomy of Systems of Corporate Governance', *Corporate Governance: An International Review* 7 (1999), 152–66

Weiss, Linda, *Creating Capitalism: The State and Small Business Since 1945* (Oxford, 1988)

Whitehead, Jack, 'Piano Manufacture in Camden Town', *Local Local History* ([London], 2012), http://www.locallocalhistory.co.uk/industrial-history/piano/page1-m.htm, accessed 14 December 2016

Whitley, Richard, *Divergent Capitalisms: The Social Structuring and Change of Business Systems* (Oxford, 1999)

Whittington, Richard, and Michael Mayer, *The European Corporation: Strategy, Structure and Social Science* (Oxford, 2000)

Wiener, Martin, *English Culture and the Decline of the Industrial Spirit, 1850–1980* (Cambridge, 1981)

Wilkins, Mira, 'European and North American Multinationals, 1870–1914: Comparisons and Contrasts', *Business History* 30 (1988), 8–45

Wilkinson, Amanda, 'Review of Periodical Literature Published in 2014: (v) 1850–1945', *Economic History Review* 69 (2016), 341–51

Williams, Bridget, *The Best Butter in the World: A History of Sainsbury's* (London, 1994)

Williamson, Oliver, *The Economic Institutions of Capitalism* (New York, 1985)

———, 'The Modern Corporation: Origins, Evolutions, Attributes', *Journal of Economic Literature* 19 (1981), 1537–68

Wilson, John, *British Business History, 1720–1995* (Manchester, 1995)

———, 'Review of: *Europe's Advantage: Banks and Small Firms in Britain, France, Germany, and Italy Since 1918*', *Business History* 48 (2006), 605–6

Wilson, John F., Anthony Webster and Rachel Vorberg-Rugh, *Building Co-operation: A Business History of The Co-operative Group, 1863–2013* (Oxford, 2013)

Winstanley, Michael J., *The Shopkeeper's World 1830–1914* (Manchester, 1983)

Woltjer, Pieter, *The Great Escape: Technological Lock-In vs Appropriate Technology in Early Twentieth Century British Manufacturing*, GGDC Research Memorandum 141 (Groningen, 2013)

Worswick, George, and David Tipping, *Profits in the British Economy 1909–1938* (Oxford, 1967)

Woytinsky, Wassily, *Die Welt in Zahlen*, vol. 4 (Berlin, 1926)

Zahra, Shaker A., Donald O. Neubaum and Bárbara Larrañeta, 'Knowledge Sharing and Technological Capabilities: The Moderating Role of Family Involvement', *Journal of Business Research* 60 (2007), 1070–9

Zaloom, Caitlin, *Out of the Pits: Traders and Technology from Chicago to London* (Chicago, 2006)

Zamagni, Vera, *The Economic History of Italy, 1860–1990* (Oxford, 1993)

Zingales, Luigi, *Does Finance Benefit Society?*, NBER Working Paper 20894 (Cambridge, MA, 2015)

Index

Tabula in Memoriam

Gerben Bakker
Youssef Cassis
Andrea Colli
Malcolm Dick
Paolo Di Martino
Barry Doyle
Elaine Fulton
Nigel Goose
Leslie Hannah
Matthew Hilton
Steve Hindle
Jane Humphries
Willem M. Jongman
Ken Lipartito
Alex Mold
Anne L. Murphy
Lucy Newton
Giandomenico Piluso
Noelle Plack
Andrew Popp
Alberto Rinaldi
Peter Scott
Anna Spadavecchia
Jim Tomlinson
Michelangelo Vasta
James Walker
Chris Wickham
Simon Yarrow

PEOPLE, MARKETS, GOODS:
ECONOMIES AND SOCIETIES IN HISTORY

ISSN: 2051-7467